Through Times
of Trouble

Russian, Eurasian, and Eastern European Politics

Series Editor: Michael O. Slobodchikoff, Troy University

Mission Statement

Following the collapse of the Soviet Union, little attention was paid to Russia, Eastern Europe, and the former Soviet Union. The United States and many Western governments reassigned their analysts to address different threats. Scholars began to focus much less on Russia, Eastern Europe and the former Soviet Union, instead turning their attention to East Asia among other regions. With the descent of Ukraine into civil war, scholars and governments have lamented the fact that there are not enough scholars studying Russia, Eurasia, and Eastern Europe. This series focuses on the Russian, Eurasian, and Eastern European region. We invite contributions addressing problems related to the politics and relations in this region. This series is open to contributions from scholars representing comparative politics, international relations, history, literature, linguistics, religious studies, and other disciplines whose work involves this important region. Successful proposals will be accessible to a multidisciplinary audience, and advance our understanding of Russia, Eurasia, and Eastern Europe.

Advisory Board

Books in the Series

Understanding International Relations: Russia and the World,
    edited by Natalia Tsvetkova
Geopolitical Prospects of the Russian Project of Eurasian Integration, by
    Natalya A. Vasilyeva and Maria L. Lagutina
Eurasia 2.0: Russian Geopolitics in the Age of New Media, edited by Mark Bassin and
    Mikhail Suslov
*Executive Politics in Semi-Presidential Regimes: Power Distribution and
    Conflicts between Presidents and Prime Ministers*, by Martin Carrier
Post-Soviet Legacies and Conflicting Values in Europe: Generation Why, by
    Lena M. Surzhko-Harned and Ekaterina Turkina
Through Times of Trouble: Conflict in Southeastern Ukraine Explained from Within, by
    Anna Matveeva

Through Times of Trouble

Conflict in Southeastern Ukraine Explained from Within

Anna Matveeva

LEXINGTON BOOKS
Lanham • Boulder • New York • London

Published by Lexington Books
An imprint of The Rowman & Littlefield Publishing Group, Inc.
4501 Forbes Boulevard, Suite 200, Lanham, Maryland 20706
www.rowman.com

Unit A, Whitacre Mews, 26-34 Stannary Street, London SE11 4AB

British Library Cataloguing in Publication Information Available

Library of Congress Cataloging-in-Publication Data

ISBN 978-1-4985-4323-1 (cloth : alk. paper)
ISBN 978-1-4985-4325-5 (paperback)
ISBN 978-1-4985-4324-8 (electronic)

∞™ The paper used in this publication meets the minimum requirements of American National Standard for Information Sciences Permanence of Paper for Printed Library Materials, ANSI/NISO Z39.48-1992.

To All Who Died In Donbas Conflict

Map of Eastern Ukraine. ID 40860225 © Mycolors | Dreamstime.

Contents

Foreword, by *Michael O. Slobodchikoff*   ix

Acknowledgments   xi

Abbreviations   xiii

Introduction: Talking Donbas, Not Putin   xv

  1 Framing the Issues: A Conflict among Other Conflicts   1

  2 Laying Grounds for Confrontation   23

  3 Faultlines in Crimea   47

  4 Donbas: A Much-Unloved Powerhouse   69

  5 Russian Spring: Bolsheviks and Monarchists, All Welcome!   93

  6 Free Guerrillas: "Novorossiya be!" *Ghosts* and *Somalis*
    Take the Stage   121

  7 "Hot Summer": Military Campaign   145

  8 Consolidation amid the New (Dis)order   169

  9 New Symbolism in the Digital Era   193

 10 Power of the State, Power of Ideas   215

 11 Rebellion in Ukrainian Context: Inviting in or
    Shutting the Door?   239

 12 What Is Donbas for Russia?   271

Final Thoughts: Imperfect Peace Is Better than a Good War   293

Appendix A: Interviewees   301

Appendix B: Notes on Methodology   305

Bibliography   311

Index   325

About the Author   337

Foreword

Ukrainian Crisis

View from Eastern Ukraine

Following the collapse of the Soviet Union, little attention was paid to Russia, Eastern Europe, and the former Soviet Union. The United States and many Western governments reassigned their analysts to address different threats. Scholars began to focus much less on Russia, Eastern Europe, and the former Soviet Union, instead turning their attention to East Asia among other regions. With the descent of Ukraine into civil war, scholars and governments have lamented the fact that there are not enough scholars studying Russia, Eurasia, and Eastern Europe. Scholars must again turn their focus on this extremely important geographic area. There remains much misunderstanding about the politics of the region. With tensions between governments at heightened levels unprecedented since the Cold War, scholarship addressing the politics of the region is extremely vital. The Russian, Eurasian, and Eastern European Politics Book Series aims at remedying the deficiency in the study and understanding of the politics of Eurasia.

In 2013, the world witnessed the first major post–Cold War crisis between the United States and Russia. Ukraine had been vacillating between signing an association agreement with the European Union or maintaining close ties with Russia. Moscow had made it clear that if Kyiv signed the association agreement, it would cut off aid to Kyiv as well as raise gas prices. As further incentive, Moscow agreed to provide further loans to Ukraine if it would agree not to sign the association agreement. Ukrainian president Viktor Yanukovych agreed and stated that he would not sign the agreement. Following that announcement, protesters began filling the Maidan Square in Kyiv, demanding an end to corruption and closer ties to the European Union. In the weeks that followed, Yanukovych fled the country, a new government assumed power, and signed the association agreement. Moscow in turn sent troops to Crimea, and Crimea soon voted to secede from Ukraine. Civil war broke out as Donbas region also tried to secede. Kyiv sent forces to quell the rebellion, and Moscow and Kyiv found themselves in the most serious military altercation since the collapse of the Soviet Union.

In the United States, the seceding regions of Ukraine were portrayed as being merely puppets of a newly assertive Russian government. In fact, the Russians were seen as pulling all of the strings in the rebellion against Kyiv. This book provides a unique perspective on the conflict in Ukraine. The author was able to speak with many of the insurgents in the seceding territories. Drawing on a very unique experience, the author is able to offer a perspective on the Ukrainian crisis that has been lacking in the West.

This book is a vital account that should be read by anyone interested in the current conflict between the United States and Russia. It should be used in all classes that examine democratic transition, as well as regional classes that focus on Russia and Eastern Europe.

Michael O. Slobodchikoff
Series Editor
Lexington Russian, Eurasian and Eastern European Politics Book Series

Acknowledgments

This book is a truly collective undertaking. I was amazed and enormously grateful to discover how many people believed in this publication to be a worthwhile effort and were prepared to offer their assistance, share critical insights, and generously let me benefit from their knowledge. Richard Sakwa provided encouragement for writing the book and led by example. Krista Zongolowicz, who had a great trust in my pursuit, helped to make the characters acquire their voices in English and come to life. Anthony Foreman contributed with valuable editorial suggestions, always trying to bring me back to the ground and find balance in this complex story. Christopher Langton advised on complicated military and security aspects of the conflict, the field in which he has unrivalled expertise. Stephane Prevost was a huge inspiration for the book and contributed with his insights throughout the long process of writing. Elizabeth Teague encouraged me to be confident about my voice and was my thorough, meticulous reader. My friends and colleagues—Marc Berenson, Peter Nasmyth, Fiona Frazer, Craig Oliphant, Anna Munster, Robert Stephenson, and Jonathan Cohen—gave me useful suggestions and their opinions on the subject matter. I would like to thank Michael Slobodchikoff, commissioning editor at Lexington Books, for support and guidance throughout the process. My sincere thanks also go to Joseph Parry, Madhu Koduvali and their colleagues at Lexington Books and at Deanta for their support and professionalism throughout the publication process.

Russian journalist Vladimir Dergachoff from Moscow shared his in-depth knowledge of the subject and helped with some of the key contacts, while military historian Yevgenii Norin from Perm' let me benefit from his field research. I would also like to acknowledge the contribution of the "Union of Donbas Volunteers" and "Novorossiya Movement" in Moscow. The nature of the book is such that some of my contributors and helpers have to remain anonymous, but I would like to extend my gratitude nevertheless. They know who they are.

And finally, my heartfelt thanks go to my childhood friend Svetlana Stephenson for her indefatigable encouragement, critical, but fair eye while reading the drafts of the chapters, for our long intellectual conversations and for being always at my side when I needed it most.

Much of the narrative is written on the basis of firsthand material collected through interviews, ongoing conversations, travel and observations taken by the author in Ukraine and Russia, as well as following the coverage of developing stories. It provides the opinions of the key actors, as well as of others who played less prominent but nevertheless crucial roles in the events as they unfolded. This is the first time when the voices of direct participants will be heard in Western literature. Interviews were held by the author with fifteen ex-combatants and with two Ukrainian politicians involved in Donbas who did not participate in fighting. Out of combatants, nine were from Russia, four were from Ukraine, one from Azerbaijan, and one from South America. Interviews, and individual and group conversations with other respondents from Ukraine included ordinary Donbas residents who were not politically involved in the conflict but whose lives have been changed by it, of different leanings. Political experts with diverse and sometimes opposing political orientations were interviewed in Kyiv. Interviews in Moscow were conducted with scholars and political analysts, journalists and bloggers who covered the conflict.

Research for the chapter on Crimea was based on interviews and group discussions in 2012 with participants of the Crimea Policy Dialogue who represented three different communities of the peninsula. Other respondents in Crimea, most of them Simferopol-based, were interviewed at the time, and follow-up interviews were conducted in Kyiv in 2015. Interviews were supplemented by written sources. Where possible, an event reported in an interview was confirmed by published information, and this public source was cited. The study uses opinion polls, which are illustrative of trends and allow confirming or denying information from interviews.

Abbreviations

AIFV	Armored Infantry Fighting Vehicles
APC	Armed Personnel Carrier
ARC	Autonomous Republic of Crimea
ATO	Anti-Terrorist Operation
CAF	Charity Aid Foundation
CIS	Commonwealth of Independent States
CPD	Crimea Policy Dialogue
DCFTA	Deep and Comprehensive Free Trade Agreement
DNR	Donetsk People's Republic
DSB	Dutch Safety Board
DTEK	Donbas Fuel and Energy Company
DOSAAF	Russian equivalent of Territorial Army associations
EEU	Eurasian Economic Union
FSB	Russian Federal Security Service
GCAs	Government-Controlled Areas (of Donbas)
GRU	Russian Military Intelligence Directorate
HRMM	UN Human Rights Monitoring Mission
ICG	International Crisis Group
ICRC	International Committee of the Red Cross
IDP	Internally Displaced Person
IUD	Industrial Union of the Donbas
JIT	Joint Investigation Team
LDPR	Liberal-Democratic Party of Russia
LNR	Luhansk People's Republic
MANPADS	Man-Portable Air Defense Systems
MGIMO	Moscow State Institute of International Relations
MLR	Multiple Launch Rocket

MoI	Ministry of Interior
MoD	Ministry of Defense
NATO	North Atlantic Treaty Organization
NGCAs	Non-Government Controlled Areas (of Donbas)
OCHA	UN Office for the Coordination of Humanitarian Affairs
OSCE	Organization for Security and Co-operation in Europe
OUN	Organization of Ukrainian Nationalists
PATRIR	Peace Action, Training and Research Institute of Romania
PoR	Party of Regions
RNU	Russian National Unity
RSFSR	Russian Soviet Federative Socialist Republic
SAM	Surface-to-Air Missile
SBU	Security Service of Ukraine
SCM	System Capital Management holding
SMM	OSCE Special Monitoring Mission
SSR	Soviet Socialist Republic (Union Republic)
UKIP	UK Independence Party
UNHCR	UN High Commissioner for Refugees
UN OHCHR	UN Office of High Commissioner for Human Rights
UPA	Ukrainian Insurgent Army
UOC MP	Ukrainian Orthodox Church under the Moscow Patriarchate
VCIOM	Russian Public Opinion Research Center
VGTRK	Russian State Broadcasting Company
WWII	World War II

Introduction

Talking Donbas, Not Putin

Our reaction to events is not a result of the events themselves, but of our opinions of them. (Epictetus)[1]

Every recent book about Ukraine or Russia is a book about Putin. This one will be different. It tells the bottom-up story of the rebellion in Ukraine's Donbas region, concentrating on its internal dynamic and explaining the perspectives of its participants—the local rebels opposing Kyiv, volunteer combatants who came from Russia and elsewhere, and ordinary residents who were caught up in the events and divided by the war. This is a book about a human tragedy on a biblical scale which happened in the twenty-first century in Europe where the principles of liberal peace seemingly triumphed making a war no longer possible. It unfolded in front of video cameras and in the era of mass communications, and yet created a humbug of misinformation, distortions, and fantasies.

The book aims to tell the story of the conflict in Donbas from the point of view of the pro-Russian rebels, who sought and continue to seek either sovereign independence from Ukraine or unification with Russia. It provides a unique insight into their thinking and motivations. The book does not try to put both sides of the argument, albeit referencing it where appropriate, not because it is unimportant, but because much is written about the perspective of Kyiv already, while the rebels remain in the shade covered by a fog of war. The side of the Ukrainian government and its support base have been presented by many knowledgeable academics, such as Andrew Wilson and others.[2] The author is aware that the account can be viewed as one-sided. Yet, such views must be understood without prejudice not only from the point of historical narrative, but also because they are important if we are ever to resolve the conflict. It is worth bearing in mind that civil wars never have absolute villains and saints, but it is rather the logic of armed struggle which leads the parties into taking actions and counter-actions that were unthinkable for them at the beginning.

Those who were making and remaking the conflict are placed in the center of the story which gets up closer to the combatants. It shows volunteer fighters, driven by a wide and diffuse set of motivations, who emerged from within Ukraine, Russia, and from the world outside that stood at the heart of the rebellion. The book seeks to bring out the participants' own voices and personalities to give the flavor and provide an opportunity to explain their thinking and actions. Rather than summarizing their stories, the characters' speech is preserved in the way of expression, as much as it was possible to do so in translation.

The book starts with scene-setting explaining identities in Ukraine through references to historical legacies, language, culture, religion, and political developments since the time of independence, and how the events at Euromaidan in 2013–2014 transformed them. The process developed rapidly when the constants which seemed fixed started moving under the pressure of circumstances. The book then goes into the internal situation on the Crimean peninsula and explores contestation of identities through history and modern politics. The story also zooms in on Donbas region, describing its origins, the place it occupied in Ukraine, and grievances the center and the periphery had vis-a-vis each other, before introducing the outbreak of the uprising.

The main part of the book follows the conflict trajectory as it went from the initial skirmishes to a full-fledged war and establishment of the unrecognized rebellious territories. The narrative concentrates on the insurgency from April 2014 onwards, going through the stages of assembling different conflict ingredients together, the rebellion's zigzagging fortunes when it became apparent that Moscow was not going to repeat the Crimea scenario in Donbas, the key military battles and the tactics the warring parties deployed against each other, and how the active phase of the war drew to a close. It further analyzes the military and political situation that shaped up in the rebellious territories and the internal processes that they underwent to arrive at these results. The book sheds some light on the developments in Moscow—although reliable data are scarce and a great deal of misinformation, ideology and propaganda obscures the picture—and discusses the phenomenon and implications of the *Russian Spring* movement.

The last part is dedicated to three themes. The first is the conflict subculture, symbolism, narrative, and communications that the insurgency produced. The rebels were making efforts to identify who they were and to spread their side of the story, which was made possible by the digital age and the internet-savvy population. The set of ideas which fed Donbas conflict are analyzed in the following chapter, as well as the power of these beliefs and ideas to act as a pull factor for people from different parts of the world. The second theme is to situate Donbas conflict within the developments in Ukraine, including how it affected the lives of the ordinary residents, and how the state and society addressed the war and peace dilemma. Thirdly, Russia's role is mentioned throughout the book and analyzed in the last chapter, as well as the effects that the conflict produced on Russian politics and society. It does not go deep into national-level politics in Ukraine and Russia, again well-researched subjects, but covers what is relevant for the understanding of the conflict and its future resolution. The book concludes with the prospects and challenges for peace.

The book reiterates that the history of Ukraine's conflict did not start in 2014. Without acknowledging the past, it is difficult to understand the present and the extent it holds the actors in conflict a hostage to it. Thus, invoking Walter Benjamin:

> the Angel of History must look just so. His face is turned towards the past. Where we see the appearance of a chain of events, he sees one single catastrophe, which unceasingly piles rubble on top of rubble and hurls it before his feet. He would like to pause for a moment so fair, to awaken the dead and to piece together what has been smashed. But a storm is blowing from Paradise, it has caught itself up in his wings and is so strong that the Angel can no longer close them. The storm drives him irresistibly into the future, to which his back is turned.[3]

NOTE ON TERMINOLOGY

The use of academic terms is explained in chapter 1 on "Framing the Issues." Rebels' self-designations of "Novorossiya," "Donetsk People's Republic," or "DNR," and "Luhansk People's Republic," or "LNR," are used to describe the actions and positions of the protagonists where relevant in the context, while the term "Non-Government Controlled Areas" (NGCAs) stipulated in the Minsk Agreement is used for more general descriptions with respect to the rebellious territories. "*De facto* authorities" is applied to the leaderships of the NGCAs. Ukrainian spellings are used with the exception of direct quotes when people spoke in Russian or when individuals and organizations had Russian names or titles.

NOTES

1. Epictetus (AD 55–135) was a Greek-born slave of Rome in the first century. His teachings are based in Stoic philosophy. The quote appeared (in Greek, then Latin) in "The Enchiridion" which was written by Arrian, a student of Epictetus, and was re-translated into many languages.

2. Andrew Wilson, *Ukraine Crisis: What It Means for the West* (New Haven, CT: Yale University Press, 2014). See also Special Issues of *Southeast European and Black Sea Studies*, 16, no. 1 (2016) and *Europe-Asia Studies*, 68, no. 4 (2016).

3. Walter Benjamin, *On the Concept of History* (Frankfurt am Main: Gesammelte Schriften I: 2. Suhrkamp Verlag, 1974), in translation.

Chapter 1

Framing the Issues

A Conflict among Other Conflicts

The conflict in Donbas attracted massive international attention because of Russia's involvement.[1] The significance of the crisis in Ukraine for international relations is certainly an acknowledged reality[2] which will continue to influence Russia-West relations for years and decades to come, and well beyond a "Putin era."[3] What set the conditions for it, as stated by Richard Sakwa, was the failure to create a stable and durable European security order, of which the conflict in Ukraine was the most vivid manifestation and a symptom of.[4] Majority of the literature on Ukraine explains the developments through the aggressive Russian policy and/or through the weakness of Ukrainian state which created an enabling environment for disturbances in the region.[5] These works which became an orthodoxy in Western scholarship primarily reflect the pro-Ukrainian perspective and rely on Ukrainian official interpretation of the conflict.[6] Some present strong political views on Russia, interpreting the events from a value-driven standpoint which can obscure research.[7] However, narratives of a "new Cold War" unhelpfully render Ukraine something of a chess piece on the geopolitical board. Geopolitics becomes what the whole story is about.[8] Without negating Russia's role in the crisis in Ukraine, it is worth noting that most conflicts which proceeded into civil wars experienced some degree of external interference,[9] either by foreign powers and regional states[10] or by diasporas, such as in Kosovo, Karabakh, and Chechnya.[11]

The argument of this book is that an exclusive focus on the Russian government masked Donbas rebellion's own features, making the social process of conflict merely a function of the Kremlin's policy. Such focus overlooks its parallels, commonalities, and contrasts with other conflicts around the world, the study of which can enrich our understanding not only of this conflict, but also of how insurgencies work. Analysis of internal dynamic brings us closer

1

to understanding of other postmodern conflicts where issues of identity and non-state actors are paramount—even the rise of the Islamic State (IS)—and how they can ultimately be resolved.

This book regards the events in Donbas as a prismatic affair and does it through four main prisms. Firstly, violent conflict cannot be explained solely through actions and interactions between states, and ordinary people rather than elites can become a decisive force in it, surprising outside observers. Secondly, while many of the interstate conflicts of twentieth century were interpreted as "ethnic," this lens is barely applicable to Ukraine, where the conflict was about politicized identity, broadly understood, in which ethnicity played less of a role, and a talk about an "ethnic Russian minority" is misleading. Thirdly, Donbas tells us something about why large numbers of people make a decision to take part in a collective violent action, when material rewards are low or nonexistent, and mortal risks are high. Fourthly, it is about how ideas and narratives are constructed to provide meaning to a struggle.

PEOPLE MAKE CONFLICT

The book situates its narrative of Donbas in an interrelationship between the past and violence that, in Karl Marx's terminology, played a role of a "midwife of history." The focus is on the sub-state actors from Ukraine, Russia, and further afield who have been a major force in igniting the rebellion and turning it into a larger uprising, into which the Russian state got embroiled. It approaches the events as a civil war defined as "armed combat within the boundaries of a recognised sovereign entity between parties subject to a common authority at the onset of the hostilities."[12] Kalyvas points that the actual dynamic of civil war has seldom been the object of examination, noting an ontological problem, that is, that "almost every macrohistorical account of civil wars points to the importance of pre-existing popular allegiances for the war's outcome, yet almost every micro historical account points to a host of endogenous mechanisms, whereby allegiances and identities tend to result from the war or are radically transformed by it."[13] The book seeks to unlock these endogenous mechanisms, although studying Donbas conflict is challenging as it has a mixture of irregular and conventional warfare elements.

The approach of characterizing Donbas rebellion as a civil war is by no means unique; for example, the Uppsala Conflict Data Program (2016)[14] classifies this conflict as intrastate. Kudelia attributes the rebellion to internal political factors: "events inside Ukraine, which were not only outside the direct control of Moscow, but often ran counter to the interests of the Russian leadership." He lists such factors as violence perpetrated by Euromaidan activists, the "show of force" by the new Ukrainian government who came to power as a result of Euromaidan, their encouragement to involve members of nationalist groups in the fighting, and provision of the Ukrainian military with "carte blanche" to use indiscriminate weaponry in densely populated areas. "All these events were superimposed on Donbas's recent political history, the structure of patronage in the region, and the system of values and political preferences of its residents. The result was the collapse of the legitimacy of the Ukrainian authorities in the eyes of a significant part of the local population, and this accelerated the region's militarization against Kyiv. Without question, Russia exploited these events, but it did not define them."[15] Katchanovski concludes that all national and international actors, including Russia and the United States, contributed to the start and escalation of the violent conflict, but that "regional political culture in Donbas and Russian ethnicity were strongest determinants of support for separatism."[16]

Conflicts often tend to be interpreted through the realm of elites and grand politics: the assumption is that elites determine the course of group actions,[17] and that their strategic actions, such as scheming of oligarchs and political forces aligned with them, shape the events. Elites are blamed for machinations aimed at increasing their hold or acquiring power, which account for subsequent violence.[18] Wilson pursues this line of argument in relation to Donbas conflict,[19] as well as does Malyarenko.[20] The problem is that although this is a valid lens for analysis of national-level politics of Ukraine,[21] it does not help to improve our understanding of what happened in Donbas in 2014, as the elite influence quickly went down when the events turned violent. The non-elitist nature of the uprising also questions the centrality of "elite bargain" for understanding of the issues of conflict and peace.[22]

The book zooms in onto a leaderless uprising started by individuals with hardly any political careers or significant military roles. "Leaderlessness" can be characterized in more than one way: as a normative extension of horizontal, or as a consequence of marginalized population turning to collective action or/and the choice of social actors who prefer to safeguard their identities.[23] This pattern is not as uncommon as believed. Arab Spring is characterized as a leaderless revolution, in which many actors chose to remain nameless and faceless. The Northern Ireland conflict was sustained by ordinary men and women,[24] and its subsequent leaders Martin McGuiness and Gerry Adams quickly rose to prominence after joining the clandestine movement from fairly ordinary backgrounds.

By far, not everybody who lived in Donbas at the time joined the rebellion, but this does not imply that it did not have local roots and indigenous activists. Rid and Hecker characterize stratification at the early stages of conflicts in the following way: "during an insurgency the population falls into three groups: a small and disenfranchised fringe group initially supports the insurgency; on the other side are those who want to see the counterinsurgent and the government to succeed; in the middle between the two is the largest group, which is neutral, uncommitted and apolitical."[25] This is consistent with the fact that participation in civil wars seldom involves large proportions of population, since insurgents cannot rely on conscription. However, in order to gain momentum, a rebellion has to acquire a sufficient backing of grass-roots society which provides logistics, new recruits, emotional support, and information. For instance, when such support in the wars in Chechnya was available, resistance was hard to conquer, but when the insurgency acquired a distinct Islamist streak, general support waned down, making it possible for Moscow to force its way through.[26]

TRAJECTORIES OF VIOLENCE

As we will see, violence in Donbas conflict was not inevitable, but nonviolent options were quickly closing down. What makes people pursue the more violent options? The concept of security dilemma offers a possible interpretation. Amid fast-moving events and in the conditions of uncertainty, the parties are faced with a perceived choice: strike first, or you will be killed. They can resort to preemptive violence if they see the other party's intentions as existentially threatening.[27] The question is whether Donbas theoretically could have seceded through a nonviolent route when Ukrainian politics underwent a radical shift. Evangelista points out that although the barriers are formidable, secession is not entirely impossible if a central state agrees to it or is too weak to resist it,[28] but this is hard to imagine in Ukraine's case.

International law regards anti-government rebellions as illegitimate and sides up with the rights of the state rather than aspirations of the insurgents. However, can there be specific circumstances when an uprising might have some default legitimacy? Do people have a right to rebel in certain circumstances which could be understood if not accepted, for example had the Chechens any moral right to stand up to the Russian state?[29] Halliday offers a rough guide on "when it is legitimate to take up arms, when the non-state actors have a *jus ad bellum*. Certain principles apply: the group must claim, plausibly, to represent a significant and definable community. It must have exhausted or found impossible nonviolent means, it should be open to negotiations."[30] These questions form a hotly contested ground between the parties to the conflict, with the government side typically answering these criteria in the negative in order to deny nascent legitimacy to a rebellion while the insurgents claim exactly the opposite.

A war follows a dynamic of escalation, where own mechanisms apply. War is a distinct phenomenon as it signifies a break with the default condition, that is, peace, and does not arise solely from prewar cleavages, but also from interactions during conflict gestation when actors start to populate the stage, local cleavages get intertwined with master cleavages, and mobilization occurs. Existence of a previously politically shaped movement is not a pre-requisite for grassroots mobilization, but when it shapes up through violence and creates internal bonds, it becomes a force that does not easily go away. This is true of Liberation Tigers of Tamil Elam,[31] Free Aceh Movement or GAM,[32] and Irish Republican Army.[33] Thus, war takes logic of its own, not always connected to the original causes, while political actors use civilians for their purposes, and civilians use political actors to settle their own private conflicts.[34] This creates a messy reality of a civil war, in which idealism and banditry get mixed together.

Conflicts are akin to living organisms and follow specific trajectories, going through the hurdles to establish themselves. The first trajectory is political: "one of the most difficult stages for an insurgent movement is the transition, or expansion, from a violent militant group to a politically influ-ential group. It takes a skilful insurgent leader, a person with solid military skills, sound political instincts and charisma to make such a transition."[35] The book explores the key personalities which were instrumental in mak-ing this transition happen. The second is about establishing control over the territory and forces which make up the rebellion. Irregular war is defined by the twin processes of segmentation (territory divided into zones controlled by rival actors) and fragmentation (zones where their sovereignties overlap). Both can be fruitfully researched in Donbas because it had a vast terrain, and uprising developed in multiple centers simultaneously. Fragmentation is interesting not only in relation to examining the course of military actions, but also because attention to actor fragmentation unlocks the complexities of collective identity and the contingency of the linkage between identity and action.[36] Actors were driven by complex and diffuse sets of motivations, and not necessarily were easy bedfellows. The rebellion had to overcome this fragmentation and achieve a degree of consolidation if it were to have a chance to survive politically and militarily. If the counterinsurgent state is interested in peace building, it needs to steer this process in the right direction to improve the chances for it.[37]

IDENTITY AND WAR

When asked by the author as what divides them from their compatriots in Donbas, my respondents from among Kyiv intelligentsia kept answering, "this is a difference in mentality." "Mentality" is not a salient category in social research, but it made sense for Ukrainian interlocutors who were trying to comprehend the turbulent events around them, and it is necessary to unlock what it means. The book interprets it in terms of identity. "Identity" is a highly politicized term. Social scientists emphasize the role of self and identity in the causes and consequences of intergroup hostility, although the meaning and nature of these social constructs have been contested by scholars from different traditions. There is an agreement that social identities create and exacerbate intergroup conflict, while intergroup conflict influences social identity.[38] The most common is Tajfel's definition of identity as "that part of an individual's self-concept which derives from his knowledge of his membership in a social group (groups) together with the value and emotional significance attached to that membership."[39] At the same time, identities are not merely individual but emerge in their sociocultural and political contexts.

Ukraine is not the only country in Europe which contains different, at times opposing, identities within a single state. Belgium is one such case where Flemish and Wallonians form distinct groups, whereas the state has to accept a mere overarching role.[40] The conflict in Northern Ireland between "Catholics" and "Protestants" is not about religion,[41] but between different identity groups which historically associated themselves with a faith congregation.[42] The conflict emerged due to differences in opinion surrounding the constitutional state of the island, with religious identity representing a badge of difference[43] bound up in political ideologies. Northern Irish research demonstrated how, once these labels are accepted, the strength of the in-group identity can impact on emotions, cognitions, reasoning, and behaviors, such as influencing in-group bias, prejudice, and discrimination.[44]

Political identities are not constants, and can rise and fall in significance depending on evolution of the states and their environments: a pro-independence Scottish identity was a fairly marginal commodity in the early 1990s in the United Kingdom, but by 2014 was shared by nearly half of Scotland's population.[45] A new identity of a frustrated Muslim emerged in Europe. Most of time, different identities do not clash with each other, even if sometimes they produce group alienation, and differences are resolved through political means, but they lay the grounds for mobilization if conditions alter. In other words, existence of identity differences is a prerequisite for conflict, but the conflict happens only when one or both identity groups feel sufficiently threatened by the other.

Conceptualization of identity beyond its definition in terms of ethnic or civic belonging is elusive and interpretative although common features include the processes of self-identification, development of self-knowledge, modes of self-representation, and coming to understand oneself as belonging to a collective.[46] Sinisa states that "identity has tended to replace older collective concepts such as 'social consciousness,' 'race,' and 'national character,' and has tried to fulfil the same all-purpose goal of expressing collective difference and individuality in terms that everyone can understand and feel."[47] Social identity refers to the facts of one's self image that derives from salient group memberships. Definition of self and "other,"—whether other is conceptualized as hostile or friendly—are aspects of identity formulation. Contingent nature of identities is reflected by the situation that groups with different identity projects will assert the validity and truth of their version of identity, and assign to other groups particular identities that suit their needs.[48] Thus, there are no "objectively verifiable" identities as the processes of definition and redefinition are always ongoing.

Anthony Smith proposes a symbolist approach to the study of identity aiming to enter the "inner world" of the participants and understand their perceptions and visions. This approach analyzes communities, ideologies, and sense of identity in terms of their constituent symbolic resources, that is, the traditions, memories, values, myths, and symbols that compose the accumulated heritage of cultural units. It highlights the role of subjective and symbolic resources in motivating ideologies and collective actions against the emphasis on material and political domains. Smith argues that symbolic realm offers a fuller and more balanced account of nationalist movements than modernist analyses that identify the structural conditions, as it brings out the appeal of different motifs—myths, memories, symbols, and values.[49]

Theorists of ethnic conflict tend to apply an inclusive definition of ethnicity, which combines racial, linguistic, and religious differences in determining group cohesion.[50] Empirically, bringing together different political and cultural elements means that political community has to have a certain ethnocultural basis.[51] Beyond ethnicity, layers of identity are multiple and can include culture, religion, historical roots, and language, but also political notions and geopolitical orientations, if they are strongly held and convey emotional resonance. They cannot be equated with "national" identities as post–Cold War era favored the emergence of "non-national" identities at the subnational and transnational levels.

But what happens to identity in a violent conflict—does one precondition the other? Social identity theory says that they are mutually reinforcing. Tajfel outlines a dynamic approach to social identity, which is understood as intervening causal mechanism in the situations of social change: "there will be some social situations which will force most individuals involved, however weak and unimportant to them may have been their initial group identifications, to act in terms of their group membership."[52] Such situations of upheaval and social turmoil can bring to life to life memberships in groups which were dormant before while positive feedback from other group members enhances such identifications. Identities are not static and essentialist, but can be fluid and situationally enacted. Reicher proposes a perceptual approach that conceptualizes identities both as processes and products, avoiding "objectifying" them. Instead, identities are changed and transformed through conflict, and the task of a researcher is to explore when and how fluid categories harden into fixed meanings.[53] Fearon and Laitin discuss a constructivist approach toward social construction of identity and violence.[54] In Ilya Prizel's observation, "while the redefinition of national identities is generally a gradual process, under situations of persistent stress even well-established identities can change at a remarkable rate, and a people's collective memory can be 'rearranged' quite quickly."[55]

Polarization of identities is the process which both precedes and exacerbates conflict, referring to divisions between groups "when a large number of conflict group members attach overwhelming importance to the issues at stake, or manifest strongly held antagonistic beliefs and emotions towards the opposing segment, or both."[56] It is consistent with observation that the outbreak of conflict and war takes people by surprise, that polarization is abrupt and unexpected,[57] but individuals and groups can move quickly to occupy extreme positions if they are convinced that their core values are at stake. This is because polarized conflicts are about not "specific gains or losses, but over conceptions of moral right and over the interpretation of history and human dignity."[58] They are "the kind of intense and divisive politics one may refer to by the name of absolute politics,"[59] where objectives of conflict parties are perceived as zero-sum.

Literature tells us that in-conflict group behavior can differ significantly from how individuals behave toward bearers of other identities in the time of peace: social behavior in extreme situations "will be to a large extent independent of personal relationships which may exist in other situations between individual members of the two groups." Acting in terms of group rather than self cannot be expected to play a predominant part unless a clear cognitive structure of "us" and "them" is present.[60] Giuliano observes that people with different ethnic identities, even those that are strongly felt, do not automatically respond to the ethnic appeals of politicians.[61] She argues, in relation to Ukraine, that because the porosity of cultural boundaries and language repertoires in Ukraine were not static, it is not worth centering on static ethnic and linguistic identities outside of political and socioeconomic context, whereas violence tends to harden identities and attitudes.[62] Moreover, salience of ethnicity as a clear-cut identity marker has been repeatedly questioned, especially in the cases when groups intermix and intermarriage is widespread, as is the case in Ukraine. Ethnic or cultural closeness is a poor safeguard against an outbreak of conflict, but can make it actually more vicious: "the more similar groups are in their values and aspirations, the more acute the intergroup social competition."[63] Instead, when a conflict breaks out, individuals with ambivalent identities are forced into making choices which group they belong to.

Another relevant layer of identity is supra-national. Huntington conceptualizes such identities as "civilizational" which transcend ethnic and state boundaries. He argued in 1993 that differences between civilizations were more fundamental than between political ideologies and regimes, that civilization-consciousness was increasing, and predicted that the main source of conflict would be cultural. Huntington's civilizations encompass divergent views on the relations between the citizen and the state, shared or separate history and visions of future, and language and culture. In Ukraine's case, state borders did not follow the divide between "Eastern" and "Western" civilizational identities, but went through it, making it prone to a conflict along "civilizational" lines.[64] From this perspective, "the Russian World is often promoted as a supra-national or civilisation-level tier of identity."[65] Huntington's understanding of "civilization" as a mega concept of culture has been robustly criticized as implying a theory of social (global) conflict, as essentialist and covering too much ground. It was observed that more people die in conflicts within civilizations than between them. Bridging from "civilizations," Avruch proposes a narrower focus on culture as a way of looking inside so-called civilizations. It focuses on historically situated individuals, images, and symbols formulated by them through immediate living experience.[66] However, recent developments, such as emergence of global jihadi movements or the *Russian World*, make us recognize the validity of Huntington's theory for interpretation of modern conflicts.

To sum up, the book sees the roots of the conflict in polarization of identities in Ukraine where plural forms of association and belonging used to coexist with each other peacefully, but tensions lay underneath. They were not irresolvable, and skillful political craftsmanship could have transformed them into an inclusive citizenship. However, polarization during Euromaidan sharpened the divide, which was largely of a nonethnic, but "civilizational" character, and transpired when people felt seriously threatened, emerging as the grounds for grassroots mobilization. The conflict actors in Donbas saw their "civilization" as a cultural entity expressed in language, history, religion, customs, institutions, and subjective self-identification of people which were important for them. We can condemn their version of these things as backward, authoritarian, illiberal, or nonexistent, but still it made sense to them.

VOLUNTEERING FOR COMBAT: WHY PEOPLE JOIN A REBELLION

The outbreak of any conflict cannot be solely explained by a presence of underlying cleavages and grievances without a reference to human agency which turns the course of events in a certain way. This can happen in the matter of days, and decisions and actions taken in this crucial time depend on the personalities whom the political wave brought to the surface and who chose to do something in that hour. These may not be members of the elite, but previously unknown individuals who were prepared to act on the strength of their convictions, moral beliefs, and self-interests. Actions, aspirations, calculations, and dreams of thousands of individuals caught up in the events at the critical moment made no less a bearing upon sliding down the road toward bloodshed than political leaders or presidents. This calls for exploration of anthropological and psychological features of organized violence which interweaves political actions with military ones.

The situation was that the social process of conflict involved a large measure of improvisation, chaotic creativity, and alliance-building, when its participants used what they had at hand combining the elements of spontaneity, deliberation, daring, caution, and opportunism. As it went on, it attracted more and more people into it driven by different motivations—standing for a homeland, protection from outside "invaders," altruism, solidarity, revenge, willingness to change the country's borders and join Russia, and ideology of a global opposition to liberalism and Euroatlanticism. Resistance was enacted through a release of collective emotions that came out of these motivations. They molded into a new quality as they went through the war and survival, and this emergent mold made enough sense to the conflict actors, so that a man from Luhansk and a man from Santiago sat in the trenches together and were prepared to give up their lives for each other.

The rebellion attracted a great deal of individuals who chose to participate in fighting, and the question is how they should be named. They are typically called "Kremlin militias" in the West while their self-designation is of "volunteers." Irish Republican Army (IRA) members were also known as "volunteers" and were concentrated in Northern Ireland, although a smaller number were based in the Republic of Ireland and there were cells in the United Kingdom. IRA volunteer cells also operated in the United States and other overseas locations.[67] Malyarenko and Galbreith, using the Scobell and Hammit's definition,[68] attribute the term "paramilitaries" to members of territorial battalions who fought on the Kyiv side alongside the regular armed forces,[69] but this definition does not adequately describe those who fought on the opposite side.

The other concept is of "irregular fighters" which as Scheipers notes, originated in mid-eighteenth century, although their status in the twenty-first century became contested. The use of irregulars as auxiliary by the regular side played a vital role in the Western strategy in Afghanistan, Libya, Iraq, and Syria. While negative attributes such as indiscipline and propensity to loot are characteristic of them, regular armies can do so as well. Moreover, the relationship between regular and irregular is inherently tense: the regular side can suddenly drop and sideline individual irregular leaders and warlords if the perception of the local situation changes. Another—negative—term is of "unlawful combatant" which acquired notoriety with Guantanamo Bay, but here "moral hierarchy emerged, equating irregular fighter with illegitimate combatant. In reality, irregular fighters can be both illegitimate combatants and useful auxiliaries, depending on the perspective of the respective parties."[70]

Malet, who researched voluntary participation in foreign conflicts, uses the terms "transnational insurgent"—noncitizen of conflict states who join insurgencies during civil conflicts—and "foreign fighter" interchangeably to characterize these individuals. His research shows that foreign fighters participated in more than one in five civil wars over the past 200 years.[71] For Hegghammer, "foreign fighters" have four characteristics: they lack affiliation to an official military; are unpaid; do not share the citizenship of factions involved in conflicts, nor do they have kin connections to fighting groups.[72] Given the definitional complexities, this book applies the term "volunteer combatant" to those who came from the Soviet successive states, including other parts of Ukraine, and "local rebel" to natives or individuals with roots in Donbas to instances when differentiation between groups needs to be made. The use of "foreign fighters" follows Hegghammer's line to describe conflict participants who came from outside the former Soviet countries, although some had a kinship connection to them.

Significance of non-state actors for the events in Donbas must be appreciated. In other conflict theaters, non-state actors operated in ways that affected political outcomes both within states or as transnational institutions operating on global arena.[73] In Donbas, non-state actors believed that they were pursuing a revolutionary warfare—a specific version of an insurgency, designed to use guerrilla warfare combined with political action to further an ideology.[74] Whiteside reminds us that the demise of revolutionary warfare turned out to be a fantasy[75] and Donbas may occupy a place in a revolutionary continuum. Non-state actors inspired by ideas feed into so-called spiritual insurgencies as opposed to those driven by a clear material or political interest, which are more likely to occur in the states of heterogeneous identity of ethnicity, race, or religion.[76]

What makes people participate in such high-risk activity as rebellion? Conflicts have been explained by the ideological and identity-based mobilization of groups which experience a fear of subrogation[77] or respond to symbols, myths, and discourses.[78] Earlier research attributed such decisions to economic incentives or peer pressure, while rationalist approaches center on greed and grievances paradigm.[79] These concepts may be able to explain some conflicts, but not all conflicts, and hardly apply to a large, territorially dispersed insurgency which attracted large numbers of external participants.

Malet questions significance of material interests for such cases: "empirical evidence indicates that recruiters rarely promise foreign fighters material incentives. Most transnational volunteers received very limited or no order of compensation but still engaged in costlier military actions than did local fighters."[80] External participation in civil wars is likelier when more universal values, such as ideology or religion, are at stake. Potential recruits are told that their common group is under existential threat and their participation is necessary for the survival of their people and themselves. Thus, an imagined community is formed on the basis of this transnational identity, such as the one that emerged during the Spanish Civil War.[81] Another motivation includes altruism and responsibility to protect which is often cited in relation to solidarity fighters who join the war theaters in the Middle East.[82]

Scholarship draws attention to ideology, a seemingly redundant concept in the post–Cold War era. Ideational factors are systems of beliefs that can be expressed as structured ideologies or general ideas of justice. Ugarriza and Craig define ideology as a set of political beliefs that promotes a particular way of understanding the world and shapes relations between members of a group and outsiders, and among members themselves. They understand ideology to be a corpus of thought that incorporates and arranges a series of specific elements present in armed conflict, such as doctrines, narratives, symbols, and myths.[83] Their research on Columbian armed groups shows that ideology continues to be relevant and plays a role in the internal dynamics, and that a combatant's ideological development is influenced not only by pre-enlistment experiences but also by participation in a group. Ideology is significant as a motivation to fight, and in maintaining internal cohesion within armed groups as an organizing and motivating factor.

Costalli and Ruggeri further show that ideologies and emotions play essential roles in causing the outbreak of civil war. Indignation and radical ideologies are crucial non-material factors in violent collective action, and are essential components of nonethnic civil wars being promoted by political entrepreneurs and through ideological networks. Such networks transform ideas into action, providing the organizational tools, while collective identities serve as a decisive component for the process of armed mobilization, during which group identities may be shaped and activated. Importance of emotions and belief systems should be emphasized as emotions and ideologies create bridges between context and individuals.[84] Power of collective emotions[85]—anger, shame, fear—as well as a moral value of solidarity can go a long way in conflict if suitably shaped. Social movement theorists underline processes of construction or redirection of emotions to achieve a necessary reframing of reality, when social movements target them toward the support and opponent bases.[86] Petersen links the emotions of fear, hatred, and rage to violence in ethnic conflicts.[87] However, emotions do not change people's underlying values; they only clarify and activate them.

Beyond the most commonly cited emotions of solidarity and anger, Costalli and Ruggeri stress the importance of indignation in the process of armed mobilization, that is, a wrong done to a third party. Indignation accounts for the sense of community and underscores the relationships between an individual and the surrounding people based on shared conceptions of right and wrong. When an emotional shock hits the links between individuals and their communities, a larger part of the population, which was not previously captured by radical ideologies, becomes available to consider it.[88] The book outlines the key events which triggered such emotional shocks and produced waves of mobilization.

Karagiannis argues, in his research on membership in paramilitary formations on the Kyiv side, that the power of ideas, sociopolitical norms, and collective emotions has been the key drivers for participation. These mechanisms functioned simultaneously reinforcing each other.[89] Wood stresses moral outrage, and claim to dignity, pride, and pleasure as motivating factors for participating in the El Salvador rebellion, when doing so was highly dangerous. Desire to assert one's dignity and defiance through the act of rebellion brought out a profound role of agency when the assertion itself constituted part of the meaning of those acts, a constitutive and expressive reason. These in-process benefits, that is, emotion-laden consequences of action, could be experienced only by those participating in it.[90] Similarly, early in Donbas war, some acted in order to act, to prove that they as empowered individuals were capable of launching a challenge. It is important to treat the combatants' emotions nonjudgmentally. Like love, moral outrage does not have to be directed at a worthy object for the emotion to be real and for individuals to act upon it. The book passes no judgment on whether the participants were justified in feeling what they felt, that is, whether Kyiv was indeed as guilty as they thought it was. If they genuinely acted in line with their values, beliefs, and emotions, they are accepted as valid.

MYTH-MAKING, SYMBOLISM, AND NARRATIVE

Culture does not cause conflict, but it is the lens through which the causes of conflict are ultimately refracted,[91] although it is often overlooked in empirical studies of conflict. Cultural elements ensure a degree of consciousness during crisis and rapid change, sharpen social boundary and opposition to outsiders, and wedge a division between "us" and "them."[92] A rebellion experiences a need to form a collective personality with its distinct culture to define "who we are." Symbols are required to remind of common heritage, and strengthen

cultural kinship and a sense of common identity and belonging. The process
of self-definition reflects a fusion of cognitive and expressive aspects, and
establishment of links with wider sentiments and aspirations. In such context,
collective rituals are being born, and their ceremonial and symbolic aspects,
if they take root, can demonstrate remarkable durability.[93] Donbas material
allows us to follow their birth: as Hobsbawn and Ranger point out, no tradition has "always" existed; there is a particular starting point in time, often
quite recent.[94]

Symbols of resistance are constructed by invoking historical memories, but
while the use of historical narratives and concepts is important, they may not
be sufficiently tangible to fill an initially barren space. Walzer writes in connection with the state, that as it "is indivisible, it must be personified before
it can be seen, symbolised before it could be loved, imagined before it can be
conceived."[95] Thus, symbols provide nodal points around which people can
eventually develop a common political identity.[96] Bolt developed a concept
of opportunity spaces that allows formation of networks of shared meaning
among those who adopt the same symbols, values, and beliefs. In crisis, ideas
are not so much lying around as get strategically placed in position. Narrative
frames that draw on simplified explanations of the "world out there" come into
play and contest those manufactured and disseminated by the state. Stories
become the revolutionary's strategic tool in fighting the asymmetric war of
ideas and images.[97] Such opportunity space opened in Donbas, where the formation of myths and symbols was chaotic and contradictory. The process was
bottom-up and individuals with ideological credentials were busy fighting as
well as creating content. Examples of leadership, notions of resistance and sacrifice became strategic tools in myth-making produced out of raw material at
hand. Hence, creation of iconic images and legendary figures was a necessary
part when it was difficult to tell fiction from reality. Marxist logic of dialectic
contradiction can explain this confusing juxtaposition of narratives and truth.

Following on from the focus on Russia's role in the conflict, most research
in cultural domain concentrated on the influence of Russian national media[98]
and on the "information warfare" directed at the opponent. Zhukov and
Baum analyze actor-specific and tactic-specific reporting bias in Ukrainian,
rebel, Russian, and international coverage.[99] Laurelle explores myth-making
process in Russia which Donbas gave impetus to, aimed at Russian nationalist base at home,[100] and O'Loughlin et al. present their survey data on support for *Novorossiya*[101] in the government-controlled areas of Ukraine.[102]
Pioneering research by Driscoll and Steinert-Threlkeld outlines a picture
of a heterogeneous set of political beliefs within the *Russki Mir* (Russian
World) constituency in Ukraine showing that strategic locals are constantly
competing in narrative production efforts, interfering with that of the Russian
government.[103]

As the conflict derived from the confluence of factors ranging from local to global that came together at one junction, their mutual influence and reinforcement created a distinct phenomenon and developed its own narrative. The conflict was "new" in a sense that it did not have a long prior history of resistance, but came about very quickly, and had a weakly articulated narrative to justify its claim. The rebellion had to organize this narrative, symbols, and communications in order to construct its version of self and of its cause, and for it to be appealing enough for people locally and globally to respond to it. There has been little work on how the rebellion defined itself for its own support base, sought to construct its version of an "imagined community" and led the battle for "hearts and minds" of the initially ambivalent population. This is not to deny the power of the Russian national media which was locked in a competition with the Ukrainian one, but to unveil a more complex reality on the ground. Typically, a rebellion has to engage in a competition for the trust and support of the civilian population when "both the insurgent and the government compete for this group's support. The insurgent's most valuable resource is a political cause that can mobilise the uncommitted masses. If the insurgent succeeds, the counterinsurgent loses the population's goodwill."[104] Therefore, insurgents' efforts must be directed toward winning over and controlling a variety of locally and sometimes globally dispersed sympathizers and populations.[105] Otherwise the supply of recruits, money, and logistics cannot be maintained.

New media played a noteworthy role. In modern warfare, non-state insurgents benefit more from new media than do the governments. Peer-to-peer technologies empower activist individuals, a trend known as Web 2.0,[106] where mass media and social interaction are merged into one. This technology replicates the principles of insurgent movements: initiative, anonymity, self-recruitment, varying levels of participation, self-motivated participants, often self-funded, fuelled by idealism, not orders.[107] Message control is weakened as audiences receive and transmit emotive messages between themselves, investing them with enthusiasm, inciting shared values and inviting collective action.[108] Collectively, this forms a certain subculture, locally produced, that appeals to subaltern identities or to those outside of hegemonic power structures. It uses anti-geopolitics, that is, inverting the categories created by hegemons, mimicry, and hybridity, and extensively relies on new media, influencing change in people's identities as a result of their engagement with it. What is propaganda and what is not is determined not by its content, but rather by the identity of the consumer.[109]

The book looks at the rebels' communications following the approaches developed by scholarship on the IS.[110] It identifies central themes of messaging: war, solidarity, anti-fascism, or binary oppositional themes—heroic/cowardly, truth/falsehood—as a way of triggering collective emotions, such as solidarity and desire for revenge.

AND LASTLY

Not everything can be explained through rigid conditionality and social science paradigms. When events unfold very quickly and in spontaneous ways, and history is made in a matter of days, there is also a question of human agency, the role of daring and charismatic personalities, actions and reactions, and a degree of coincidence and fortuitous circumstances. Why, for example, the city of Mariupol did not fall into the rebels' hands in the end, although it was a part of the original uprising? Was it because no charismatic field commander appeared at the right moment? Or was it because the Ukrainian security services promptly reacted and dispelled the nascent protests? Was it because of a weakness of anti-Kyiv feelings among the residents? Or was it because the local rebels could not lay their hands on arms quickly enough and were outgunned? All these—and maybe others—were contributing factors, while different observers attach different weight to them, depending on where they are situated in the conflict context. What is certain is that the present is a space of radical contingency, and history is produced within it in piecemeal fashions as opposed to being inevitable.

The narrative, experiences, and solidarity that Donbas unleashed would not go away even when the conflict is eventually resolved. The crisis in Ukraine will have far-reaching consequences, far beyond Ukraine's and Russia's internal developments. Thus, it should make us pause and think that it may be something more complex than the narrative which holds the conflict to be little less than an unmitigated act of Russian aggression perpetrated by the ugly and authoritarian regime of Putin.

NOTES

1. Michael McFaul, "Faulty Powers: Who Started the Ukraine Crisis?," *Foreign Affairs*, November/December 2014, Roy Allison, "Russian "deniable" intervention in Ukraine: how and why Russia broke the rules," *International Affairs* 90, no. 6 (2014): 1255–1297, DOI: 10.1111/1468-2346.12170, Taras Kuzio, "Ukraine between a Constrained EU and Assertive Russia," *Journal of Common Markets Studies* 55, no. 1 (2017): 103–120.

2. Gerard Toal, *Near Abroad: Putin, the West and the Contest over Ukraine and the Caucasus* (Oxford: Oxford University Press, 2017).

3. Rajan Menon and Eugene B. Rumer, *Conflict in Ukraine: The Unwinding of the Post–Cold War Order* (Boston: The MIT Press, 2015), Richard Sakwa, *Frontline Ukraine: Crisis in the Borderlands* (London: I.B. Tauris, 2015), special issue of *The Soviet and Post-Soviet Review* 44 (2017), koninklijke brill nv, leiden, DOI: 10.1163/18763324-04401002, H. Haukkala, "From Cooperative to Contested Europe? The Conflict in Ukraine as a Culmination of a Long-Term Crisis in EU-Russia Relations," *Journal of Contemporary European Studies* 23, no. 1 (2015): 25–40.

4. Richard Sakwa, "The death of Europe? Continental fates after Ukraine," *International Affairs* 91, no. 3 (2015): 555.

5. Andrew Wilson, *Ukraine Crisis: What It Means for the West* (New Haven, CT: Yale University Press, 2014). Czuperski, M., Herbst, J., Higgins, E., Polyakova, A., & Wilson, D. "Hiding in plain sight: Putin's war in Ukraine," (Washington, DC: Atlantic Council, 2015) http://www.atlanticcouncil.org/images/publications/Hiding_in_Plain_Sight/HPS_English.pdf

6. Andrew Wilson, "The Donbas in 2014: Explaining Civil Conflict Perhaps, but not Civil War," *Europe-Asia Studies* 68, no. 4 (2016): 631–652.

7. Stathys Kalyvas, *The Logic of Violence in Civil Wars* (Cambridge: Cambridge University Press, 2006), 33.

8. Samir Puri, "Human Security and Dialogue Challenges in Ukraine's Donetsk Region," Report (London: Peaceful Change Initiative, 2016).

9. Patrick M. Regan, *Civil Wars and Foreign Powers: Interventions and Intrastate Conflict* (Ann Arbor, MI: University of Michigan Press, 2000).

10. The data incorporate 150 conflicts during the period 1945–1999, 101 of which had outside interventions. In Patrick M. Regan, "Third Party Interventions and the Duration of Intrastate Conflicts," *Journal of Conflict Resolution* 46, no. 1 (2002).

11. Maria Koinova, "Diasporas and secessionist conflicts: the mobilization of the Armenian, Albanian and Chechen diasporas," *Ethnic and Racial Studies* 34, no. 2 (2011): 333–356, DOI: 10.1080/01419870.2010.489646

12. Kalyvas, *The logic of violence in civil wars*, 5.

13. Kalyvas, *The logic of violence in civil wars*, 3.

14. Uppsala Conflict Database, http://ucdp.uu.se/#country/369

15. Serhiy Kudelia, "The Donbas Rift," *Russian Politics & Law* 54, no. 1 (2016): 5–27, DOI: 10.1080/10611940.2015.1160707

16. Ivan Katchanovski, "The Separatist War in Donbas: A Violent Break-up of Ukraine?" *European Politics and Society* (2016). doi: 10.1080/23745118.2016.1154131

17. Kalyvas, *The Logic of Violence.*

18. Paul R. Brass, *Theft of an Idol: Text and Context in the Representation of Collective Violence* (Princeton, N.J.: Princeton University Press, 1997), Stanley, Tambiah, "Leveling Crowds: Ethnonationalist Conflicts and Collective Violence in South Asia," (Berkeley: University of California Press, 1996), Bruce Kapferer, *Legends of People/ Myths of State: Violence, Intolerance, and Political Culture in Sri Lanka and Australia* (Washington, DC: Smithsonian Institution Press,1988).

19. Wilson 2016, "The Donbas in 2014," 643–646.

20. Tetyana Malyarenko, "A gradually escalating conflict: Ukraine from the Euromaidan to the war with Russia," The Routledge Handbook of Ethnic Conflict, 2nd edition, eds. Karl Cordell and Stefan Wolff (Abingdon: Routledge Handbooks, 2016).

21. Slawomir Matuszak, "The Oligarchic Democracy: The Influence of Business Groups on Ukrainian Politics," OSW Studies no. 42 (Warsaw: Centre for Eastern Studies, 2012).

22. Most work on "elite bargain" was developed on case studies in Africa and the Middle East, for example, Malik Mufti, "Elite bargains and the onset of political liberalization in Jordan," *Comparative Political Studies* 32, no. 1 (1999): 100–129,

Stefan Lindemann, "Inclusive Elite Bargains and the Dilemma of Unproductive Peace: A Zambian case study," *Third World Quarterly* 32, no. 10 (2011): 1843–1869, DOI:10.1080/01436597.2011.610585. For literature review see Jonathan DiJohn and James Putzel, "Political Settlements," GSDRC Issues Paper (Birmingham: University of Birmingham, 2009).

23. Neville Bolt, *The Violent Image: Insurgent Propaganda and the New Revolutionaries* (New York: Columbia University Press, 2012), 214.

24. Brendan O'Leary, "The IRA: Looking Back, Mission Accomplished," 191–228 (203–210), in *Terror, Insurgency, and the State: Ending Protracted Conflicts*, ed. Marianne Heiberg, Brendan O'Leary and John Tirman (Philadelphia: University of Pennsylvania Press, 2007).

25. Thomas Rid and Marc Hecker, *War 2.0 Irregular warfare in the Information Age* (Westpoint: Praeger Security International, 2009), 1.

26. Anna Matveeva, "Chechnya: Dynamics of War and Peace," in *Problems of Post-Communism* 54, no. 3 (2007): 3–15.

27. Rui J. P. de Figueiredo, Jr., and Barry R. Weingast, "The rationality of fear: Political opportunism and ethnic conflict," in *Civil Wars, Insecurity, and Intervention*, eds. Walter and Snyder (New York: Columbia University Press, 1999), 261–302, Russell Hardin, *One for All: The Logic of Group Conflict* (Princeton: Princeton University Press, 1995).

28. Matthew Evangelista, "Paradoxes of Violence and Self-determination," *Ethnopolitics* 14, no. 5 (2015): 451–460, DOI: 10.1080/17449057.2015.1051811

29. For exploration of this issue see *Chechnya: From Past to Future*, ed. Richard Sakwa (London: Anthem Press, 2005).

30. Fred Halliday, "The romance of non-state actors," (21–37), 35, in *Non-state Actors in World Politics*, eds. Josselin and Wallace (Basingstoke: Palgrave, 2001).

31. Brendan O'Duffy, "IRA: Irish Republican Army (Oglaighnah Eireann)" in *Terror, Insurgency, and the State: Ending Protracted Conflicts* eds. Marianne Heiberg, Brendan O'Leary, and John Tirman (Philadelphia: University of Pennsylvania Press, 2007), 250–284.

32. Edward Aspinall, *Islam and Nation: Separatist Rebellion in Aceh, Indonesia* (Stanford: Stanford University Press), 2009.

33. Benedetta Berti, *Armed Political Organisations* (Baltimore: John Hopkins University Press, 2013), 130–175.

34. Kalyvas, *The Logic of Violence*, 12.

35. Rid and Hecker, *War 2.0*, 216.

36. Wendy Pearlman and Kathleen Gallagher Cunningham, "Nonstate Actors, Fragmentation, and Conflict Processes," *Journal of Conflict Resolution* 56, no. 1 (2012): 3–15.

37. Jesse Driscoll, "Commitment Problems or Bidding Wars? Rebel Fragmentation as Peace-Building," *Journal of Conflict Resolution* 56, no. 1 (2012): 118–149.

38. Marylinn Brewer, "Ingroup Identification and Intergroup Conflict: how does ingroup love become outgroup hate," in Social Identity, Intergroup Conflict and Conflict Reduction, eds. Richard Ashmore, Lee Jussim and David Wilder (Oxford: Oxford University Press, 2001), 3–16.

39. Henri Tajfel, *Human Groups and Social Categories: Studies in Social Psychology* (Cambridge: Cambridge University Press, 1981), 255.

40. Maddens, Bart et al. "The National Consciousness of the Flemings and the Walloons. An Empirical Investigation" in *Nationalism in Belgium: Shifting Identities, 1780–1995*, eds. Kas Deprez and Louis Vos (Basingstoke: Palgrave McMillan, 1998).

41. John McGarry and Brendan O'Leary, "Explaining Northern Ireland: Broken Images," (Oxford: Blackwell, 1995).

42. Neil Ferguson and Shelley McKeown, "Social Identity Theory and Intergroup Conflict in Northern Ireland" in Understanding Peace and Conflict Through Social Identity Theory, eds. S. McKeown et al. (Peace Psychology Book Series, Springer International Publishing Switzerland 2016), DOI: 10.1007/978-3-319-29869-6_14

43. Edward Moxon-Browne, "National identity in Northern Ireland," in *Social Attitudes in Northern Ireland: The First Report*, eds. P. Stringer and G. Robinson (Belfast, Northern Ireland: Blackstaff Press, 1991).

44. Ed Cairns, *Children and Political Violence* (Cambridge: Blackwell, 1996); Ed Cairns, J. Kenworthy, A. Campbell and M. Hewstone, "The role of in-group identification, religious group membership, and intergroup conflict in moderating in-group and out-group affect," *British Journal of Social Psychology* 45 (2006): 701–716, DOI: 10.1348/014466605X69850, Neil Ferguson, "The impact of political violence on moral reasoning: Socio-political reasoning in Northern Ireland," in *On Behalf of Others: The Morality of Care in a Global World*, eds. S. Scuzzarello, C. Kinnvall and K. Renwick Monroe (Oxford: Oxford University Press, 2009), 233–254.

45. Carol M. Glen, "Nationalism, Identity and Scotland's Referendum, Contemporary European Politics," 1 (2015), "Who feels Scottish?" National identities and ethnicity in Scotland" study found that 83% of population of Scotland felt 'Scottish,' (Manchester: University of Manchester, ESRC Centre on Dynamics of Ethnicity (CoDE), 2014).

46. Rogers Brubaker and Frederick Cooper, "Beyond Identity," *Theory and Society* 29, no. 1 (2000): 1–47.

47. Malesevic Sinisa, *Identity as Ideology: Understanding Ethnicity and Ideology* (Basingstoke: Palgrave Macmillan 2006), 32.

48. Celia Cook Huffman, "The role of identity in conflict," 19–31, in *Handbook of Conflict Analysis and Resolution*, eds. Dennis J. D. Sandole et al. (Abingdon: Routledge, 2008).

49. Anthony D. Smith, "Ethno-symbolism and Nationalism: A Cultural Approach," (London: Taylor & Francis, 2009).

50. Donald L. Horowitz, *Ethnic Groups in Conflict* (Berkeley: University of California Press, 1985), Nicholas Sambanis, "Do Ethnic and non ethnic civil wars have the same causes?," *Journal of Conflict Resolution* 45, no. 3 (2001): 259–282.

51. Taras Kuzio, "The Myth of the Civic State: A Critical Survey of Hans Kohn's Framework for Understanding Nationalism," *Ethnic and Racial Studies* 25, 1 (2002).

52. Tajfel, *Human Groups*, 239.

53. Stephen Reicher, "The context of Social Identity: domination, resistance, and change," *Political Psychology* 25 (2004): 921–45.

54. James D. Fearon and David D. Laitin, "Violence and the Social Construction of Ethnic Identity," *International Organization* 54, no. 4 (2000): 845–877, 874.

55. Ilya Prizel, *National Identity and Foreign Policy: Nationalism and Leadership in Poland, Russia and Ukraine* (Cambridge: Cambridge University Press, 1998).

56. Eric A. Nordlinger, *Conflict Regulation in Divided Societies* (Cambridge, MA: Center for International Affairs, Harvard University, 1972), 9.

57. Kalyvas, *The Logic of Violence,* 81.

58. Seymour Martin Lipset and Stein Rokkan, *Party Systems and Voter Alignments* (Toronto: Free Press, 1967), 11.

59. Victor M. Perez-Diaz, *The Return of Civil Society: The Emergence of Democratic Spain* (Cambridge: Harvard University Press, 1993), 6.

60. Tajfel, *Human Groups*, 239–244.

61. Elise Giuliano, *Constructing Grievance: Ethnic Nationalism in Russia's Republics* (Ithaca: Cornell University Press, 2011).

62. Elise Giuliano, "The Social Bases of Support for Self-determination in East Ukraine," *Ethnopolitics* 14, no. 5 (2015): 513–522, DOI: 10.1080/17449057.2015.1051813

63. Marilynn Brewer "Ingroup identification and intergroup conflict: when does in-group love become outgrip hate?," 25.

64. Samuel P. Huntington, "The Clash of Civilizations?" *Foreign Affairs* (1993): 22–49.

65. Victoria Hudson, "Forced to Friendship? Russian (Mis-)Understandings of Soft Power and the Implications for Audience Attraction in Ukraine," *Politics* 35, no. 3–4 (2015): 330–346, 335.

66. Kevin Avruch, "Culture Theory, culture clash, and the practice of conflict resolution," 241–255, in *Handbook of Conflict Analysis and Resolution.*

67. Sean Boyne, "Uncovering Irish Republican Army," *Jane's Intelligence Review*, 1996.

68. Andrew Scobell and Brad Hammitt, "Goons, gunmen, and gendarmerie: Toward a reconceptualization of paramilitary formations," *Journal of Political and Military Sociology* 26 (1998): 213–227.

69. Tetyana Malyarenko and David J. Galbreath, "Paramilitary motivation in Ukraine: beyond integration and abolition," *Southeast European and Black Sea Studies* 16, no. 1 (2016): 113–138, DOI: 10.1080/14683857.2016.1148414

70. Sibylle Scheipers, *Unlawful Combatants: A Genealogy of the Irregular Fighter* (Oxford: Oxford University Press, 2015), 191, 223.

71. David Malet, *Foreign Fighters: Transnational Identity in Civil Conflicts* (Oxford: Oxford University Press, 2013), 10.

72. Thomas Hegghammer, "The Rise of Muslim Foreign Fighters: Islam and the Globalization of Jihad," *International Security* 35, no. 3 (2010–11): 57–58.

73. Daphne Josselin and William Wallace, "Non-state actors in World Politics: a Framework," in *Non-State Actors in World Politics*, eds. Josselin and Wallace (Basingstoke: Palgrave, 2001).

74. Bernard Fall, "The Theory and Practice of Insurgency and Counterinsurgency," *Naval War College Review* (Winter 1998): 46–57.

75. Craig Whiteside, "Lighting the Path: the Evolution of the Islamic State Media Enterprise (2003–2016)," (The Hague: ICCT Research Paper, 2016).

76. Steven Metz, "Insurgency after the cold war," *Small Wars and Insurgencies* 5 (1994): 63–82.

77. Donald Horowitz, *Ethnic Groups in Conflict* (Berkeley: University of California Press, 1985).

78. Stuart J. Kaufman, *Modern Hatreds: The Symbolic Politics of Ethnic War* (Ithaca, NY: Cornell University Press, 2001).

79. Ibrahim, Elbadawi, and Nicholas Sambanis, "How Much War Will We See? Explaining the Prevalence of Civil War," *Journal of Conflict Resolution* 46, no. 3 (2002): 307–34; James D., Fearon, and David D. Laitin, "Ethnicity, Insurgency, and Civil War," *American Political Science Review* 97, no. 1 (2003): 75–90, Paul Collier and Anke E. Hoeffler, "Greed and Grievance in Civil War." Oxford Economic Papers 56, no. 4 (2004): 563–95.

80. Malet, *Foreign Fighters*, 3.

81. Malet, *Foreign Fighters*, 92–126.

82. Randy Borum and Robert Fein, "The Psychology of Foreign Fighters," *Studies in Conflict and Terrorism* 40, no. 3 (2017), 248–266, doi: 10.1080/1057610X.2016.1188535

83. Juan E. Ugarriza and Matthew J. Craig, "The Relevance of Ideology to Contemporary Armed Conflicts: A Quantitative Analysis of Former Combatants in Colombia," *Journal of Conflict Resolution* 57, no. 3 (2012): 445–477, 450.

84. Stefano Costalli and Andrea Ruggeri, "Indignation, Ideologies, and Armed Mobilization Civil War in Italy, 1943–45," *International Security* 40, no. 2 (2015): 119–157, doi: 10.1162/ISEC_a_00218

85. John Deigh, "Cognitivism in the Theory of Emotions," *Ethics* 104, no. 4 (2000): 824–54; Peter Goldie, *The Emotions: A Philosophical Exploration* (Oxford: Oxford University Press, 1994).

86. Helena Flam, "Emotions' map: a research agenda,"19–40, in *Emotions and Social Movements*, eds. Helena Flam and Debra King (Abingdon: Routledge, 2007).

87. Roger D. Petersen, *Understanding Ethnic Violence: Fear, Hatred, and Resentment in Twentieth-Century in Eastern Europe* (Cambridge: Cambridge University Press, 2002).

88. Costalli and Ruggeri, "Indignation, Ideologies, and Armed Mobilization."

89. Emmanuel Karagiannis, "Ukrainian volunteer fighters in the eastern front: ideas, political-social norms and emotions as mobilization mechanisms," *Southeast European and Black Sea Studies* 16, no. 1 (2016): 139–153, DOI: 10.1080/14683857.2016.1148413

90. Elizabeth Jean Wood, "The emotional benefits of insurgency in El Salvador," 267–280, in *Passionate Politics: Emotions and Social Movements*, eds. Jeff Goodwin, James M Jasper and Francesca Polletta (Chicago: University of Chicago Press, 2001), 268.

91. Kevin Avruch, *Culture and Conflict Resolution* (Washington, DC: US Institute of Peace Press, 1998).

92. Anthony D. Smith, *Ethno-symbolism and Nationalism: A Cultural Approach* (London: Taylor & Francis, 2009), 25.

93. Anthony Smith, *National Identity* (London: Penguin, 1991).

94. Eric Hobsbawn and Terence Ranger, *The Invention of Tradition* (Cambridge: Cambridge University Press, 1992).

95. Michael Walzer, "On the role of symbolism in political thought," *Political Science Quarterly* 82, no. 2 (1967): 191–204, 194.

96. Pal Kolstoe, "National Symbols as Signs of Unity and Division," in *Ethnic and Racial Studies* 29, no. 4 (2006): 676–701.

97. Bolt, *The Violent Image*, 105, 108–110.

98. Peter Pomerantsev, *Nothing Is True And Everything Is Possible: The Surreal Heart of the New Russia* (New York: Public Affairs, 2014).

99. Yuri M. Zhukov and Matthew A. Baum, "Reporting Bias and Information Warfare," International Studies Association Annual Convention conference paper, Atlanta, GA, 16–19 March 2016.

100. Marlene Laruelle, "The three colors of Novorossiya, or the Russian nationalist mythmaking of the Ukrainian crisis," *Post-Soviet Affairs* 32, no. 1 (2016): 55–74, DOI: 10.1080/1060586X.2015.1023004

101. The term is explained in chapter 2.

102. John O'Loughlin, Gerard Toal and Vladimir Kolosov, "The rise and fall of "Novorossiya": examining support for a separatist geopolitical imaginary in southeast Ukraine," *Post-Soviet Affairs* 33, no. 2 (2017): 124–144, DOI: 10.1080/1060586X.2016.1146452

103. Jesse Driscoll and Zachary Steinert-Threlkeld, "Alternative Facts: Social Media as Propaganda in Post-Maidan Ukraine" (March 8, 2017), at *SSRN*: https://ssrn.com/abstract=2825452

104. Rid and Hecker, *War 2.0*, 1–2.

105. Bolt, *The Violent Image*, 47.

106. Tim O'Reilly, "What is Web 2.0?" http://www.oreilly.com/pub/a/web2/archive/what-is-web-20.html

107. Rid and Hecker, *War 2.0*.

108. Bolt, *The Violent Image*, 8.

109. Jason Dittmer, *Popular Culture, Geopolitics and Identity* (Lanham: Rowman and Littlefield, 2010).

110. Whiteside, "Lighting the Path," Charlie Winter, *Documenting the Virtual Caliphate* (London: Quilliam, 2015).

Chapter 2

Laying Grounds for Confrontation

POLITICIZATION OF IDENTITY

The conflict in southeastern Ukraine has to be understood by paying attention to the complex and shifting terrain of identities and past struggles in the region. Its ideological and identity-based grounds can be traced back to Soviet time and early independence years. Known in academic scholarship, these grounds had been largely overlooked by policy discourse on the developments in the former USSR before violence broke out.[1] This was because Ukraine remained largely peaceful throughout independence while violence flared up elsewhere, but tensions festered under the surface. However, the Maidan events of 2013–2014 served as a catalyst for an explosion of the deep societal rifts that had been growing over years. They resulted in fierce confrontation in Donbas, the country's industrial region located on the border with Russia.

Most explanations center on Russia's desire to destabilize Ukraine, deny its independence, prevent it from joining North Atlantic Treaty Organisation (NATO), and make it follow its geopolitical designs.[2] There is also a body of work which looks inside Ukraine. Combination of political events that exacerbated identity cleavages, elite actions, and involvement of external forces form a more Ukraine-centered interpretative framework. Identity issues have prominently featured in previous studies on Ukraine, with some authors defining them through a postimperial prism which was inherently conflictual. In 2001, Taras Kuzio saw Ukrainian identity as threatened by "Other," that is, Russia, regarding Ukraine as a postcolonial state and a former dependency, which had to assert its identity and sovereignty vis-a-vis the former metropolis. Others warned of dangers of this approach: "ultimate challenge to Ukrainian sovereignty may be neither military, political nor economic. Rather, it seems likely to be cultural, spiritual, and psychological. . . . Does their [Ukrainians] contaminated legacy truly divide them from the Russians?"[3] Explaining the conflict later, Petro argued that Donbas was the most serious fault-line in Ukrainian identity politics and that "the peremptory removal of President Yanukovych violated the delicate balance of interests forged between Galicia and Donbas. It was thus seen as a direct threat to the core interest of Russophone Ukrainians."[4] This book follows an internally centered line of argumentation as it seeks to situate the conflict in broader Ukraine's context.

HISTORY AND DEMOGRAPHICS

Following its independence in 1991 and before the Euromaidan of 2013–2014, Ukraine was run by four presidents, all elected through an internationally recognized democratic process. As a broad-brush description, Leonid Kravchuk (1991–1994) and Victor Yushchenko (2004–2010) were associated with policies of change toward Ukrainization in linguistic and cultural spheres and Euroatlantic geopolitical orientation, and had their support base in the west of Ukraine. Leonid Kuchma, originating from Dnepr (Dnepropetrovsk until 2016) in the east (1994–2004), was located more at the center of Ukrainian politics and pursued a "multi-vector" approach. He rectified some excesses of his predecessor, but made fewer concessions than expected by his supporters in the east, and drove toward greater centralization and diminished power of the regions.

Elections reflected the pattern of polarization. Yushchenko's election in 2004 was preceded by controversy which caused the first Maidan protests when thousands gathered at Kyiv's central square to demonstrate against a supposedly stolen victory of their candidate. Protests were effective and Yushchenko was confirmed as president. His was a narrow victory against Viktor Yanukovych, who followed him as the next president (2010–2014), but Yushchenko ruled in a way as if a vast majority in society shared his vision for cultural and geopolitical transformation, with insufficient regard to the views of the constituency which supported his rival. Yanukovych's electoral victory in 2010 was a score for the east as he came from Donetsk. His election was recognized by the Organization for Security and Co-operation in Europe (OSCE) as "free and fair." However, it did not heal the divisions. Ukraine's political system was no doubt democratic, but remained particularly unstable compared to many other post-Soviet states.[5]

Fear of secession and conflict were not new in Ukraine, and there were predictions of violence in earlier period of independence. They were explained by such factors as state strength/weakness and the effects of geography, statebuilding, and democratization. However, d'Anieri argued that because control of the Ukrainian government was open to the eastern elite, when in power they had a stake in preserving the state's integrity and it made no sense for them to split the east when they had a chance to control the whole country. Continuous unity relied on a largely liberal and tolerant state approach.[6]

However, politics rested upon a complex pattern of cleavages in society. Before President Yushchenko came to power, most of the society paid little attention to identity differences, and Russian-facing and Polish-facing sides of Ukraine went along with each other.[7] Identity was affiliated more with region than with ethnicity. Ethnicity is a poor marker in Ukraine, and loyalty and identity are weakly correlated with it. Many people are ethnically mixed, and members of the same family can have different identities, depending on their formative experiences. Moreover, identity is not a fixed category and can be shifted under the pressure of circumstances.[8] It was also influenced by localism: in Donetsk, a Ukrainian national identity was far less pronounced than local identity and roughly equaled in salience to those defined by gender and social status.[9] Kulyk, writing in terms of "titular" nation and language, treats identity both as culturally and geographically conditioned, and at the same time dynamic. He concludes that in Ukraine, "ethnocultural elements of the national identity content were more strongly contested than civic ones"[10] and Ukrainian society was characterized by the uneasy coexistence of two roughly equal territorial "halves" with their respective divergent identities and policy preferences. Situation in Donbas was distinct, as the preference for national identity significantly decreased between 2012 and 2014 surveys, with a simultaneous gain in the salience of regional identification. In 2014, alienation of Donbas from Ukraine manifests itself in worsening attitudes toward its symbols.[11]

Poll data indirectly confirmed that identity was far from straightforward in Ukraine. A survey by Kyiv International Sociology Institute published in 2010 revealed that the composition of Ukrainian society differed significantly from official statistics if self-ascribed identities were taken into account: 60–62 percent identified themselves as monoethnic Ukrainians, 23–25 percent as bi-ethnic Ukrainian–Russian, 9–10 percent as monoethnic Russians, and about 5 percent as belonging to other ethnic groups.[12] In another survey in 2012 every tenth citizen considered themselves a Soviet person rather than Ukrainian or Russian.[13] People with different identities—Ukrainian monists, Ukrainian pluralists, "cultural" Russians, and those politically oriented toward Russia—have lived throughout the country. Their ratio has simply been different in each region. People of "pro-Ukrainian" orientation, or "monists," were to be found in the East and in Crimea, but were in the minority there.[14] Sakwa describes "monism" as an emphasis on the singularity of the Ukrainian experience, fulfillment of Ukraine's destiny as a nation state, which is officially monolingual, culturally autonomous from other Slavic nations, and aligned with the Atlantic security community.[15]

One factor accounting for this situation was the movement and intermixing of people during the Tsarist and Soviet eras through state-sponsored projects.[16] This movement resulted in ethnic Russians settling in Ukraine, while Ukrainians found themselves in places such as the Far East. At present, Russians and Ukrainians form large minorities in their respective countries: according to 2010 census in Russia, Ukrainians were almost 2 million and amounted to 1.4 percent of the population.[17] Russians in Ukraine comprise the largest minority in the country, and their community forms the biggest single Russian diaspora in the world. In the last Ukrainian census of 2001, 17.3 percent of the population identified themselves as "ethnic Russians."[18] Western Ukraine has fewer people who identified themselves as "ethnic Russians" than the East and the South, but has its own intermix with Poles, Hungarians, Austrians, Czechs, Slovaks, and Romanians.

Identity differences existed under the surface in Soviet times, and the authorities were conscious of them, giving concessions to balance them against one another and used to relieve pressures in society. For example, a monument to Alexander Pushkin could not be built in a Ukrainian town unless there was also a monument to Ukrainian poet Taras Shevchenko. On a popular level, while many in society easily went along with Russians throughout the USSR, there was a perception in some quarters that an image of an ethnic Ukrainian was derogatory and that Ukrainians were looked down upon by Russians.[19]

The ingredients of identity are several. Firstly, the contemporary identities derive from different histories of Ukraine's populace. The major legacies which left their various imprints include the Russian/Soviet system, the Polish-Lithuanian Commonwealth, and Habsburg Austria. Prior to their incorporation into the Habsburg monarchy, the three regions of Ukraine's west had disparate political histories—Galicia as a part of Poland, Bukovina as a part of Romania/ Moldavia, and Transcarpathia as a part of Hungary— and did not present a single historical unit.[20] Developments during the Civil War (1917–1921) and World War II (1939–1945) pitted parts of the country against each other as they joined opposite sides, and these wounds were far from forgotten in some circles.

Western regions of Ukraine were incorporated into the USSR in the 1940s, and the armed resistance to Soviet rule subsided only in the 1950s.[21] Even in the 1980s, visitors from "Russia" felt uncomfortable there in Soviet times.[22] Unsurprisingly, attitudes toward the Soviet system, which was seen as "Russian," were negative and were epitomized by the discourse that presented Ukraine as a victim of Russian colonization. It was first articulated in historical terms by dissident intellectual Ivan Dziuba[23] and got prominence among liberal national-democratic constituency when rewriting of Soviet history started after independence.[24]

A special place in history was occupied by Stepan Bandera, more of a symbol than a person, that "became a focus of impassionated debate between those who wish to elevate him as a national hero and those who regard him as the epitome of evil."[25] Bandera's role was seen diametrically different in the east and west, and became a divisive symbol, later used at Maidan and in construction of conflict narratives described later. Bandera was a nationalist who regarded Russia as a principal enemy of Ukraine and was prepared to sacrifice all for the single goal of gaining independence from it. At the onset of World War II, his Organization of Ukrainian Nationalists (OUN) sought cooperation with the German authorities, particularly with *Abwehr* and the German army, believing that "the Germans would support an independent Ukraine against Russia, because the ideology of national socialism and Ukrainian integral nationalism were similar."[26] Two militant groups within the OUN were created in 1941 for the struggle against the Bolshevik USSR. However, the Germans backtracked and withdrew their support for OUN and Bandera, keeping him in incarceration until 1944, until they decided to collaborate with the Ukrainian nationalists again. The Ukrainian Insurgent Army (UPA) was formed in 1942 and its activities during the Nazi occupation and the incidents of collaboration remained the most controversial episodes which divided historians.[27]

If Bandera was merely confined to a regional figure revered in western Ukraine, this would not have been a big issue, in case Ukraine remained pluralistic and its different parts were allowed to continue with their different versions of history. The problem developed when Bandera was presented as a national hero that could be imposed upon the parts of society which had a profound discomfort with the version of Ukrainian national project that Bandera was associated with. Construction of a new national identity based on Bandera's legacy meant a significant redefinition of the existing one and no wonder caused a considerable strain, given that memories of the past were strong and the traumatic events of the War fairly recent.

LANGUAGE AND FEAR OF ASSIMILATION

Unlike in a number of post-Soviet states where Russian is spoken by a large portion of the population and where it is allocated a status of an "official language," Ukraine did not make any official concessions to bilingualism until 2012. Russian, although widely spoken on the street, suffered significant setbacks in the public visual space, especially during Yushchenko's presidency. As Protsyk noted, "debates on the status of the Russian language have been the most politically salient linguistic issue throughout the post-communist period. One indicator of its salience is the frequency with which each issue is raised in the Ukrainian parliament."[28] Russian has dominated in Central and Eastern Ukraine, and in big cities, while the countryside was more Ukrainian speaking. At the onset of independence, Russians and other Russian-speaking minorities made up a solid majority in Donbas: 67 percent in Donetsk and 63 percent in Luhansk oblasts. Only few of them claimed proficiency in the Ukrainian language.[29]

The policy of "Ukrainization," or a state drive to decrease the presence of Russian language in the public sphere and in education began in 1990s under the presidencies of Kravchuk and Kuchma. Although there was no resentment of Ukrainian per se and many understood it even without being proficient, the pace of change in education was rapid and top-driven, and as Fournier demonstrated, caused considerable resistance in Central and Eastern Ukraine.[30] Under this policy, many "Russian" schools, that is, those in which all subjects were taught in Russian with some hours allocated to teaching of Ukrainian, were closed down. In 1989 (last Soviet-era figures) 1,058,000 pupils (Russian and Russophone) in Kyiv were studying in Russian out of 2,572,000 pupils in the city in total.[31] In 2014 only five such schools and one gymnasium remained in Kyiv,[32] where, according to the 2001 census, 13.1 percent of residents declared themselves "Russian" by ethnic affiliation. In 2004, 4.7 percent of schoolchildren studied in Russian, as compared to 22 percent in 1996.[33]

The data of Ukraine's Ministry of Education and Science illustrate the process.[34] According to its 2015 nationwide data, schools with Russian medium of instruction constituted 47.8 percent in the academic year 1991–1992, but in the year 2014–2015 there were only 3.5 percent such schools in the Government-Controlled Areas (GCA) of the country. The figures in Table 2.1 confirm that the main wave of "Ukrainization" took place under Kravchuk and Kuchma.[35]

Russians in eastern Ukraine formed an "accidental" "diaspora"—a social group that shared a cultural rather than an ethnic identity, was Russian speaking, closely tied with the Russian cultural heritage, and favored deep cooperation between Ukraine and Russia.[36] Many of them lived in Donbas which consisted of two *oblasts* (administrative regions)—Donetska (in Ukrainian, Donetskaya in Russian) and Luhanska (in Ukrainian, Luganskaya in Russian). It was Yushchenko's presidency that dealt a decisive blow to Russian language in the region. Shift in language policy and a threat of losing access to education in the mother tongue were of concern to the local society. Minister of education, Ivan Vakarchuk, launched an accelerated transfer to Ukrainian as a medium of instruction at schools and universities. Only 26.6 percent of schoolchildren studied in Ukrainian in Donetsk oblast in 2004 when Yushchenko took office, and in 2012 they already numbered 48.4

Table 2.1   Change in Language of School Instruction in Ukraine, 1991–2015

Schools/ school year	1991/92				2001/2002				2013/2014				2014/2015			
	Number of schools	% of schools	Number of pupils, in thousands (ths)	% of pupils	Number of schools	% of schools	Number of pupils, in thousands (ths)	% of pupils	Number of schools	% of schools	Number of pupils, in thousands (ths)	% of pupils	Number of schools	% of schools	Number of pupils, in thousands (ths)	% of pupils
Ukrainian as language of instruction	15536	51.4	3516.1	51.4	16937	80.2	4511.3	73.5	16045	85.8	3352.8	81.8	15696	88.6	3281.6	87.3
Russian as language of instruction	13364	47.8	3257.9	47.8	1732	8.2	1560.8	25.4	1275	6.8	703.5	17.2	621	3.5	356.2	9.4

Source: The data of the Ministry of Education and Science of Ukraine.[37]

percent, almost twice as much. In a decade from 2001 to 2011, the number of Russian-language schools in Donetsk oblast reduced from 518 to 176, with the process accelerating since 2004. Many families had no choice but to send their children to Ukrainian schools, and this caused resentment in them.[38]

In Donetsk city, where in the 1990s nearly all schools were teaching in Russian, by 2012 there were 18 Ukrainian schools, and another 63 schools became mixed with some classes in the same year being instructed in Russian and others in Ukrainian, while 70 stayed as Russian. In the city of Makiivka (in Ukrainian, Makeevka in Russian), situated next to Donetsk, there were no Ukrainian schools at the time when the USSR broke up, while by the beginning of the conflict in 2014, 68 out of 72 city schools taught in Ukrainian.

The situation was similar in the neighboring Luhansk Oblast. In the 2001 census 68.8 percent of the oblast population declared Russian as their mother tongue. In 2005, 29.5 percent of schoolchildren of Luhansk Oblast studied in Ukrainian, but in 2009 they already made up 48.5 percent, although two-thirds of the population considered Russian as their native language. Higher education underwent a similar process. In 2000, 75.7 percent of university students in Luhansk oblast studied in Russian, but in 2013 they constituted only 37 percent. In 2001 a decision was made to transfer instruction at the Luhansk Pedagogical Institute from Russian into Ukrainian, and to study Russian as a foreign language.[39] This prompted some well-to-do parents to send their children for education abroad.

Still, many among the intelligentsia in Kyiv believed that "language was not an issue":[40] everybody understood Ukrainian even if they preferred to speak Russian. Presumed bilinguism of the capital prevented Kyiv intellectuals to see the real language barrier further east. Gradually, Russian diminished in official use and individuals had to Ukrainianize their name spellings. Since formal communication was conducted in Ukrainian, for example, in courts, those who could not write in it, were disadvantaged, and court hearings sometimes proceeded in Ukrainian even if defendants could not understand it.[41] Language remained an issue of contention even after the Languages Law was adopted in 2012 which allowed bilinguism on a regional level with significant minority representation. Still, Yanukovych's electoral promise of making Russian the second state language which had a wide support in Crimea and Donbas was not fulfilled.

CULTURAL RIVALRY AND THE ROLE OF INTELLIGENTSIA

The most important identity pillar was culture. Creation of nationhood necessitated some sort of a "cultural nation" at the heart of it,[42] and Prizel, for example, urged segregation from Russian culture: "for Ukraine it is essential to distance itself from Russia and reassert a separate identity."[43] This was, however, difficult—and in the view of many citizens, unnecessary—as both high and low culture of Central and Eastern Ukraine had a great deal of commonality with Russian and often was barely distinguishable. Nikolai Gogol is as much a Ukrainian as a Russian writer.[44]

Omnipresence of "Russianness" continued after 1991. Independence did not bring a great deal of separatedness, as few barriers in society existed to the penetration of modern Russian culture. The use of Russian language in everyday interaction, cinema and pop culture, open borders, ease of travel and education, business ties, mutually understandable life strategies and prominence of Russian TV channels meant that Russian cultural influence was in abundance throughout the independence period and society was readily absorbing it. As fewer news programs became available in Russian on Ukrainian TV, it was natural for Russian-speaking citizens of Ukraine to watch channels from Russia until they were banned in 2014.[45]

Organized religion in a society where faith matters emerged as an arena for cultural contestation, since the time when the Christian Orthodox Church was divided in 1991 into two main administrative cum existential branches[46]— Ukrainian Orthodox Church under the Kyiv Patriarchate led by metropolitan Filaret, with a minority of parishes, and a larger Ukrainian Orthodox Church under the Moscow Patriarchate (UOC MP) headed by metropolitan Onuphrii, to which the majority of Orthodox Christians adhered. Filaret was an enthusiastic political player since the early 1990s and a supporter of both Maidans, who sought to take his church with him. Given its symbolism for the *Russian World*, the UOC MP stood for the other end of the spiritual spectrum. At the same time, the UOP MP has the broadest powers of autonomy and enjoys internal diversity. It is as diverse a Church as Ukraine is and gained indigenousness during Ukraine's independence.

The role of western Ukrainians in cultural identity-building was significant because they had more religious diversity and a culture distinct from the Russian/Soviet one. Thus, a regional culture got promoted as a national one to provide a legitimization to the nationhood, but as it was based on rural/pastoral roots of Western Ukraine, it found little resonance in big Russian-speaking industrial cities, socially distant from it.[47] While most of mainstream society unconsciously went along with closeness to Russia, many members of the politicized "national-democratic"[48] intelligentsia was concerned with a sense of cultural vulnerability of the new nationhood vis-à-vis the Russian colossus. In this paradigm, cultural closeness was viewed not as a natural state of affairs, but as a political and existential threat to own distinctiveness, because, as journalist Alexander Chalenko, who originated from Donbas, told me: "a Ukrainian who loves Russian culture and speaks Russian, becomes a Russian."[49] As Paul Kolstoe predicted already in 1995:

> Culturally, . . . authorities may carry out a linguistic and educational Ukrainization process which proceeds so fast, or goes so deep, that the Russians begin to fear for their cultural identity. This danger is emanating primarily from certain sections of the cultural intelligentsia . . . who are bent on turning the political liberalisation of Ukraine into a cultural triumph for ethnic Ukrainians at the expense of other groups.[50]

Politicians and intelligentsia share responsibility for polarization. Ukrainian successive presidents did not try very hard to create a unified national identity, instead basing their credentials on either Eastern or Western orientation. Consequently, as put by Oleg Tsaryov, formerly a Ukrainian MP—and later a chair of Novorossiya parliament, – "Ukraine was very diverse, split into two constituencies, with staunch pro-Russian and pro-Ukrainian supporters at its flanks and a passive mass in the middle."[51] A move toward "Ukrainization" under Kravchuk in the 1990s was understandable, reflecting a common trend in the ex-Soviet republics to promote their nationhood. However, this alienated those citizens who did not feel the need for cultural separation from Russia and felt disaffected by Kravchuk's strident anti-Russian escapades. The vote for Kuchma, who succeeded Kravchuk and promised language and cultural concessions, reflected this disaffection. Kuchma's efforts were inconclusive and some key promises in education, language and cultural spheres were not kept, but attitudes softened and a default consensus emerged.

The 2004 Orange Revolution, or the first Maidan, emphasized divisions along identity lines. The national-democratic intelligentsia became more vocal under Yushchenko, as identity politics occupied the public space, manifested by the erection of monuments to Stepan Bandera,[52] renaming of streets,[53] introduction of new national celebrations and other symbols. An opposition to the ideology of Ukrainization also emerged under Yushchenko. Under Yanukovych, identity contestation continued, but two discourses counterbalanced one other, to a certain extent. While intellectuals largely grouped around the Ukraine-centered national-democratic camp, the ruling politicians promoted an independent Ukrainian statehood with a cultural closeness to Russia.[54] Characterization of Yanukovych as "pro-Russian" is simplistic and in fact misleading: while it was true that he balanced off some excesses of the Yushchenko period, he also sought to make concessions to the west of the country, especially in cultural sphere, which did not vote for him. Nevertheless, he failed to become a unifier.

Two opposing camps were shaping up. Kuzio explains that since Ukraine did not inherit a uniform national identity, its post-Soviet nation- and state-building project revolved around a debate over how this identity will be constituted and which of its neighbors will be "Others ."[55] An attitude toward Russia with everything it represented has become the identity marker in politicized circles[56] and was important in the formation of the "western" and "eastern" constituencies. Many citizens believed that Ukraine's foreign policy orientation had consequences for internal balance of power between Russian and Ukrainian language and culture, because the internal and the external were intimately interlinked. Sensitive to cultural diffusion, those who feared cultural Ukrainization at home, supported closer ties with Russia and sought to protect the sphere of mass communications where culture wars were played.[57]

Émigrés of Ukrainian descent contributed to articulation of the "away from Russia" narrative which often reflected their own histories. The bulk of Ukrainians who emigrated to the West after World War II came from the areas of Western Ukraine where anti-Russian sentiment was strong. At the end of the War, such people stood to lose from the encounter with Stalinist victors and had an incentive to leave for the West when the Soviet troops were approaching. This "generation of 'displaced persons' took over Ukrainian community organisations in North America, establishing the anti-communist political profile of the Ukrainian diaspora."[58] The legacy survived through generations and found its political expression when Ukraine acquired independence and started to explore its non-Soviet connections and roots.

A large part in the identity rift was played by a segment of politicized intelligentsia who got involved in asserting nationalist superiority long before the second Maidan. Anti-Russian discourse was prominent among the liberal elite, and media, think tanks, and the expert community articulated it loudly and clearly.[59] It was hard to make a career in the Ukrainian intellectual milieu speaking for the Eastern identity and interests, as accusations of being a "Kremlin agent" could easily follow.[60] Although numerically small, this constituency was vocal and tended to dominate public discourse before the events of 2013.

Representatives of the pro-Russian constituency maintained that, unlike the West, Moscow did not support its loyalists among intelligentsia through grants, publications, roundtables, and other soft tools. Chalenko recalls an example that a writer Vladimir Kornilov could not obtain some meager Russian funds for promotion of his history book on Donetsk-Krivoroj republic. In this narrative, the West was subtle, but moving steady with its soft power and thinking long-term. "Western assistance to civil society formed a cohort of supra-national people who were not dependent on the Ukrainian job market and had little stake in domestic realities. A circle of the like-minded was formed with a backing by foreign embassies who could afford 'to think freely,' without taking responsibility for outcomes."[61] One confirmation for this belief was Victoria Nuland's, the US Assistant Secretary of State's, statement that the United States had "invested" over $5 billion in democracy promotion, civil society development, and good governance in Ukraine since 1991.[62]

Identity faultlines culminated in the Second Maidan which had a passion-ate anti-Russian streak, despite all social and cultural closeness between Ukrainian and Russian societies. Hudson's 2011 research indicates that "on the level of values, Ukrainians share a common well of social values with Russians, which could support a case for a sense of common civilisational belonging."[63] Sociological research conducted in Ukraine and Russia indi-cated that although commonalities between people in both countries were strong in family and cultural values, political differentiation was growing. By 2014 Ukrainians had lower levels of belonging to a unified nation than Russians and feared civil war more than Russians. When comparing the dynamics of change in values, Ukrainians felt that their government and institutions became increasingly nonrepresentative of the peoples' needs over time.[64]

EUROMAIDAN: FOMENTING IDENTITIES FOR CONFLICT

Euromaidan was a momentous event in the history of Ukraine while the issues that were at stake are interpreted in many different ways. Predominant Western explanation of the Euromaidan movement is that Ukraine sought to choose a West-looking democratic governance over the post-Soviet authori-tarian government associated, in their view, with Russia, but Moscow would not have it because "President Vladimir Putin retains a zero-sum mentality to foreign policy that looks for 'winners' and 'losers' in any interaction."[65] Russian view was that skirmishes were masterminded by oligarchs who rivaled Yanukovych and exploited nationalist sentiments of patriotic groups in their struggle for power.[66] Putin called the outcome an "unconstitutional coup," but added that he understood people who demonstrated at Maidan as they were protesting against corruption and demanded radical change.[67] Involvement of the West led by the United States to pull Ukraine from the Russian orbit was also a widespread explanation.

The crisis started when two economic association agreements became a bone of contention—one was an Association Agreement with the European Union (EUAA) and the other with the Russia-led Eurasian Economic Union (EEU). The latter was based on the Customs' Union whose members were Belarus, Kazakhstan, and Russia and envisaged creation by 2015 of four freedoms of movement, that is, of capital, labor, services, and goods.[68] The EUAA had the Deep and Comprehensive Free Trade Agreement (DCFTA) in the heart of it, as a result of which Ukraine and the European Union would gain a privileged access to each other's markets, and tariffs and trade quotas between the European Union and Ukraine would be eliminated. Ukraine would be able to sell its goods to the EU countries on the condition that they satisfied the EU quality control standards and were competitive against other producers, while the European Union would get a reciprocal access for its goods on the Ukrainian domestic market. Such agreements were signed with Georgia and Moldova without much political ado. This option, however, appeared incompatible with Ukraine's existing free trade agreements with Russia within the Commonwealth of Independent States (CIS) framework unless a solution was negotiated between all parties. Russia feared that a flood of tariff-free EU goods through Ukraine would undermine its domestic producers and sought to delay the signing by Kyiv. Moscow offered $15 billion in immediate support and preferential gas tariffs to Ukraine. For that, Yanukovych had to maintain the traditional CIS free-trade links and postpone the signing of the EUAA in November 2013 until a solution harmonizing the two options could be found. There was no obligation to join the EEU immediately as long as the status quo was preserved. Ukrainian goods were to enjoy tax-free access to the EEU market and its citizens would not face restrictions on migrant labor in Russia.

After Maidan, there were different perspectives whether the two offers were mutually exclusive, or whether a tripartite arrangement between Brussels, Kyiv, and Moscow could have been worked out on how provisions on certification of goods and standards should be applied. Sakwa describes that reaching an inclusive compromise was not tried and Moscow's various proposals were rebuffed. The proponents of the association in the European Union insisted on making a choice.[69] As Sakwa notes, "the concept of 'choice' thus became deeply ideological and was used as a weapon against those who suggested that countries have histories and location, and that choices have to take into account the effect that they will have on others."[70] As a result, as a European Parliament's study acknowledges, "for all these countries [of the EU Eastern Partnership[71]], a choice for east or west has meant a loss: a loss of trade policy sovereignty for some; a loss of the vital and once-fluid exchanges with the EEU for the others."[72]

However, what a politically minded Ukrainian public read into the EUAA was much more than a trade deal. Many Ukrainians believed that prospective EU membership was on offer, and the EUAA was a step toward it. Brussels fudged over the issue of prospective accession, stating that "we take note of recent opinion polls which show that a majority of Ukrainians supports future EU membership,"[73] although an authoritative IFES survey in December 2013 returned data that only 37 percent wanted to join the EU.[74]

The issue had a polarizing effect because popular attitudes toward "Eurointegration" were influenced by the "values" aspect rather than economic considerations, and reflected distinct identities of western and eastern Ukraine. In 2013, EU integration was supported by 72.2 percent in the West and by 20.7 percent in the East, where 50.4 percent supported integration into the EEU.[75] Pavel Gaidutsky, director of Strategic Assessments Institute at the Kuchma Foundation, commented in June 2013 on the EU and EEU integration options writing that "in the European direction, civilisational values have a much higher priority for Ukraine over the economic ones, than on the Eurasian direction."[76]

Yanukovych hesitated which way to go, then in November made a volte-face after an encounter with President Putin in Sochi and announced the postponement of the signing to allow more time for talks. This happened in already highly politicized environment in Ukraine, where a wave of peaceful protests called by journalist Mustafa Nayyem[77] unfolded urging the Ukrainian president to go with a Euro-association. The government forces used violence, triggering the swelling of protests, and on December 1 half a million people demonstrated on Maidan. Following that, several attempts to overtake public buildings turned into brutal clashes. The government tried to forcefully disperse the protestors who by then blocked the city center, set tents, and organized self-defense committees. The stakes were upped by Nuland who travelled three times to Kyiv during Euromaidan events and on December 5 handed "cookies" to the demonstrators, producing an impression that the United States had a hand in Maidan's script.

As violence escalated, the government passed the "anti-riot laws" through the parliament on January 16, 2014, which were quickly repelled. The first death occurred in Kyiv on January 22, when a protestor was killed. After that, the protestors seized administrative buildings in western Ukraine.[78] Militant groups became noticeable among their ranks, such as the Right Sector[79] which led confrontations with *Berkut* special forces of the Ministry of Interior. Use of force generated more militancy, including occupation of public buildings in Kyiv and taking their staff hostage, as at the Ministry of Justice on January 26. Protests gained in ferocity, and on February 18, 2014, twenty-eight people were killed in Kyiv, including ten *Berkut* troopers, buildings were set on fire, and military arsenals were raided in western Ukraine. Mass riots culminated on February 20 when most fatalities occurred. Altogether, ninety-eight Maidan protestors—the "Heavenly Hundred"—were confirmed dead, according to the Social Policy minister Liudmila Denisova.[80]

Alarmed by the scale of the crisis, the foreign ministers of Germany, France, and Poland facilitated the deal between Yanukovych and three protest leaders in Kyiv. On February 21 the agreement stipulating the steps toward peace was signed, being witnessed by the EU ministers who provided their assurances to the Ukrainian president. In several hours, the deal was rejected by the Maidan protestors and the government troops retreated. Activists occupied the parliament, where several pro-government MPs were brutally beaten. Yanukovych felt a mortal danger and fled the capital, which Putin advised him against.

Euromaidan represented different things to different people who came together in one historical junction, and any single definition runs a danger of being simplistic. It had civic values and aspirations which were not entirely anti-Russian at the onset. For some, it was a protest against corruption, general malfeasance of Yanukovych regime and his nexus between politics, business and law enforcement which exercised an overwhelming control and left little chance to the honest outsiders. There was a strong quest for prosecution of corrupt officials of the Yanukovych government. Older people were frustrated with the failure of the first Maidan's promise of liberal reforms,[81] but younger protestors had little awareness of that. For others, Euromaidan expressed a speedy entry into the European Union and associated benefits of access to the single market and good governance.

Pro-European discourse allocated different attributes and advantages to European integration with little explanation of the specifics, because the national-democratic elites have not formed a coherent national project aimed at Europe in the earlier period, thus giving rise to a fusion of what it in reality entailed. It could be understood as building effective institutions in law, politics and social relations, or as overcoming the Soviet legacy and history of incorporation into the Tsarist Russia. One view was that while the essence of the "European choice" was a move away from participation in Eurasian geopolitical projects, it also reflected a vacuum in indigenous designs.[82] As noted by Sakwa, "the 'European choice' is, paradoxically, precisely not European—it is Atlanticist."[83] In 2015, when the realities transpired more clearly, the "European vision" came under criticism from opposition politicians, such as Viktor Medvedchuk, leader of *Ukraine's Choice*, who called it a "myth" based on an unrealistic foundation.[84]

There were those, for whom Euromaidan epitomized a struggle for a denied Ukrainian identity sabotaged by the iron fist of the Russian state. Internal political choice came to equal the external one: toward or away from Russia as far as possible.[85] Distancing from Moscow was considered by a large segment of the Maidan constituency as an essential prerequisite for progress down the European path: "we have a very negative example—Russia, a place we want to leave, push back from."[86] However, the anti-Russian sentiment that Maidan unleashed was perceived as deeply problematic by those citizens who empathized with the anti-corruption stance but were alienated by the behavior and rhetoric of some pro-Maidan activist groups. Some were outright frightened, as I learnt during my own visits to the region in 2014.

OPENING THE ROAD TO VIOLENCE

Opposing groups became more shaped and were preparing to clash with each other. The pro-Russian one, which previously expressed itself rather passively, was awakened by Yanukovych's runner. Although anti-Maidan rallies took place before the president's ouster, they did not generate a popular movement and some participants were believed to be paid by Yanukovych (so-called *titushki*), although several later said that they participated voluntarily. When Maidan was going on, its opponents felt that it was the state's responsibility to address the protests and that it had resources in its disposal to do so.

This changed with the Maidan victory when tables were turned. *Berkut* which defended the government during the protests, in the course of which seventeen servicemen died and many suffered firearms wounds, became one of the first casualties because the winners were angry at *Berkut* for shooting down protestors.[87] The remaining force was hunted down, beaten up, and shot at, and some of their arms were apprehended by Maidan activists. The next move was the vote in Supreme Rada (parliament) to abolish the Languages Law which was initiated by a nationalist *Svoboda* (Freedom) party. Although the bill was never signed into law, the damage was done and the rhetoric of the moment was exclusionary.[88] Pro-Maidan activists were keen to capitalize on their victory and dispel resistance in the parts of southeastern Ukraine.

In response to the Maidan victory, protests, disturbances and low-level confrontations broke out in the parts of the country where pro-Russian identity was strong, including Crimea, Donbas, and Odesa. Resistance in these regions must be situated against a wave of anti-Russian sentiment and moves of the new power-holders in Kyiv after Yanukovych fled. Protesters feared that their policies would see Russian language marginalized and more Russian schools closed amid attempts to break free of Russian influence more generally. These policies were directed not against a small minority but against a significant body of Ukrainian citizens, who held the opposite views from those of pro-Maidan activists.

The tragic events on May 2 in Odesa are of crucial significance because they had the same effect on the Russian world as the downing of the Malaysian airliner had for the Western public opinion, as it was received as a collective shock and as an albatross of things to come. Given contradictory accounts—some of which blamed the victims[89]—it is prudent to use the UN Office of High Commissioner for Human Rights' (UN OHCHR) outline of what happened. According to it, two rallies were held—a 2,000-strong pro-Maidan one that included the Right Sector activists, "self-defence" militias, and football supporters wearing helmets and masks, and armed with shields, axes, sticks, and some with firearms. A smaller 300-strong anti-Maidan crowd in a similar gear gathered nearby. The two crowds clashed, six men were killed by gunshots, and the anti-Maidan losers ran away chased by their pro-Maidan opponents. Some ran to the tent camp at the Kulikovo Pole square, where 200 of their supporters had gathered, but it offered poor protection and they took refuge in the Trade Union Building. Their rivals burnt their tents and threw Molotov cocktails at the building. Gunshots were heard coming from both sides. Anti-Maidan protestors barricaded themselves in the building, after which a fire broke out inside. According to the investigation by the "2 May Group," the fire started spontaneously at the main entrance and in the foyer where the anti-Maidan activists built a makeshift barricade out of furniture and wooden panels which quickly started burning on coming into contact with petrol.[90] The fire brigade which had its base located 650 meters from the scene took 40 minutes to arrive after receiving the first phone call. As a result of the fire, forty-two people died, thirty-two were trapped and burnt alive, and ten, including a woman and a minor, died jumping from windows. Some pro-Maidan protesters were beating up those who were escaping the burning building, while others were trying to actively help them. A total of 247 people were brought from the scene requiring medical assistance.[91]

There were different perspectives on who was to blame for the events. One could attribute the blame to the pro-Maidan activists—many of whom came from outside Odesa—for setting the building on fire, or to the emergency services for not responding to it, or to police for the failure to stop the rival rallies earlier and letting the groups clash. They were some who had no sympathy with the anti-Maidan victims, but expressed that they fell on their own sword. The reaction of civil activists in Kyiv was divided and, sadly, there were voices that endorsed violence.

As a result of these turbulent events, the gap in society widened, when many who preferred not to make identity choices, were forced into them. Two opposing political camps which were implicit before, got crystallized. They cannot be interpreted in terms of ethnicity because individuals of the same blood line could find themselves on the opposite sides of the divide. Not everybody in Ukraine fits into these categories, but the actors in the conflict do, and it is useful to explain them as they will be used later in the book. It applies the terms "pro-Ukrainian" and "pro-Russian" while acknowledging that they are not perfect. However, alternatives have own shortcomings. "Pro-Maidan" and "anti-Maidan" definitions characterize differences in relation to the event, that is, Euromaidan, but they cannot be fully extrapolated to all that went on before and after it. The term "pro-European" Ukrainians implies that their opponents did not feel "European" which was not true because they believed Russia to be a part of Europe. Other descriptions, such as "pro-EU/ NATO" and "anti-EU/NATO" supporters, do not give justice to what was really important to different identity bearers, only defining them in relation to geopolitics.[92] The other possible terms are "Ukrainophones" and "Russophones" used, for example, in Wilson's earlier works, but they have poor readability. "Pro-Ukrainian" identity stood for the Ukrainian unitary statehood, facing away from Russia and making a radical break with it. It comprised the elements of its past history which were not associated with Russia or those which exemplified a struggle against it, and a future vision of the entry into NATO and the European Union as its core pillars. A forward-looking perspective was the idea of European integration based on "democratic civilisational" values which was presented as an alternative to the *Russian World*. These signifiers were aimed to replace the memory of the past and aspirations for future associated with the Soviet Union/Russia.

The opposing pro-Russian identity stood for cultural and political belonging to *the Russian World* as a community of peoples who felt a connection to Russia, association with a "Russian civilisation" and was distinct—but not necessarily hostile—to the West. In Ukraine, many of its bearers felt that Russians and Ukrainians are essentially the same people (народ), in which they form distinctive cultural groups, but broadly share a historical destiny, and feeling "Russian" and "Ukrainian" at the same time did not present a contradiction in terms for them. Generally, a popular understanding of the *Russkyi Mir* existed long before Maidan which included such notions as the preservation and promotion of the Russian language, recognition of Russian culture as a part of one's own, social and cultural attraction to the way of life associated with Russia, interest in Moscow's positioning in world affairs, and anger when its actions were unjustly criticized. Richard Sakwa sensed its emergence long before it actually came out, giving it a codename of *Russonia* as a virtual community united by language and culture. Many who settled around the globe, formed a *Russkyi Mir* whose members, although living elsewhere, are still oriented toward Russian culture and values. One does not have to be an ethnic Russian to associate themselves with the Russian World, as, for example, some Germans with the Soviet roots who became recent citizens of Germany, the same sometimes happens in Israel, etc. The concept indicated the presence of a transnational community with little formal institutional identity, but which has a cultural resonance in its host states and Russia. When one part of *Russkyi Mir* is attacked, the whole community endures a collective chill.[93] I return to the use of the *Russian World* by the Russian state in chapter 12.

To conclude, Ukraine could have remained stable on the basis of acceptance of pluralism and identity differences as an essential part of the nature of the state. However, the attitude of intolerance and polarization that followed Maidan posed a threat to the delicate equilibrium characteristic of the past, and was detrimental in the country with diverse political cultures and orientations. If differences could not be accommodated in a legitimate discourse, they were bound to come out by other means. Thus, attempts at redefinition of the country's identity which was shared by a significant segment of society were likely to encounter resistance, and it did not take long to erupt.

NOTES

1. The exception was the work of the OSCE High Commissioner on National Minorities in Crimea in the 1990s, but it was focused on a specific issue.

2. Andrew Wilson, *Ukraine Crisis: What It Means for the West* (New Haven, CT: Yale University Press, 2014); Edward Lucas, "I hope I'm wrong but historians may look back and say this was the start of World War III," *Daily Mail*, 16 April 2014.

3. Paul G Holman Jr., "Russo-Ukrainian Relations: The Containment Legacy" in *Ethnic Nationalism and Regional Conflict. The Former Soviet Union and Yugoslavia*, eds. Duncan Raymond W. and Holman Paul G. Jr (Boulder: Westview Press, 1994): 95.

4. Nikolai N. Petro, "Understanding the Other Ukraine: Identity and Allegiance in Russophone Ukraine," in *Ukraine and Russia: People, Politics, Propaganda and Perspectives*, eds. A. Pikulicka-Wilczewska and R. Sakwa (E-International, 2015), 3, http://www.e-ir.info/wp-content/uploads/2015/03/Ukraineand-Russia-E-IR.pdf.

5. Andrew Wilson, *Ukraine Crisis: What It Means for the West* (New Haven, CT: Yale University Press, 2014), 39–49.

6. Paul d'Anieri, "Ethnic Tensions and State Strategies: Understanding the Survival of the Ukrainian State," 25–30, in *Democratic Revolution in Ukraine: from Kuchmagate to Orange Revolution*, ed. Taras Kuzio (Abingdon: Routledge, 2009).

7. Bremmer, Ian, "The Politics of Ethnicity: Russians in the New Ukraine," *Europe-Asia Studies* 46: 2 (1994).

8. On complexities of identity in the first decade of independence see Graham Smith and Andrew Wilson, "Rethinking Russia's Post-Soviet Diaspora: The Potential for Political Mobilisation in Eastern Ukraine and North-East Estonia," *Europe-Asia Studies* 49, no. 5 (1997): 845–886.

9. Yaroslav Hrytsak, "National Identities in Post-Soviet Ukraine: The Case of Lviv and Donetsk," *Harvard Ukrainian Studies* 22 (1998): 263–288.

10. Volodymyr Kulyk, "National Identity in Ukraine: Impact of Euromaidan and the War," *Europe-Asia Studies* 68, no. 4 (2016), 588–608.

11. Kulyk utilises data from surveys by the Kyiv International Institute of Sociology (KIIS) in 2012 and 2014, in "National Identity."

12. Khmel'ko Valery E,"Социальная основа расхождения электоральных предпочтений двух частей Украины на выборах 2004–2007 годов" (Kyiv: Aidos, 2010): 398–408.

13. "Каждый десятый украинец считает себя гражданином СССР," *Research and Branding Group survey*, October 5, 2012. http://news.finance.ua/ru/news/-/288874/kazhdyj-desyatyj-ukrainets-schitaet-sebya-grazhdaninom-sssr

14. Razumkov Centre findings in 2009 in Crimea were that "only 27.3% of representatives of the Slavic [Russian and Ukrainian] community consider themselves

members of the Ukrainian political nation, while 44.2% do not feel like that," *National Security and Defence* 5 (Kyiv: 2009): 5.

15. Sakwa, *Frontline Ukraine*, ix.

16. Kolstoe, Paul, *Russians in the Former Soviet Republics* (London: Hurst & Company, 1995).

17. "Ethnic Composition of Population of the Russian Federation according to the 2010 National Census," (Moscow: State Statistics Committee, 2010).

18. "National Composition of Population General Results of the Census," (Kyiv: State Statistics Committee, 2001).

19. Ihor Semyvolos, interview by the author, Kyiv, November 2015. Kuzio stretches this perception to language, but does not provide evidence for his argument that "to many Russians the Ukrainian and Belarusian languages are 'provincial,' 'peasant' languages unfit for state elites, culture or the technical sciences," in Taras Kuzio, "Identity and Nation-building in Ukraine: Defining the 'Other,'" *Ethnicities* 1, no. 3 (2001), 348.

20. Himka, John P, "Western Ukraine in the Interwar Period," *Nationalities Papers* 22, no. 2 (1994): 347–363.

21. Armstrong, John, *Ukrainian Nationalism*, 2nd edition (New York: Columbia University Press, 1963), Himka, "Western Ukraine," "Organisation of Ukrainian Nationalists and the Ukrainian Insurgent Army," (Kyiv: Institute of Ukrainian History, Academy of Sciences of Ukraine, 1978): 385–386.

22. Kharlamov, Sergei. December 2014. Interview with the author, Moscow; personal experience in 1984, Lvov.

23. Dziuba, Ivan, *Internationalism or Russification? A Study in the Soviet Nationalities Problem*, trans. from Ukrainian, edited M. Davies (London: Weidenfeld and Nicolson, 1968).

24. On early historiography see Mark von Hagen, "Does Ukraine Have a History?" *Slavic Review* 54: 3 (1995): 658–673. For critical perspectives see History Project by Heinrich Boell Foundation in Ukraine, http://ua.boell.org/uk/categories/history

25. David R. Marples, "Stepan Bandera: The Resurrection of a Ukrainian National Hero," *Europe-Asia Studies*, 58: 4 (2006): 565.

26. Marples, "Stepan Bandera," 561.

27. Marples, "Stepan Bandera."

28. Oleh Protsyk, "Majority-Minority Relations in the Ukraine," *JEMIE* 7 (Flensburg: European Centre for Minority Issues, 2008): 21.

29. Paul Kolsoe, *Russians in the Former Soviet Republics* (London: Hurst & Company, 1995), 171.

30. Anna Fournier, "Mapping Identities: Russian Resistance to Linguistic Ukrainization in Central and Eastern Ukraine," *Europe-Asia Studies*, 54: 3 (2002), 415–433.

31. Data compiled by Kolstoe, Russians, 183, from *Natsional'nyi sostav naseleniia SSSR* (Moscow, 1991), 78–86; and *Shkoly Ukrainy* (Odesa: Iug, 20 January 1993), 3.

32. http://doshkolenok.Kyiv.ua/srednie-shkoly-rus.html

33. http://www.igpi.ru/info/people/malink/1111152776.html

34. Data were provided to the author by the Ministry Science and Education of Ukraine in December 2015. The 2015 figures do not include Crimea and the NGCAs of Donbas.

35. Data were provided to the author by the department of general secondary and pre-school education, Ministry of Science and Education of Ukraine, Kyiv, November, 2015.

36. Ivan D. Loshkariov and Andrey A. Sushentsov, "Radicalization of Russians in Ukraine: from 'accidental' diaspora to rebel movement," *Southeast European and Black Sea Studies* 16, no. 1(2016): 72, DOI: 10.1080/14683857.2016.1149349.

37. Data were provided to the author by the Ministry of Education and Science of Ukraine in December 2015. The 2015 figures do not include Crimea and the NGCAs of Donbas.

38. Author's interviews in Donbas, 2014.

39. Alexei Volynets, "Язык из Киева уведет: украинизация на востоке," *Rus Balt News Agency*, May 13, 2014. http://rusplt.ru/world/ukrainskiy-yazik-9782.html

40. Sergey Volkov, Kyiv-based expert, interviews with the author, 2014 and 2015, Kyiv–London (by Skype).

41. Marina Kurktchyan, Oxford academic, interview with the author, London, 2013.

42. Anthony D. Smith, *National Identity* (London: Penguin, 1991).

43. Ilya Prizel, "The Influence of Ethnicity on Foreign Policy: the Case of Ukraine," in *National Identity and Ethnicity in Russia and the New States of Eurasia*, ed. Roman Szporluk (New York and London: M. E. Sharpe, 1994), 116.

44. Nikolai Gogol was born in Dikan'ka in eastern Ukraine and although he wrote in Russian, his earlier work, such as fairy tales, and burlesques and humorous stories are much influenced by Ukrainian folklore and imagery. His later works, which brought him an international fame, such as *Dead Souls*, are written using Russian material.

45. Channels started to be banned by Kyiv since Russia's annexation of Crimea; 14 main Russian TV channels were prohibited in August 2014 by a joint decision of the Ministry of Interior and the National Council on Television and Radio Broadcasting. Police were given enforcement powers in eliminating Russian channels by the Ministry of Interior decree of 19 August 2014. "Какие российские каналы запрещены в Украине и какие провайдеры плюют на запрет." August 21, 2014.*UNIAN* http://uainfo.org/blognews/378702-kakie-rossiyskie-kanaly-zaprescheny-v-ukraine-i-kakie-provaydery-plyuyut-na-zapret.html

46. The other protagonist is Ukrainian Autocephalous Orthodox Church, also on conflictual terms with the Church under the Moscow Patriarchy.

47. Dmytro Vydrin interview with the author, Kyiv, 2014.

48. [National-Democrats] is a self-designation of Maidan-supporting intellectuals in Ukraine. The previous widely used term "Orange Coalition" [referring to a coalition of political parties and leaders] acquired a derogatory connotation associated with the failed attempt at reforms during Yushchenko presidency.

49. Author's interview with Alexander Chalenko, Moscow, May 2016.

50. Kolstoe, *Russians*, 180.

51. Oleg Tsaryov, former chair of Novorossiya Parliament, interview with the author, April 2017, via Skype.

52. Eleanore Narvselius, "Polishness as a Site of Memory and Arena for Construction of Multicultural Heritage in L'viv," 84, in *Whose Memory? Whose Future?*, ed. Barbara Tornquist-Plewa (New York: Berghahn Books, 2016).

53. In January 2010 President Yushchenko signed a decree on "Commemoration of participants in the struggle for Ukraine's independence in 20th century," 29 January 2010, https://censor.net.ua/n111277. In June 2009 a street in central Kyiv was named after Simeon Petlyura despite protests from Jewish organisations.

54. Oleh Protsyk, Ukrainian scholar, interview with the author, June 2015, by Skype.

55. Kuzio, "Identity and Nation-building."

56. Denys Kiryukhin,"Roots and Features of Modern Ukrainian National Identity and Nationalism," in *Ukraine and Russia: People, Politics, Propaganda and Perspectives*, eds. Agnieszka Pikulicka-Wilczewska and Richard Sakwa (E-International Relations: 2015), http://www.e-ir.info/2015/03/06/edited-collection-ukraine-and-russia-people-politics-propaganda-perspectives/, 57–65, 60.

57. Stephen Shulman, "Cultures in Competition: Ukrainian Foreign Policy and the 'Cultural Threat' from Abroad," *Europe-Asia Studies*, 50, no. 2 (1998): 287–303.

58. Serhy Yekelchyk, *The Conflict in Ukraine: What Everyone Needs to Know* (Oxford: Oxford University Press, 2015), 22.

59. Author's interview with Mikhail Pogrebinskiy, director of Kyiv Centre of Political Studies and Conflictology.

60. Dmytro Vydrin, interview with the author, Kyiv, 2014.

61. Alexander Chalenko interview with the author, Moscow, May 2016.

62. Nuland in remarks at the US-Ukraine Foundation conference at National Press Club, said on December 13, 2013: "the United States supported the Ukrainians in the development of democratic institutions and skills in promoting civil society and a good form of government–all that is necessary to achieve the objectives of Ukraine's European. We have invested more than 5 billion dollars to help Ukraine to achieve these and other goals. "The US official aid to Ukraine was the third largest after Israel and Egypt. For examination see James Dean, "Ukraine: Europe's Forgotten Economy," *Challenge*, 43, no. 6 (2000).

63. Victoria Hudson,"Forced to Friendship?" Russian (Mis-)Understandings of Soft Power and the Implications for Audience Attraction in Ukraine," *Politics* 35, nos. 3–4 (2015): 330–346. doi: 10.1111/1467-9256.12106.

64. Ekaterina Turkina, "Russia-Ukraine Crisis:Value-Based and Generational Perspective," *Studies in Ethnicity and Nationalism* 15, no. 1 (2015), 189.

65. William E. Pomeranz, "Ground Zero: How a Trade Dispute Sparked the Russia–Ukraine Crisis," in *Roots of Russia's War in Ukraine,* eds. Elizabeth A. Wood, William E. Pomeranz, E. Wayne Merry, and Maxim Trudolyubov (Washington, DC: Woodrow Wilson Center Press, 2016).

66. Dmitry Trenin, "The Ukraine Crisis and the Resumption of Great-Power Rivalry," *Russia in Global Affairs*, 14 July 2014, http://eng.globalaffairs.ru/book/The-Ukraine-Crisis-and-the-Resumption-of-Great-Power-Rivalry-16806. Other Russian view see in Paul J. Saunders "How Russia Sees the Ukraine Crisis," *The National Interest*, October 13, 2014, http://nationalinterest.org/feature/how-russia-sees-the-ukraine-crisis-11461 and Anatolii Tsyganok, *Donbas: Unfinished War. Civil War in Ukraine (2014–2016)* (Moscow: AIRO-XXI, 2017), 39–48.

67. "Vladimir Putin responded to questions from journalists," 4 March 2014, http://kremlin.ru/events/president/news/20366

68. Nicu Popescu, "Eurasian Union: the real, the imaginary and the likely," *Chaillot Paper* 132 (Paris: EUISS, 2014)

69. Sakwa, *Frontline Ukraine*, 42–43.

70. Sakwa, *Frontline Ukraine*, 40.

71. Eastern Partnership countries are Armenia, Azerbaijan, Belarus, Georgia, Moldova, and Ukraine.

72. Pasquale De Micco, "When choosing means losing The Eastern partners, the EU and the Eurasian Economic Union," European Parliament Policy Department, Directorate for External Policies, Brussels, March 2015.

73. European External Action Service, "Myths about the Association Agreement—setting the facts straight," undated, http://eeas.europa.eu/archives/delegations/ukraine/documents/myths_aa_en.pdf

74. IFES, "Public opinion poll shows dissastisfaction with sociopolitical conditions," December 2013, http://www.ifes.org/news/ukraine-2013-public-opinion-poll-shows-dissastisfaction-socio-political-conditions

75. Democratic Initiative Foundation and Razumkov Centre, May 2013, quoted in Haran Olexiy, Zolkina, Maria, "Трудный путь Украины к европейской интеграции." *PONARS Eurasia analytical memo* 311 (Kyiv, 2014) http://www.ponarseurasia.org/sites/default/files/policy-memos-pdf/Pepm_311_rus_Haran_Feb2014.pdf

76. Pavel Gaidutsky, "Украина—ЕС: проблемы интеграции," June 7, 2013, http://gazeta.zn.ua/international/ukraina-es-problemy-integracii-_.html

77. Mustafa Nayyem, "Uprising in Ukraine: How It All Began," Open Society Foundation, April 4, 2014. https://www.opensocietyfoundations.org/voices/uprising-ukraine-how-it-all-began

78. "Ukraine unrest: Protesters storm regional offices," *BBC*, 24 January 2014, http://www.bbc.co.uk/news/world-europe-25876807

79. Right Sector was formed based on several Ukrainian nationalist organisations, including UNA-UNSO, Trident, Ukrainian Patriot, and White Hammer. On 22 March 2014 the Right Sector became a political party based on the Ukrainian National Assembly.

80. June 3, 2014, http://podrobnosti.ua/978812-kolichestvo-pogibshih-na-majdane-ofitsialno-uvelichilos-do-98-chelovek.html

81. On the developments see Lucan Way, "Between National Division and Rapacious Individualism Ukraine before and after the Orange Revolution," *The Brown Journal of World Affairs*, 14: 2 (2008): 253–264.

82. Volodymir Lipatsy, interview with the author, Kyiv, November 2015.

83. Richard Sakwa, "The death of Europe?" 559.

84. Viktor Medvedchuk quoted by *RBK Ukraine*, "Медведчук назвал "мифом" евроинтеграционные обещания украинской власти," November 25, 2015, http://www.rbc.ua/rus/news/medvedchuk-nazval-mifom-evrointegratsionnye-1448442623.html

85. Author's interview with Sergei Markedonov, Moscow, June 2016.

86. Author's interview with Ihor Semyvolos, Kyiv, November 2015.

87. They appealed to The Hague International Tribunal accusing Berkut of crimes against humanity. The Tribunal, however, ruled that although human rights violations

took place, they could not be qualified as "crimes against humanity." See, for example, "Суд в Гааге реабилитировал «Беркут» и не признал, что на Майдане совершались преступления против человечности." November 13, 2015. *Antimaidan.* http://antimaydan.info/2015/11/sud_v_gaage_reabilitiroval_berkut_i_ne_priznal_chto_na_majdane_sovershalis_420001.html

88. International Crisis Group, "Ukraine: Running out of Time" *Europe Report* 231 (2014).

89. For reporting, see Pavel Koshkin, "Odesa incident: The media battle for Eastern Ukraine," May 4, 2014, http://www.russia-direct.org/analysis/odessa-incident-media-battle-eastern-ukraine, for analysis, Oliver Boyd-Barrett, *Western mainstream media and the Ukraine Crisis: a study in conflict propaganda* (London: Routledge, 2016), chapter 6.

90. *2 May Group* was set up by the then Odesa governor Igor Palitsa. ""Группа 2 мая" опубликовала отчет о пожаре в Доме профсоюзов в Одессе," May 24, 2015, http://korrespondent.net/ukraine/3495145-hruppa-2-maia-opublykovala-otchet-o-pozhare-v-dome-profsouizov-v-odesse

91. "Report on the human rights situation in Ukraine," *Office of the United Nations High Commissioner for Human Rights* June 15, 2014, http://www.ohchr.org/Documents/Countries/UA/HRMMUReport15June2014.pdf

92. Definitional issue was discussed at the Civil Society Dialogue Network Meeting on "How to make the peace processes in Ukraine more inclusive?" 28 February 2017 Vienna, Austria, EPLO meeting report.

93. Richard Sakwa, *Russian Politics and Society*, 4th edition (Abingdon: Routledge, 2008): 219.

Chapter 3

Faultlines in Crimea

Crimean peninsula has been inhabited by different civilizations since time immemorial. Ancient Greeks left a distinct mark on its material culture, and later it became a homeland of early Christians who contributed to the peninsula's spiritual heritage. It is also a cradle of Crimean Tatar people who adhere to Islam and are responsible for development of Crimea's Muslim architecture and cultural monuments. The rise of empires—the Ottoman, Russian and British—led to territorial contests, geopolitical competition and wars, changing political fortunes and altering cultural boundaries. The twentieth century was particularly turbulent in Crimea's history, with two World Wars fought on its territory. The peninsula changed its status four times in a hundred years: from a special place in Imperial Russia to an autonomous republic within the Russian Federation (RSFSR) in the Soviet Union, became a part of the Ukrainian Union Republic (SSR) for 37 years, then—an autonomous republic within independent Ukraine (Autonomous Republic of Crimea, or ARC) and subsequently—a subject of the Russian Federation, unrecognized by the international community.

The push against the Ottoman Empire under Catherine the Great witnessed incorporation of the peninsula as a Taurida Oblast into the Russian Empire where it became a part of Novorossiya, a distinct administrative unit along the Black Sea coast stretching to the Dnestr (Nistru in Romanian) river in the west.[1] In February 1954 the peninsula was unexpectedly transferred to the Ukrainian SSR to mark the 300th anniversary of Ukraine's "reunification" with Russia by Nikita Khrushchev who just succeeded Stalin as the secretary general of the Soviet Communist Party, and the pliant USSR Supreme Soviet dutifully raised its hands in favor without a debate or consultation with the people involved. The exact reasons for the transfer had not been clarified. One was that it was a form of expiation for the Soviet atrocities in Ukraine

47

committed on Khrushchev's watch and the other, more plausible reason, was economic. It was easier to supply the peninsula with water and electricity, and develop its agriculture if it were integrated into a single economic and administrative cycle with the neighboring Ukrainian SSR.[2]

Three main ethnocultural communities in Crimea—Russians, those Ukrainians who associated primarily with Ukrainian nationhood and Crimean Tatars—perceived these historical events differently. Distinct and at times mutually exclusive perspectives on history accentuated intergroup cleavages. From the perspective of people of different ethnicities who associate themselves with the Russian cultural, social, and historic space, an accident of history transformed Crimea from a prominent place of Russian culture and glory into one of the less developed regions of Ukraine. Significant parts of this group were reluctant to identify with the new Ukrainian statehood,[3] regarding it as irrelevant to their daily routines and interactions, or—worse— a threat to the future viability of social and cultural community. For them, the most regretted historic moments, in retrospect, were the transfer of Crimean jurisdiction to the Ukrainian SSR and the dissolution of the Soviet Union.

The Crimean Tatar perspective is different. The community regarded itself as an indigenous group on the peninsula and saw others—as interlopers who forced their way into the territory which they consider their homeland. Deportation to Central Asia and Siberia in 1944 as a collective punishment for an alleged collaboration with the occupying German troops and denial of the right to return en massacre during the 1950s when many formerly deported people were allowed to move to their historical lands, led to emergence of a victimization stance, through which the relations with other groups were seen. Crimean Tatars felt that they experienced a social prejudice derived from the dominant historical narrative of the World War II. Historians of "pro-Russian orientation" in their turn maintained that although deportation was an inhumane act, collaboration was real and newly opened archives confirmed that, such as the events surrounding Crimean partisans. Katchanovski noted that while no ethnic group was immune to it, "proportion of Tatars collaborating with the Nazis was much higher than the proportions of collaborators among Russians and Ukrainians."[4]

Crimean Ukrainian perspective reflected concerns over the prevalence of the Russian language on the peninsula, with few lower-level officials being fluent in Ukrainian well enough to be able to respond to citizens' requests in the state language and a proportionate deficit of schools with Ukrainian as the language of instruction.[5] Ukrainian served the purpose of identity preservation and was useful for ties with mainland Ukraine, but was less prominent in daily interactions. Interlocutors among Ukrainian-speakers admitted that public pressure made them feel uncomfortable about talking Ukrainian in public.[6] As most people valued social acceptance, they preferred to go with the flow and not to confront the dominant norm, which was to speak Russian in public. Such perspectives, with variations when it came to different cultural groups among Russians and Ukrainians, served as an obstacle to the formation of a common identity and shared vision of a future. All three groups felt as minorities in the peninsula, and its civic future was being built on a precarious foundation.

Crimea's situation can be interpreted as a time bomb inherited from the Soviet era. The region was weakly integrated into Soviet Ukraine after its transfer. Most of its command and subordination lines emanated from Moscow, which was in charge of the navy, controlled the best Black Sea resorts, and oversaw its international contacts. It also closed the whole sways of land for defense purposes making it inaccessible to the local population. Kyiv's role was confined to infrastructure and economic development with little impact on culture and education, where Russian influence was predominant. No Ukrainian schools existed and Ukrainian language broadcasts were limited. In fact, some would stress that being a part of the Ukrainian SSR did not mean much to Crimea and its people back then, other than in administrative terms. Things changed after the collapse of the Soviet Union.

When it came to the twilight of the USSR, popular attitudes toward the future were confused. It was not apparent that this was a historical turn that would seal Crimea's belonging to an independent state that could potentially be hostile to Russia. Uncertainty of the period was reflected in two votes cast in 1991. The percentage of those who voted "yes" in the December 1991 Ukrainian referendum on independence in the Crimean ASSR was 54.19 percent, the lowest in the Ukrainian SSR, followed by 57 percent in Sevastopol,[7] although independence as a total cutoff was hard to imagine. Crimea also held its own referendum on January 20, 1991 on restoring autonomy within the USSR rather than in Ukraine, in which 93.3 percent gave an affirmative answer. Movements and groups advocating unification with Russia were numerous and vocal at the time, and the peninsula could have easily turned into another secessionist conflict as did the Caucasus and Transnistria in Moldova.

However, President Yeltsin, resentful of the pro-Communist credentials of the then Crimea's leadership and fascinated by bringing Communism to a bitter end, did not make a decisive claim on the region in 1991. After the breakup, the regional leadership chose the path of an attempted referendum, solicitations of legal provisions and negotiations with Kyiv over autonomy, and did not mount enough courage for a rebellion.[8] There was no "push" of interethnic tensions between Russians and Ukrainians as none existed, and relations with Crimean Tatar returnees were seen as a local issue. Although the Russian State Duma and a number of public figures in Russia voiced support for Crimea's re-unification, their declarations had no political consequences, and the idea never got traction in the Kremlin. Kyiv's hand was stronger, and it eventually outmaneuvered Simferopol, which received few concessions in its 1992 constitution against the original demands, although its autonomy was not abolished. The new ARC's constitution, adopted in 1998 under Leonid Kuchma, further deprived the republic of many of its autonomous powers compared to the 1992 version.

DEVELOPMENT OF POST-INDEPENDENCE IDENTITIES

Crimea can be interpreted as a case of flared up identity politics that had developed since independence in the context of the evolution of Ukrainian statehood, demographic changes, and the creation of new discourses. The Soviet legacy laid the ground, but it was not solely accountable for the identities that emerged in its wake. Increasingly, they competed against one another, making the situation fragile and in need of delicate maintenance.

In 1989, according to the last Soviet census, the ethnic composition of Crimea was 67 percent Russian and 25.75 percent Ukrainian, out of whom 47.4 percent considered Russian to be their native language. Moreover, as Russian-Ukrainian intermarriage was widespread, and the format of passports permitted only one ethnicity to be registered, some of those registered as "Ukrainians" could have been more "Russian" in their orientation and vice versa. The rest of the population comprised smaller groups, such as Armenians, Greeks, Germans, while Crimean Tatars made up 2 percent. Most identified with the "Slav majority," comprising ethnic Russians, Russian-speaking Ukrainians and others, including Belarusians, Poles, Jews and people of mixed ethnicity. Initially, they took their "Russianness" for granted and as a continuation of a Soviet identity, as there was no real "other" to define against.

However, when rival identities started to make their presence felt, create discourses and future orientations, "Russianness" was contextualized differently. The promotion of the Ukrainian language in education and visual space were markers of this fundamental identity rift. Historical narratives worked to exacerbate the gap as "each new government when it came to power in Ukraine, started with re-writing history."[9] Yushchenko's rule gave a boost to an alternative version of the World War II history and introduced changes in the public space to leave a footprint on the ground, producing a divisive effect on pro-Russian and pro-Ukrainian oriented constituencies.

The key cleavage lay in relations between the pro-Russia/Soviet identity majority, including ethnic Russians, Russian-speaking Ukrainians and some Crimean Tatars, and a minority that identified with the Ukrainian state, such as Ukrainian-speaking ethnic Ukrainians, most Crimean Tatars and some new generation Russians. Public opinion research from this time showed that ethnic identity was not a defining identity marker for most—it was important for merely 26 percent of Russians—but this was different for the Crimean Tatars, 80 percent of whom found it significant.[10]

CRIMEAN TATARS: A "HOST MINORITY"

The chaotic return of some 250,000 Crimean Tatars from Central Asia in the late 1980s—early 1990s at the time when neither old Soviet, nor new Ukrainian state mechanisms were able to cope with accommodating such a number of in-migrants, created strains of absorption of new arrivals into the existing multiethnic community of Crimea. The 2001 census recorded that Crimean Tatars already made up 10 percent of the population share against 1989 and an estimated 13 percent by 2014. Their initial demand was for a Crimean Tatar national-territorial autonomy. Their main national movement, the Milli Mejlis, was traditionally in opposition to the ARC authorities. It adhered to a top-down strategy fighting to achieve "indigenous people" status from the central government, from which resolution of all other issues was to follow. Yet, the community was split into those who supported the Mejlis and those who did not, such as Milli Firca. Some favored the notion of a "Crimean identity," but a politically engaged segment disapproved, claiming that it weakened a separate "Crimean Tatar" identity and denied it a special place and recognition as the indigenous group. The role and status of the Crimean Tatar language, which suffered a heavy blow due to deportation and struggled to rise to prominence, was one of the pillars around which the community's grievances centered. This included practical issues of teaching it in schools, such as number of classes, availability and quality of textbooks, teacher training and allocated hours.

The perception that the Crimean Tatar community was claiming a special privilege on the peninsula over other inhabitants fed anti-Tatar attitudes. "Slav" grievances centered on the presumed sense of Crimean Tatars' exclusive rights:

All right, they arrived because they lived here before. We made room, but of course it was tough for them. As it was for everybody else. Remember the 90s? Nobody had jobs, there was no cash, people with PhDs were trading at street markets. So, they settled, but why say now that "we are the ones whom this land belongs to," that "we were here first." That they should have some special rights and say over it. It is as if they are somehow better than us, and we should feel guilty about it.[11]

It is often the case in divided societies that cultural manifestations by one group can cause distress to another. Construction of historical monuments and renaming of geographic locations is a key identity marker which connects the past to the present. Although Islam was present in material artifacts of the bygone era, visible signs of the Muslim way of life was a novelty, and religious tensions transpired. Changes in visual space resonated differently in different communities, for example, the erection and destruction of Christian crosses in 2011 that led to clashes between Crimean Tatars and Cossacks in Feodossia and other locations. More recently, reports implicating Tatar young men in subversive Islamist activity and of joining fighting in the Middle East portrayed them as a security threat.[12] Moreover, this group demonstrated an entrepreneurial, service-oriented culture that made their businesses successful in comparison to other locals and contributed to intergroup alienation. The communities led two parallel lives and rarely interacted with each other in a meaningful way. Their attitudes toward each other were often underpinned by fear, suspicion and prejudice.

The Crimean Tatar community was known for their mostly negative attitudes toward Russia, confirmed by various surveys in the 1990s. It represented Kyiv's stronghold on the peninsula and tended to support "national-democratic" parties with roots in Western Ukraine, whereas "cooperation between the Mejlis and nationalist/pro-Ukrainian organizations was a marriage of convenience that resulted from mutual anti-Russian orientation."[13] In 1996, asked about the status of Crimea, 54 percent of Crimean Tatars compared to 29 percent of Ukrainians and 13 percent of Russians, said that the region should be a part of Ukraine.[14] Sasse describes that "Crimean Russians have been in favor of improved links or integration with Russia. The majority of Crimean Ukrainians revealed a similar orientation. Only the Crimean Tatars have been consistently opposed to close ties with Russia."[15]

Discussing this period of relative tranquility, Kuzio claims that The confederation of Mountain Peoples of the Caucasus which had close ties to the Crimean Tatars would have intervened against Russia in the event of a Crimean conflict. "Cooperation was already well established between Ukrainian paramilitaries and the Chechen leadership in the Chechen conflict where Ukrainian paramilitaries had by then participated on the Chechen side. At least 100 Tatars fought in Chechnya from the Adalet Party led by former airborne officer Fevzi Kubedinov. Adalet had 1,500 paramilitaries who were from former airborne forces who were used by the Mejlis for security and bodyguard operations."[16]

Initial actions of the international community fed the feeling among the Slav majority that Westerners privilege "them over us." Understandably, the United Nations went to Crimea to assist with repatriation and help the new arrivals to settle, thus providing housing, income-generation and access to justice programs. Although an exclusive targeting of Crimean Tatars was later rectified and other deprived groups received aid as well, a perception of bias was created. Respondents observed that most substantial jobs at the local offices of international agencies went to the Crimean Tatars, while Russians worked as guards and drivers.

Other groups had their own vulnerabilities. Language served as a powerful conflict driver. Rapid changes in language policy, such as a considerable reduction in school hours of the Russian language, literature and history, and introduction of compulsory classes of Ukrainian language and literature produced a profound effect on the majority of Russians, making them more conscious of their identity and resolute to preserve it. Transferring all TV programs to Ukrainian in the Yushchenko period with no Russian permitted until 2012 Languages Law was passed and dubbing Russian films into Ukrainian had a negative effect. The local joke was that only TV speaks Ukrainian in Crimea. Ukrainization of names also had a psychological effect, for example, when "Anna" had to become "Janna" and Ekaterina—"Kateryna."[17] Karabanova argues that Russians' resistance to Ukrainian in Crimea was of a psychological character and the demand to be proficient in the state language found resistance rather than support. "Russian speakers consider such language politics forceful, and, because the process of Ukrainization demands quick results and presupposes the replacement of a common language, artificial."[18]

In 2010 Brunova—Kalisetskaya and Duhnich addressed the issue of linguistic distress in their "Psychological images of language and cultural threats as perceived by Crimea's city dwellers" research work, understanding threats to a language as encompassing other sociocultural factors, such as identity, belonging and interpretation of history. Russian respondents demonstrated the highest degree of emotional attachment when discussing the language issue compared to other groups.[19] They saw their language space diminishing and were dissatisfied with Kyiv's language policy and manipulations of the language issue by central and ARC's politicians. They regarded development of Crimean Tatar and Ukrainian languages as confined to these two groups and not relevant for them, while some associated the promotion of Russian as a symbol of political rapprochement with Russia and positive development of the region.

The majority of Ukrainian respondents saw the threat to their language because of its "state language" status, which attached a highly charged political weight to it. This weight was causing resistance to the use of Ukrainian in everyday interactions. Some Ukrainians felt that the widespread of Russian threatened Ukrainian and could provoke an aggression by Ukrainians in Crimea. In the eyes of other identity groups, Russian held an "asymmetric" position as it performed two functions—"neutral as a major international language and a lingua franca of the peninsula," and "negative" associated with ethnic Russians, Russia's influence and threatening integrity of Ukraine. Research concluded that each group concentrated on perceived risks to their own language and on a sense of relative deprivation that their language was losing out vis-a-vis others. Each groups saw its own claims as justified, but none conceded that other groups had valid reasons for anxiety, whose claims were considered "illegitimate" or disproportionate.[20]

The adoption of the Languages Law in 2012 was a key milestone. On August 15, 2012 the ARC parliament issued a decree on "Urgent measures on implementation of the Law on Foundations of State Language Policy" that allowed Russian to be used on par with Ukrainian, for which 80 out of 88 MPs voted in favor.[21] The Russian-speaking majority felt that the language misbalance was to some degree rectified, while Ukrainian activists feared that an elevation of the status of Russian will exacerbate the situation for Ukrainian-speakers. Crimean Tatars from the Mejlis constituency were critical of the law, mostly out of solidarity with their political allies from the Ukrainian opposition camp, and did not use it as an opportunity to elevate the status of their own language.

ISSUES OF DISCORD

There were other fault lines apart from language and culture, and one was to do with political economy. Theoretically, Crimea should have been a booming part of the country, as it had all it takes: superb geographic location for trade and tourism, developed infrastructure, physical security, agricultural lands and a high-profile cultural attraction. Successive Ukrainian governments established foundations for a market economy. And yet, the region was not living to its potential: Crimean resorts had changed little since Soviet times, unlike their Georgian and Russian counterparts, and could only attract unfussy budget tourists. Popular sentiment was that resources were taken out from Crimea by Kyiv, but in fact it was subsidized from the central budget.

Crimea benefitted slightly from the 2010 power change, as financial allocations from the central budget were coming more regularly. Investment was channeled by the Party of Regions (PoR)—affiliated oligarchs, such as Borys Kolesnikov and Dmytro Firtash. Still, fundamental reasons for poor economic performance, that is, corruption and vested interests, which controlled access to natural resources, business assets and opportunities, remained unchanged. The business climate was such that outsiders were unwelcome and significant foreign investment was hard to attract. Kyiv's resistance to Russian investment into Crimea was politically motivated. When Yuri Luzhkov in his time as the Moscow mayor offered to build twenty-two youth holiday camps and invest $3.4 billion into the project, Kyiv declined.[22]

Land was a valuable resource and a hotly contested ground. The returning Crimean Tatar population did not receive access to land in the way they felt they were entitled to and not on equal terms as the rest of the population. Moreover, significant amount of land only had institutional owners, was not cultivated, and de facto lay idle. This situation facilitated several waves of successful land-grabbing. The practice had a demonstration effect: non-Crimean Tatars realized that land could be grabbed and started applying the technique themselves. Although the majority sentiment attributed land acquisition to the Crimean Tatar community, in reality vested interests were responsible for a murky state of affairs which allowed nontransparent arrangements to fester. Corruption in land allocation was largely practiced by the Slavs in Crimea, since they had preexisting social networks that could be used for these purposes. Thus, a competition of means for acquiring land emerged—Crimean Tatars through squatting, Slavs through networks and corruption—for which each side blamed the other.

The other conflict axis was the center-periphery relations. Crimea's political establishment demonstrated remarkable continuity unlike the rest of the country which shifted with each new president. When Yushchenko was in power, Crimea was ruled by the PoR members, in opposition at the time. Yushchenko pursued a cautious stance, reluctant to interfere into the affairs of an autonomous republic, but Crimean Tatars considered his administration an ally, given the tensions between Kyiv and Simferopol. Milli Majlis tactics reflected a certain duality. While being in opposition, its key members nonetheless maintained an effective dialogue behind the scenes with the ARC authorities, until some time into the Yanukovych presidency. Successes were manifested by the ongoing presence of a Mejlis-aligned deputy premier in the Council of Ministers and a deputy speaker in the ARC parliament, as well as several roles within the ARC Council of Ministers being traditionally considered part of the "Mejlis quota," appointees for which were in effect nominated by the Mejlis. Still, when the center-periphery tensions were largely gone under Yanukovych, the Crimean Tatars lost the pole to appeal to and the international community became their primary advocacy target.

Yanukovych's victory improved the "power vertical"—the authority of the central state over the periphery—since the key ARC actors were on the same side of the Ukrainian political divide and the PoR was always strong in the region. The appointment of Anatoly Mogilev, a former minister of interior of Ukraine, following the sudden death of the ARC prime minister Vassily Jarty in November 2011, was viewed as a negative development for harmony on the peninsula.[23] Mogilev brought a cohort of PoR newcomers from Donbas to capture positions, giving them access to preferential treatment in political economy. Arrivals from Donbas were nicknamed *Makedontsy* (Macedonians), which a wordplay combines the cities of Donetsk and Makiivka. The popular sentiment was that "we don't have a single head of department left who comes from Crimea,"[24] even if this was not necessarily true. Such arguments were strongly felt, but Crimea inspired little political or policy interest among national politicians of all persuasions, apart from oligarchic appetites.[25]

Geopolitics, embedded in the history of great power rivalries formed another axis. The underlying tension between Ukrainian statehood support-ers and the pro-Russian majority revolved about geopolitical orientation, when the latter regarded Moscow as an existential center of gravity and the locus of their civilization, while the former was keen to distance themselves from the Soviet and Russian past. Often, Crimea tended to take the opposite stance on geopolitical issues to that of Kyiv. For example, Russia's actions in South Ossetia in 2008 were met with enthusiasm. On September 17, 2008 Sergei Tsekov, a leader of the NGO "Russian Community of Crimea," initiated the appeal by the ARC Supreme Council to the Ukrainian parlia-ment on recognizing the independence of Abkhazia and South Ossetia. By contrast, the Crimean Tatar community typically took the positions oppos-ing the majority, supporting, for example, the 1999 NATO intervention in Kosovo.

In 2006 Crimea was affected by a wave of protests against a potential NATO entry. Thousands of demonstrators against NATO exercises in Feo-dossia blocked uploading of troops' supplies cargo from a US military vessel for the planned Sea Breeze 2006 exercise. Protests occurred at Simferopol air-port when an Alliance airplane landed and in Alushta where 140 US instruc-tors were trapped, unable to leave the Druzhba (Friendship) sanatorium.[26] On June 6, 2006 Crimea's Supreme Soviet declared the peninsula a NATO-free zone, for which 61 out of 78 deputies voted. Taras Chornovol of the PoR proclaimed that since the Supreme Rada did not approve an annual bill to authorize foreign troops' exercises on Ukrainian soil, their arrival could be classified as aggression. On June 12 American troops left without taking part in the exercises. Geopolitical passions subsided when relations with Moscow improved under Yanukovych and a number of contentious issues concerning language and the Black Sea fleet had been resolved. However, this was a turn for the pro-Ukrainian constituency to feel dissatisfied. The signing of the Kharkiv agreement in 2010 on Russian Black Sea deployment in Sevastopol until 2042 caused strong resentment and protests by the Ukrainian opposition and their electoral base.

Ethnocultural differences fed into these issues and amplified them, lead-ing the identity groups to form distinct ideological positions. There was little cross-party voting in the republic's elections, and constituencies did not overlap. Despite frequent encounters, relations between identity groups were characterized by alienation, thinly veiled suspicions and uncertainty about their future together. Dormant in the time of peace, when they functioned as social stereotypes and formed leitmotifs in distinguishing "us" from "them," identity faultlines played a major role in fomenting the conflict when political conditions suddenly altered.

TALKING POLITICS

Crimea always had a certain political activism of Russia-oriented groups who at times enjoyed a degree of support by the republic's authorities, but also were kept at an arm's length to prevent their emergence as competitors in the ARC elections. While identity issues were a subject of passionate debate internally, the position the least represented in the discourse in Ukraine and in international scholarship, was that of the pro-Russian community. International efforts mostly targeted the Crimean Tatar minority, with the result that a well-articulated stance emerged on their side, and their representative structures demonstrated political maturity.

Relatively little attention was paid to the Russian spectrum, such as Russian Unity, Russian Bloc and Russian Community of Crimea, mostly because their electoral strength was negligible. Interestingly, the Russian Community of Crimea published a *Russkii Mir* newspaper already in the 1990s, but did not manage to articulate a good narrative outside of the circle of its supporters. Karabanova wrote that most of its concerns did not find any relevant external support: "the OSCE High Commissioner on National Minorities Max van der Stoel was not impressed by [Vladimir] Terekhov's [the organization's leader at the time] complaints ."[27]

Sasse writes that "the contrast between the failed Russian movement in Crimea and the strong resurgent Crimean Tatar national movement is particularly striking." She described the Russian movement as loosely organized and fragmented, and constructed around a confused Soviet-Russian identity with blurred political goals. It lacked symbolic figureheads who could articulate a coherent ethnopolitical project. "The Russian idea in Crimea has always remained vaguely reflected in a plethora of 'Russian' organizations that came and went without forming a cohesive bloc."[28]

Alienation of such groups from Ukrainian national politics worsened under Yushchenko and conveyed a sense that their voice could be heard only in Russia. Their demands included obtaining a state or official status for Russian, prospects for dual citizenship for Crimea's residents, and making Sevastopol belong to Russia. The election of Yanukovych gave hope that the tables would turn in their favor, but the new president instead reneged on his promise to give the status to Russian and progressively worsened relations with Moscow. He was not a friend of pro-Russian groups either, worried about the emergence of a political force which could take away his electorate. In 2012 Yanukovych halted the project of Dmitrii Rogozin, a Duma MP and former Rodina (Motherland) party leader, to strengthen ties with Crimea's Russian organizations. Rogozin abstained from visiting the region on the Ukrainian president's insistence. When Yuri Meshkov, the first Crimea's president, who had pressed demands for a greater separatedness from Kyiv, returned to the peninsula in July 2011 after sixteen years of absence, he was deported and banned from entering Ukraine's territory for five years on a Security Service of Ukraine (SBU) directive approved by a Crimean court, the move apparently orchestrated by Yanukovych.

As a result, Crimea had a core of independent pro-Russian activists who were not tarnished by nepotism and corruption of the PoR establishment. There was a nascent intellectual elite which could articulate positions and demands. Some of them were represented in the Crimea Policy Dialogue (CPD), a project by the Peace Action, Training and Research Institute of Romania (PATRIR) sponsored the Ministry of Foreign Affairs of Finland. It worked in 2009–2014 on creating a dialogue and advocacy platform for preventing conflict between three main communities in Crimea and on building mutual understanding. It sought to address the issues of conflict through a cycle of dialogues, empirical research and policy advocacy leading to practical measures targeting integration.

The CPD experience, successful in its own right, helps us to understand the advantages and limitations of dialogue interventions for peacebuilding, based on the principles of "liberal peace." The Dialogue's main vehicle—and achievement—was the establishment of a core caucus which represented three identity groups: pro-Russian, pro-Ukrainian and Crimean Tatar. Some ethnic Russians fell into the "Ukrainian" group as their political loyalty lay with Kyiv. The group was supplemented by experts from the capital with links to power-holders. The idea was to resolve the situation from within by assisting the parties in finding their ways of building a future together, in which every group had a stake. The Dialogue worked with intellectual elites and their discourses, making them talk to each other and develop a new quality on this basis. CPD was a "track II"-type of peace intervention in which the involved participants did not hold political office, but had channels of influence to the decision-making level and/or to their grassroots constituencies.

In the words of its former member,

> The issues upon which the Dialogue concentrated—history, Crimean School and land—were relevant for all. It was a unique experience in finding consensus, a lesson in how psychology of inter-ethnic dialogue can be constructed. Dialogue of intelligentsia was important to identify the points of commonality and the drivers that unite us. People with opposing views could interact in it productively.[29]

CPD was a process involving handpicked constituency representatives, skillful facilitation and eye-opening experiences of foreign travel. Russian and Crimean Tatar intellectuals started speaking to each other, which they almost never had before. Refat Chubarov, Milli Mejlis chair and Sergei Aksyonov, Russian Unity leader, went together on a study tour to South Tyrol. The Crimean trilingual School was about to open in 2014 producing an impetus for introduction of multilingual education in Ukraine beyond Crimea. Dialogue of historians gained momentum, and former fierce opponents became enthusiastically engaged in joint exploration of contested periods of the peninsula's history together. Television audiences saw prominent intellectuals from three communities articulating narratives that spoke to each other.

Still, until January 2014, neither Crimea's political trajectory nor the Dialogue process forced the participants to confront any hard choices, as the emphasis was on the points of commonality rather than discord. Congenial atmosphere of a group process tended to mask the underlying tensions. This worked remarkably well in the conditions of peace, but how much real impact the Dialogue produced on its participants' values and their commitment to mutual understanding? How the participants would behave when seriously challenged? Were the relationships built strong enough to sustain the conflict impact? To what extent did participation in peace and confidence-building dialogues affect values, or did it only produce a short-lasting impact on attitudes and behavior, which crumbles under the pressure of a major conflict? Is it reasonable to expect that people would compromise on their core values when a decisive historical moment arrives?

POINT OF DEPARTURE

In 2014, a relative political calm of Crimea was disrupted by an external shock. At first, the second Maidan was seen as of little direct bearing on the region, and the ARC leadership kept a cautious distance from the turbulence. Still, the 2013 events in the capital resonated among local society to the joy of some and dismay of others. Euromaidan supporters organized picketing of administrative buildings in Sevastopol and Simferopol, among whom Tavria football ultras featured.

Although Yanukovych was not particularly popular, majority society was still shocked by casualties among *Berkut* troops in the Maidan clashes, 150 of whom originated from Crimea, and began to feel vulnerable. In this logic, if the state could not effectively defend itself in its own capital, it could not be relied upon. In January 2014, after a wave of seizures of administrative buildings in Western Ukraine and escalating disorder in Kyiv, the Russian Community of Crimea and Russian Unity, together with Cossacks and Afghanistan war veterans, started to set up citizens' self-defense units. The Slav Antifascist Front was formed in Simferopol out of 30 Cossack, Christian and pro-Russia groups who on occasion clashed with pro-Maidan activists. Businessman Alexei Chalyi launched a pro-Russian movement in Sevastopol.

On February 4 Sergei Tsekov, the Russian Community leader, proposed to the Presidium of ARC Supreme Soviet to issue an appeal to Russia for help and protection, saying that Crimea was not only a multiethnic, but also a Russian autonomy. ARC parliamentary speaker Vladimir Konstantinov agreed to consider Tsekov's proposals, but reminded him that they were living in Ukraine. Legal claims on the legitimacy of the 1954 transfer, dormant since the early 1990s resurfaced and began to be articulated in political discourse. On February 20 Konstantinov went to Moscow to meet with Russian State Duma MPs and publicly stated that he did not exclude the possibility of Crimea's secession from Ukraine, but only if central government falls under pressure.[30] Crimean PoR deputy Nikolai Kolisnichenko spoke at the Supreme Council about the "Crimea's return to Russia" if the situation in the country is not resolved.[31]

The CPD members were not shying away from political difficulties and convened a meeting in Crimea in mid-February to turn the Dialogue into an active conflict prevention tool. However, they did not realize that they did not have the luxury of time. Acting as responsible citizens, they were resolute to intervene for peace using the skills they acquired through the CPD. One member, a Crimean Russian anti-Maidan activist sought contacts with pro-Maidan forces in Kyiv through the CPD participants based there with an intention to initiate dialogue, resolve the standoff peacefully and prevent violence. Kyiv experts agreed, but abandoned the effort later.

Events moved very quickly since. The news that Viktor Yanukovych fled his post came on February 22, and 110 *Berkut* troops in full fighting gear returned to Crimea where they were given a heroes' welcome. Meanwhile, Sevastopol and ARC authorities were not in any revolutionary mood and declared their allegiance to the Rada in Kyiv. The ARC Supreme Council, which did not include any "eagles and lions," made a timid attempt to restore the 1992 constitution abolished by Kuchma.

In these circumstances of great uncertainty, Russian activists resorted to direct action. On February 23 Crimea's Russian mass political awakening started with the celebration of Army Day[32] in Sevastopol which turned into a rally headed by the Russian Bloc. Between 20,000 and 25,000 poured into the streets pressing demands for the return to the 1992 constitution, revival of Crimea's presidency, a referendum on Crimea's independence from Ukraine and appeals to Russia for protection. Protesters deposed mayor Volodymyr Yatsuba and spontaneously voted for Alexei Chalyi, a Russian citizen, as a mayor in his place, who immediately took the reins. A "now or never!" mood was strong in the air. In the words of the blogger Boris Rozhin, writing from within the heart of the protest movement, "people are very aware that they will never again have such a remarkable chance to break free and are afraid to blow up a lifetime opportunity if they stop. People are genuinely ready to take up arms and fight—anything as long as they don't have to live under the rule of the Bandera-ites. For this reason, the demand to distribute firearms to the ranks has, today, become the number one priority."[33]

On February 24, 2014, Andrei Nikiforov of Tavrida university and a CPD member initiated a meeting of Crimean pro-Russian experts, political activists and journalists in the Russian cultural center in Simferopol. A "Letter of Fifteen" addressed to the speaker Konstantinov was drafted, urging to organize a referendum on the peninsula's status. A prominent cultural figure, director of Tavrida Museum and CPD member Andrei Mal'gin was among the draftees, but did not sign the letter. Protest activity, especially in leadership roles, could have had grave consequences, were the Maidan side to secure power, and those who threw their weight openly against Kyiv, took a considerable risk. Grassroots activists and the uprising leaders had no clue of Yanukovych being evacuated to the peninsula and that the "return Crimea to Russia" train had already been set in motion in the Kremlin.

The turbulence of these days exposed the core identity cleavage: pro-Russian Slavs against Crimean Tatars with a small but well-articulated circle of intelligentsia of various ethnic origins loyal to Kyiv. Crimean Tatars publicly expressed their pro-Kyiv position and had sufficient manpower for street protests. Political confrontation easily assumed an added ethnic element. The head of the Crimean Tatar diaspora in Moscow, Ernst Kudussov, publicly called Russians "hereditary slaves."[34]

On February 23 the Mejlis organized a rally in Simferopol, when Refat Chubarov endorsed the power change and demanded the ARC parliament in ten days to demolish all Lenin monuments and then dissolve itself. Crimean Tatars became Kyiv's most staunch defenders, as put by a young man at the Mejlis premises: "I hope that they [Kyiv] have started to understand who the real Ukrainians are here" (Надеюсь, они стали понимать, кто здесь настоящие украинцы).[35] An eyewitness described to me the events she observed regarding them as "surreal" because they exposed things unseen before:

A Ukrainian Orthodox priest was saying a prayer at the end, and the Crimean Tatar (Muslim) crowd was responding "Amen." Another surreal memory was a lots of "Allah Akbar" shouts by the Crimean Tatar crowd that day. They indeed rallied under Lenin's statue and demanded its demolition. However, there was also another rally that day. It was literally a couple of blocks away (near the Parliament). Cossacks and pro-Russian activists were all flaring up and ready to move on the Crimean Tatar rally. Some leaders managed to contain them and prevented the clash. I walked to and back between the two rallies a couple of times, quite shocked to see how close and how completely disconnected they were.[36]

On February 24 Right Sector activist and former UNA-UNSO member Ihor Mosyichuk speaking at *112 Ukraina* channel warned Crimeans that their attempts to undermine territorial integrity would be severely punished. "If the authorities are not capable of doing so, then the Right Sector will send a 'train of friendship.' We, like UNSO in the 1990s, would go to Crimea. Then such public as this lot fled like rats when an UNSO column entered Sevastopol."[37]

Russian Unity and like-minded organizations responded by a show of strength to act as a deterrent to the "trains of friendship," and a wave of rallies shook the peninsula. Pro-Russia activists regarded the Crimean Tatars as the fifth column, and wanted to start and win a fight before reinforcements arrived from the mainland. They clashed with Maidan supporters in Kerch and Yalta, where they outnumbered them, but the situation was different in Simferopol when two opposing rallies faced each other on February 26. Mejlis activists sought to enter the ARC parliament building believing that its deputies were adopting a decision to hold a referendum inside, but were opposed by Russian and Cossack demonstrators.

The leaders of both movements—Chubarov and Aksyonov—acted for peace together to separate the crowds, preventing them from fighting.[38] As a way out of the tense situation, they attempted to negotiate a power-sharing government based on a quota system. Still, this only bought time. The crowds clashed, seventy-nine demonstrators were injured, ten people were hospitalized and two died. Crimean Tatar protesters prevailed in the end, overpowered the guards with teargas and entered the building to find it empty with no parliamentary sitting in evidence.

The fate of the pro-Russian activists was uncertain, to say the least. Crimean police were demoralized and were hardly seen after Yanukovych's flight from the country. The Berkut did not join the protesters and locked themselves at their base, anticipating a storm by the Kyiv-loyal troops. Sevastopol sent three busloads of supporters, but the bulk of their activists preferred to rally in the relative safety of the naval base of the Russian Black Sea Fleet. Meanwhile, Right Sector flags were seen in February 26 clashes and more of its members were believed to be on their way to Crimea. Insecurity and anticipation of Maidan-style violence were rampant, but without riot police this time.

On February 27 *vejlivye liudi* (polite people), unidentified masked gunmen who were later admitted to be 120 Russian marines and paratroopers, appeared at public buildings. Most Russian activists did not know who they were. At the same time, volunteers from Russia flocked to the region, recruited through social networks when Maidan was turning violent. Alexander Borodai and Igor Strelkov, future Donbas protagonists, were among the arrivals from Russia (see chapter 5). According to Borodai, Orthodox oligarch Konstantin Malofeev played a key role and acted "very fast" in Crimea,[39] for example, by financing Strelkov's group. Strelkov explained:

I played a technical role in Crimea and wasn't aware of the whole plot. I thought that Moscow was leading towards some Abkhazia-type variant—separate from Ukraine, but not a part of Russia. I was a part of a large machine, but still my role was important. Aksyonov, for example, wouldn't have so easily become the head of Crimea hadn't he met me. But I did not seek any prominence. If Donbas did not happen, perhaps nobody would have known about my presence.[40]

Strelkov was instrumental in organizing the vote in the ARC Supreme Council bringing together initially hesitant deputies who ruled to hold a referendum on March 25 on upgrading of Crimea's autonomy within Ukraine, with Tsekov and Aksyonov in the leading roles in that session. Premier Mogilev was dismissed, replaced by Aksyonov who stated nonallegiance to Kyiv and appealed to Russia for assistance in guaranteeing peace and stability. Since then the Russian activists were gaining an upper hand, and their rallies proceeded mostly peacefully. Journalists reported that the protesters, many of them female, were shouting, "We were passed over as an object to Ukraine. We are against Ukrainization!"[41]

The military operation, according to Putin's own admission a year later, was supervised by him personally and was smoothly executed.[42] Troops used in the takeover were already deployed in Crimea at the Sevastopol naval base and were reinforced by up to 1,700 additional GRU (Russian acronym for Russian Military Intelligence Directorate) forces, paratroopers and marines, although their total number did not exceed the previously agreed quota on the Russian military presence. They took over civilian and military infrastructure, forcing a peaceful surrender of Ukrainian forces, some of whom chose to join the Russian army. On March 6 the referendum question and its date were altered. In violation of Ukraine's constitution, the public was asked to vote on unification with Russia. On March 11 ARC parliament and Sevastopol city council adopted independence declarations and on March 16 the referendum was held which proclaimed an independent Republic of Crimea which signed a treaty with Russia on its entry into the Federation as one of its subjects. Both the outcome of the referendum and the turnout for the vote have been repeatedly questioned since.[43]

"Volunteers" organized by the state arrived later after the insecurity peaked to ensure that the referendum was not disrupted by "provocations" of its opponents. According to a *Novaya Gazeta* investigation, on February 28, 170 volunteers were flown from Chkalovsk military airfield to Sevastopol. They were supervised by a *United Russia* MP Frantz Klintsevych, who headed the Russian Union of Afghanistan Veterans. Volunteers were transferred by *Sevastopol* vessel to a military sanatorium in Yalta which belonged to the Russian Ministry of Defense. They comprised Afghan veterans, boxers, *Nochnye Volki* (Night Wolves) bikers, members of territorial army (DOSAAF) clubs and private security guards. They collected intelligence, identified potential saboteurs, stood guard at pro-Russia rallies, "neutralised" opponents and participated in overtaking military objects and administrative buildings disguised as local residents.[44] However, their arrival was too late for a real fight, and while the spirits were high, their role was limited. On March 18 the state-sponsored volunteers were returned to Russia where many received presidential distinctions and awards.[45] Strelkov noted that his battalion was disbanded after the referendum and he was left with only few members—anti-Maidan activists from mainland Ukraine who had nowhere to return to. The period between February 26 and March 18, when the Accession Treaty with Russia was signed, was characterized by widespread lawlessness, as nobody was fully in charge. A witch hunt of pro-Ukrainian and Crimean Tatar activists was unleashed, and those detained were often tortured, while Ukrainian and foreign journalists were harassed. Several people perished in dubious circumstances.[46]

UNDER THE HISTORY WHEEL

Speaking to the author, Alexander Borodai reflected on the success of the Crimea operation which he framed in terms of history and belonging:

> Crimea is Russia. Everybody with few exceptions felt themselves Russian there, as Russians temporarily deprived of rights. This was a historical injustice which needed to be righted. So, everything went painlessly. Popular support and Russian troops had an effect.[47]

The composition of Crimea's population changed after the referendum. Politically active pro-Ukrainian intelligentsia relocated to the mainland. The largest exodus was among Crimean Tatars, some of whom feared prosecution and loathed the new regime.[48] Among the first to leave were *Hizb ut-Tahrir* members because their organization was banned in Russia.[49] Tatars who did not accept the new order, but were not engaged in activism, stayed to lead private lives, while Mejlis actors were harassed. In a VCIOM (Russian Public Opinion Research Center) opinion poll taken in February 2015, 1 year after the referendum, around half of Crimean Tatars said they would support the decision to join Russia if the referendum was to be repeated. Only a quarter said they would vote to remain in Ukraine.[50]

Out-migrants were replaced by a cohort of the displaced families from Donbas who had enough means to settle in Crimea after conflict broke down there. Exodus of much of the pro-Ukrainian element in society and political transformation along the Russian model brought a profound change. The implication of this change is that "the kind of Crimea as it used to be, no longer is, and would not be returning to Ukraine, as there is no more of it" (такой Крым, который был, уже в Украину не вернется), as reflected by journalist and CPD member Volodymir Prytula in our interview.[51] MGIMO Professor Valerii Solovei summed up the prevailing sentiment: "I cannot imagine circumstances under which Crimea would return to Ukraine."[52]

Volodymir Prytula held the opinion that the annexation was conceived long ago and could have been foreseen: "I had a sense of danger, but could not really prove it, and others at CPD did not support me." Putin himself argued the opposite—no premeditated annexation plot existed in Kremlin before the events spiraled down in Kyiv in 2014. Informed observers in Moscow agreed on this. Even if different scenarios and contingency plans were floated, the prevailing view was to support the ruling president and the territorial integrity of Ukraine.[53] When this failed and Yanukovych fled on the *Bandido* yacht belonging to his son, Putin seized the opportune moment.

Russia's takeover of Crimea was not inevitable. It was propelled by a confluence of three factors that came together at the same historical junction: a surge of ethno-nationalism unleashed by pro-Maidan forces which the new power-holders in Kyiv went along with, fears of Russian identity-bearers that this nationalism would be directed at them, and the ability of Russian leadership to react decisively and in force. The element of spontaneity, local initiative and quality of leadership played a significant role in shaping the outcome. The fire of resistance and display of a local drive for secession played an important role, and Crimea's fate was sealed in a matter of days. Disarray of Ukrainian security structures contributed, because the new Kyiv power-holders until very recently were their opponents who caused street chaos which the forces of law and order were trying to contain. Neither politicians nor the military trusted each other. However, were the standoff to last, Kyiv could have mobilized its pro-Maidan militias and loyal units among armed forces and SBU, with possibly very bloody consequences.

What about the Crimea Policy Dialogue? As one participant expressed, "the result was hellish. A tragedy took place." Another said that "when a crisis is of such scale, dialogues become redundant." The CPD members sought to do the right thing and adhered to the vision of a liberal peace which was working until it was no longer, when confronted with a realist challenge. Since March 2014 the core group split into a minority who accepted annexation/unification with Russia and the majority who did not. This spelt the end of the CPD as a confidence-building tool. Several members relocated to Kyiv where they acquired new careers, some quite prominent, and two Crimean Russian participants obtained political appointments with the de facto Russian authorities. Those who sided with the new order were viewed as collaborationists by others, embittered by the betrayal of trust: "some participants were not what we thought they were." The questions lingered: did they know in advance what was to come and were they a part of it? When they were sincere—when they sat together with the others and spoke their hearts and minds, or when they rushed to support the new order? And the most potent was whether any among the Dialogue members had links to the parties that deployed violence. These questions will remain unanswered until the protagonists have a chance to confront one another face to face.

The annexation of Crimea led to the wholesale condemnation of Russia by the West and led to imposition of the first round of sanctions. Still, the weight that history bore down on the region needs to be taken in consideration to make sense of what happened. Looking at politics of regional identity, changed jurisdictions and demographic shifts on the peninsula, the idea that Crimea was always unconditionally Ukrainian, subsequently to be invaded by Russia, misses a more complex picture. At the same time, although the weight of history hangs round the neck of the living, its trajectory can never be foretold. No preconceived state project by Putin to annex Crimea was likely to have existed, but the moment came along when the pro-Russian majority got moralized in the face of fears of moves directed against them and anticipated aggression of pro-Maidan forces. Putin can be accused of taking advantage of the situation, but it was laid out for him by the turbulent events within Ukraine and the existing pro-Russian sentiment.

In the meantime, the train of instability was moving toward Donbas.

NOTES

1. Sakwa, *Frontline Ukraine*, 11, 13.
2. Sakwa, *Frontline Ukraine*, 100–101.
3. The findings of Razumkov Centre research are that "Only 27.3% of representatives of the Slavic [mostly Russian and Ukrainian] community consider themselves members of the Ukrainian political nation ("Ukrainian people, including, according to the Constitution of Ukraine, citizens of Ukraine of all nationalities"), while 44.2% do not feel like that,"—*National Security and Defence*, Kyiv, 5 (2009): 5. Razumkov Centre together with the University of Basel's Europainstitut with the support from the Swiss State Secretariat for Education and Research.
4. Ivan Katchanovski, "Small Nations but Great Differences: Political Orientations and Cultures of the Crimean Tatars and the Gagauz," *Europe–Asia Studies*, 57, no. 6 (2005). For examination see Brian Glyn Williams, *The Crimean Tatars: From Soviet Genocide to Putin's Conquest* (Oxford: Oxford University Press, 2015).
5. There were seven such schools by March 2014.
6. Author's interviews in Simferopol, August 2012.
7. *Democratychna Ukraina*, 5 December 1991.
8. Roman Solchanyk, "The Politics of State Building: Centre-Periphery Relations in Post-Soviet Ukraine," *Europe–Asia Studies*, 46, no. 1 (1994): 47–68.

9. CPD participant, Simferopol, August 2012, author's interview.

10. Carina Korostelina, "The Multiethnic State-building Dilemma: National and Ethnic Minorities" Identities in the Crimea," *National Identities*, 5 (2003): 147.

11. Crimea's Russian activist, author's interview, Simferopol, August 2012.

12. Anna Münster, "Transnational Islam in Russia and Crimea," Research Paper (London: Chatham House, 2014).

13. Katchanovski, "Small Nations," 881.

14. USIA/SOCIS-Gallup Poll 1996 quoted in Katchanovski.

15. Gwendolyn Sasse, *The Crimea Question: Identity, Ttransition, and Conflict* (Cambridge, Massachusetts: Harvard Ukrainian Research Institute, 2007): 255.

16. Taras Kuzio, *Ukraine–Crimea–Russia: Triangle of Conflict* (Stuttgart: Ibidem-Verlag, 2007), p. 195–96.

17. Anna Munster, correspondence with the author, May 2017.

18. Viktoriya Karabanova, "Linguistic Tools for Nation State Building: The Relationship between Ukraine and Its Russian-Speaking Crimea," *Polish Sociological Review*, 144 (2003): 417–433.

19. Research included a survey among 320 respondents and focus groups in 9 cities of Crimea including Sevastopol. Five groups were identified based on self-designation: Russians, Ukrainians, Crimea Tatars, Russian-speaking Ukrainians and Russian-speaking Crimea Tatars.

20. Irina Brunova-Kalisetskaya and Ol'ga Duhnich, "Психологические Образы языково-культурных угроз в восприятии городских жителей Крыма," in *Crimea Policy Dialogue* (Moscow, 2011): 150.

21. Igor Livanov, "Крым готовится к внедрению региональных языков," *Коммерсантъ-Украина*, August 15, 2012, http://www.kommersant.ua/doc/2002246

22. Op. Ed. "Острый Крым" http://www.gazeta.ru/comments/2014/02/19_e_5915897.shtml

23. CPD participants, author's interviews, Simferopol, August 2012.

24. CPD participant, author's interview.

25. Natalia Mirimanova, CPD co-director in interview with the author, 2015: "in 2011 the project brought the Dialogue core group from Crimea to Kyiv and extended invitations to representatives of political and intellectual elites of different persuasion—and none responded." February 25, 2014.

26. "Ukraine: opposition creates tempest over "Sea Breeze" in Crimea," June 6, 2006, *Wikileaks*, US Embassy in Ukraine, https://wikileaks.org/plusd/cables/06KIEV2190_a.html

27. Karabanova, "Linguistic Tools," 429.

28. Sasse, *The Crimea question*, 254.

29. CPD Core Group member, author's interview, Simferopol, August 2012.

30. *Interfax*, February 20, 2014, http://www.interfax.ru/world/359837

31. "Депутаты Крыма предложили вернуть полуостров России," February 19, 2014, *Lenta.ru* https://lenta.ru/news/2014/02/19/crimea/

32. Officially called "Defender of the Motherland Day."

33. February 25, 2014, http://colonelcassad.livejournal.com/1432097.html?thread=103997729

34. http://www.regnum.ru/news/polit/1770039.html

35. Vladimir Dergachoff, Sergei Zinchenko, "Если Россия не займет Крым, это сделают США" http://www.gazeta.ru/politics/2014/03/04_a_5934745.shtml

36. Anna Munster, in correspondence with the author, London, May 2017.

37. «Правый сектор» отправит в Крым «поезд дружбы» 24 February 2014, https://lenta.ru/news/2014/02/25/crimea Игорь Мосийчук, осуждённый за терроризм в 2011: «Попытки разорвать территориальную целостность Украины будут жёстко наказаны. Если власть на это не способна, то „Правый сектор" сформирует „поезд дружбы". Мы, как в 90-м УНСО, поедем в Крым. Тогда публика, подобная этой, как крысы убегали, когда колонна унсовцев входила в Севастополь...»

38. https://www.youtube.com/watch?v=lp_g9sXyHs0

39. Borodai in interview with the author, Moscow, May 2016.

40. Igor Strelkov in interview with the author, Moscow, May 2016.

41. Dergachoff, Zinchenko "Если Россия" http://www.gazeta.ru/politics/2014/03/04_a_5934745.shtml

42. Interview with Vladimir Putin by Andrei Kondrashov in documentary "Crimea. Homebound," *BBC*, March 9, 2015, http://www.bbc.com/russian/international/2015/03/150309_putin_crimea_annexion_film

43. Paul Gregory, "Putin's "Human Rights Council" Accidentally Posts Real Crimean Election Results," *Forbes*, May 5, 2014, http://www.forbes.com/sites/paul-roderickgregory/2014/05/05/putins-human-rights-council-accidentally-posts-real-crimean-election-results-only-15-voted-for-annexation/#27ad61e110ff

44. Sergei Kanev, "Герои под грифом «Секретно»" *Novaya Gazeta*, June 16, 2014 http://www.novayagazeta.ru/inquests/64030.html

45. http://www.novayagazeta.ru/inquests/64242.html

46. "Report on the human rights situation in Ukraine" *Office of the United Nations High Commissioner for Human Rights*, April 15, 2014; "Crimea: Attacks, 'Disappearances" by Illegal Forces. Rein in Units Operating Outside Law," *Human Rights Watch* March 14, 2014, https://www.hrw.org/news/2014/03/14/crimea-attacks-disappearances-illegal-forces

47. Borodai in interview with the author.

48. In October 2014 17,794 Crimean IDPs were officially registered on mainland Ukraine, UN OHCHR 6th Report on the human rights situation in Ukraine, 16 September 2014.

49. Anna Munster, correspondence with the author, May 2017.

50. http://old2.wciom.ru/fileadmin/news/sobytiya/Krblm2015.pdf

51. Volodymyr Prytula, author's interview, Kyiv, November 2015.

52. Valerii Solovei, author's interview, Moscow, February 2016.

53. Vladimir Zharikhin, deputy director of the CIS and Diaspora Institute, author's interview, Moscow, February 2016.

Chapter 4

Donbas

A Much-Unloved Powerhouse

FROM WILD FIELDS TO INDUSTRIAL STRONGHOLD

Donbas has always been a distinct region due to its history of emergence out of Russian/Ukrainian borderlands and connectedness to Russia. The lands which comprise the current Donbas historically have been sparsely populated due to harsh climate, infertile soil, and distance from major routes. They stretch from the Donets (little Don, a tributary of the Don River) hills toward the Don River, and across the coastal plains to the Azov Sea. The lands were known as Dikoe Pole (Wild Fields) and were roamed by Russian (Don) and Ukrainian (Zaporijie) Cossacks, as well as the Ottomans whose legacy is felt in past monuments and place names, such as Bakhmut. Coal was discovered in 1721 which turned the region's fortune and provided with its present name which means the Donets Coal Basin.[1]

The first general census of the Russian Empire in 1897 recorded the multiethnic character of the region: 52.4 percent Ukrainians, 27.8 percent Russians, 6.4 percent Greeks, 4.3 percent Germans, followed by Jews, Tatars, Poles, etc. The "who-was-there-first" rivalry of historical narratives sprang out at the onset of Ukraine's independence. In the pro-Ukrainian version, the region was mostly Ukrainian-populated with an implication that, as argued by Wilson, "history should take precedence over the wishes of postwar immigrants and the *false consciousness* of local Ukrainians."[2] The key point in Russophone historiography was that Russians were not recent "immigrants" in Donbas brought in by the Soviet system, but a "rooted people" in a multiethnic region. As expressed by Alexander Borodai, it was a kind of Klondike:

Donbas was a region of Novorossiya which was joined by Potemkin and Suvorov and had scarce population. As the Russian Empire was developing it, colonisers of all kinds headed there, not exactly crème-de-la-crème. It had a distinct frontier lifestyle with an intermix of cultures, criminal traditions and abundance of marginal elements. Soviet power added resettlers from Western Ukraine. The Civil War was fought in very brutal ways there, and this is being repeated now.[3]

The region had a free-spirited reputation and was often a home for serfs who managed to escape from their owners. Even after the abolishment of serfdom in 1861 and accelerated industrial development, Donbas remained a somewhat unruly territory true to its unbending traditions. Historian of Donbas Kuromiya wrote that

> The Donbas, the steppe land once controlled by Cossacks, symbolized freedom both in popular imagination and in the perception of Moscow (or Kyiv). I use the term freedom in its "negative" sense, namely, "freedom from" and not "freedom to." With its highly developed underground (both literal and symbolic), Donbas collieries served as a refuge for freedom seekers.[4]

Whichever historical interpretation one takes, by the time of independence the power of ethnicity was not particularly relevant for Donbas to act as a collective emotional bond. Its identity has been more civic as it derived from the region. In pre-conflict period, Zimmer found that "people in Donetsk region strongly identify with their region. The self-definition and self-symbolisation of Donetsk regional elite and population is local in nature and set the region apart from the rest of Ukraine. Imagined community as a construct is defined in socio-economic rather than ethnic terms."[5] This is echoed by Hudson: "those in Donetsk were more inclined to express a specifically local Donetsk identity or a diffuse cosmopolitan, transborder sense of belonging."[6] Few in Donbas had deep local roots, because its population was transient and people were brought in from different parts of Russia and Ukraine to participate in industrial works throughout the Soviet era. Development under the Soviet system which attached a great economic significance to the region produced profound social consequences. A large-scale mining and industrial expansion brought a population influx and propelled rapid urbanization. Between 1926 and 1932, the Donetska oblast population had grown by 39 percent and its urban population by 129 percent.[7]

Displacement during the World War II and population losses, especially severe in Donbas where partisan resistance was the most ferocious, added to diversity as newcomers were resettled after the War. While censuses identify Ukrainians and Russians as the dominant groups, impressionistically, the traces of intermix with Tatars, Caucasians, Greeks, and others can be observed in the features of its inhabitants. Ukraine's formerly richest man Rinat Akhmetov is a Tatar from Donbas, who nevertheless was perceived in the region as "one of us."

PROSPERITY AND ITS PRICE

By January 1, 2014, Donbas was a home to 15 percent of Ukraine's 45.4 million population, of which 4.3 million lived in Donetska oblast and 2.2 million in Luhanska oblast. Donetska oblast was the center of metallurgy, while mineral products and chemicals, as well as transport equipment were important industrial sectors in Luhanska. When the shock of privatization and market economy arrived to Donbas, it found, after initial disarray, an entrepreneurial cadre ready to capitalize on the emerging opportunities. This gave impetus to the rise of the new business elite, often fairly young. They were responsible for turning around Donbas industries which returned to growth at least two years earlier than Ukraine's industrial sector in general. This is when, according to Mykhnenko, a shift toward the capitalist values of profit-making and accumulation of capital through investment began to transpire: "the basis of the new Donbas ideal has become 'freedom to own.'"[8]

Donbas's indicators improved as compared to its performance in the Soviet times. In 1988 the region's GDP per capita was 32.5 percent lower than generally in Ukraine. By 2002, the GDP per capita was 26.7 percent higher than the national average, indicating a 60 percentage point positive change. The region cumulatively accounted for 25 percent of Ukraine's sales of industrial products and 27 percent of its exports.[9] The real wage growth trajectory in Donbas indicated an almost constant up-ward slope significantly higher than the national average.[10] Economic might was reflected in better living standards.

New prosperity came at a price. Several prominent business leaders perished in a wave of assassinations of the 1990s which were widely attributed to the oligarch and former prime minister Pavlo Lazarenko[11] backed by the-then president Kuchma. Both originated from Dnipro (formerly Dnipropetrovsk in Ukrainian, Dnepropetrovsk in Russian) in eastern Ukraine and were keen to take over Donbas's lucrative productive assets. A remedy against a hostile takeover had to be found quickly, and this entailed a region-wide rather than an individual response. Local business elites when they came under threat understood the wisdom of a "united we rise" mantra. Consolidation of assets into holding companies, such as Industrial Union of Donbas (IUD –Sergei Taruta, Sergei Levochkin, Viktor Yanukovych) and System Capital Management (SCM – Akhmetov) proceeded to form a collective shield around the region's assets. Economic defenses soon were backed by political leverage, as business elite realized that any central government in Kyiv could try to replicate the predatory tactics of Kuchma's period of the late 1990s. The PoR led by Yanukovych, one of the region's oligarchs, emerged in 2001 as a vehicle for political protection. It outperformed expectations when it became the second largest party in the Verkhovna Rada in the 2002 parliamentary elections. This sealed "the final friendly takeover of Donbas political economy from the central authorities by the local elites."[12]

The Donbas's emergence as Ukraine's powerhouse can only partly be explained by the inherited capacities and institutions. Entrepreneurial elites who managed to fight off the outsiders, as well as strong economic ties with Russia should be credited as well. The outcome was a merger between politics and business that characterized Donbas's power-holding, when the PoR-affiliated oligarchs, Borys Kolesnikov, Rinat Akhmetov, Sergei Kluev, Alexander Yefremov, produced a direct impact on how the region was ruled. National oligarchs were also represented in the region, such as Dmytro Firtash who owns Azotnitrogen chemicals producer and used to sponsor Luhanska oblast media. Russian companies co-owned many assets in Donbas together with Ukrainian businessmen. All in all, the region was going upwards and expected the trend to continue. Still, this prosperity did not earn Donbas recognition in national and international expert discourse. The region was often characterized as locked in neo-patrimonialism and ruled by opaque financial industrial groups. This could not explain why Donbas socio-economic record was far better than of other Ukrainian regions if it was governed the worse. Swain and Mykhnenko find the predominant critique of Donbas unjustified and debunk the stereotypes associated with it.[13]

The attitude toward the oligarchic class was not straightforward in the region, and wealthy individuals are seldom popular in post-Soviet societies. Yanukovych's presidency was well-received in Donbas at first when he was elected in 2010, but after he failed to make Russian the second state language and carry out a decentralization reform as promised, attitudes got lukewarm as his presidency unfolded. His PoR appointees were not popular either. Luhansk governor Alexander Yefremov in particular was seen as doing little for the oblast where public infrastructure appeared poorer than in its Donetsk neighbor, and he was accused of engagement in personal enrichment projects, some quite petty.[14] Akhmetov was perhaps more respected than others, as he was known for his contributions to prestige projects, such as construction of the Donetsk airport and Donbas Arena stadium, the best football grounds in Ukraine and probably in Eastern Europe. However, the origins of his wealth and earlier life in the troubled period of the late 1980s—early 1990s remained obscure and gave rise to speculation.[15] His business empire penetrated deep into the region's social fabric including integration of its security sector: Akhmetov's head of security Vladimir Malyshev was an ex-chief of Donetska oblast police.[16]

COSSACK LEGACY

Parts of Donbas are endowed with a strong Cossack ancestry which can be interpreted as positive or negative, depending on one's perspective. Opinions on the Cossacks are divided. For some, as the Soviet doctrinal image goes, they present a retrograde force famous for their role in Jewish pogroms and suppression of revolutionaries in Tsarist Russia. For others, they are romantic free-spirited warriors living by their own law and an ideal of justice rather than one imposed by the state. The activities, outlook and mannerisms of the Cossacks served to dismay of the Russian liberals.

The original Cossacks were believed to be serfs who succeeded in escaping from the landlords. Historically, Cossacks existed in Russia and Ukraine, and their settlements were later founded in Central Asia when the Russian Empire expanded. In Russia, the main Cossack area was at Don River and the Azov Sea basin which was the seat of the Don Host and comprised Rostov, Volgograd and Voronezh oblasts in Russia, and parts of Donetsk and Luhansk oblasts of Ukraine. Until 1708 Don Host was an independent self-ruled formation when it was incorporated into the Russian Empire under Peter the Great. Other sizeable Cossack settlements could be found in the east in the lower Volga and the Urals.

They formed their own communities of "free farmers," lived in *stanitsas* (makeshift villages) which reflected the initially temporary nature of their settlements and had only loose social stratification. They elected their own leaders and made main decisions by popular assemblies of all adult men (*krug*). As they settled in risky frontier conditions, they had to become peasant warriors too, holding the buffer between Turkic and Caucasian groups and Russia proper. In doing so, Cossacks came into close contact with other groups, and the words "Cossack" and "ataman" (Cossack leader) are of Turkic origin. At first, Cossack settlements had a prevalence of men, who used to abduct women from their neighbors, intermixing with them in this way, and thus considered themselves distinct from "Russians." In Ukraine, the Cossacks migrated to the undeveloped south where they established paramilitary settlements and by the sixteenth century formed a territorial formation called the Zaporizhian Host, based on the same direct democracy principles.

The arms of the Tsarist Empire at first did not stretch far enough to bring the Cossacks to order, but subsequently it realized the usefulness of their presence at the frontiers acting as a collective border guard which largely sustaining itself out of farming income. Their conservative and devout

Christian beliefs enabled the government to steer them against the possible oppositionists to the Tsarist rule, such as Jews, students, worker's rights movements, political party activists, etc. and they were awarded with privileges for their service to the state. The tables were reversed when the policy of "elimination of the Cossacks as a class" was ordered by Lenin soon after of the Bolshevik Revolution. It led to mass executions of adult male Cossacks and dispersal of the survivors around the Soviet Union in the 1920s to eradicate their distinct settlements. Descendants of Cossack officers were limited in their civil and political rights, and had to identify themselves in the official papers as such. The rights were restored to the whole of the Soviet population in 1936, but the requirement for self-identification held until the 1960s. Cossacks were finally rehabilitated in November 1989 during *perestroika*.

After the fall of the USSR, the Cossack traditions were revived, although it could be argued that claiming a direct ancestry could be done only with a high degree of approximation as the blow wrecked in the 1920s was too severe. There are some who believe that the present Cossack groups have little to do with historical Cossack roots of a hundred years away and view the modern Cossacks with skepticism as a large fancy dress party which sometimes toys with guns. Nevertheless, there was a desire to reclaim pre-Soviet roots when the Soviet system was falling apart. Cossack renaissance swept Russia and Ukraine with equal force. Those identifying with the Cossack ancestry and its traditions were present in different parts of Ukraine post 1991 and different Cossack organizations and clubs were established. Some participants in Maidan protests in Kyiv referred to it as a Cossack *Sich* (gathering). Activists sang the national anthem at Maidan which ends on the words "we, brothers, are of the Cossack nation."[17] However, Cossacks in Southeastern Ukraine were historically connected to the Don Host rather than Zaporizhe and had their loyalties on the other side of the political divide. In the 1990s the Luhansk Cossacks refused to swear loyalty to Ukraine, choosing instead to give it to the Great Don Host.[18] Overall, Cossacks in modern Ukraine have not been a unified force, and Donbas war split them further.

In Russia, Cossack groups were set up in the South where they were viewed as folk history clubs at first. However, instability in the Caucasus brought about their old role of "civilian armed protection." The Cossacks were given a status in 1995 by a presidential decree on a temporary state registrar of Cossack society in Russia. In July 2008 a State Policy Concept on Cossacks was adopted under Dmitrii Medvedev's presidency and they were allowed to set up an equivalent of territorial army forces via the Cossack Union.

"OTHERING DONBAS": ATTITUDES AND STEREOTYPES

The situation in the region was already pregnant with grievances stored up since early independence in 1991, and the fear of being swept up by Ukrainian nationalism did not spring out only as a reaction to Euromaidan. Such fear gripped society in the south-east in 1991 when the Soviet Union was heading toward disintegration, but the election of Soviet apparatchik Leonid Kravchuk calmed the situation down.[19] Still, in 1993 "the Movement for the Rebirth of Donbas' demanded a restructuring of the Ukrainian state on federal lines, the elevation of Russian to the status of second state language and closer integration for Ukraine into the CIS."[20] Overall, population of the southeastern Ukraine was showing weak association with the new statehood. A July 1994 poll returned the data that 47 percent of respondents would have voted against independence of Ukraine if a referendum was conducted at the time, and only 24 percent would have voted "yes" in it.[21] In 1994 the oblast councils (regional parliaments) conducted referenda on making Russian a second state language in Ukraine and on federalization of the country.[22]

"Soviet" identity in a sense of belonging to a large multiethnic space, being supranational and civil rather than ethnic, encompassing all peoples of the Soviet Union as its members, and having common expectations on the state institutions, education system, and the relationship between citizen and the state derived from the Soviet era, remained strong throughout the independence period. Hrytsak writing in the 1990s noted that it was "the 'Sovietness' of the Ukrainian population that provided the Ukrainian leaders with an opportunity to keep the country together,"[23] an effect which lasted as long as the Soviet identity remained sufficiently strong. Many in Donbas were reluctant to come to terms with the dissolution of the USSR as a single country which they shared with the Russians. As expressed by a local resident,

Donbas never considered itself the real Ukraine. Historically, it had many Cossack settlements. When we got up one day [when the USSR ended] and were told that we now live in Ukraine, many despaired that the border would unnaturally divide us from Russia.

Before the conflict, tensions between identity groups within the region were hardly noticeable for an outside observer. Smith and Wilson wrote that "in Donbas, there is a powerful, but ill-defined sense of community" with a "fragmented diaspora,"[24] although the pro-Russian constituency were unhappy to be characterized as "diaspora" given that they were not recent migrants and had local roots. By the time of the second Maidan, the process of political identity-formation in Donbas was far from complete. Diversity of identities reflected pluralism in a society, which had a fairly high degree of tolerance to accommodate different views. The main faultlines were to do with language accompanied by an underlying fear of assimilation—losing viability as a distinct community, – opposing positions on the cultural heritage and history, – shared or not with Russia, – and choice of geopolitical orientations associated with particular developmental models. As a rough generalization, the region was made up of three constituencies: those with opposing pro-Russian and pro-Ukrainian political orientations, and those who hardly reflected on these matters and would adapt to either Russia or Ukraine as long as security, jobs and welfare were available, and cultural and language rights were ensured.[25] Many of this ambivalent group felt culturally Russian, but a part of Ukrainian citizenry. Quite a few people with a strong Ukrainian identity, many among middle class, left the region at the beginning of the insurgency.[26]

People with a pro-Russian identity based their orientation on three key notions: a demand for the use of Russian in official communication and public sphere, the right to education in that language, and preferably making Russian the second state language; acceptance of their choice to associate with a common history and culture with Russia and not being challenged that they are some "inferior and insufficiently patriotic" Ukrainians; and appreciation of higher living standards in the adjacent regions of the Russian Federation. Cross-border demonstration effect was vivid and it is not surprising that they wanted to live better themselves. As labor migration to Russia was rife and local incomes were supplemented by remittances, the migrants used to bring good money and happy stories on public sector salaries and benefits that favorably compared to home. Differences in economic performance between Russia and Ukraine were pronounced.[27]

Pro-Russian sentiment was reinforced by a social distance that Donbas felt from Kyiv where it often perceived looked down upon. Economic success, industrial modernization, investment into infrastructure, scientific achievements of Donbas scholars, and political organization did not translate into credit for the region on the national scene. Distancing was also fed by a perceived "invasion" of the capital by Donbas moneyed class and the unpopular PoR elite which managed to get access to lucrative appointments. The image of Donbas as a crime-ridden land, poor, full of lumpen elements, socially dysfunctional (*bydlo*), isolated, untraveled and living in the Soviet past has been a frequent narrative.[28] This is, for example, how Ukrainian author Zhurzhenko presents the region: "people have either left to work in Russia, joined smuggler gangs or turned to small-scale subsistence agriculture."[29]

These attitudes and stereotypes, which had been measured in stable times, came out during the crisis, as Maidan protests brought out derogatory images previously too extreme to be articulated in public space. Graffiti appeared in

Kyiv "do not pee at the entrance, you are not from Donbas" and was seen as a good joke.[30] The international community in Ukraine had to acknowledge the strength of negative feelings when its humanitarian operations began: "a great deal of stigma and negative stereotyping is associated with people from Donbas region, and has resulted in challenges securing accommodation and employment for IDPs (internally displaced persons)."[31] The feeling of being unloved and considered inferior resonated in the region, while the policy of Ukrainization was interpreted as a collective payback for its distinctiveness. In the words of a local resident,

> Kyiv didn't do much for us to get to love it. We paid taxes—and they were stolen, put into offshore accounts. They considered us mindless slaves and used to talk like "they are slaves, so let them work for us, and we will live off the proceeds." And culture. Kyiv did a lot to provoke us. I don't mind Shevchenko, but we did not want monuments to heroes like Bandera here. My grandfather was killed fighting *banderovtsy*. People really hated it. Why did we have to watch a Russian film Taras Bulba with Ukrainian subtitles? My husband hasn't been to a cinema since this started. Just couldn't stomach it.

Certainly, there were other views as well and a constituency associating themselves with Ukrainian statehood was growing. The region of a population of 6.5 million was not homogeneous and the rural areas especially in the North had a prevalence of ethnic Ukrainians and a higher association with the Ukrainian statehood. There were pro-Ukrainian public intellectuals who threw their weight with West-looking Ukraine, such as Hryhoriy Nemyria, originally from Donetsk, who was elected to Rada in 2006 on Yulia Tymoshenko Bloc's mandate. He made a career in the "national-democratic" camp becoming a deputy premier in charge of European integration during the Yushchenko presidency.

POLITICAL AND CIVIC ACTIVISM

In the first decade of Ukraine's independence, sustained regional mobilization was weak, with a limited potential for collective action. Generally, people in Donetsk were much less politically mobilized than their Lviv counterparts. Scholars noted weak organizational and activist capacities of pro-Russians before the emergence of PoR: "between elections Russophones with their weaker and more complex sense of identity tend to lose ground to better organised and better motivated nationalist Ukrainophones."[32] Hrytsak had believed that even if the Donetsk people were willing to reunite with Russia, it was unlikely that they could organize a significant movement for this end.[33] Later, Donbas's independent political and civic activism was so overshadowed by the PoR that it went hardly noticed. However, it raised its head when fears of Ukrainian nationalism resurfaced in 2004 in Donbas and protest rallies took place in response to the Orange Revolution in Kyiv. As a reaction to the first Maidan victory, various initiatives flourished.

That time, it was all resolved by elites. An anti-Maidan Congress was held in Sievierodonetsk in November 2004 under Viktor Yanukovych chairmanship after he lost the presidential electoral battle. An idea of a South—Eastern Autonomous Republic was launched, but Yanukovych supporters were cautious about pushing it too far. A memorandum between Yushchenko and Yanukovych in 2005 put an end to the nascent tendency of Donbas's distancing itself from Kyiv. The Donetsk-based elite was the main driving force behind the federalization agenda.[34] The federalization debate surfaced on and off in the "Orange" period but its most ardent and politically salient proponent Yevgen Kushnarev, the head of Kharkiv oblast administration, was killed under mysterious circumstances during a hunt in January 2007.

Although regional elites enjoyed considerable self-confidence in politics and business, the region lacked a sufficient mass of humanist intelligentsia to project its own version of history and identity to counter the nationalist historiography emanating from Kyiv and western Ukraine. Donbas's academic resources to elaborate its own narrative were insufficient and its most able politically salient representatives left for careers in Russia. PoR dominated the political landscape, absorbed many of those interested in pursuing a political career and put a lid on development of an alternative activism which it would be unable to control. While Donbas had a distinct regional identity, it could not have a local irredentist project since the emergence of the PoR with its national agenda, which would have contradicted it. Moreover, it is hard to set up a "revolutionary movement" for preservation of a status quo unless one is seriously challenged.

In this limited space, it was cultural personalities who were speaking for the East such as prolific fantasy novelist Fyodor Beryozin from Donetsk who later joined the ranks of the rebellion. However, Donbas intellectuals were of no consequence for political elites in Russia who were not interested in cultivating them. Ukrainian scholars from Kyiv and beyond, in their turn, often ignored Donbas own voice and concentrated on opposing a "Russian influence," when discussing center-periphery relations. This lack of appreciation that Donbas may have an indigenous perspective that was not being masterminded by Moscow became politically relevant later when most of the Western commentary found it difficult to accept that the 2014 rebellion might have local roots which had been growing since the Soviet period.

One common assumption about Donbas is that its civil society was rather thin and fragmented, and it was difficult to find partners for the international development community. In actuality, strong organizations existed in the region, but they were reluctant to seriously challenge the ruling establishment who kept at a distance from civil society. Independent trade unions were a more demanding force, but were marginalized. Authentic grassroots activism, such as an anti-pollution campaign in Mariupol or consumer rights movement in Donetsk, sprang out on and off, but were unsustainable as they resisted institutionalization and were reluctant to apply for grants.[35] Business leaders also sponsored the causes they believed in or found strategically expedient, for example, DTEK (Donbas Fuel and Energy Company) had a corporate social responsibility operation and supported civil society.

Nevertheless, grassroots irredentism was not entirely wiped out by PoR dominance. One such grassroots movement with a nascent irredentist agenda was *Interdvijenie* (International Movement of Donbas) in Donetsk, which was pressing for Donbas autonomy throughout the 1990s and early 2000s. In the 2000s the idea that southeast was distinct from Kyiv and the rest of Ukraine started to be discussed in pro-Russia intellectual circles of Odesa, Dnipro, Donetsk, and Kharkiv. This did not imply breaking away from Ukraine, but sought to maintain cultural and historical connectedness with Russia.

Novorossiya also featured, although its political meaning was evolving over time. The term was first used by Count Potemkin under Catherine the Great and means "New Russia." Contrary to a popular belief, "Novorossiya" as a political project was not invented by Putin after Crimea but emerged during the dissolution of the USSR. In Odesa, a "Democratic Union of Novorossiya" was established in 1991 and campaigned for a "special state status" within its historical boundaries.[36] The idea did not presuppose joining Russia, but was a kind of new beginning for the lands that comprised it. Alexander Chalenko launched in 2005 an initiative of an autonomy for Novorossiya League—modeled on the Italian Lega Nord, with Kharkiv as its capital. He explained that "Novorossiya was an idea of pro-Russian people in Ukraine who felt these lands to be a historical part of Russia."[37]

In 2011 Chalenko gave an interview to Ukrainian *Novyi Region* news site advocating Novorossiya's autonomy within Ukraine. He spoke about it in March 2014 *Izvestiya* article when ideas from Donbas finally got attention in Russia.[38] Juchkovsky also stresses that the idea of Novorossiya did not come out of an empty space, but existed historically. He goes much further

Novorossiya is an idea of preservation of Russian identity in the conditions of Ukrainian state and a subsequent return to Russia of some sort of a confederation of eight oblasts, where people speak and think Russian and want to live with Russia. It is an anti-Ukrainian idea.[39]

A short-lived *Donetsko—Krivorojskaya Respublika* of 1918 which was established in the territories of the South-East when they refused to join

Ukrainian state of hetman Skoropadsky[40] was used as a political legacy
to base the region's claim to its separate path upon. Vladimir Kornilov, a
historian of Donbas who researched the *Respublika*, supplied Novorossiya
with its foundation "myth of the past," and when the uprising took off later,
expressed that the myth was becoming a means to the right end.[41] However,
Donbas intellectuals were not at the heart of the rebellion when it began.
Andrei Purgin was the only one among the 2014 protest leaders with a credible claim of past political activism. Purgin was reputed as an idea's person,
but his latest employment was of a hardware shop-keeper and he changed
over 70 jobs prior to that. He was a member of the Born by Revolution Union
which in February 2005 set up a protest tent camp in Donetsk and launched
twelve political demands, including federalization of Ukraine and the status
of a second state language for Russian.[42] Back in 2005, Purgin established a
Donetskaya Respublika public organization with six branches. Its objective
was to achieve a special status for the eastern oblasts of Ukraine and create a legacy entity to the Donetsko-Krivorojskaya Respublika. Purgin also
promoted the *Novorossiya* initiative within Donbas as an island of a separate
identity with a political and cultural connection to Russia. This, however,
remained underdeveloped and in 2007 *Donetskaya Respublika* was banned by
the government. These moves had little public prominence outside the region.

CONFLICT GESTATION: RESPONSE TO MAIDAN

According to a Research & Branding poll of December 2013, 81 percent
of population in Donbas did not support the Maidan.[43] The speed and ease
of Yanukovych's downfall shocked the region. The 2014 Maidan events
unleashed strong fears throughout southeastern Ukraine that victorious
nationalists would move to stamp out their way of life. A wave of pro- and
anti-Maidan rallies opposing each other swept through the region. The Rada's
move to abolish the Law on Languages prompted concern that Donbas communities would be forced to accept an interpretation of history and cultural
symbols that they did not share, and which were alien to them. This is not
to say that this adequately reflected the intentions of pro-Maidan forces, but
people tend to overestimate the differences at the moment of perceived danger and to ascribe more extreme views to their opponents than they actually
might have.

When Maidan was going on, the vast majority of the population could
not imagine a separation from Kyiv, but after protests ousted Yanukovych,
many felt that they would be regarded by the rest of Ukraine as potentially
rebellious and disloyal citizens, and as Yanukovych supporters who harbored
revenge. They feared that they would be scape-goated as a backbone of the

old regime, which inflicted casualties on protestors in Kyiv, whom they would come to avenge upon: "they will finish with *Berkut* in Kyiv and come to get us" was commonly said. As salaries were higher in Donbas, many suspected that they would be squeezed to subsidize the poorer Western regions, who won at Maidan. Rumors circulated that a "special toll" will be levied for "Maidan needs." Widely televised instances of unruly behavior of the Right Sector and thuggish groups[44] conveyed worrying signals to the East. The region went from confident and powerful to feeling extremely vulnerable in no time.

Lines deepened, and people started to confront identity choices they had not been previously conscious of. Generational differences did not appear to be a significant determinant. A Rubizhne respondent in Luhanska oblast noted that at the beginning of 2014 a group of 16–17-year-olds she was giving lectures to, was evenly split along pro-Russian and pro-Ukrainian identity lines. Many ordinary people preferred conflict avoidance and withdrew from discussions which might touch upon sensitivities. Still, politization was going on, and mothers and sons, husbands and wives started to find themselves on the opposite sides of the divide, in which case the only way to maintain a personal relationship was to confine conversations to private matters. People did not know how to talk about the divisions safely and were afraid to open the door which may lead into abyss. An interviewed civil activist expressed that

I am close to my brother and moreover we work together, but we have the opposite views on who was right and wrong on Crimea and how it affects our region. We agreed that the only way to preserve the family relations was not to mention these subjects at all.

Protests and public expressions of anti-Maidan views affected a larger area than Donbas. Now ousted PoR politicians had hopes that differences would be resolved through some sorts of informal power-sharing as they were in 2004–2005 after the first Maidan. PoR at root was a party of business interest protection and had few real political credentials to show when a decisive moment arrived. They were more inclined toward bargaining rather than radical protests, lacked grass-root support and quickly lost control over the action. The new powers in Kyiv were not enthusiastic about negotiating with their defeated rivals who tried to attract attention to themselves. While the PoR members did not work with the street, Kyiv did not see them as a credible force to be reckoned with, and was not sure whom they represented apart from their own interests. As Tsaryov recalled,

We at first thought that it'd be like the Congress in Severodonetsk in reaction to the 1st Maidan. There were a lot of people among regional elites, administrators and security services who were aware that they would lose their positions with Maidan's victory. We had three demands: federalization, amnesty for those who took part in the first disturbances and to make Russian the second state language. Then a Coordination Council of South-East was set up which included representatives of several regions [not only Donbas]. It kept launching demands on Kyiv to stop bloodshed, while it was still possible to prevent the country from sliding into large-scale violence.[45]

The situation quickly went out of control in early March when younger and previously unknown figures came out to fill the void, such as Pavel Gubarev and Denis Pushilin. A hardly known 31-year-old Gubarev ignited the unfolding wave of rallies, having supplied a political passion to the first protests in Donetsk, which subsequently created connections with other cities. As he explains in his informative Torch of Novorossiya (Факел Новороссии) book,

> We were inspired by a great dream of unification of Russian lands. We considered that Donbas will pave the way to Russian Risorgimento, as the Garibaldi army fighters called unification of Italy a century and a half before us. And we ignited the Torch of Novorossiya.[46]

When political crisis in Kyiv deepened, Gubarev organized a "People's Defence of Donbas" group and, when he was proclaimed a "people's governor of Donetsk oblast" on March 1, 2014, demanded a referendum on its status. In field commander *Prince's* later characterization of Gubarev,

> Revolution is always in the hands of half-crazed people because a normal man would be scared of responsibility. Such people think differently—bad is the soldier who does not want to be a general. We will take the power and then will learn to govern somehow.[47]

Moscow which was used to dealing with the ruling establishment had no clue who these people were. Gubarev was eventually found by the Russian Federal Security Service (FSB) through the *V Kontakte* social network website. He was originally from Sievieredonetsk and turned out to be a history graduate who worked as a private businessman in advertising and as a children events' organizer with an artist wife Ekaterina, and was known in Donetsk as a "Father Frost" as the Gubarev couple used to visit families and hand over gifts to children on New Year's Eve. Ekaterina was the one who first met with Strelkov in Rostov to discuss the future plan of action. On that occasion, Strelkov declined her suggestion to meet in a cafe and instead made her walk fifty loops around a park while talking to him, while she suffered in her high heels. Ekaterina became the first "minister of foreign affairs" of the separatist "republic." The ruling elite in Russia was not aware of the Novorossiya idea, and initially used the term "South-East of Ukraine." Russian nationalist circles neither also did not recognize any potential for indigenous activism in Donbas until mass rallies broke out, as Alexander Juchkovsky later reflected.[48] Borodai became aware of Novorossiya idea only when he was already in Donetsk:

> The political project of Novorossiya didn't exist before. Novorossiya was thought as a part of Russia, not a separate country. It was discussed in a small circle of people interested in politics, and the population largely didn't know about it.[49]

However, the immediate concern was security. Pro-Russian activists in Donbas believed that the region should be prepared to defend itself from nationalist militias, but it could not rely on the central apparatus for protection. The security sector was in disarray and many commanders were distrustful of the new authorities. Their local branches either sympathized with the anti-Kyiv side because they shared their sentiments, or sought to keep their distance to support the eventual winner. Senior officers were Yanukovych-era appointees and were afraid that they would follow *Berkut's* fate. Later on such fears turned out not to be entirely groundless when the minister of interior Arsen Avakov ordered the dismissal of nearly 600 Donbas police officers against whom prosecution cases were launched while a further 242 were investigated.[50]

My respondents from among ordinary residents of Donetsk oblast who did not take part in the conflict noted their support for federalization idea as conducive for the conditions in the region with its distinct economic and social features, and as a part of Ukraine. They expressed regret that the notion was rejected without serious consideration. Instead, the conflict dynamic escalated in an action-reaction process in which each side came to see the other as an existential threat. Violent clashes between pro- and anti-Maidan groups took place in Donetsk, in which Maidan supporters got a severe battering and made few overt displays in the city since. The first deaths in the South-East occurred in March 2014 when a young *Svoboda* member Dmytro Chernyavskyi was stabbed at a clash between pro- and anti-Maidan activists in Donetsk. The next day two anti-Maidan protesters Artyom Judov and Alexei Sharov died in a Rymanky street skirmish in Kharkov. The most prominent case was of *Bat'kivshina's* political party deputy Volodymyr Rybak who was abducted on April 18 while attempting to place a Ukrainian flag at the Horlivka city hall. His tortured body was found in a water reservoir together with the body of Kyiv student and Euromaidan activist Yurii Popravko who traveled to the region.[51]

At the time, each action or posture taken by the anti-Maidan protestors served to heighten the fears of the government in Kyiv of the disintegration of the country and further territorial losses. After Crimea, which Kyiv surrendered with almost no fight, it watched the same mechanics underway in eight other regions of the South-East. It seemed that not only Donbas, but Kharkiv, Dnipro, Kherson, Zaporizhe, and Odesa might seek to separate. However, violence only happened in Donbas. Kyiv's response was to use force rather than to identify local leaders, try to address the region's grievances and negotiate a solution. Instead, SBU began arresting local political activists as early as the first days of March.

While in the conflict in Moldova over Transnistria in 1992 the uprising was led by the regional leadership backed by its industrial elite, Donbas establishment was not interested in the rebellion, but keen to secure their assets and profits. The region's oligarchy did not receive guarantees of securing their assets under Maidan rulers after Yanukovych's ouster. They had a vested interest in putting pressure on Kyiv to preserve some of their influence and negotiate a coalition government, and in this context it is believed that some initial rallies included protesters paid by the wealthy elite such as Akhmetov, Sergei Kurchenko, remnants of Yanukovych Family and others associated with the PoR. However, slogans on joining Russia quickly appeared and spread through the masses. They were counterproductive for the oligarchic cause as "joining Russia was not in their interests as they would not have been able to pursue their corrupt financial schemes, given that they would have been outsiders there."[52]

Elites came to appreciate that the game was over: they blackmailed Kyiv and outplayed themselves. The regional elite quickly fell into disarray and their reaction was to flee from a dragon's den. The PoR leadership was discredited; others were not prepared to go all the way toward an open confrontation. Those PoR MPs, such as Nikolai Levchenko who initially was seen at anti-Maidan rallies and campaigned for the status of the Russian language, were seen as disloyal by both sides in the end. Levchenko and other PoR figures who wanted to instrumentalize the rallies were shocked that the protests quickly adopted the demand to join Russia rather than put pressure on the new authorities in Kyiv to give them more say on the national scene. Attempts to influence the activists to follow their agenda were sternly rebuffed and Levchenko tried to first bribe and then threatened Gubarev with a gun to steer the protests in the direction he wanted.[53] Politicians who moved to Kyiv at the onset of disturbances and expected to come back found themselves out of place. The elite did not cover themselves in glory in the eyes of the population: "the elite only thought about their wealth. Look at it—both Yefremov and Kravchenko ended up in Kyiv."[54]

The regional elite played their cards badly, and the old politics/ business network was quickly dismantled. Ex-head of the PoR parliamentary faction oligarch Alexander Yefremov, the former Luhansk governor, sided with Kyiv but was put on trial there for his role in the adoption of "16 January" 2014 laws restricting civil freedoms in response to Maidan protests. Alexander Lukyanchenko, mayor of Donetsk, left with an untarnished reputation only to join the officials-in-exile club struggling to maintain relevance. The former Luhansk mayor Sergei Kravchenko was less fortunate as he was detained by Ukrainian *Aidar* territorial battalion (see chapter 6) as he attempted to leave for Russia. Nevertheless, the pattern of oligarchic stranglehold continued. In March 2014 Sergei Taruta, board chair of IUD, which he co-founded in 1995, was appointed by Oliksandr Turchinov as the new pro-Maidan governor of Donetska oblast. It was believed that the position was first offered to Akhmetov, but he refused and proposed Taruta instead, although neither of them confirmed this. Taruta demonstrated his apparent lack of touch when the rebellion was just raising its head. He learnt about his removal from governorship from a presidential speech announcing his successor in October 2014.

The exception among the elite losers was Rinat Akhmetov, formerly Ukraine's wealthiest man with assets in steel and mining. He found himself at the beginning of the conflict with a Hobson's choice. Unlike the protest leaders who were ordinary people, Akhmetov had a lot to lose from any prospective Western punitive actions. Had he sided with the rebels, he risked asset seizure in the West and a travel ban. If he turned against the rebels, they would have destroyed his productive capabilities. Akhmetov hesitated, but on May 19 came out in condemnation of Donetsk rebels, urging his workforce to strike.[55] Apparently, this was a reaction to a potential PR-disaster, because a few days before one of his companies *Metinvest* signed a memorandum of understanding with the local authorities and the rebel representatives in Mariupol on maintenance of order and public safety.[56] Still, informal links apparently were kept because his personal property was not raided, despite growing disorder. By squaring the circle, Akhmetov secured a place in Kyiv while his enterprises in Donbas continued functioning for three years of 2014–2017.

EXPLANATIONS

The "thinking class" was trying to come to terms with what was happening in spring 2014. Ukrainian writer Konstantin Skorkin from Luhansk refers to the "Soviet" identity as he seeks to interpret the polarization while stressing a non-ethnic character of identities in Ukraine. He sees the dividing line as between those who wanted to go into a new future and those who preferred to stay with the Soviet past. He wrote that

This is not an ethnic hatred because these people can hardly be called Russians or Ukrainians—these are Soviet people, and resentment is between them and non-Soviets. Crimea and Donbas were prepared to live in the Soviet Ukraine, but don't know how to live in the other Ukraine. This process of discord prompts "barbarisation"—hatred, rise of xenophobia and intolerance in society. We take on the "us"—"them" (свой—чужой) logic of a civil war which we also apply to culture. This finds its expression in a division into Ukrainian and anti-Ukrainian, Donbas and anti-Donbas.[57]

Different scholars and opinion-makers offered their views on what produced the conflict. Minority of authors look for internal causes. Zhukov offers a political economy perspective arguing for a causal relationship between the prospects for machine-building industry and gestation of the rebellion, because that industry had more to lose from potential disruption of economic relations with Russia.[58] However, hypothetical economic losses are unlikely to be a sufficient motivating factor when matters of life and death are concerned, especially before they become a tangible prospect. A "branch of economy under threat" also fails to explain large volunteering for participation in conflict by a whole host of different people. In fact, all industries lost and the one which lost the most was coal. Giuliano also sees an economic side to the conflict, such as the material interest of industrial workers in preserving ties to Russia, but also points to contextual identity factors such as nostalgia for the Soviet Union strengthened by developments which emphasized an exclusivist Ukrainian national identity, and gave voice to the ultranationalists in politics.[59] Richard Sakwa in *Frontline Ukraine* states that "a new relationship was required with Donbas, but it was not forthcoming. . . . The Ukrainian revolution of February 2014 and Donbas rebellion fed off each other, and were then exacerbated by geopolitical tensions."[60]

A popular explanation is elite competition that went wrong. It is an interesting and plausible argument, although is lacking in hard evidence. This is how it is seen on the Russian nationalist spectrum, as put by Yegor Prosvirnin, the editor of Russian website *Sputnik i Pogrom*:

Opposition between eastern and western Ukraine does not explain all of it: the conflict is a triangle rather than a dichotomy. It had three driving forces: Donetsk and Dnepr clans which existed since the Soviet times, and western Ukrainians who did not have a financial and industrial grouping of their own. Donetsk clan stayed with a pro-Russian sentiment and pro-Soviet ideology, weakly defined. What happened was the collision between Donetsk and Dnepr financial-industrial groupings, and Dnepr clan utilised western Ukrainian version of national identity to legitimise its bid for power. It was used instrumentally, because the land which produced Brezhnev, did not have a strong connection to this identity. Many among the key Maidan figures were from Dnepr, such as (Dmytro)Yarosh[61] (the Right Sector) and (Ihor) Kolomoyskyi (as well as Yulia Timoshenko, in prison at the time), while commander of Azov Andriy Biletsky is from Kharkov.

If this was merely a confrontation between Lvov and Donbas, then a mass of simple guys from the western Ukraine would have been just slaughtered because they lacked the money, organisational capacities and an experience of killing others, such as the oligarchs of Donetsk and Dnepr clans had. Ukrainian nationalism started to get more flesh on the bones during independence, but it was nowhere near the stage when they could seriously challenge the Soviet-rooted clans. Is it possible that such seasoned predators as Yanukovych and Akhmetov got frightened of pot-wearing democratic protestors? I think they got scared of Kolomoyskyi and [Hennadyi] Kernes (Kharkiv governor) who were of the same mould. So, it was a "mafia state conflict," into which Russian nationalists and irredentists got involved.[62]

The "it is all Putin" narrative occupies the mainstream discourse. It often relies on official Kyiv's stance although the evidence base is not always convincing. Even the first-hand accounts of the region which characterize the conflict as "Putin's double punch" fail to present proof that the Russian government organized the rebellion.[63] Wilson writes that while history and identity were "baseline" factors, they were not enough in themselves to explain the outbreak of war in 2014. The local state was weak, but far from collapsed; it was also permissive and enabling. However, the same can be said about many other conflicts which were not inevitable, but happened nevertheless, while few conflicts do not have outside connections. According to Wilson, demonstrators and hooligans were bussed in from Russia, but there is no real proof and no Russian citizens were arrested in Donbas during the early rallies. The resulting argument is that Euromaidan was a genuine popular movement, but the protests in Donbas opposing it were not, and all the key triggers that produced all-out war were provided by Russia.[64] Russian popular narrative is a mirror image which presents Euromaidan as externally generated and uses Nuland's cookies as "evidence."

Opinion surveys are used to prove that no strong movement to join Russia had existed, but many of them were taken in different circumstances. Moreover, surveys are merely one of the tools rather than a litmus test unequivocally establishing a fact. The same as with the voting outcomes, surveys can predict wrong results. Yekelchyk in *The Conflict in Ukraine: What Everyone Needs to Know* based his argument that the external dimension was decisive[65] on an attitudal survey of 900 respondents taken in southeastern Ukraine *outside the rebel areas* in December 2014, in the period after the major hostilities were over.[66] It should be mentioned that a direct question on joining Russia was not the one typically asked by pollsters before Crimea, because it seemed irrelevant although this does not prove that the sentiment was absent.

Instead, the population was frequently polled on their opinions on joining the European Union, thus creating the impression that this was a real option on the table.[67]

This is of course not to say that the Russian government did not play a role, and it will be addressed in the subsequent chapters. However, a "Putin double punch" theory of conflict does not explain for what strategic goal the Kremlin would want to create devastated rebellious territories on Russia's borders and receive over four million refugees. If indeed the region was flooded with hundreds of GRU agents and modern weapons since March 2014, it is surprising why the rebels did not quickly take over the whole of Donbas when the Ukrainian armed forces were in disarray. When an operation was organized by the Russian state and overseen by Putin, as it was in Crimea, it proceeded smoothly, but Donbas rebellion instead turned into a bloodbath.

To conclude, as a result of elite exodus, concerned with its own narrow interests and fearing a threat to life and assets, society was left leaderless, but already sufficiently empowered to wanting to take action although not knowing how to do so. While no political project of irredentism existed under Yanukovych, and Donbas's different constituencies co-existed peacefully together, this did not continue when the circumstances massively changed. The attempt to radically redefine the country's identity and geopolitical orientation encountered staunch opposition to it. Many among population were prepared to live in an imperfect, but pluralistic and largely tolerant Ukraine of Yanukovych, but were reluctant to follow the new "European Choice" trajectory which was taking them elsewhere. Ukraine could have continued as a pluralist country and stayed at peace, but this required statesmanship which was not available, and the events took a different course. The next chapters demonstrate that the conflict that unfolded was a complex phenomenon which had local, all-Ukrainian, Russian, and international layers to it, which no single actor could have orchestrated.

NOTES

1. Ukrainian form of the name is Donets'kyi Basein, Russian is Donetskii Bassein.

2. Andrew Wilson, "The Donbas between Ukraine and Russia: The use of history in political disputes," *Journal of Contemporary History*, 30, no. 2 (1995): 283.

3. Alexander Borodai, interview with the author, May 2016, Moscow.

4. Hiroaki Kuromiya, *Freedom and Terror in Donbas* (Cambridge: Cambridge University Press, 1998), 2.

5. Kerstin Zimmer, "Trapped in past glory: self-identification and self symbolisation in Donbas," 97–121, in *Re-Constructing the Post-Soviet Industrial Region: The Donbas in Transition* , ed. Adam Swain (Abingdon Routledge, 2007), 103.

6. Hudson, "Russian Soft Power," 341.

7. Cited in Vlad Mykhnenko "From Exit to Take-Over: The Evolution of Donbas as an Intentional Community," Paper for Workshop no 20. The Politics of Utopia: Intentional Communities as Social Science Microcosms, 13–18 April 2004 Uppsala.

8. Mykhnenko,"From Exit."

9. Compiled from Ricardo Giucci, Robert Kirchner, "The Economy of Donbas in Figures," German Advisory Group, Berlin/Kyiv, June 2014.

10. Mykhnenko "From Exit."

11. Lazarenko was sentenced to nine years in prison by a US court for extortion, money-laundering through American banks and fraud.

12. Mykhnenko "From Exit."

13. Adam Swain and Vlad Mykhnenko, "The Ukrainian Donbas in 'transition,'" 7–46, in *Re-Constructing the Post-Soviet Industrial Region: The Donbas in Transition*, ed. Swain Adam (London: Routledge, 2007).

14. Former Luhansk resident interview.

15. "Скелеты в шкафу Рината Ахметова. Нераскрытые убийства," 22 June 2014, CRiMEArchive, http://crime.in.ua/statti/20140622/skelet-akhmetova

16. "Начальник охраны Ахметова опровергает свое задержание," Korrespondent.net, 22 April 2005, http://korrespondent.net/ukraine/events/119957-nachalnik-ohrany-ahmetova-oprovergaet-svoe-zaderzhanie

17. Nicolas Kozloff, "Note to Ukraine: Time to Reconsider Your "Cossack" Pride," 25 November 2014, Huffington Post, http://www.huffingtonpost.com/nikolas-kozloff/note-to-ukraine-time-to-r_b_6220554.html

18. Svetlana Bolotnikova, "Cossack against Cossack," 30 July 2014, *Open Democracy*, https://www.opendemocracy.net/od-russia/svetlana-bolotnikova/cossack-against-cossack

19. Prizel, "The Influence of Ethnicity."

20. Kolsoe, *Russians*, 189; Wilson, Andrew, "The Growing Challenge to Kiev from Donbas," RFE/RL Research Report 2, no. 33, August 20, 1993.

21. Kutsenko quotes Halyna Bekeshkina, Kucheriv, Nebozhenko, "Політичний портрет України. 1994." Sociological service of the "Democratic Initiatives" centre/ Kyiv, 201.

22. Sergei Vlasov and Valerii Popovkin, "Проблема Регионализма в Структуре Государственной Власти и Политике Украины," in *Ethnic and Regional Conflicts in Eurasia. Book 2. Russia, Ukraine, Belarus*, eds. Alexei Zverev, Bruno Coppiters and Dmitrii Trenin (Moscow: Ves' Mir, 1997), 154.

23. Yaroslav Hrytsak, "National Identities in Post-Soviet Ukraine: The Case of Lviv and Donetsk," *Harvard Ukrainian Studies* 22, Cultures and Nations of Central and Eastern Europe (1998): 263–281, 277.

24. Graham Smith and Andrew Wilson, "Rethinking Russia's Post-Soviet Diaspora: The Potential for Political Mobilisation in Eastern Ukraine and North-East Estonia," *Europe-Asia Studies* 49, no. 5 (1997): 845–864, 854, 861.

25. This is a simplified version. For the complexity of factors that initially shaped identity see Paul S. Pirie, "National Identity and Politics in Southern and Eastern Ukraine," *Europe-Asia Studies* 48, no. 7 (1996): 1079–1104.

26. " Влезь или Умри (Climb in or Die)," www.gazeta.ru

27. Men were sending home 10,000 hryvna per month which was good money in Donbas before 2014. Interviews in Donbas, 2014.

28. Vividly depicted in Эти ужасные «донецкие», или Правду ли говорят украинцам о жителях Донбасса?, 17 July 2014, http://timer odessa.net/statji/ti_ujasnie_donetskie_ili_pravdu_li_govoryat_ukraintsam_o_jitelyah_donbassa_626.html. Several comparative studies of different regions of Ukraine alluded to this; see Antonina Tereshchenko, "Regional Diversity and Education for "National" Citizenship in Ukraine: the Construction of Citizenship Identities for Borderland Youth," in *Naturalization Policies, Education and Citizenship: Multicultural and Multi-Nation Societies in International Perspective,* ed. Dina Kiwan (Basingstoke: Springer, Palgrave, 2013).

29. Tetyana Zhurzhenko,"From Borderlands to Bloodlands," http://www.iwm.at/read-listen-watch/transit-online/borderlands-bloodlands/

30. Alexei Tokarev, author's interview, Moscow, May 2016.

31. Humanitarian Country Team, "Ukraine: Humanitarian Needs Overview 2015," December 2014, http://reliefweb.int/sites/reliefweb.int/files/resources/2015_HNO_Ukraine_20141205_0.pdf

32. Smith and Wilson, "Rethinking," 855.

33. Hrytsak, "National Identities," 276.

34. Protsyk, "Majority-Minority Relations."

35. Kirill Savin interview, Heinrich Boell Stiftung, Kyiv.

36. Roman Solchanyk, "The Politics of State Building: Centre-Periphery Relations in Post-Soviet Ukraine,"*Europe-Asia Studies* 46, no. 1 (1994): 47–68, 59–60.

37. Alexander Chalenko, author's interview, Moscow, May 2016.

38. "What is Novorossiya?" *Izvestiya*, 20 March 2014 http://izvestia.ru/news/567843

39. Alexander Juchkovsky, author's interview, 2017.

40. Vladimir Kornilov, *Donetsko—Krivorojskaya Respublica: the Assassinated Dream.* http://kornilov.name/kniga/, for alternative history see Yekelchuk, 135–137.

41. Maxim Edwards, "Symbolism of the Donetsk People's Republic," Open Democracy, 9 June 2014 https://www.opendemocracy.net/od-russia/maxim-edwards/symbolism-of-donetsk-people%E2%80%99s-republic-flag-novorossiya

42. http://novorosnews.ru/persons/biografiya-andreya-purgina/

43. *Research & Branding Group* polling December 2013, 12 February 2014. http://reporter-ua.com/2014/02/12/81-zhiteley-vostoka-ukrainy-ne-podderzhivaet-sobytiya-na-maydane-i-zahvat

44. "Leader of Far-Right Ukrainian Militant Group Talks Revolution With *Time* Simon Shuster," *The Time*, 4 Feb 2014. http://time.com/4493/ukraine-dmitri-yarosh-kiev/

45. Oleg Tsaryov in interview with the author, April 2017, vi Skype.

46. Pavel Gubarev, *Факел Новороссии* (St. Petersburg: Piter, 2016).

47. Prince in interview with the author, Moscow, May 2016.

48. 15 November 2015. http://sputnikipogrom.com/review/46747/the-torch-of-novorossiya/#.V8WuiVQrK70

49. Alexander Borodai, interview with the author, Moscow, May 2016.

50. "Аваков уволил почти 600 милиционеров Донецка, не прошедших проверку" *RIA Ukraine*, 15 July 2015 http://rian.com.ua/politics/20140715/354862428.html

51. "Кто и как погиб на Донбассе: Список жертв противостояния," 30 April 2014, http://podrobnosti.ua/972868-kto-i-kak-pogib-na-donbasse-spisok-zhertv-protivostojanija-foto-video.html

52. Inga Zueva, author's interview.

53. Gubarev, *Torch of Novorossiya*.

54. Inga Zueva, author's interview.

55. "Ахметов призвал своих рабочих бастовать против сепаратизма," 19 May 2014, http://podrobnosti.ua/976753-ahmetov-prizval-svoih-rabochih-bastovat-protiv-separatizma.html Video of Akhmetov's statement is available on the website

56. "Эксперты: Ринат Ахметов-таки-сотрудничает с террористами," 16 May 2014, http://crime.in.ua/news/20140516/akhmetov-terroristy

57. Skorkinin interview to Ukrainian *Forbes*, "Как Майдан наконец развалил УССР" May 22, 2014, http://forbes.net.ua/opinions/1371550-kak-majdan-nakonec-razvalil-ussr

58. Yuri M. Zhukov, "Trading Hard Hats for Combat Helmets: The Economics of Rebellion in Eastern Ukraine," *Journal of Comparative Economics*, 44 (2016).

59. Elise Giuliano, "The Social Bases of Support for Self-determination in East Ukraine," *Ethnopolitics* 14, no. 5 (2015): 513–522, DOI: 10.1080/17449057.2015.1051813

60. Sakwa, *Frontline Ukraine*, 149, 182.

61. Yarosh was born in Dneprodzerjinsk.

62. Yegor Prosvirnin in correspondence with the author, May 2017.

63. Anna Reid, *Borderland: A Journey Through the History of Ukraine* (London: Weidenfeld & Nicolson, 2015).

64. Andrew Wilson, "The Donbas in 2014: Explaining Civil Conflict Perhaps, but not Civil War," *Europe-Asia Studies* 68, no. 4, (2016): 631–652, DOI: 10.1080/09668136.2016.1176994

65. Serhy Yekelchyk, *The Conflict in Ukraine: What Everyone Needs to Know* (Oxford, Oxford University Press, 2015), 141.

66. Paul Chaisty and Stephen Whitefield, "Support for separatism in southern and eastern Ukraine is lower than you think," *The Monkey Cage* blog at *Washington Post Online*, February 6, 2015.

67. In IFES poll in December 2013, 37 percent wanted to join the European Union, http://www.ifes.org/news/ukraine-2013-public-opinion-poll-shows-dissastisfaction-socio-political-conditions. In 2010, 50 percent of Ukrainians expected their country to join the European Union in the next ten years, in DW-Trend/IFAK Ukraine, December 2010, http://www.dwworld.de/dw/article/0,,14767626,00.html

Chapter 5

Russian Spring

Bolsheviks and Monarchists, All Welcome!

The conflict in Donbas is distinct from other post-Soviet conflicts, as it was leaderless and not spearheaded by an elite. Instead of benefitting elites, the conflict created a political vacuum for society to act, even if in violent and extreme form when it got to appreciate that power was in its own hands. The insurgents believed that when significant elements in local society resisted the redefinition of their country's identity, they should turn from the objects of history into becoming its movers and shakers. With an absence of recognized politicians, the conflict witnessed local entrepreneurs as frontline actors who fostered mobilization in what used to be an atomized and politically alienated environment that flourished under the dominance of the PoR. As the uprising fought its way, survived, and got entrenched, it led to what Cheng calls a formation of "conflict capital."[1]

While the predominant Western narrative saw the hand of the Russian state, I argue that the conflict was a powerful indigenous phenomenon and that it provoked an expression of popular activism in modern Russia not seen since *perestroika* days. Russia's takeover of Crimea opened a window of opportunity unthinkable since the era of the USSR break up when changing borders through expression of popular mobilization suddenly appeared possible. The grievances against Kyiv combined with an expectation that Moscow's handling of the Crimean situation would be mirrored in Donbas generated huge hopes of unification with Russia for some and fears of invasion for others. A local Luhansk resident, in an interview with the author, expressed her sentiments at the time as joy, hope, and fear:

Crimea gave hope. In 2014 ordinary people got to feel themselves Russians, part of Russian polity. People were crying, hoping, news coverage was projected on big screen TVs and everyone was watching. It was a purely people's uprising.

The authorities had nothing to do with it. When a miners' column marched
through Lugansk protesting against an arrival of pro-Maidan activists even I
got scared. But a popular uprising would have exhausted itself if material help
had not come.

Certainly, not everyone in Donbas felt the same way, but public rallies and
demonstrations were visible and attracted people from all walks of life.
Expectation of events to come was in the air.

RUSSIAN SPRING

As the disturbances in Donbas escalated, the local insurgents were supplemented by figures from Russia, who had more political experience, were better educated, well-spoken, and some—with fighting experience. A volunteer
combatant movement had existed in Russia since the conflict in Transnistria,
and later Russian volunteers fought in Bosnia and the Caucasus, but their
numbers were modest and they had little publicity. This time, the situation
was of a different magnitude. The response to Maidan was a resonant event
which provided a huge boost to the *Russian World*. It inspired a strong identity movement that called itself the *Russkaya Vesna* (Russian Spring),which
brought about a solidarity wave in Russia combined with the Ukrainian element disaffected with the post-Maidan outcomes. In Donbas, it acquired its
first real-life rather than historic heroic figures, as its actors were seen by their
support base.

The term *Russian Spring* in an analogy with the Arab Spring appeared in
early 2014, generated by the events in Ukraine and symbolizes a collective
awakening after a long winter when the essential "Russianness" had been
dormant. It acquired a mobilizing power and a calling in Russia and beyond.
Unlike the *Russian World* civilizational and statist concept, the *Russian
Spring* reflected a sense of dynamism: the *Spring* was needed for the *World*
to wake up. It was a statement that people could act and their actions could
change the course of history. The *Russian Spring* can be also interpreted as
a reaction to what its followers perceived as an existential threat not experienced since the World War II by the Russians and the peoples who were
allied with them. The previous long period of a relative peace diminished the
sense of a collective danger, but in 2014 it arrived at the doorstep.

The Russian Spring unleashed an energy in a society when old and young, –
the age of volunteers ranged from seventeen to seventy, – and even those
more accustomed to armchair philosophizing, were geared into direct action.
The interviewed Russian volunteer combatant *Strannik* (Pilgrim) expressed
that: "the Russian Spring allowed us a breath of fresh air." Alexander

Borodai, a Russian conservative thinker and one of the key figures of the Russian Spring, defined it as "the desire of the Russian people for reunification in their natural borders." The phenomenon had an autonomous existence from the state, and its vector was pointing away from the West, back to a reconstruction of the past: "*Russian Spring* reflected traditional values, within an idea of Christianity."[2] Strannik lived up to the image—blond, high cheek-boned and with a goatee, he could be easily placed in a Dostoevsky novel, if dressed in a cloak and emerging from a monastery, reminiscent of an older version of Alyosha Karamazov.

Malet in his research on foreign fighters notes that the kind of people who is likely to be more susceptible to the idea of standing up for a wider community cause "are individuals who are highly active in the institutions of that community and identify closely with it, but who tend to be marginalized within their broader polities."[3] The main characters of the Russian Spring fit into this characterization. Crucial roles in the formation of armed struggle were played by Igor Ivanovich Strelkov (*nom de guerre*, real name Igor Vsevolodovich Girkin, born in 1970) and Alexander Yurievich Borodai (born in 1972), prompting some commentators to conclude that, had they not arrived in Donbas at the pivotal moment, the rebellion probably would not have developed as it did.[4] Neither considered themselves the "heroes" of the Russian Spring in Donbas, characterizing their roles more as participants who made several "tactical moves" which changed the course of events.

Both were humanities graduates from Moscow and men of ideas on Russia's development and its role in history. High-strung, passionate and handsome Strelkov finished the Moscow Institute of History and Archives and was a war history fan, reading *The Art of War* by Sun Tzu and taking part in historical battle reconstruction games; he modeled himself on a White Army officer with the code of honor and in appearance. Russian patriotic circles portrayed him as "the Hero of Our Times," in the reference to Lermontov's character. Strelkov fought as a young volunteer in Transnistria, then in the Balkans, and, already as a security serviceman, in the North Caucasus. Strelkov was an active journalist and Borodai's long-time friend, with whom he travelled to Dagestani Wahhabi villages in the late 1990s as *Zavtra* conservative newspaper correspondents. Subsequently, Strelkov graduated from the FSB school specializing in frontline intelligence and counterintelligence, and worked for the FSB's Department of Protection of Constitutional Order, but he left the service long before the Ukrainian calamity began. Informed observers commented that he was probably too idealistic and values-driven to fit into the system at the time, while others stressed that his independence streak and "lone wolf" temperament were hard to manage. He also had a reputation for cruelty, later confirmed by sources in Donbas during his time as the DNR "minister of defense" (April–August 2014).

Cool and superior Borodai, the first DNR "premier" (May–August 2014) was a graduate of the Philosophy Department of the Moscow State University, one of the top schools in Russia, and a son of the well-known Russian philosopher, Yuri Borodai. He was a political strategist with military experience, such as volunteering in Transnistria at the age of 19, and an active author on the Russian conservative political spectrum. Strelkov and Borodai were connected to the oligarch Konstantin Malofeev, the owner of the Marshall Capital investment fund, for which Borodai provided PR services and Strelkov headed private security. According to Borodai, Malofeev rendered considerable humanitarian assistance to Donbas through his charitable foundation,[5] but the situation there was that of war rather than politics, and Malofeev had little direct participation.

Apart from these two pivotal figures, solidarity-driven volunteers of all kinds had been flocking to Donbas in the chaotic conditions. Several Russian citizens arrived into the region as early as February. They came for a mixture of reasons, including family, initial pro-Maidan sympathies which turned into their antidote when the outcome transpired, and a sense of adventurism which smelled disorder and an opportunity for action. They were mostly graduates, business people, private sector employees, and people of creative professions, such as PR-specialists and media workers, and there were also students. Some had a military background, such as off-duty and reserve personnel recruited via the Union of Russian Officers, military-patriotic clubs, such as *Varyag* and the Russian Union of Afghanistan War Veterans. Many, among them retired officers with technical skills, took their own decisions and got to Donbas assembled through informal social networks. Later on, some "active holiday-makers" were those Russian servicemen who answered "yes" to the call to go, and they took the leave of absence from their regular military duties. Borodai explains that,

> Many who came had real fighting experience. There had been plenty of local wars in the last 20 years and a lot of people had gone through them. They had come under fire and could kill other people, which gave the rebel forces a big advantage over the adversary. Donbas only had Afghan war veterans, but they were over 50 by then, while we brought in younger veterans from the two Chechen wars, the counter-terrorist operation in Dagestan, and the 2008 war in South Ossetia. On the other hand, some volunteers didn't know how to fight at all—like Strelkov and I were when we first arrived in Transdniestria.[6]

At the other end of the spectrum there were total beginners who had not even served in the conscript army and had to be taught on the spot how to shoot. Some of them could hit a target only by accident, but others rapidly mastered combat skills. One volunteer, who later commanded over 200 men and received an award for shooting down a military helicopter, had only served as a conscript soldier in Russia and played at military strategies in his childhood. *Strannik* said to me that:

> People came from different social groups. About a half hadn't served in the army, couldn't shoot, and didn't know how to use weapons. Some got scared when they had to go into a real fight and were paralyzed with fear. Commanders used to put them in the pits to think about why they had come to Donbas. There was a lot of untrained people and no time for team building. Some went back home very soon.

They were people of different ideological persuasions – right-wing nationalists, monarchists, spiritual heirs of "White Russia," ultra-leftists, National-Bolsheviks and Communists, with political ideas of an oppositionist mold. They were far from being Kremlin stooges. Many were inspired by a sense that the war and the collapse of the old regime had cleared the ground and opened a unique opportunity to build the kind of political order that had failed in Russia with its oligarchic capitalism, social polarization, corrupted elites and dubious patriotism of the rulers. This was a chance to start anew with an alternative state-building project baptized by fire which did not copy Western designs, but reflected the revolutionary spirit of the moment. This aspiration matched the anti-oligarchic, anti-elitist, "power to the people" sentiment of Donbas rebels. Some volunteer combatants were liberal oppositionists, such as Commander *Prince,* who was detained by Russian police in 2014 for his participation in Bolotnaya anti-Putin protests which happened two years ago. His office in Moscow was searched several days before our interview. Friendly, young and approachable, *Prince* came from a liberal Moscow background. This was his third war, as he has been through South Ossetia and Syria conflicts engaged in humanitarian missions, but he volunteered for Donbas as a combatant. *Prince* reflected that:

> Very idea-driven people were going to Donbas in order to build something there that didn't work here. They weren't regime loyalists, they were opponents of the system here. They went to change the situation. They tried to live up to standards—be cultured, polite, protect the local population.

Another group of Russian volunteer combatants identified themselves with the region's Cossack heritage of the Great Don Army and saw their mission as a revival of their ancient "free warriors" role. They were recruited via the Union of Cossack Forces of Russia and Abroad, but anybody could claim a Cossack ancestry and join the fight regardless, such as a detachment of "Moscow Cossacks" who arrived into Luhanska Oblast. Don and Kuban Cossacks were reported to be bold and the most reckless.

Not all volunteers who came from the Russian side were ethnic Russians. A military chief of staff of the Sloviansk brigade *Mikhailo* was a former Azeri officer with an allegiance to the *Russian World* and a strong anti-Western sentiment. "Chechen volunteers" have been visible among the rebel ranks.[7] Apart from ethnic Chechens, they include other Caucasians. According to *Prince*, Dagestanis were the first to arrive in Sloviansk as pro-Russia identity among them was high and they were among the most fearless fighters. They came out of their own accord as individuals and were very motivated, while Chechens organized in groups appeared later. They had an Islamic battalion, which congenially coexisted with overtly Orthodox Christian groups. Abkhaz held the border in Luhanska Oblast. Ethnicity and faith made no difference, as volunteers molded into a single fighting milieu. As put by *Prince* in our interview, "Buryats, Kazakhs and all the others were sitting together in the same trenches and were prepared to give up their lives for each other. You get to appreciate your mates who won't betray you, but save you. The first losses were the most painful."

As the uprising was gaining momentum, volunteers started to arrive in groups and some had good kit they procured in Russia, even if not all were sure how to use it. Field commanders typically split such groups and dispersed them throughout the fighting squads, so that outsiders would intermix with locals and prevent the formation of separate teams, a line which volunteers at first did not like. Volunteers were of a variety of orders—troopers, generals, and civilians who were not combatants, but were eager to help with building the proto-governing structures. In the words of a Swiss-educated lawyer from Moscow, "I could see that there was nobody to do any planning and institution-building. So I went there to draft the new laws." *Prince* regards this as a lost opportunity to capitalize on the enthusiasm and professionalism of high-skilled altruists because the local context was not ready to absorb their input:

> There were a lot of volunteers who contacted us saying that they were ready to come to build the republics. One man wrote from Singapore, where he had a senior position in a bank, that he was ready to drop everything, come to the LNR and establish the new banking system. But they refused his help because the low-brain LNR leadership saw spies everywhere. Another man left a good job in an IT company in China to set up management systems at LNR, but it was a madhouse and his efforts led to nothing. The IQ level was low and conspiracy theories were flying high.[8]

No single list of volunteer combatants exists. Some were known by their call signs only, with their true identities concealed because a command-and-control structure was not yet established. An informal estimate by the Russian Union of Donbas Volunteers is that perhaps about 50,000 people went through Donbas who were non-citizens of Ukraine, and out of them 30,000 were combatants. Many of them did not stay long—there were people who came for two weeks or a month which they took as holiday. Their combat effectiveness mostly was not great, but they manned the ranks and generated a spirit of solidarity.

The figures of losses are, as expressed by a respondent, "a mystical subject." Norin suggested that 3000–3500 may have been killed on the insurgency side, but this includes the losses among local rebels, and this is a very rough estimate. Information gathered from individual commanders gives more precise figures on losses in their units, but they are too patchy to draw wider conclusions. Former commanders said that losses were mostly sustained in key engagements; for example, *Russian Orthodox Army* lost about fifty men, mostly at Debaltseve cauldron, and in battles at Avdiivka, Piski, and Yelenovka; battalion *Viking* lost nineteen (thirteen in fighting at Spartak village). *Prince* recalls that "most were buried where they fell. Many graves have no names, only a commander's initials. It was very hard to explain to their parents that 'he was not sent there by the Ministry of Defense.'" Some of their families were helped by other volunteers, but there was no assistance from the state. Yet, the proportion of those who came from Russia among the overall rebel forces was fairly modest. Rebel sources estimate that about 50 percent of the fighters were local to Donbas, 30 percent came from the rest of Ukraine including its western part, 10 percent were from Russia, and 10 percent from a variety of other countries. The impression of a massive presence of Russian combatants was created because many were in commanding roles, especially at first before indigenous commanders emerged, and they had social media profiles, feeding battlefield news to their supporters outside Donbas.

MOTIVATIONS: RESPONSIBILITY TO PROTECT

Altruism and a feeling of the "responsibility to protect," as well as strong emotions of indignation, were among the most powerful drivers for the volunteer combatants who came from outside. The sensation was that Russia had raised the hopes of the people who trusted the country to take care of them, but that Russia turned its back when the people had come under attack, and that was not right. These people were culturally and politically close— members of the same historical "Russian World" community with shared language, mutually understandable life strategies and social aspirations. There was hardly any social distance. Seeing their world turned upside down felt like watching one's friends and family in distress. Hearing the battlefield news which mentioned the names of Russian settlements rather than faraway places in Afghanistan and the Middle East had a shocking effect. The feeling was that if the state was not acting, somebody had to come forward. This, of course, does not justify the actions and atrocities that followed, but suggests that an imperialist expansion or recreation of the USSR was not what was driving the volunteer movement.

Combatants stressed that they were idea driven. They also maintained that common identity in their view does not imply negation of "Ukrainian-ness" and that a cultural conquest or a territorial homeland was not what they were fighting for. In their narrative, it was the predatory elite supported by the West who acted against the interests of Ukrainians by starting a fratricidal war. As put by Andrei Pinchuk, one of the DNR's first leaders: "Kiev unleashed an aggression against their own people, who are fraternal and friendly to us. We are not anti-Ukrainian; on the contrary, many of us, like Borodai, Pinchuk, Beryoza, have some Ukrainian roots."[9] From this perspective, Yanukovych and Poroshenko were essentially two sides of the same coin, who let society pay the price while Moscow walked away. *Prince* told me in our interview:

> My quest was not to fight but to protect. People in the south-east were betrayed by Russia, which had sort of promised to protect them. So, I considered it my duty to go there. When it all started, I was on Maidan, supporting protests against Yanukovych and the legitimate desire of the people to get rid of the corruption in their country. When people were seizing administrative buildings in Lvov or in Donetsk, Lugansk, Antratsit—these were essentially the same people fighting for political order (мироустройство) the way they understood it. If Yanukovych would have won, the same process [as took place in Donbas] would have started in western Ukraine and the West would have defended the people there. Poroshenko with his tanks is no better than Yanukovych with his APCs (armoured personnel carriers) on Maidan. If Kiev had not made rushed decisions, most probably nothing would have happened. Still, I understand the Ukrainian authorities: they were under considerable pressure from the right-wingers among Maidan participants who had enough power to stir up trouble. Kiev was afraid of the "patriots."[10]

Most volunteers underscored that the Odesa fire served as a trigger for their decision to go: "this was a shock for many of us. We were very emotional, terribly upset those days. Many just ran amok to Donbas after 2 May."[11] "Odessa" became their battle cry and emerged as a symbol of the martyrdom of innocents which formed an important part of the rebellion narrative. The Novorossiya Movement (Движение Новороссия) subsequently set up by Strelkov in Moscow has an Odesa commemoration plaque at its entrance hall. *Strannik* mentions Odesa when he describes his values of sacrifice, justice and the identity bond that prompted him to go to join the ranks of combatants. Juchkovsky described his feelings at the time: "I had a moral urge. I came to protect Russian people who found themselves in conditions of oppression for thinking differently, for the use of Russian language, for their pro-Russia sympathies." What he witnessed in Donbas was something unseen before: "for the first time in my life, I saw not the amorphous Soviets, but rebellious Russians."[12]

Religion was important on an individual level for many volunteers and local rebels. Many were reinforced in the feeling that they were in the right by personal religious convictions symptomatic of the faith revival in the post-Soviet world and believed that "God is with us." *Strannik* expressed that Christian Orthodox faith was his main pivot which gave him strength to go through all trials and tribulations of the conflict. In his words,

> Volunteers flocked to Donbas to protect, out of solidarity with the suffering of the people we identify with. There was a post-Crimea momentum that created a powerful romantic-patriotic drive. Some volunteers came from Crimea and several were in the region already. I went to fight for the Russian World. For me, Odessa was the point of no return. My values are self-sacrifice and fighting for justice, which are Russian Orthodox values. The volunteer movement motto was *For our brethren* (За други своя), meaning that you should be prepared to give up everything, even your life, to protect others. This is the highest calling of a Russian.[13]

There were of course some young people who just wanted to be "heroes" and were not quite clear about what they were doing. A 19-year-old man from a Moscow upper-middle class family disappeared one spring day, leaving parents a note that he went to fight in Donbas. The parents were so well connected that they managed to contact FSB asking to find and return their son, but FSB curtly replied that their hands were rather full already. The youngster reappeared in September, tanned and decorated with awards, and resumed his studies in an elite Moscow university. A highly motivated and fairly numerous cohort was formed by people from different parts of Ukraine outside of Donbas, many of whom were anti-Maidan activists with a strong sentiment against new Kyiv power-holders.

Strangely, several Russians said that they had an advance sensation that a war of this kind was coming, as if they were reading from some imagined script. One volunteer combatant—a civilian—told Yevgenii Norin that several years before the events in Crimea he went there to survey the terrain for future combat and to get a sense of how guerrilla operations could be staged. Juchkovsky talked about the same, moving from aspiration to recruitment:

> I'd an inkling for a long time before the military actions in Ukraine took place, that something like this may happen and I'll have to take some part in it. Apart from my political activism, I was developing a sideline in military and physical training for quite some time. We set up a club in St. Petersburg where I and my

mates were learning how to handle weapons, act in extreme situations and such-like. When it was starting in Crimea, me and my mates arrived to support the locals, but our help wasn't needed. The Russian state took everything under control very soon. We went to Donbas from that club's base—I went in early May, and my mates were preparing and equipping groups in St. Petersburg. They sent about 20 groups which arrived in June. Alas, not everybody returned.[14]

REBELLION'S LOCAL MOMENTUM

Although disturbances and seizures of administrative buildings had affected large parts of the south-east since March 2014, they were too sporadic and disorganized to seriously challenge Kyiv. A public display of strength was meant to drive the point across that "we are angry with Kyiv" and "don't mess with us" rather than start a fully-fledged conflict. Regional elites, some of them hesitant at first, remained loyal at Kyiv. The only politician of standing who openly rebelled was Oleg Tsaryov who explained to me that

> I sided with the anti-Maidan forces because I realised that if Maidan wins, it"ll bring about Yugoslav scenario. There was little chance to prevent this, but I thought it was worth trying to do something about it nevertheless. I spoke out in support of *Berkut*, and so did several other PoR deputies. Then I came to Donbas as a part of my electoral campaign in the presidential race. We launched appeals, assembled dignitaries and tried to turn the process away from violence and into politics. We declared our demands at every public space. This was going nowhere, and I resigned as a presidential candidate.[15]

The Donetsk People's Republic (DNR) was proclaimed on April 7, 2014, in Donetsk in these messy circumstances. However, a violent protest movement does not have a capacity to sustain itself without the formation of military units. Prompted by the events, in March–April 2014 idealists and conflict entrepreneurs emerged to mobilize identity fears and created armed capabilities out of local civilians and remnants of the security personnel. Altogether they put together an assortment of guerrilla forces in the spirit of the Spanish Civil War, with no uniforms and a patchy collection of weapons. As the elites made themselves scarce, a Mr. Common Guy came to replace wealthy power-holders. Working class men prevailed in the ranks of local rebels, but there were also educated middle class and businessmen as well. The conflict attracted participation of women, including in combat roles. The local rebels explained their motivations of why they joined and fought by a desire for unification with Russia, as a struggle for "good Ukraine" because they believed that "now we have 'bad Ukraine.' They were also claiming that they needed to fight the 'battle against fascism.' In their worldview, what was happening was 'civil war,' in which they 'fight against junta' [new authorities in Kyiv]."[16] At first, many rebels were not showing their faces, wearing balaclavas that concealed their identities and some Ukrainians from outside Donbas feared for their families which stayed on the territories controlled by Kyiv.

Several guerrilla battalions were formed, headed by men of Donbas origin. *Oplot* (Stronghold) was established in January 2014 as an anti-Maidan group in Kharkiv by Yevgenyi Zhilin and later became a battalion led by Alexander Zakharchenko, the future DNR premier. On April 16, 20 *Oplot* activists occupied Donetsk city council to demand a referendum on the region's status. *Oplot* was a reasonably well behaved force from the start as compared to some overtly unruly groups, and had helped to release hostages and abductees from detention. *Vostok* (East) battalion was headed by Alexander Khodakovsky, a former SBU Alpha commander, with its core made up of the ex-members of Ukraine's special branch. *Vostok* made its first public appearance at May 9 Victory Day parade in Donetsk numbering up to 500 men.

Initially, there was a lot of ambivalence and events sometimes developed without any grand design. In Luhansk, Valerii Bolotov emerged as a military leader. He was originally from Stakhanov and at one point worked as a driver of the son of the Luhansk governor Alexander Yevremov.[17] Still, Bolotov was a graduate and held two university degrees—in economy and in engineering, and worked in small business before the conflict. He reportedly chaired the paratroopers' union of Luhanska oblast because he had served in the Soviet times in the Vitebsk paratrooper regiment which participated in the operations in Nagorno Karabakh and Georgia in late 1980s. Bolotov and his club members, the same as Strelkov, had an interest in military reconstruction games and took part in staging of 1943 battle for Voroshilovgrad (Soviet name of Luhansk). When protests started, Bolotov recorded four video appeals to the Luhansk residents. At first he wore a mask, but in his statement on April 5 when he called on people to rise up against Kyiv and seize buildings, he showed his face for the first time. SBU officers tried to arrest him the day before, and he had not much to lose.[18] However, an armed raid on SBU premises on April 6 seemed more of an improvisation than a thoroughly planned operation. In the words of a local Luhansk resident,

> The attack on the SBU was what altered the course of events. Security services kept arresting those whom they suspected of disloyalty and sending them to Kiev. When they arrested the "Afghantsy" [veterans of the war in Afghanistan], their mates with Bolotov as their head went to set them free. They attacked the SBU building, freed their guys, seized weapons and wanted to flee. But local people came out and said "no," somebody has to head the revolt. As you started, you have to go ahead.

Bolotov and his group risked a lot when they raided the SBU building because they could have been easily killed. Tsaryov recalled that Bolotov was suffering from this trauma which he tried to suppress, and it was unsurprising that he died aged 47 as a result of heart failure in January 2017.[19] On April 21 Bolotov was proclaimed by protesters as a "people's governor," became the first head of the LNR, and by April 29 Luhansk was under rebel control.[20] A local resident recalls that a hope for a peaceful resolution held on for a long time:

> Bolotov and his mates tried to negotiate with Kiev for a month and a half in the period under Turchinov [6 April–25 May]. People wanted to join Russia, but there was no real hatred of Ukraine then. Calls for separation emerged only after shelling started. When Poroshenko came to power, this brought hopes that now we will sit down to talks and sort out everything. But soon Lugansk was blockaded and we were trapped inside.

Despite their forceful actions, Bolotov's group in Luhansk attempted talking to Kyiv.[21] Kyiv engaged on and off, but made no breakthrough. The dual situation of proclamation of *de facto* independence and efforts at negotiation with the adversary to try to find a resolution, both going on at the same time is not internally contradictory. In fact, this typically occurs during conflict gestation when insurgents are often not clear what exactly they want, how far they are prepared to go and how much support they really have. They can be persuaded to drop maximalist demands in exchange for concessions and recognition of some of their grievances as valid. Such talks often help to calm down nascent irredentism before it reaches a truly violent stage. This happened when the Soviet Union was fracturing and different bids were being launched, but few situations developed into fully-fledged conflicts because many were negotiated down.

The situation in Donetsk in spring was not straightforward as there were different views and constituencies pulling in different directions. "Pro-Ukrainian" parties had their modest followings in the region, with several local council deputies elected on their tickets; and party headquarters and friendly NGOs oriented towards Maidan and Kyiv continued to operate. It is symptomatic that Donbas branch of the Voters" Committee of Ukraine led by Serhii Tkachenko attempted to organize the vote in the Ukrainian presidential election on May 25, 2014, in Donetsk despite harassment by DNR pressure groups.[22] Voting in the presidential elections did not proceed in 14 electoral districts out of 22 of Donetsk oblast and 10 out of 12 districts in Luhanska oblasts. Apart from the situation in Sloviansk and Kramatorsk, this cannot be explained exclusively by activities of the rebel armed groups because at that time their numbers were tiny compared to general population and by far not sufficient to be able to disrupt the elections to such degree. For example, Donetsk had 1000 rebels at most[23] in a 1 million city and a Kyiv-appointed governor in sitting.

Part of the society hardly cared about political events: an expectation that politicians would find a way out somehow as they always had done, and society should carry on regardless, generated passivity among large segments of the population who was slow to get going. How much support for the rebellion existed in Donbas in spring 2014 is a controversial subject. It can be said that it was weaker on the territories where referenda did not go ahead, that is, in rural areas and small towns of the north of Luhanska and the north-western edges of Donetska oblast. This does not mean that there were no sympathizers, but they were disorganized and not numerous, while the local authorities acted quickly enough to curb their nascent expressions. Borodai recalls that when he arrived in Donetska oblast in spring, he found that

> Initial support in Donbas was less than in Crimea. There were some who thought that Donbas was already Ukraine, not Russia, and others who thought that Donbas was Donbas, and still think that they are Donbastsy (донбассцы). It had its own specifics, regional character, and own patriotism.[24]

Despite grievances against Kyiv, enthusiasm for the rebel cause in the pre-Poroshenko period was lukewarm, until political differences transformed into combat lines. Even as violence was gaining momentum, a pattern of resolve and ambivalence with a mixture of motives prevailed. Ideas and ideological platforms were fluid and were frequently changing. Still, the bottom line was that many in Donbas perceived Russia as "Motherland" and expected that "Motherland would give us a shoulder." There was a sense among this constituency that after Maidan something fundamentally wrong was happening with Ukraine. They were not irredentists to start with and were prepared to live in an old Ukraine, but the trajectory it followed after Maidan was not shared by a sizeable segment of Donbas society and they felt that their paths diverged. Kyiv's actions, such as a move to abolish the Languages Law, display of fascist symbols by some Maidan activists as well as Gay-Europa image as a future geopolitical orientation resonated negatively, while Odesa created a sense of direct threat.

The war was also a tremendous opportunity for individual self-realization, for finding a new meaning. Miners formed a large contingent of rebels because "we risk our lives every day when we go underground. Now we can do this for a cause." An interviewed twenty six-year- old man from Kostiantynivka in Donetsk oblast explained that his life had no meaning before the war, but the conflict gave him that meaning. He used to paint icons for sale; it was his only skill. Being an orphan, he was allocated a tiny barrack room and, as he maintained, the Ukrainian state could not care less about him. He enlisted on May 5 and was taught how to shoot by his new comrades-in-arms.

WAS THERE A PLAN? THE SLOVIANSK STORY

The armed conflict began at the northwestern town of Sloviansk, and the arrival of Strelkov's group served as a trigger. Strelkov, speaking to me in our interview said that he had assumed that a powerful military demonstration would supply the necessary momentum, because "the rebellion would have quickly exhausted itself without an armed struggle as happened in Odessa and Kharkov, but with more victims."

Strelkov and his group seized some weapons from Crimea's arsenals and advanced on Sloviansk before the border was fully closed. A corridor to protect their movement must have existed, but in a way that would not implicate the Russian authorities. Still, they had to traverse large swathes of Ukrainian territory on their own to get to Sloviansk and crossed not where they were expected. On the strength of the gathered evidence, it is possible to conclude that the intentions of Strelkov and his comrades-in-arms were probably known in Moscow but the mission was not ordered, although he was observed and a communication line was open. "The Kremlin is not a monolith, but has twenty towers. It can be enough if one tower nodded in approval."[25] That allowed for the Kremlin to distance itself from the armed group in case their adventure would not generate local traction.

On April 12, 2014, fifty-two armed volunteers arrived into Sloviansk, led by Strelkov. Six or seven out of them had Russian citizenship and the rest were from Ukraine, including Crimea. They walked for 15 kilometers across the border area until they were met by a local activist who hired a Ukrainian postal service delivery vehicle to transport the group to Sloviansk. Importantly, they brought with them 250 military uniforms which gave the would-be rebels an image of an organized force with a hand behind it, although this was a bluff. Strelkov's group included *Motorola* whom he met in Crimea and selected from among Russian volunteers who came to support the protesters there. *Motorola* (real name Arsenii Pavlov), a working class lad who acquired a legendary fame as a fighter, was a Russian citizen born in Komi who served in Chechnya as a contract trooper in communications, – hence the sign *Motorola*, – and worked as a security guard in IKEA store and at a car wash in Rostov. He was hardly an assuming character, short and plain.

Joined by the local activists on arrival, Strelkov's force raided the police station and then—an SBU office. City administration offered no resistance and let the insurgents occupy it. In a few hours the city was in their hands without any casualties. In Strelkov's account, the dash to Sloviansk was a big improvisation and his own initiative. The Kremlin's intentions at the time remained opaque to him:

> I was fully certain that Russia would repeat the Crimea scenario in Donbas. Putin crossed the Rubicon in Crimea and had to continue since bridges with the West were already burnt. I thought that if they had gone that far, it meant they would go all the way. During Crimea, I thought that Putin was in charge of the situation, but when Donbas was happening, I had the feeling that I didn't know where things were going. At some point I stopped understanding anything.[26]

However, the scarcely known town of Sloviansk (in Ukrainian, Slavyansk in Russian) was not an obvious choice, although the symbolic significance of the name contributed to its selection, as well as its proximity to Christian Orthodox holy sites. Strelkov explains his logic for the choice:

> Some medium-sized town was needed that would be visible and have its own activists to provide support. We would have been lost in a large city like Donetsk. Unlike in my other wars, I barely knew the local terrain and had no information sources of my own. I toured the south of Russia, went to Rostov, Taganrog, and asked for advice, but it was not clear who I could believe and I didn't have my own network. We thought about going to Shakhtyorsk at first, but were told that there were no local supporters there. So we decided to go to Slavyansk. There was no time to prepare.[27]

One plausible explanation of the advance on Sloviansk was its strategic location on the highway to Kharkiv, but it made sense only if a Russian military intervention aimed at Ukraine's second largest city was to follow. Much to Strelkov's regret, this did not happen, although he argued that the course of history could have been changed: "if I had been given 500 machine guns and trained people, I could have taken Kharkov when there was still an element of surprise. By the time I got something, it was too late because the Ukrainian army came to their senses and started to fight." This sentiment is echoed by *Prince*: "our loss was that we did not occupy Kharkov during the chaos when administrative buildings were changing hands back and forth. This could have been done, and Ukraine would have negotiated seriously in that case."

Otherwise, Strelkov observes, "Slavyansk was a difficult location for our purpose, as it was a town located at the far northern end [of Donbas], easy to surround and hard to defend." By going there, Strelkov was plunging into the unknown, because if the adventure found no local support, it would have made no sense, but:

> Slavyansk did not fail our expectations—200 people enlisted on the first day. The religiousness of the population and the Orthodox Church, which blessed our

cause, played a role. Although Slavyansk isn't an industrial town but a resort, the local support was greater there than in Kramatorsk, where it took longer to get going. At that moment, I was glad when anybody—even fancy-dressed Cossacks—turned up, because everything was needed here and now.[28]

When Sloviansk fell into the hands of the rebels and uprisings erupted in other cities, the next day—on April 13, 2014—the Anti-Terrorist Operation (ATO) was launched.[29] It was announced by Rada's speaker and acting president Oliksandr Turchynov who said that "we're not going to allow Russia to repeat the Crimean scenario in Ukraine's East."[30] Kyiv escalated the conflict by declaring the other side "terrorists," with whom no talks could be held. The challenge to Strelkov did not take long to come, and the Ukrainian attack started immediately. First fighting casualties were sustained in Sloviansk on April 13 when Ukraine's security service officer was killed and another five wounded.[31] At least one pro-Russian activist –local rebel Ruben Avanesyan from Donetsk was also killed in the gunfire and two injured. Several young local rebels were killed in different episodes during April in the ATO attacks on their block posts[32] outside Sloviansk. It is believed that one of the key combat roles in the armed action in Sloviansk was played by *Romashka* (call sign "Daisy," real name Sergei Jurikov), a Ukrainian citizen born in Sevastopol who lived in Kyiv. *Romashka* was a church bell ringer and not a tough paratrooper as many who met him at the time thought. *Romashka* came with Strelkov from Crimea and was killed in the second serious bout of combat in May.[33] On May 2–3, Kyiv attempted an offensive but lost in the first hours two Mi-24 helicopters which were firing at the rebel positions. One helicopter was shot down by *Granddad*, a 76-yer old Afghan war veteran from Russia and Strelkov's mentor. When the ATO forces failed to take the city by storm as planned, they halted further direct infantry assaults.

While Sloviansk raised the banner of resistance, the larger, industrialized Kramatorsk remained ambivalent. Strelkov maintained that only after he sent twenty machine gunners to seize the administration building did things start to move. The ATO command decided to deploy troops there to prepare an advance on Sloviansk, but the tactics backfired. Ukrainian spetznaz troops took a nearby airfield, but the convoy of 25th airborne brigade reconnaissance company was blocked by local residents who used own cars to barricade roads. The army which was not prepared to use force against civilians, stopped and was forced to negotiate. After a tense stand-off lasting for several hours, Strelkov's detachment from Sloviansk arrived and disarmed them, seizing a number of heavy armored vehicles, a Nona 120 mm self-propelled artillery piece, and a large quantity of small arms and light weapons. These guns were used for defense of Sloviansk.[34] Strelkov acknowledges his personal role in this key incident:

If I hadn't taken charge of disarming a convoy of Ukrainian forces near Krama-torsk myself, we wouldn't have taken the armoured vehicles. Local residents ran up to us saying that we should take 11 APCs from the National Guard and Ukrainian armed forces, which were surrounded by civilians. But we were wor-ried that if we started shooting, they would open fire on civilians because of us. We retreated, but they started shooting at civilians later, one person died, and we engaged then.[35]

In *Prince's* view, support for the rebel cause in Kramatorsk was half-and-half, but one incident which left imprint on his memory, produced a triggering effect. A 91-year-old woman armed with a hunting rifle had set up a blockpost of her own, all her pose saying "Не пущу!" (I won't let you pass!). Ukrainian artillery struck and killed the babushka. This altered the mood provoking anger and indignation, and local recruitment accelerated. Chalenko in our interview expressed his view that had Kyiv not overreacted to the initial uprising, most probably the protests would have died out, but the first casualties among locals triggered a more violent response than would have been otherwise:

The population was expecting the Russian army to enter, but Russia was at a loss at that moment. People were largely always pro-Russian, but when Russia did not come, they were not sure what to do and were not particularly keen on fighting. But then the ATO forced them into it. Pro-Maidan politicians decided to spill blood (пошли на кровь) at the time when Donbas inhabitants were ready for protest rallies but not for blood."[36]

At first, the rebel forces were small. A trickle of volunteer combatants from the Russian side was arriving in April-May, but many did not get as far as Sloviansk, and stayed in Luhanska oblast, closer to the border. Getting to the territories from the Russian side was not easy because the border was patrolled by Russian border troops and the Ukrainian side introduced check-points on the main roads. *Prince* describes his journey:

We only managed to cross on the second attempt because we were turned back and fined by the Russian guards at the first try. Once we got through, there was no real plan. Locals explained how to get to Lugansk and get in touch with the rebels. There wasn't much to do there, and we decided to proceed further. We took several locals with us who were not keen on simply protecting sandbags [manning the barricades] and wanted action. When we got to Donetsk city, we met the people we'd been in touch with before, and they then had advised us to go to Slavyansk. The Ukrainian side had already blocked the roads and we travelled through the green zone.[37]

On arrival, they joined Strelkov's forces. Strelkov's role was more of a political leader of the uprising, in which he landed almost by default as he was prepared to face the cameras while most other rebels covered their faces with balaclavas. *Prince* recalls that "at first, everybody was afraid to show their faces. Only Strelkov and Vitalii Ponomarev [the 'people's mayor' of Sloviansk] feared nothing." Strelkov says that he had no political ambitions of his own and regarded his function more as a catalyst than as the head of the rebellion:

> I didn't intend to play any leadership role, or be in the spotlight myself. My mindset is that of a special service operative. I am a counter-intelligence officer and always stay in the shade. My plan was to find a local leader in Donbas, inject some organisation, help with the referendum—and vacate the seat. But no such cadre could be found locally. So I had to do it.[38]

However, field commanders emerged quickly, and prior experience was not necessary.

> There was a group of nine of us who arrived in Slavyansk, including a 17-year old boy, and we were sent to Semyonovka. They asked who the commander was, and the others pointed at me. After that, I had 200 under me in Slavyansk and more in Snejnoye.[39]

Most volunteers from Russia had scarce knowledge of Donbas and were not sure what they would find there, but

> there was a lot of support from the local population. Residents were giving us a lot of lard (*salo*). Each shop had a collection box. If we knew of an impending artillery strike in Semyonovka, we visited households, warning them and inviting them to our bomb shelter. Bombardments all happened at night, people worked their garden plots in daytime."[40]

Old people sought to pull their weight: a rebel from Luhansk remembered an old man with a prosthetic leg coming every day to chop wood for them. The rebels recalled that they ate better as they learnt to procure food quickly while the Ukrainian army often did not have their food deliveries and went hungry. An old woman was baking *pirojki* (pastries) for volunteers at Semyonovka all the time, and they were so embarrassed that they tried to give her some money. An old man armed with a machete tried to stop tanks at Krasnodon. Local population, especially mothers, played active roles to prevent an escalation of hostilities. "They besieged military regiments where their sons were serving as conscripts saying 'we take our children with us and then leave.' Local activists did the same, rightly, in my view."[41]

Although people were joining DNR groups in safer areas, recruitment in Donbas to go and fight in Sloviansk was inadequate. On May 17 Strelkov appealed to the people of Donbas, in which he shamed its men. Strelkov was pretty hard-hitting: "if you wish your freedom, fight for it. Don't wait for the Russian army or crazy volunteers to arrive and solve your problems."[42] He said that because young men and those with military background prefer to vent out their frustration with Kyiv in comfort and safety, and are slow to arrive to Sloviansk barricades, he decreed that women can be enlisted and put in combat duties if they wished so. He appealed the same day to "all Russian men and women" saying that Sloviansk is the center of the *Russian World*, it needs them to defend it; all who can, get up and come to Sloviansk.[43] The first who answered his call were those volunteer combatants who were already in Donbas. Juchkovsky recalls that there were two queues at the border: able-bodied, but unmotivated Donbas men evacuating to Russia, and highly motivated volunteer fighters crossing from the Russian side. He said that he was "philosophical" about it: rather than being a sign of an absence of local resolve, this was a typical situation in histories of civil wars, and even in the Russian Civil War (1917–1921) relatively few people took direct part.

The Russian volunteers had to mix with the locals to form a single movement, but found them less motivated than expected and sometimes confused as of what they really wanted.

> The locals were very different, not as motivated as volunteers from Russia. Many simply wanted to have better living standards, like in Russia. There were "weekend rallies." For example, two miners in Donetsk took a two-weeks' vacation to join a rebel group, but said that if nothing happens, "we will return to the mine." Locals showed a complete lack of independent decision-making capacity. They were not ready to take responsibility for their choice. They wanted to get rid of the Maidan forces, and did not know what to do next.[44]

REFERENDA

In spring 2014, Moscow was proposing a federalization solution to the spreading unrest, but in the words of *Prince*, "I have not seen any 'supporters of federalisation' as Moscow was calling protesters in Donbas at the time. I only saw the supporters of joining Russia." After Crimea, everybody was convinced that a plan aimed at unification with Russia existed. Strelkov's arrival and his actions were interpreted as an advance party preparing grounds for the Russian army to enter; however, he soon started to realize that this was not going to happen. Strelkov:

> In early May, just before the referendum, I stopped understanding what scenario Russia was planning. It was obvious that troops weren't going to be sent. There was an attempt by Moscow to cancel the referendum, but it was too late by then. Instead, the question was changed from the original one on joining Russia.[45]

Moscow was elusive, zigzagging and non-committal, and, while preparations were underway, President Putin on May 7 called for a postponement of the referenda. Some already knew that the original question on joining Russia has been changed to an ambiguous "self-rule." The rebellion was already in full swing by that time, with people dying for its cause. Eyewitnesses said that the momentum was unstoppable by then. In practice, most people who voted expected a quick Russian takeover, a deployment of Russian troops, and Moscow taking them under its wing. The impression was reinforced by the involvement of volunteers from Russia among the active organizers. In the words of a volunteer combatant in charge of the referendum in Starobesheve (Donetska oblast), a Russian in his thirties,

> Enthusiasm was high, turnout was 100 percent and even patients were transported from a hospital by bus. The voter lists were brought in from Krasnoarmeisk and handed over to the local electoral commissions made up roughly of the same people as in previous elections. Sometimes we had to coerce them into what needed to be done [for example, providing voting lists and stamps]. Our role was to provide security to avoid any incidents and first aid.

In these uncertain conditions and with no apparent promise from Russia, referenda were organized on May 11, 2014, in large parts of Donetska and Luhanska oblasts with a "yes or no" question: "Do you agree with the Act on *самостоятельность* of the Donetsk People's Republic (DNR)/ Lugansk People's Republic (LNR)?" The chosen term was elusive: it could imply independence, but could mean "self-rule" or "sovereignty." A turnout reported by DNR and LNR central electoral commissions amounted to 75 percent, with an overwhelming (89 percent in Donetska and 96 percent in Luhanska) vote in favor. Low turnout of 28 percent was observed in Mariupol which was already affected by growing insecurity. Tsaryov, with hindsight, argued that "irredentist moods were strong in Donetsk, but I tried to calm them down. I insisted that the referendum question is framed in terms of "self-rule" for Donetsk and Luhansk rather than independence, and that this "self-rule" can be interpreted differently depending on how the events shape up."[46]

It seems reasonable to assume that participation was voluntary and reflected the popular will. The rebels' earlier doubts whether people would turn out in numbers were dispelled. This does not mean that all the electoral commission members participated willingly and some provided stamps and ballot boxes under pressure. The turnout figures are easily disputed, as well as legitimacy of the whole enterprise, although the rebels were not numerically strong enough to be able to coerce large numbers of people into voting. The international community condemned the referenda and the then UK foreign secretary William Hague mocked them saying that Eurovision results were more credible.[47] The fact that a section of the community were prepared to fight, kill and die for the cause they voted for, in their eyes enshrined their credibility in blood. They would point to the fact that referenda were not such an unheard of idea in the context of a rebellion: citing examples from the Zapatista movement in Mexico, which organized a referendum in March 1999, in which over three million people voted for a wide autonomy for Chiapas.[48] Moreover, as Boyd-Barrett observes, the referenda organizers sought to ensure transparency—it was a public vote, in glass ballot boxes, and some western journalists were present.[49]

No action followed after the announcement of results, and the referenda only served to provoke Kyiv. Many people felt betrayed that the takeover did not happen and it became apparent that the Kremlin was in no hurry to do that. The insurgency had to find its own way in politics. Direction of travel rather than an end picture influenced the evolution of the movement. This direction became "Novorossiya," a political ideal of a land they were fighting for. It was floated in spring and was noticeable in public statements and in the news, even President Putin referred to it on April 17, 2014.[50]

The idea of Novorossiya originally comprised a larger area than Donbas, but the rebellion established it on the basis of the territories under their control which got loosely joined into a "Novorossiya" confederation. It was established by six DNR and LNR representatives in May 2014 on the basis that most of the internal powers stay at the "republics,"[51] but it would hold a united front vis-a-vis Kyiv. The Novorossiya parliament in theory could include representatives of other regions if they wished to join. Oleg Tsaryov became the parliament's chair and started drafting a "constitution." Originally from Dnipro, Tsaryov used to be a prominent PoR MP in several consecutive Radas and put forward his candidacy in May 2014 presidential elections, but was harassed and beaten, and withdrew from a race against Poroshenko. Tsaryov explains to me that

> Novorossiya was a confederation and its only organ was its parliament. We took turns to hold sessions in Donetsk and Luhansk. There were many idealists among this first wave of deputies. I deliberately took the parliament out of the military side of things because I reckoned that sooner or later some political process of getting to an agreement would have to start, and we'll need a body untarnished by war for this.[52]

Otherwise, the insurgents were local, mostly working-class men, poorly educated and often unruly, with a background in private security, skilled labor, small business, and low-level administrations. Few were professional middle class. For example, the future DNR "defence minister" Vladimir

Kononov used to be a judo instructor in Sloviansk. The new wave of Robin Hoods—the indigenous commanders and leaders of future republics"— emerged from that conflict milieu, with personal charisma and battlefield reputations being their distinguishable characteristics. As Noah Sneider wrote, "the separatists are scores of men, mostly locals, who believe—truly, madly, willing-to-die believe that they are doing the right thing. These are not the mustachioed villains you see on television. These are factory workers and mechanics who now man checkpoints and lead military operations."[53]

The rebels were not paid and were self-financing through different avenues, including collecting voluntary contributions, levying toll on local businesses for a war chest, raiding banks, intercepting cash deliveries from Kyiv, benefitting from private donations and from benefactors in Russia and globally. Some insurgents had funds of their own which they put into their cause, like Pavel Gubarev and other like-minded people in Donetsk whom he describes.[54] This is similar to how the Chechen rebels, especially in the first campaign of 1994–1996, sustained themselves, before sponsorship from abroad started to play a bigger role during the second war. Still, even then local sources were perhaps predominant. Private donations were used for the procurement. During Sloviansk siege, some pay was distributed to rebels on two occasions. Otherwise individual commanders were handing over one-off payments to their fighters when they managed to obtain something. Overall, rebel fighters were not receiving regular payments until mid-2015 when formal structures started to be set up.[55]

The downside was that people who suddenly acquired guns and the power that comes with them felt liberated from conventional social norms. Many were not angels, but free-spirited bandits. Chalenko explained to me that

it was *makhnovshina* [disorder under Nestor Makhno" Insurgent Revolutionary army during the Civil War][56] at first. The borderline between heroism and banditry was thin. A person could be a fearless war hero one moment storming some fortified height and the next moment he could be raiding a business and locking hostages in a private dungeon for ransom. It was a disaster.[57]

When the Russian takeover did not materialize, there was no overall plan and everybody was fighting their local war. The rebels found out that nothing was more difficult than supervising an insurgency because it was territorially dispersed, nobody was in overall command and the leaders were disinclined to take orders from each other. At the same time, the conflict fostered the development of political personalities of the "people's republics" amid societal mobilization around resistance. They had to put across the message that they were in charge. Then physical survival and management of unpredictability loomed large and side-lined the end goals of the rebellion. Although it was clear what the fight was against, no certainty existed what it was for. The longer it progressed, the more rebels got convinced that they were fighting for no return to Kyiv, ever.

Politically, the rebellion can be interpreted as a revolutionary movement as it sought radical social change against the established order. The movement had a strong anti-oligarchic streak: oligarchs should not be involved in politics but should "mind their own business." It was a kind of a "revolution from below" because it had an aspiration for political change beyond one's cultural identity, and a socio-psychological power of moral impulse. The grounds for this political agenda were already laid when the elites abandoned the region and ordinary people were left to fend for themselves. Leftist values, that is, social justice, power to people at the local level, rebuilding Donbas on an egalitarian basis and anti-elitism formed its all-important pillars. In commander Mozgovoi's words, "Novorossiya be! Oligarchs out. Power to genuine, ordinary people. This is our chance in many decades to build a fair, human and humane state."[58] In this, the Novorossiya ideology had commonality with Maidan in its anti-corruption and anti-oligarchic aspiration, and an idealistic demand for the voice of ordinary people in politics to be heard.

What made them different was the attitude towards the *Russian World* which was a source of inspiration for the rebels. It conveys a sense of belonging to a larger historic, political and cultural community, bringing them to the imagined roots of the pre-revolutionary Russia. Christian Orthodox faith, traditional values such as family, Russian language, and an image of the treacherous West were the main pillars of this socially conservative ideology. In the words of Pavel Gubarev: "we aspire to a new social model based on Russian civilizational identity and fair political order."[59] Thus, identity politics became reconfigured to produce something bigger than a mere desire to shake off Kyiv's rule, and the connection to the *Russian World* formed a powerful emotional bond.

The rebel narrative, which Wilson calls "a morphed Russian–Orthodox–Soviet absolutist nationalism"[60] absorbed different ideological ingredients from monarchism to Sovietism, reflecting the kaleidoscope of identities which came together in a single social movement. Monarchist ideas somehow got combined with the Soviet history which reflects the legacy of Sovietism in the *Russian World*. Eventually, more coherent ideas and identities started to crystallize out of this chaotic torrent. Lack of coherence made no difference in 2014 when the rebels implicitly understood what united them. However, it created tensions later when the situation stabilized and ideological differences transpired. This was especially true for the volunteer combatants from Russia upon their return home. Borodai was skeptical of the caliber of indigenous political designs. He acknowledged the quest for social justice to be an important driver of the rebellion:

There were some idiots who were saying that "let us build Novorossiya without any Russia"—they had to be dealt with later. There was no real Communist Party, just a bunch of imbeciles with no serious convictions. Social justice was important as it is also in demand in Russia where the gap between rich and poor is very great. Resentment of oligarchs was felt in Donbas.[61]

Strelkov, Borodai, and Bezler brought a degree of organization into DNR, but the disarray was worse in Luhansk, as Kyiv-loyal forces did not wither away entirely, and the oblast Interior Ministry department was apprehended only on May 19. Bolotov was wounded in an assassination attempt on May 13 as a US$1 million reward was believed to have been put on his head on the Kyiv side. He left for treatment in Russia and was detained by the Ukrainian border guards when attempting to cross back into Luhansk. The guards reportedly informed Kyiv of this important find and asked for reinforcements, but Luhansk rebel militia got there first, engaged with border guards, and rescued Bolotov and his team. Ukrainian army helicopters, when they arrived, found that the bird has already flown.[62]

My respondents emphasized Bolotov's unsuitability for a leadership role and remember him as a heavy drinker with no sense of how to govern. On May 6 *Prince*, in his recollection, advised him not to close branches of the *Privat* bank which belonged to the pro-Maidan Ukrainian oligarch Ihor Kolomoyskyi, because the population drew pensions and salaries from it. He urged, on the contrary, to get as much credit from it as possible as the money may never have to be returned.

I spoke to people at *Privat* bank who were prepared to transfer any sum to any account, but nobody among the LNR "leadership" had the nerve to OK it. I was telling them that "don't expect that Russia will come and take over. You aren't needed in Russia, you are just the knife at Ukraine's throat. You are only interesting for Russia when you are a part of Ukraine." But Bolotov's guys didn't believe this.

There were few adequate people who could act or build something. They were all paranoid about spies, although they couldn't hide their own communications. They spoke on Ukrainian free-access mobile networks calling bombs "sugar": "we've put some 'sugar' under a bridge." Vladimir Gromov [the head of LNR Counter-intelligence department] who considered himself a superspy, locked several Russian volunteers in a pit for alleged spying for Kiev. Local revolt leaders at heart were scared that the Ukrainian powers would return and they would have to answer for what they had done. Then they, for whatever reason, started issuing a medal for taking Kiev (медаль за взятие Киева). In short, Bolotov and a few other characters in Lugansk should've been removed forcefully straight away. Decisive action was required.[63]

To conclude, the Russian Spring made a strong statement of its emergence and catalyzed the local protests to grow into an insurgency. By the time

President Poroshenko was elected on May 25, 2014, territorial configuration was in the rebels' favor. They controlled most of Donbas's large industrial cities, although the uprising was running out of steam in Mariupol. Countryside was left to its own devices, with local authorities in charge of daily business. It was already a rebellion with a political face which was attracting recruits, but the situation had not turned into a war and has not affected each and every person yet.

NOTES

1. Christine Cheng, "Conflict Capital," British International Studies Association conference paper, June 19, 2015.

2. *Strannik*, author's interview, May 2016.

3. Malet, 5.

4. Ilya Barabanov, *Kommersant* journalist, author's interview, May 2016.

5. See also "Бизнесмен Малофеев рассказал о связях со Стрелковым и Бородаем" 13 November 2014, http://slon.ru/fast/russia/biznesmen-malofeev-rasskazal-o-svyazyakh-so-strelkovym-i-borodaem-1183830.xhtml

6. Alexander Borodai, author's interview, Moscow, May 2017.

7. Memorial Human Rights Centre, September 30, 2014. http://www.memo.ru/d/211293.html

8. Prince, author's interview, May 2016.

9. Conference of Union of Donbas Volunteers, Moscow, February 27, 2016.

10. Prince, author's interview, Moscow, May 2017.

11. Alexander Juchkovsky, author's interview, April 2017, via Skype.

12. Alexander Juchkovsky, "Story of our author who went to war in Novorossiya," 19 May 2014, https://sputnikipogrom.com/war/12544/heroes-of-sputnik-and-pogrom/

13. *Strannik*, author's interview, Moscow, May 2016.

14. Alexander Juchkovsky, author's interview, May 2017, via Skype.

15. Oleg Tsaryov in interview with the author, May 2017, via Skype.

16. Author's interviews with ex-combatants.

17. *Liga.net*. Болотов руководил копанками регионала Ефремова–Ландик. 20 August 2014. http://news.liga.net/news/politics/2995373-bolotov_rukovodil_kopankami_regionala_efremova_landik.htm; Глава ЛНР Болотов был «смотрящим» Ефремова, 12 June 2014. http://uapress.info/ru/news/show/27503

18. "Первый глава ЛНР умер под Москвой, 27 January 2017," https://www.gazeta.ru/politics/2017/01/27_a_10496633.shtml#page3

19. Tsaryov interview.

20. Anton Lavrov, "Civil War in the East," in *Brothers armed: military aspects of the crisis in Ukraine*, eds. Colby Howard and Ruslan Pukhov, Centre for Analysis of Strategies and Technologies (CAST), Moscow (Minneapolis : East View Press, 2015), 202–227, 206.

21. Bolotov's statement on readiness to talk see "ЛНР уже готова к переговорам с Киевом, если будет прекращена АТО," 21 May 2014, http://korrespondent.

net/ukraine/politics/3366626-lnr-uzhe-hotova-k-perehovoram-s-kyevom-esly-budet-prekraschena-ato. Also in Anton Lavrov and an interview with a politically-connected local resident

22. Serhii Tkachenko interview, Kyiv, 2014, see also Tkachenko in Radio Svoboda on 25 May 2014, http://www.svoboda.org/a/25398049.html

23. Lavrov, "Civil War," 206.

24. Alexander Borodai, author's interview, Moscow, May 2016.

25. Alexei Tokarev, author's interview, May 2016, Moscow.

26. Igor Strelkov, author's interview, May 2016, Moscow.

27. Igor Strelkov, author's interview, May 2016, Moscow.

28. Igor Strelkov, author's interview, May 2016, Moscow.

29. Turchynov speaking at Ukraine's Security Council, *CBS*, 13 April 2014. http://www.cbsnews.com/news/ukraine-to-launch-large-scale-operation-against-pro-russian-forces/

30. *CBS*. 13 April 2014. Turchynov speaking at Ukraine's Security Council. http://www.cbsnews.com/news/ukraine-to-launch-large-scale-operation-against-pro-russian-forces/

31. "Ukrainian, Pro-Russian Militia Sustain Casualties in Slovyansk Gunfire," 13 April 2014, Voice of America, http://www.voanews.com/a/ukrainian-prorussian-militia-sustain-casualties-in-slovyansk-gunfire/1892393.html

32. The block post is a small tactical sub-unit designed to check or delay reconnaissance forces or advance guards of enemy forces. Often they were manned by "cannon fodder"; the expendable and not so well trained troops.

33. "Один из лидеров ополчения Славянска "Ромашка" погиб," 3 May 2014, *RIA*, http://ria.ru/world/20140503/1006339733.html

34. Lavrov, "Civil War," 205–206.

35. Igor Strelkov, author's interview, Moscow, May 2016.

36. Alexander Chalenko, author's interview, Moscow, February 2016.

37. Prince, author's interview, May 2016, Moscow.

38. Igor Strelkov, author's interview, Moscow, May 2016.

39. Prince, author's interview, Moscow, May 2016.

40. Prince author's interview, May 2016, Moscow.

41. Prince author's interview.

42. Appeal of Igor Strelkov, 17 May 2014, https://www.youtube.com/watch?v=KIHdrSm6jrU

43. https://sputnikipogrom.com/politics/12436/to-all-russian-men-and-women/

44. Prince, author's interview, Moscow, May 2016.

45. Igor Strelkov, author's interview, Moscow, May 2016.

46. Oleg Tsaryov, author's interview.

47. 12 May 2014, https://www.theguardian.com/world/video/2014/may/12/eurovision-votes-more-credible-ukraine-referendum-william-hague-video

48. George Allen Collier, Elizabeth Lowery, *Quaratiello 'Basta!: Land and the Zapatista Rebellion in Chiapas* (Oakland, CA: Food First Books, 2005).

49. Oliver Boyd-Barrett, *Western mainstream media and the Ukraine Crisis: a study in conflict propaganda* (London: Routledge, 2016), chapter 6 "Crimea, Odessa and Eastern Ukraine."

50. Transcript: Vladimir Putin April 17 Q&A, *The Washington Post*, 17 April 2014, https://www.washingtonpost.com/world/transcript-vladimir-putins-april-17-qanda/2014/04/17/ff77b4a2-c635-11e3-8b9a-8e0977a24aeb_story.html?utm_term=.124293ae7de5

51. http://rusvesna.su/recent_opinions/1432801159

52. Oleg Tsaryov, author's interview, April 2017, via Skype.

53. Noah Sneider, "Huddling With Ukrainian Rebels in a Bunker on the Front Lines," 24 July 2014, https://newrepublic.com/article/118837/huddling-bunker-ukrainian-rebels-aftermath-mh-17

54. Gubarev, *Torch*.

55. Juchkovsky, author's interview, 2017.

56. Michael Malet, *Nestor Makhno in the Russian Civil War* (London: Macmillan, 1982).

57. Alexander Chalenko, author's interview, Moscow, February 2016.

58. *Colonel Cassad*. September 4, 2014. http://colonelcassad.livejournal.com/1764917.html

59. *Novopressa*. http://novopressa.ru/articles/pavel-gubarev-buducshee-novorossii.html

60. Wilson, "The Donbas in 2014."

61. Alexander Borodai, author's interview, Moscow, May 2016.

62. "Первый ушел: Чем запомнился Валерий Болотов—один из лидеров ополчения Донбасса," 27 January 2017, https://lenta.ru/articles/2017/01/28/bolotov/

63. Prince, author's interview, Moscow, May 2016.

Chapter 6

Free Guerrillas

"Novorossiya be!" Ghosts *and* Somalis *Take the Stage*

This chapter sets the stage for the key military action and describes the beginnings of the road toward irreversible violence. It explores who were the rebels and their opponents, how they organized themselves, where they initially got their weapons from, how they governed the areas they held, and what distinguished them from each other. Their assemblage was far from a proper army, but was highly adaptive and resilient, despite its irregular nature.

COMBAT-NOT-READY: A RELUCTANT START

Neither side expected a full-scale war, until they gradually slid down into one. The ATO was ordered as a joint operation of the SBU and the Ministry of Interior, and the Army was also used from the start. However, fighting was of low intensity until when Petro Poroshenko came to power and the conflict turned into a full-fledged war. At the start of the ATO, Ukrainian armed forces were in a state similar to that of the Russian army in 1994 when President Yeltsin invaded Chechnya, with poor maintenance, supplies, and command.[1] Crucially they were not trained for the task and were as reluctant to fight as the Russians had been in Chechnya. In the end they used similar tactics, with the same disastrous consequences, including heavy troop losses and civilian casualties.

The assemblage of the rebel forces was far from a strong adversary at first, and it is interesting to note why the Ukrainian army took so long to make progress against them. In these early stages, even small groups of highly motivated people could be very effective and had an advantage over the ATO forces because such combatants were idea driven and were fighting willingly. Strelkov and other commanders explained that the rebels had a core group

121

of mostly Russian combatants who could fight from the word "Go," while
the Ukrainians lacked combat experience. The last war in which they were
involved was in Afghanistan (1979–1989) and its participants were now
too old. The insurgency had an advantage that it was highly adaptive and
resilient, despite, or maybe because of its irregular nature. Insurgents tried to
exploit every crisis moment as an opportunity and to move into void spaces.
Imagination and "thinking outside the box" were their important tactics. For
example, a fear of ferocious "Chechens" that existed among the Ukrainians
was picked by *Motorola* who instructed the Sloviansk rebels to imperson-
ate "Chechens," grow beards, shout "Allah Akbar!" on radios, and call their
military vehicles *jihad-mobil*. Bolt notes that "insurrectionists must maximise
limited tactical resources: they must imagine what opportunities could arise,
and recognise them when they come. Innovation, imagination and opportunity, and the endless production line of sympathisers and fighters that emerge
out of population are the insurgent's weapons."[2]

The rebels exploited psychological weaknesses of the Ukrainian side. One
was that they expected an arrival of the Russian army as happened in Crimea
and some believed that they were already in Donbas. They were not prepared
for a head-on military confrontation with them. Indeed, Moscow imitated
troop movement along the border. Ground attack forces and artillery systems
appeared ready to cross, but the moves were later declared to be "military
exercises." The ATO command also overestimated the rebels' fighting capabilities believing that there were Russian regular troops behind the front line
of rebels, and so they were reluctant to launch ground attacks. The other one
was army's unwillingness to use lethal force against their fellow citizens,
toward whom they did not feel hostility.

The initial relations between the rebels and the Ukrainian military around
the main theatre of action in Sloviansk were largely devoid of aggression.
There was often contact between the two sides to reduce escalation. Rebels
at Semyonovka (a suburb of Sloviansk) where their frontline defenses were
located, conveyed the message to the Ukrainian side that they would deploy
on the heights, but would not shoot at them. *Prince* recollects that evacuation of mental health patients from Semyonovka hospital was arranged after
extensive talks with the military. Negotiations at Sloviansk were frequently
happening. As *Prince* described to me, the Ukrainian officers sometimes
contacted the rebels to say that

we do not want to shoot you, we will shoot in the air and our troops will draw
lots on who will get their arm or leg shot to imitate battle casualties. We would
leave some armoured vehicles, you should burn them, and we will report that we
engaged in armed combat. We are under orders to conduct warfare, but you can
send your observer to stay with us to monitor that we stick to the deal.[3]

Some armored vehicles in a convoy that was sent to Kramatorsk were filmed raising Russian flags because their crews expected that Moscow would act. Some troops were changing loyalty, siding with the rebels or were prepared to do so, as many did not see the new power-holders in Kyiv under Turchinov as a legitimate authority. There were voices among the military who were saying to the rebels "let's join forces and advance together on Kyiv to get rid of the people who seized power there." In *Prince*'s view, the Ukrainian military in Donbas should have been proactively encouraged to relocate to Russia at that time until troubles were over, but Moscow made no such move.

The situation changed when Ukrainian territorial battalions appeared on the scene. As was the case among the rebels, a parallel process of armed citizens' participation in the conflict took place on the Kyiv side which was encouraged by the state. Territorial battalions[4] were set up, starting with some pro-Maidan activists who got armed and on the basis of some preexisting paramilitary groups. These battalions solved one immediate problem of absorbing overenthusiastic Maidan participants who continued to rally in Kyiv, thus driving them away from the capital. The activists found it harder to justify their protests in the capital when the country needed them on the battlefront. The government and some politicians, such Kyiv's mayor Vitaly Klitschko encouraged and sponsored their formation. Appeasing such forces was inevitable in the short-term out of the fear that the activists could hit back at Kyiv and, in that case, it was not clear who would defend the government.

On April 13, 2014, Arsen Avakov issued a decree authorizing the creation of the new paramilitary forces from among the civil population. Altogether forty-four battalions were identified,[5] although the real number may be higher. Several, such as *Aidar*, were sponsored by the Ukrainian oligarch Ihor Kolomoyskyi, who was the main financial backer of the battalions. They were informal armed formations attached either to the Ministry of Defense (MoD) or to Ministry of Interior (MoI), but privately sponsored or self-financed. National Guards were reestablished, also under the MoI system. Formally, the battalions under the MoI were the "second echelon" forces vested with securing territory cleared by the army and had no heavy weapons or vehicles at their disposal. They hunted down rebel suspects and spies, manned check points, secured important facilities etc. Those under the MoD, such as the *Aidar* battalion in Luhansk oblast, were considered combat forces and had military-style weapons and equipment.

The reality was more obscure. All battalions performed police functions whenever they could, and there was often a fine line between policing and criminality.[6] They also became involved in frontline fighting alongside the army, when several battalions suffered heavy losses. The difference was that unlike the regular forces, the "irregular" elements had no publicity restrictions and their leaders could engage in the most brazen PR through social media. In the eyes of the public which consumed the news through Facebook, Twitter and YouTube, most fighting was done by battalions rather than the Army, which was not the case as the war progressed. Their commanders became the new celebrities, some even acquiring a *nom de guerre* for this purpose, such as Semyon Semenchenko, the leader of *Donbas* battalion who abandoned his real Russian-sounding name Konstantin Grishin.

Crime bosses demonstrated their "patriotic" credentials, sponsoring or joining the battalions. Criminals were already visible during the 2013–2014 protests. For example, Sashko Bilyi (real name Alexander Muzychko), the Right Sector leader in Vinnitsa who attacked a prosecutor, served two sentences for violent offences and was eventually killed in March 2014. Nikolai Kolesnik, aka *Tyson*, a crime boss from Krivorizhie, was associated with the *Krivbas* battalion and claimed to be backed by it in his parliamentary election campaign.[7] The Konstantinovskye (aka brothers *Karamazov*), who became wealthy businessmen and restaurant owners in Kyiv, occupying the 41st place in *Focus* magazine rankings, started their career as hitmen in the 1990s.[8] Brother Vyacheslav spent time with the *Kyiv-1* battalion, having offered his Rolls-Royce for sale as sponsorship, and campaigned in the October 2014 parliamentary election under the "Sold the Rolls, Went to Front" slogan.

The battalions were thoroughly despised by the rebels as willingly waging the war, unlike the army which had no alternative but to fight when ordered. *Aidar* was the leader of negative ratings. Battalions were not amenable to negotiations. These were idea-driven men who made a conscious choice to go to fight for their motherland on their own terms. Rebels who fought against them said that they were very brave, but had no knowledge how to fight and sustained heavy casualties. The rebels at one point apprehended Donbas battalion flag, which *Prince* returned with a war captive from that battalion during the prisoner exchange.

Hundreds of people were taken prisoner, and commanders on both sides sought to the exchange them for their own fighters, thus keeping private prisons. Situation was breathing of criminality. Trade in people, alive and dead, was not unheard of, and some were held for ransom. *Amnesty International* documented ill-treatment and torture of prisoners held by both sides.[9] *Prince* describes the situation in 2014 from a rebel perspective:

There were cases of outright deceit. Some [Ukrainian] volunteers got in touch with me claiming that people were taken to Russia to Adygeia and put into slavery, but then we found their corpses at Ilovaysk [after August 2014 counteroffensive]. We gave their bodies to the Red Cross. These volunteers were just making money. There were cases when Ukrainian volunteers sold bodies to relatives for $200 claiming that they need money for refrigerators. But not everybody was like that. There were decent people as well. Such cases occurred on our side as well.[10]

As the war progressed, hatred emerged on both sides because civil wars brutalize combatants, destroy the psychological mechanisms of self-sanction and lower the cost of violent activity.[11] They allow the rise in prominence of people with a propensity for violence. Atrocities committed by territorial battalions[12] had a provocative effect on the rebels. A rebel *Nemets* (German) originally from Lysychansk who married into Kharkiv and had a German grandfather, – hence the call sign, – pointed out that he decided to join the resistance so that "those battalions don't shoot there." When battalion fighters shot down a convoy of civilians fleeing Lysychansk, among them his father, *Nemets* went to a rebel conscription point in the city to enlist. The rebels were afraid to surrender to the battalions because they had a reputation of being very cruel. Many rebels carried a last hand grenade to blow themselves up if a capture by a territorial battalion was imminent. It was considered possible to surrender to Ukrainian regular armed forces: one was likely to get roughed up, but then the prisoners would be normally handed over to the SBU. In the words of a Russian volunteer, "there you will live and would not end up crippled for life."

The Ukrainian army, in their turn, was angered by the first real assault on one of their block-posts by the commander Bezler-led group (see below) on May 22, 2014, at Volnovakha district on the road between Volodymyrivka (in Ukrainian, Vladimirka in Russian) and Ol'hynka (in Ukrainian, Ol'ginka in Russian) when 16 troops were killed and over 40 injured. This provoked the military into a forceful response and provided the impetus to fight back. The attack was criticized in rebel circles as unnecessarily cruel and politically wrong because the chances for peace with the Ukrainian military had not been lost yet.

The main theatre of action lay in the North in Sloviansk, allowing time for the rebellion to organize itself. Although Sloviansk was the main focus of attention, violence was breaking out elsewhere. Events were moving very quickly then, with casualties occurring daily. A former rebel fighter noted that "it was striking how little time passed from the first rallies to the first fire." The weakest area was in the South on the coast of the Sea of Azov. On April 16 three men were killed in Mariupol in what Minister of Interior Arsen Avakov said had been raids on a military base, but the relatives believed that they were innocent civilians. Tensions led to violence on the Victory Day (May 9) as ten unarmed civilians were shot by Ukrainian National Guard forces during skirmishes when some local police sided up with the protesters.[13] The group of insurgents there was not very big and barely had arms, also was geographically cut off from the main centers of rebellion in Donetsk, Makiivka and Horlivka. When the group came under attack, it could not be supported by others. Mariupol never managed to set up a real battlefield command and its weak rebel units were overpowered and dispersed when on June 13 territorial battalions Avoz and Dnipro-1 launched a successful assault. Mariupol was a significant loss for the rebel cause because it was an important city—perhaps more than Luhansk, since it has sea access, and developed industry and infrastructure.

EARLY WEAPONS' ACQUISITION

As the demand for arms appeared in March, they found their way into Donbas and armaments left from World War II, including a tank which formed a war memorial, were also used.[14] Some were brought by volunteers from Russia, some apprehended from the Ukrainian arsenals, police and the military, and others were procured on the black market after arsenals in Western Ukraine were raided by Yanukovych opponents.[15] Local Interior Ministry troops have been disarmed by rebels who seized their weapons often with little resistance, and some sided with them. Interviewed rebels underscored that initially, especially in Donetsk oblast, there were more people willing to fight than arms available. A Russian volunteer combatant said that

> I only had a 1933 pistol but no bullets for it. We went to the local history museum and confiscated bullets of that period. We gave the museum a formal note that bullets were requisitioned for defense needs.[16]

Local residents were proactive in weapons' grabbing. In the early days of the conflict, three reconnaissance armory vehicles were seized by civilians from troops and handed over to Strelkov's forces at Sloviansk. The same way as it had happened in the Russian army during the first war in Chechnya, the military were selling weapons to their opponents or trading them for goods. A local rebel told me a story that a boy on a scooter exchanged foodstuffs and vodka for a *Mukha* grenade launcher with Ukrainian soldiers, which was later used against the same troops. Borodai recalled the time when such acquisition of weapons was possible if one had the nerve and determination:

> we harvested (*otzhali*) some and some were bought from Ukrainian troops. I remember one episode when we exchanged a modern APC in good condition for a collectable revolver, a German knife, and a bottle of good whisky. The Ukrainian military even filled a full tank of petrol for us. When we laid our hands on military vehicles, the situation changed.[17]

Before full-scale military actions started in mid-summer, supplies from Russia were negligible. The rebels at that period had obsolete weapons brought in from Crimea with the possible complicity of the Russian authorities. However, modern weapons were absent and many existing arms had technical defects; for example, a rebel recollects that a *Luna* (Moon) night vision optical device would not switch on when needed in the field. But then procurement in Ukraine got underway: "it was impossible not to find weapons in Ukraine. It is the territory of the former Kyiv Military District, it had an abundance of arms depots."[18] Every opportunity was seized. When Sloviansk engaged a large concentration of the ATO forces in Donetsk oblast, the rebel forces attacked from the rear in the southeast and seized the Artemi-vsk (presently Bakhmut) arms depot. This was a major breakthrough. Rebels seized the compound of the 156th AA Missile regiment's 1st battalion outside Donetsk airport and apprehended a Buk-M1 SAM system.[19] The first three tanks from Russia arrived on June 12.

Connection to Russia was important not only as a source of weapons, but also for fuel required for the armored vehicles, and for battlefield medical supplies. Already in spring the rebels had managed to gain control over a section of the Ukrainian border with Russia in Luhanska Oblast where the Ukrainian border troops put up minimal resistance and agreed to capitulate in return for safe passage out. On June 4 the rebels took two border guard bases when Ukrainian troops surrendered. Ammunition was taken from the base, and the remaining border guards were allowed to leave. The National Guards' base near Luhansk surrendered when its defenders ran out of ammunition and the troops withdrew. The highway from Izvarino checkpoint via Krasnodon to Luhansk was now in rebels' hands.

This capture allowed the Russian volunteers to make deals with Russian traffickers who helped them to move stuff across the border. Interestingly, Russian smugglers did that out of altruistic and solidarity motives without charging for their "services," although the rebellion disrupted their business. Ukrainian smugglers, on the contrary, tried to charge combatants for helping to move their cargo across the border, and they decided not to deal with them. Russian and transnational society contributed to acquisition by sending money in, and Moscow initially averted its eyes to informal supplies, although measures to stop them were also made and some of such deliveries failed. Alexander Juchkovsky, coordinator of "non-humanitarian aid," and *Prince* were among prominent activists who organized procurement:

Periodically Juchkovsky and I went to Russia from Donbas to procure what was needed—uniforms, ammunition, written-off APCs. The Russian army frequently rotates their armoury and writes it off for agricultural use. It was possible to buy an APC for 3.5 million roubles, and a good quality reconnaissance infantry armoured vehicle cost 1.5 million. However, procuring ammunition was more problematic. We reckoned how we were going to move the APCs, and decided to bluff our way through: we bluntly took off the number plates, dressed in military uniforms and drove across the Russian–Ukrainian border. On seeing men in uniform, Russian border guards assumed that this was a bona fide deal and let us through. Subsequently they realised what was going on and blocked that channel.[20]

Prince also remembers Russian law-abiding servicemen among the troops deployed at the border who were keen to join in, but only with permission. "As we were crossing illegally, some paratroopers gave us a lot of combat advice and sounded wildly enthusiastic. "Do it like this and that," they would say. They asked me to write to their commander so that they could be released to go to Donbas. When I said "just take time off duty and come straight away with us," they grew timid: "but there are no orders," they said."

Russian volunteers at times were frustrated with the low skill base of Donbas rebels, as many from Ukraine did not even serve in the conscript army and could not use the modern systems. One block post had an AGS-17 *Plamya* (Flame) 30-mm automatic grenade launcher, but kept it in the basement because nobody knew how to use it. Prince said that

> We brought the first drone which flew for 20 km, not any worse than those the Ukrainians had. Then we discovered that it was lying idle because nobody could read instructions in English. We had to look for a person in Russia who could come to teach the locals how to use it.

ON THE ROLE OF PERSONALITY IN HISTORY

The rebels described the early period of idealism, when the role of charismatic personalities was a significant factor: "those were genuine volunteers who were ready to face death. In order to attract and unite such people, extraordinary human qualities were needed. Strelkov and Mozgovoi were such leaders."[21] Charismatic figures were pulling the insurgents together and this is how the first groups of fighters emerged. Three characters were of crucial importance for establishing a military-political order at the DNR– Strelkov, Borodai and Bezler. If Mariupol had somebody of that caliber, the course of events in the city could have been different.

Strelkov in Sloviansk provided a degree of military organization in the areas which he controlled. He organized a "Slavyansk brigade," numbering at its height, according to him, 1,100 fighters in Sloviansk, 500 in Kramatorsk, 150 in Druzhkivka and 150 in Kostyantynivka. However, his geographical location was dire and, as he maintained, it was hard to sustain fighting with capabilities he had at his disposal. Intelligence-gathering was deficient: Strelkov said that they began to listen to the adversary communications only after the rebels apprehended a Ukrainian reconnaissance vehicle and two SBU staff switched their allegiance to them. A general mobilization could not be ordered because Strelkov had no powers to do that. Many local recruits were motivated but had no military background and the deficit of combat-ready cadres was acute: "I had one experienced local officer to head our air defenses and my logistics chief was an elderly retiree from Ukraine. Only three out of the 30 Afghan veterans in town joined us."[22] *Strannik* adds that "logistics remained a big problem throughout because outside volunteers were coming to Donbas keen to fight rather than organise procurement, while the locals did not have the skills required for troop support operations." This is of course a rebel view on the opportunities and limitations, assets and constraints at their disposal.

On June 2 Ukrainian territorial battalions launched an offensive on Sloviansk, but it was repelled. At first, the Ukrainian side used air power to bomb the town, but the rebels managed to close the airspace fairly early on when they seized *Igla* and *Strela* portable surface-to-air missile (SAM) defense systems [Soviet equivalents of *Stinger*] from the Ukrainian side. Most aircraft were shot down near Sloviansk, the first as early as in May, when one was downed by a shot from a heavy machinegun. The first Ukrainian helicopter was lost in April when it was destroyed on the ground at the Kramatorsk airfield. Rebel capabilities grew with the acquisition of heavy armor through seizures from ATO troops and contraband from Russia, and their military operations moved to a qualitatively new level. At the same time, the Sloviansk brigade was a poor match to the ATO after the Ukrainian war effort was considerably upgraded following Poroshenko's election, and it had superiority in terms of firepower and the number of military vehicles, let alone fuel supplies.

With few modern weapons and trained fighters, Strelkov had to manage with the assets he had, and his theatrical personality and counter-espionage skills came in use. He acted as an imaginative leader and his various past experiences served in staging a gigantic bluff which was an important part of his method of warfare. The Western and Ukrainian media provided him with the much-needed frightening public image of a simultaneous FSB and GRU (Main Intelligence Directorate of the Russian Ministry of Defense) Colonel, and the EU sanctions list identified him as a serving GRU officer, although this was not even remotely true. Strelkov told me that:

My [defense] tactics were disinformation and intimidation, so that the opponent thought that there were more of us and that we were better armed [than we really were], and that Russia was behind us. We bluffed, pretended that Russian spetznaz [special forces] were fighting with us and that rebels only made up the first line of defence. The Ukrainian side feared that we would begin an offensive, and this deprived them of willpower.[23]

Prince and Borodai agree that it was hard to see from outside that the Emperor had no clothes. In Borodai's remarks:

> Strelkov was perceived both as a Russian volunteer and on a mission from Moscow. He exploited his image of an FSB colonel, although it later became clear that he was a volunteer. But he played his part, and became a symbol. Here he appears at a press conference—so handsome, mysterious, in camouflage, reading yet another [military news] brief. It looked arty; the patriotic media did what they could to portray him as a Russian folk hero.[24]

Installed as a military leader, Strelkov had to supervise the internal situation and construct an order of governance which was in tune with his ideological convictions of moral purity, the way he understood them. It was also important to demonstrate that he was really in charge. Strelkov issued an order to execute looters, and two executions took place, publicized as a deterrent to others. It was prohibited to use expletives in radio calls, although this was largely ignored. Drunkenness was punishable by 10 days of digging trenches. A formal confiscation act which had to be signed in three copies, was introduced which was used when the rebels seized private assets for their needs, such as vehicles, and which provided evidence for compensation later. It is hard to know whether this affected the criminal situation much other than drunkenness in public and the drugs trade, which almost stopped but it is for this that Strelkov is remembered. When he and his Sloviansk brigade arrived later in Donetsk, they were appalled by what they viewed as a moral decay of the rebel leadership there.

BEZLER IN HORLIVKA

Defenses were well organized at Gorlovka by the battalion of influential commander Igor Bezler (call sign *Bes* translated as Demon) who was praised the most for his military talent by the rebel sources. Bezler, unlike Strelkov and Borodai, remained an enigmatic figure whom the *New Republic* slapped as a "battle-hardened Mr. Potato Face" after Bezler's refusal to take its photo shoot directions.[25] Indeed, with "a walrus moustache, a fiery temper and a reputation for brutality, Bezler was one of the most feared commanders" who did not give Western journalists an easy time.[26]

Bezler was not a native of Donbas but a Russian citizen originally from Crimea and of German descent, who lived in Gorlovka long before the conflict and had a Ukrainian residency permit since 2003. In 1994–1997 he studied at Dzerzhinsky military academy in Moscow. In Ukraine, Bezler worked at *Prostor* funeral parlor and in private security guards at the Horlivka machine-building factory. He headed the Horlivka ex-paratroopers' association and had his paramilitary network ready which later proved instrumental. In 2013 Bezler visited Crimea where he was involved in the events preceding the Russian takeover. He was highly praised for the organization and discipline of his troops when he controlled Horlivka and partially Makiivka. By mid-July Bezler's battalion had shot down 4 Ukrainian military aircraft. In interlocutors" accounts, Bezler had been better at military organization than Strelkov and consequently Horlivka and Yenakijeve which he controlled held on longer than other places.

This is as far as certainty goes, as Bezler was a hero of many legends. "Bezler was a good and brave commander who enjoyed a huge respect among his troopers. He was also sometime short-tempered and unjust, but this is a feature of a civil war. He would have looked good as some medieval fief who ruled his fiefdom."[27] He was much feared even in rebel circles and "Bezler's dungeons" were remembered with trepidation even by war-brutalized fighters. He had the reputation of a military professional with ties to the GRU, although this was never confirmed as a fact. One theory heard in Moscow was that Bezler was planted as a GRU sleeper to be activated when the time came. It seems too much of a conspiracy theory that the GRU already knew in 2003, when President Kuchma was in power, that Bezler's military skills would be required in Horlivka in 2014, and stuck him into a funeral parlor from where he was in the end sacked.

Among other things, Bezler was a master of deception and impersonation using these tools to compensate for the rebels' weaknesses. In April, he released a video of himself giving orders to the defecting Horlivka policemen, in which he made a plausible performance, authoritatively communicating the words they were waiting to hear: "I am a lieutenant colonel of the Russian Army. Your mission: keeping the peace, not allowing looting, not allowing unsanctioned seizures of buildings." He looked the part and was persuasive, how were they not to believe him and suspect that this was a bluff?

Bezler projected his messages through video and they helped to build up his formidable reputation. He kept hostages and prisoners as a "currency" to trade for his fighters seized by the Kyiv side. In June, he released filming of the execution of two blindfolded men by firing squad whom he tried to exchange for his captured man but the Ukrainian side refused, and he ran out of patience. In July, Bezler demonstrated the supposedly executed prisoners to cameras explaining that they were dummy bullets meant to produce psychological effect. This happened at the time when ISIS was doing the same in Iraq, with the difference that their executions were real rather than mock, and TV coverage probably gave Bezler the idea. One of the characters who was a victim of the mock execution was met in Horlivka by *the Guardian* journalist Shaun Walker later.

BORODAI IN DONETSK

Although the city had indigenous activists, volunteers from Russia played an organizational role in Donetsk fairly early on. When one of the interviewed volunteers who later emerged as a rebel army commander came to Donetsk for personal reasons in February 2014, he remembers witnessing mass demonstrations. Many locals, in his opinion, were not committed to anything in particular but were hanging out to watch the action. In April and early May, chaos prevailed. "I could see they need organisational help. My message was—guys, please move a bit and give us some room. We need to make a stand here, for the *Russian World*."

Borodai was not the only prominent Russian in Donetsk, but he was the key leader who started building up of the "republic." He served as the DNR premier from May 16 to August 7, 2014. Borodai tells a story similar to Strelkov's of an initial reluctance of the local rebels to claim political leadership and of his unexpected role as a creator of a "proto-republic," without the velvet gloves:

> I came as an adviser and organiser, but realised that a structure was needed. Nobody wanted to be a figurehead. I suggested this role first to Khodakovsky, then to others, but no one wanted to do it. They all refused because they weren't sure that the uprising wouldn't collapse. They were personally brave and ready to fight, but unwilling to assume political responsibility.
>
> My role was of a military leader. I sometimes had to stop panic and kick battalions back to the frontlines, especially the locals who hadn't seen war before and would run away at the first sign of shelling and death. What I did in Donetsk was first to set up a headquarters, then start managing, then disarming. If anyone didn't obey, I had them shot in the legs. A few were grateful afterwards. Everything was out of the ordinary. For example, the rebel Prosecutor General's Office had its own tank because it had a reconnaissance and saboteur (разведовательно-диверсионный) company of 500 troops. We used to joke that this was the only prosecutor's office in the world with its own armoured forces.[28]

Borodai facilitated the arrival of the security team once involved in Transnistria who were no longer welcome in the breakaway region after a leadership change there in 2011. Vladimir Antiufeev, a Transnistrian ex-security chief, became the first deputy chair of the "DNR Council of Ministers" responsible for the security bloc (July–September 2014) and his lieutenants, Oleg Beryoza and Andrei Pinchuk were appointed "ministers" of interior and security, respectfully. Borodai valued their contribution to the establishment of the security infrastructure, and Pinchuk and Beryoza lasted into 2015, after Borodai and Antiufeev were gone. In Borodai's words:

Antiufeyev was a volunteer general. He played his role decently and left in time. My bodyguard squad was composed of volunteers who protected me and indispensable ministers, such as Antiufeev, Pinchuk and Beryoza. We were serving the same cause. He was responsible for the security bloc that included the interior and security ministries and the prosecutor's office. He was a professional because he had been in charge of these issues in Transdniestria. The work advanced considerably after he came with his team.[29]

The necessity to build nascent governance arrangements on the rebel-held territories was realized fairly early on. Although field commanders were in charge of their areas and the rebellion was territorially dispersed, institutional constructivism proceeded along "an imagined state" script from ground zero. A quasi-state infrastructure with various "ministries," "state committees," and "prosecutor's offices" was set up. Donetsk was the capital and tried to act as a center of power for other parts under the DNR control. This was state-building at its most raw. Borodai appointed himself DNR "prime minister and commander-in-chief," and Strelkov was "minister of defence." There were plenty of other positions, especially in the defence and security sphere, to satisfy everybody's ambition, which did not dictate that responsibility and authority was to follow. Sometimes the performances bordered on the ridiculous. Borodai:

> I made lots of appointments. Sometimes not the best ones, as I could later see, but this was because I didn't know the people and the context. Overall, I treated appointments lightly. The only regret I have is that I failed to appoint an admiral. Antiufeev said that he would be the first in line for this. I agreed and said that we'd make him a uniform which absolutely must include a parrot.[30]

Apart from volunteers of the opposition or with independent-minded streaks, interviews show that seemingly there was another kind of *Russian Spring* men. These were the people who had had security sector careers in the past but had discontinued service well before the Ukraine crisis. They went to Donbas of their own volition and risk, but continued to maintain contact with their former outfits and, from time to time, fulfilled certain tasks for them: such as intelligence gathering on the rebels" affairs, identification of promising local leaders and those who could turn into liabilities, streamlining of military organization, and information on crime and disorder which might affect Russia itself.

Local "Stars" Rising

As the conflict progressed, battalions rose to prominence out of smaller units, and with the exception of *Motorola* were all headed by the locals. *Somali* in

Donetsk was led by Mikhail Tolstykh (call sign *Givi*)[31] in his early thirties
who was born in Ilovaisk and trained as an industrial rope access technician
with his last job as a heavy truck factory driver. *Somali* later got famous for
fighting in Ilovaisk and Donetsk airport. *Sparta* emerged in Donetsk from
Motorola's unit of "Slavyank Brigade." *Kalmius* battalion, named after the
river Kalmius, was set up by staff and miners of Donetsk Metallurgic Factory.
It was headed by several different leaders and fell under Strelkov's overall
command during his time in Sloviansk. *Kalmius* became known for its fighting at Savur-Mohyla and Debaltseve.

Vostok controlled, together with *Oplot*, Donetsk, Snizhne (in Ukrainian,
Snezhnoye in Russian) and Shakhtarsk (in Ukrainian, Shakhtyorsk in
Russian) until July 9, 2014, when Khodakovsky argued with Strelkov who
arrived to Donetsk from Sloviansk. This resulted in the splitting of *Vostok*
with one part going to Makiivka, and the other joining Strelkov. Borodai
explains that

> There were no DNR and LNR in any serious way at first, the idea was to join
> Russia. The "republics" came together from small fighting detachments. I
> used to joke that we have feudalism of some sorts: Gorlovka khanate, Donetsk
> fiefdom, Sloviansk principality. *Oplot* and *Vostok* were the largest units, but
> there were all sorts of groups, like the Russian Orthodox Army with up to 600
> troops, such exotic thing as Russian Orthodox Sunrise, a separate DNR Cossack
> brigade etc.[32]

Tensions between groups and the way they aligned themselves were
evident from the start. Relations were characterized by rivalry, making it
hard to establish a command and control structure. A Military Council was
founded by Strelkov in an attempt to unite the main DNR groups whose
members included Strelkov, his chief of staff *Mikhailo,* Mozgovoi from LNR,
Khmuryi (*Gloomy,* call sign of general Petrovsky also known as *Bad Soldier*)
and Bezler, but Zakharchenko, the commander of the *Oplot,* was present
only twice and Khodakovsky of *Vostok* did not wish to conduct joint operations with them at all. They were pulling in a different direction to center
everything on Donetsk and did not want to bow to the authority of outsiders. *Mikhailo* recalled that he believed that Zakharchenko and Khodakovsky
were diverting weapons which were destined for Sloviansk when they finally
started to be sent from Russia, and they were outgunned as a result.

Although the security situation in Luhansk oblast was slightly better than
in Donetsk due to its location further away from Kyiv, the uprising suffered
from the proliferation of dozens of groups dispersed throughout the oblast
who did not recognize any overall command. Some Luhansk militias aligned
with Strelkov rather than with the LNR leadership, although he in theory was

a DNR forces' commander, because they sought to maintain their independence. At least three centers contested power, which continued into the period of relative stabilization. LNR, by analogy with *semiboyarshina* (rule of seven *boyars* or princes in pre-Petrine Russia) was known as *semibattalionshina* (rule of seven battalions).

The main Luhansk battalion was *Zarya* (Dawn) commanded by Igor Plotnitsky, later the LNR premier. Plotnitsky with no security background used to be head of a market checking department of the Luhansk oblast consumer rights inspectorate. *Zarya's* core was made up of the former security personnel with an anti-Maidan orientation and "Afghantsy," who were joined by local Luhansk men of all kinds of social origins, "from homeless to wealthy businessmen who stood shoulder to shoulder for their land."[33] There were other groups in the same city. *Batman* was established by Alexander Bednov, a former night club bouncer, and *Leshii* (Troll) was led by Alexei Pavlov.[34]

Charismatic commanders emerged in other parts of the oblast, such as Mozgovoi, Dremov, Ishenko, and Malyi. *Prizrak* (Avenging Ghost) battalion which operated outside of the LNR command occupied a special space in the rebellion history both inspirationally and as a combat force. It was set up in Stakhanov and later based in Alchevsk. *Prizrak* was headed by Alexei Mozgovoi from Svatove (in Ukrainian, Svatovo in Russian) in Luhanska oblast. Mozgovoi in his civilian incarnation was a local singer and used to perform in a club in Svatove. Chalenko characterized him as artistic, a Facebook creation and a "YouTube hero" whose reputation was made up by social media in search for stars. In *Prince*'s description, "Mozgovoi was a colourful personality. He called himself a battalion answerable to nobody. What he was thinking militarily was unclear. I asked him why he would not launch an attack to capture Antratsyt, to which he replied that 'there was no need to take it now.' Why, I could not comprehend. He tried to be close to his fighters, but simultaneously strict; this did not quite work. It was not very serious somehow." Mozgovoi established contacts with Vladimir Zhirinovsky, the leader of the Liberal-Democratic Party of Russia (LDPR), and his camp was filled with LDPR T-shirts and other memorabilia. A "Zhirinovsky Tiger" tank managed to make its way to Mozgovoi in May, although border guards were under orders not to allow such things through.[35]

Mozgovoi had no fighting experience, but his deputies had, and it enabled *Prizrak* to conduct military operations. In *Mikhailo's* account, Mozgovoi was an idealist who fought for the liberation of Ukraine from illegitimate Maidan victors, as he saw the new Ukrainian government. He opened a dialogue with Kyiv which was not without success, but it was *Prizrak's* own initiative not endorsed by the LNR leadership. Talks were held in summer 2014 via Skype with Ukrainian military representing the Kyiv side. A participant from Mozgovoi's entourage noted that "there was such excitement that we finally got to a negotiation table, that we would now resolve our problems. This sadly did not happen."

Already in March, according to an eyewitness account, Mozgovoi with his group was active in weapons' seizure from army troops, but this acquisition did not seem to have a clear purpose.[36] Early on, Mozgovoi came into conflict with Bolotov in Luhansk and left for Lysychansk to avoid confrontation. In May 2014 *Prizrak* allied with Strelkov's overall command and their units were stationed together in Siversk in Artemivskii district. One rebel who fought with it expressed his disappointment saying to me that "*Prizrak* perished under the tanks at Lysychansk, it was all downhill after that." Eventually, *Prizrak* developed into a large battalion, had a stream of international volunteers, and even a French-Serbian unit.

COSSACKS

In 2014 up to 60 percent of LNR territory was controlled by the fighters who identified themselves as Cossacks and served under their own atamans and also at *Prizrak*. Cossack presence was a mixture of attraction to Cossack historical traditions which finally found a modern application, romanticism and unruly behavior as long as the groups had the "right values" at heart. This can explain the ability to call many recruits under arms who identified as "Cossacks." They were associated with lawlessness, courage and shortage of combat skills. Nikolai Kozitsyn, the chief ataman of Don Cossack Army, originally from Donetsk oblast but living in Russia, deployed with his Cossack volunteer group at Antratsyt in May 2014. Kozitsyn had a colorful biography and started as a prison guard in the notorious Novocherkassk "Buhanwaldt" jail before his Cossack warrior career, which left him decorated with 28 awards, including a medal from Mauritius.[37] He and Pavel Dremov in the north commanded the largest forces. Dremov was from Stakhanov in Luhansk Oblast where he had worked as a stone mason and lived with his mother. He had reportedly been to Transnistria before. Both were a law unto themselves and did not recognize the authority of the LNR leadership. Cossack behavior often worked to discredit the rebels' reputation. In *Prince*'s recollection,

> Cossacks presented a big problem. DNR also had a smaller Cossack presence and they were badly behaved. They were brave when they were drunk, and they were drunk mostly at night. They would say—why don't we go for a stroll at Donetsk airport? So they went out in their Niva [car] to chase a Ukrainian APC, and nobody saw them after that. There were many Kozitsyn people who were not taken seriously, locals and outsiders.[38]

Dremov's forces were called the 1st Cossack regiment named after a legendary Don Cossack ataman Matvei Platov. It numbered 1176 by January 1, 2015, according to the LNR "ministry of defence." Dremov led a large fighting force and enjoyed a controversial reputation. Volunteers who served under Dremov's command disagree that he was such a notorious figure, stressing his honesty, great emotional appeal and the respect he commanded. A local rebel speaking in his defense stated that, when Dremov's troops entered Debaltseve, Dremov did not seize cash from banks as was the usual practice of the time, but instead ordered banks to be safeguarded.

Cossacks tried to govern the territories they controlled in the way they could. After the retreat from Sievierodonetsk (Ukrainian, Severodonetsk in Russian) in July 2014 Dremov's troops occupied his native Stakhanov. They apprehended branches of *Privat* Bank in Pervomaisk and Stakhanov, and started to pay salaries and pensions. They introduced a Cossack radio station with songs allowed only in Russian in the areas where electricity was cut off and people could not watch TV. They attached their own "observer" (смотрящий) to Sergei Zhevlakov, a former mayor of Stakhanov until 2010, for whom the rebellion offered a second chance to return to power, and levied taxes on the remaining businesses to pay into the city budget to run schools and municipal services.

In Pervomaisk, a Cossack group armed with machineguns confronted and nearly gunned down its mayor Boris Babyi who had been loyal to the rebels and led organization of the referendum.[39] The population in Antratsyt was terrified of the Cossacks. There was no love lost between the Cossacks and the LNR leadership. Cossack commanders resented the LNR "minister of defence" Plotnitsky, a "prime minister" since August 14, who hardly ruled the territory outside Luhansk. They quarreled with the LNR leadership over the distribution of Russian aid as only single trucks out of a hundred from humanitarian convoys typically reached the northwestern towns of Stakhanov and Pervomaisk, the most remote from the Russian border.[40] The LNR leadership, in their turn, alleged that Kozitsyn was stealing coal. Ataman Kozytsin and his people were believed to control coal smuggling in three districts under his rule which were less affected by fighting.

Cossacks were obsessed with spy mania and saw Kyiv spies everywhere. One volunteer combatant from Moscow was locked twice in a dungeon and then falsely accused of treason because of a failed prisoner exchange. Only love and high-level intervention from Russia saved him from a sure execution at the hands of Dremov's Cossacks:

> I came under suspicion in the battalion and some people tried to put me into detention while I was carrying out certain tasks. Then a commander's brother was not included into the group presented for exchange by the Ukrainian side at

the last minute, and I was accused of orchestrating this. I had concussion at the time and lay bed-ridden in hospital. Little I could do.

Before that, I met a local Cossack woman at the frontlines who was in the rebel movement and we fell in love. The Cossack woman learnt that suspicion fell on me and warned me to run away. Then she started calling everybody in Russia she could think of who could protect me. When she learnt that Dremov was going to drive to the hospital and kill me, she charged at him, trying to stop him. Dremov tried to strangle her, they fought and another commander broke up the fight and rescued her. He was locked in a dungeon for several days for that.

I could have run away from the hospital. But I decided to stay put because that would have amounted to an admission of guilt and I was not guilty. I am a deeply religious person. I resorted to prayer as I thought: "If I die at the war, I will go to heaven, but I have to be pure before Him." My faith is my compass, my guiding force, and I sought strength in my faith at that hour.

Dremov arrived after a few hours later to say that everything was sorted. He added that he had no clue that such people [from Russia] were prepared to vouch for me.

GOVERNING THE TERRITORY

When protests turned militant in spring 2014, many heads of administration ran away, leaving their mostly female deputies to govern in the interim, and others went on perpetual sick leave. But others stayed and, like Sloviansk mayor Nelly Shtepa, publicly stated their allegiance to the "people's republics," only to change their mind later when it became apparent that Kyiv's power may not be over. Mariupol's mayor Yuri Khotlubey originally supported the rebellion but switched sides before his reputation in Kyiv's eyes was stained by collaboration. In some places "people's mayors" were appointed to oversee the actions of administrative personnel who did not dare to disobey people with guns. Still, the managerial elite largely left, and the rebel republics were left with few cadres with any governing capabilities.

The only individuals with recognizable political careers on the rebel side were Tsaryov and Luhansk mayor Manolis Pilavov who had been a deputy mayor before the conflict. Pavel Gubarev was quickly detained by the SBU on March 6, kept for two months until he was exchanged in May 2014, and missed the conflict gestation. Borodai told me that in his view, Gubarev suffered from a shock resulting from his captivity and the time spent at the SBU. He disappeared from public eye on his release, so that Moscow got concerned that he was repressed by DNR's "big bad wolves" and urged Borodai to find and present him, alive and well.

Until July 2014 the rebels coexisted relatively peacefully with the old administrators who were left in peace to perform their duties, but the latter failed to negotiate with them. Governor Taruta worked in Donetsk virtually unobstructed until the end of May 2014. In the meantime, the rebels were only growing stronger. This dual-power changed when Strelkov arrived in Donetsk where, in his view, the elites were either neutral or did not support the rebel cause, and there was a deficit of suitable military cadres everywhere. He decided to show who was in charge and called the mayor of Donetsk, Alexander Lukyanchenko, to press him to make a choice which side he was on. As a result of speaking to Strelkov, Lukyanchenko left the city for Kyiv at the end of July, after the security situation deteriorated. Borodai considers that dismissing Lukyanchenko was Strelkov's mistake which they quarreled about afterwards:

Lukyanchenko was a city manager and didn't bother us. Let him do what he was good at, my policy was. What he thought about ideology didn't interest me. While he was in place, Kyiv continued to pay public sector salaries. Lukyanchenko had only one request from us to move a checkpoint so that a trolleybus could pass through the street. We agreed to this as we also wanted to support the normal functioning of the city. I spoke to him once at the end of May and told him that "this is all serious and for the time to come. Don't think like that today I arrived here, tomorrow will leave and there will be a yellow-blue [Ukrainian] flag again. No, it won't." Lukyanchenko replied that he loved the city, but would not take the oath. I said, "OK, stay as you are. Call Kyiv every day if you like. Tell them that 'I don't cooperate with them, make sabotage, throw yeast into their toilets every day'"—but so that they keep sending money under you.

He left because when I went on a trip to Moscow, Strelkov in my absence shouted and stomped at him. Tried to force him to take an oath of allegiance to us. But if he took the oath, Kyiv'd stop money transfers. I asked him "Igor, dear, who would pay salaries to municipal workers now, have you thought about this? Who would run the city?" Strelkov brought me some ideologically sound field commanders as mayoral candidates, but they couldn't manage anything. We needed managers in these positions rather than some ideological бодяги (imbeciles) with machineguns.[41]

The rebels eventually got a handle on running civilian affairs, and order and service delivery was maintained through wartime measures. In Torez rubbish collection had never been that good. In Horlivka, in the words of Bezler, "Mr. Klep remains a mayor with a stamp and a signature. I protect and take care of him [he is under guard]—head shaven, dressed for the moment, sings the Soviet anthem in the morning, rises at 6 a.m. and bed at 22.30. He is being morally cleansed and learns to live within his means, not taking bribes."[42]

The disorder unleashed crime, although before July 2014 isolated incidents across a fairly large territory were too small to give the rebels a banditry image. The crime wave accelerated when the war intensified and the guerrillas were running out of money and so had to finance themselves.[43] Taking hostages for ransom, raiding businesses, expropriating cars, breaking cash machines, robbing banks and intercepting cash deliveries were widespread. Borodai estimated that around 150 assassinations happened between April and August 2014 within the rebel ranks, a phenomenon, in his view, that typically characterizes guerrilla warfare. As *Prince* tells,

> There were many dubious characters. One guy in Lugansk had been through five trials in Ukraine before. He had to be apprehended with tanks when he got out of hand in the end.[44]

At the same time, tough justice was enforced, often by cruel means, in a merciless fight against crime. In the worst case, hostage-taking, looting and rape could be punished by death, even within one's own ranks. Public executions of perpetrators periodically took place especially since the rebels could not afford to keep prisons running for long. In a few cases prison doors were opened and the inmates were offered the opportunity to join the rebels while those serving life sentences for violent offences were executed. Curfews were introduced, the sale of alcohol restricted, drunkenness in combat areas was strictly prohibited and was punishable by "community service" for civilians, such as digging trenches. The fight against drugs was conducted with great effectiveness, and most channels were ruthlessly blocked, with users left to hang out to dry.[45] When Dremov's Cossacks occupied Sievierodonetsk at the onset of the rebellion in 2014, drug dealers were shot dead and those who survived fled.

Captives were taken by both sides. *Prince* said that he sought to treat prisoners decently, forbade making them work, let them call relatives, and told them that they were not going to be killed. He explained that many army soldiers were simply law-abiding citizens who were told to go to war, and so they went. Some changed sides while in captivity. Sappers detained in Snizhne stayed with the rebels and showed them the mine fields which they had laid against them. Some captives were transferred through "green routes" into Russia, given money and explained how to reach Ukrainian consulate. There were also not so happy moments. The most gruesome were the instances when people surrendered alive and later were found dead, killed in captivity. There were also some ugly cases of mutilating prisoners by the rebels just out of drunkenness. When exchanges started, the Ukrainian side presented all sorts of people for exchange, such as rebels' relatives who stayed in the government-controlled areas, rather than actual combatants. *Prince* explained that:

I created lists of detainees. Negotiations on prisoner exchanges were very difficult. Sometimes I had information that such and such person, for example, in Komsomolsk held captives in a private dungeon and wanted to exchange them for his fighters rather than for any Ukrainian prisoners. We would then contact the commander of a person put forward for an exchange, launch a verification procedure and seek documental proof. There were also cases on both sides of trade in captives for a price of 10,000 *hryvnas*.[46]

The situation was complicated by the fact that the rebels at the beginning did not have a complete list of their own fighters because many were known only by call signs and there were no records of real names. These unidentified rebels if they were kept in private Ukrainian captivity had no means of letting their commanders know that they were alive, while the commanders did not know whom to ask for. This was especially true in the case of combatants from Russia.

Hence, the early stage of rebellion resulted in the main protagonists being formed, many of whom until recently could not imagine that they would be doing any real fighting. Quasi-governance structures popped out and propped up the (dis)order, but personal rivalries between commanders were too great, and the insurgency remained horizontally organized. The rebels improvised, using what they had in hand, from military vehicles to outright deceit, and created an insurgency of highly motivated but irregular forces, some of whom were tempted by the spoils of war. The war had indeed started.

NOTES

1. Anatol Lieven, *Chechnya: Tombstone of Russian Power* (New Haven and London: Yale University Press, 1998).

2. Bolt, 262.

3. Prince, author's interview.

4. The "battalion" was a self-designation. It does not imply a regular unit of the Army, but a more loosely organised formation of a basis of volunteer mobilization. The term is used in this sense throughout the book.

5. "Know your volunteer battalions," Kyiv Post, 9 September 2014, http://www.kyivpost.com/article/content/ukraine/know-your-volunteer-battalions-infographic-363944.html

6. Amnesty International, "Ukraine: Abuses and War Crimes by the Aidar Volunteer Battalion in the north Luhansk region," September 8, 2014. Investigation was opened into behaviour of some of its members.

7. The battalion denied its support for Kolesnik's race. See http://ru.golos.ua/uncategory/14_09_25_lider_opg_tayson_kolesnik_reshil_ispolzovat_batalon_krivbass_v_predvyiborno Golos.ua 2014

8. "Братья «Карамазовы» или от биты к байтам," October 4, 2014, http://antikor.com.ua/articles/15393-bratjja_karamazovy_ili_ot_bity_k_bajtam

9. *Amnesty International,* "Ukraine: Breaking bodies: Torture and Summary Killings in Eastern Ukraine," May 22, 2015, https://www.amnesty.org/en/documents/eur50/1683/2015/en/

10. Prince, author's interview, Moscow, May 2016.

11. Kalyvas, *The logic of violence,* 56–58.

12. According to UN OHCHR 14th report, "since 15 March 2014 until February 2016, the Office of the Military Prosecutor has investigated 726 crimes committed by members of the territorial defence battalions, including 11 crimes of killing, 12—torture, 27—arbitrary deprivation of liberty, 29—creation of a criminal gang, 6—banditry. 622 people were charged." Report on the human rights situation in Ukraine 16 February to 15 May 2016, http://www.ohchr.org/Documents/Countries/UA/Ukraine_14th_HRMMU_Report.pdf

13. Dubovoi, 198–199.

14. Jonathan Ferguson and N.R. Jenzen-Jones, "An Examination of Arms & Munitions in the Ongoing Conflict in Ukraine," Armament Research Services Research Report no. 3 (2014).

15. Author's interviews in Kyiv with eye witnesses, and in Donbas, 2014.

16. Mid-range ex-commander, author's interview, Moscow, February 2016.

17. Alexander Borodai, author's interview, Moscow, May 2016.

18. Borodai, author's interview.

19. Lavrov, "Civil War," 216.

20. Prince, author's interview, Moscow, May 2016.

21. Juchkovsky, author's interview.

22. Strelkov, author's interview. He presumably meant Dmitry Kupriyan, see a report in "Батю гривны погубили," https://www.gazeta.ru/politics/2016/03/20_a_8130713.shtml

23. Igor Strelkov, author's interview, Moscow, May 2016.

24. Alexander Borodai, author's interview, Moscow, May 2016.

25. Julia Ioffe, "I Met Igor Bezler, the Russian Rebel Who Said, "We Have Just Shot Down a Plane," 18 July 2014, https://newrepublic.com/article/118770/who-igor-bezler-russian-rebel-implicated-malaysia-flight-17

26. Shaun Walker, "An audience with Ukraine rebel chief Igor Bezler, the Demon of Donetsk," 29 July 2014, https://www.theguardian.com/world/2014/jul/29/-sp-ukraine-rebel-igor-bezler-interview-demon

27. Juchkovsky, author's interview.

28. Alexander Borodai, author's interview, Moscow, May 2016.

29. Alexander Borodai, author's interview, Moscow, May 2016.

30. Alexander Borodai, author's interview, Moscow, May 2016.

31. *Givi* is not Georgian. He claimed that he got his nickname when he had served in the Ukrainian army because of his Caucasian looks.

32. Alexander Borodai, author's interview, Moscow, May 2016.

33. Donbas resident, author's interview.

34. *Russkaya Vesna.* October 10, 2014. http://rusvesna.su/news/1413015517

35. Alexander Juchkovsky in his memories for *Sputnik i Pogrom*.

36. Author's interview in Kyiv with a Luhansk woman who happened to travel the road when one such episode took place and intervened to negotiate.

37. "Атаман, академик и князь," July 18, 2014, *Novaya Gazeta*, http://www.novayagazeta.ru/society/64479.html

38. Prince, author's interview, Moscow, May 2016.

39. Alexander Chalenko, "Экс-мэр Первомайска Борис Бабий о горячем лете 2014 года в ЛНР," 3 September 2015, http://www.politnavigator.net/ehks-mehr-pervomajjska-boris-babijj-o-goryachem-lete-2014-goda-v-lnr.html

40. *Strannik*, author's interview.

41. Alexander Borodai, author's interview, Moscow, May 2016.

42. Cited in *Colonel Cassad*. September 25, 2014. http://colonelcassad.livejournal.com/1811415.html

43. On criminal situation in Donetsk bringing the rebellion into disrepute see Pavel Gubarev, 207–208.

44. Prince, author's interview, Moscow, May 2016.

45. Dergachoff, Vladimir, "В ЛНР казаки избивали наркоманов нагайками," June 12, 2015. *Gazeta.ru* http://www.gazeta.ru/politics/2015/06/11_a_6837717.shtml

46. Prince, author's interview, Moscow, May 2016.

Chapter 7

"Hot Summer"

Military Campaign

THE WAR TOLL

The period between May 25 when Petro Poroshenko was elected president of Ukraine and September 6 when the Minsk ceasefire was signed was war, a horrible war. Heavy weapons and armed aviation were deployed, and mass casualties followed. In three years of April 2014–May 2017, 10,090 people were killed, including 2,777 civilians.[1] Sloviansk suffered from the use of multiple-rocket launchers in densely populated areas.[2] Ukraine had been saturated with weapons both because the Soviet Union was preparing to resist a Western invasion, in which Ukraine would have been in the frontline of defense and also because it is a major weapons' producer in its own right. So, while having formidable guns, the ATO commanders had no prior experience of fighting an insurgency operation in urban terrain, and perhaps did not foresee the effects that the arsenal at their disposal might produce if used in such conditions. After the war effort was upgraded, the Ukrainian army got itself into a public relations trap, as for an attacking force it is difficult to maintain a benevolent image while being engaged in combat operations. Government injustice and inadvertent mistakes were bound to provide invaluable propaganda opportunities to the irregulars.[3] Besides, such degree of escalation was unexpected. Juchkovsky notes that

> Nobody expected such level of military hostilities, as during the WWII. At first people did not even think that firearms would be used against protesters, and it was a real shock when residential quarters were shelled from howitzers. Everything that could be used, was used—aviation, tanks, even ballistic missiles. And more and more, until it became a norm, reaching a level of 1943 battles when hundreds of people died every day.[4]

In Donbas, military hostilities and civilian losses fostered the rebels' resolve to resist, achieving the opposite of the effect that Kyiv intended. The situation was the same in Chechnya when many in the republic treated general Dudayev and his political escapades with considerable skepticism, but when the Russian army and aviation started bombing them, Dudayev became a savior of the nation. In Ukraine, the government had airpower, as well as heavy artillery and cluster munitions which were used to hit large areas while irregular rebel forces mostly did not have them and in the summer of 2014 were engaged in an asymmetric warfare campaign. Illegal acts which they committed at the time included abductions, detentions, torture, murder, executions, extortion, and destruction of property are well documented.[5] However, similar abuses by the Chechen rebels against civilians in Russia in the 1990s were not documented anywhere close.[6]

Focus on looking for Russian regular troops overshadowed external analysis of the rebels' own military tactics, strategies they employed in the face of a better armed adversary led by military professional cadre, and the strengths they capitalized upon. And yet, such analysis could be useful for understanding of how modern irregular wars are conducted. The rebels' assets were high mobility of small groups, high level of initiative and improvisation, prior reconnaissance allowing for surprise effect, deception and make-belief persuading the adversary that their forces were more numerous, knowledge of local terrain, ability to operate inside the enemy territory, and fortification of city defenses. The weaknesses consisted of a lack of supplies, fighting not with weapons of choice, ill-discipline, lack of strategic depth, shortages of trained cadre, and conflicts between field commanders which resulted in a lack of coordination.

Shelling of civilian areas by the Ukrainian air force and artillery was a wake-up call that overcame the initial passivity, when citizens' militias turned into combat forces. The instinctive force was brought to life among people prepared to defend themselves with utmost aggression as they felt that their core existence was threatened. On June 2 one of the turning points of Donbas conflict occurred: eight people were killed and 20 injured in an air bombing raid on the regional administration building in the central square of Luhansk. This was the first time that civilians were killed in an attack by the Ukrainian air force who used their Su-25 "Frogfoot" ground attack aircraft.[7]

Use of firepower that hit residential areas exacerbated hostility and stimulated a desire for revenge. Moods hardened every time when something terrible happened. An iconic *Govlovka Madonna*—a 23-year-old woman killed with her 10-month-old baby girl in her hands by a Ukrainian artillery strike, became a symbol of the rebels' resistance, as *Odesa* had served as a trigger for the earlier volunteer mobilization.[8] The rebels and Donbas residents describe what they lived through: "Tochka-U [SS-21 Scarab A tactical missile] burnt a school nearby (the attack on Roven'ki in Luhansk oblast which hit residential areas). "They shelled us and dropped bombs on us. A 500 kg bomb fell into a courtyard in Lugansk."[9] A resident witness described what she saw:

> A bomb dropped, and there was a huge explosion, then screams. My husband and I ran to help the wounded. Blood was everywhere and bodies were lying on the ground. I looked up and saw something hanging from a tree. I didn't understand at first what it was, then did. It was a child's intestines. Something I'll never forget. We were trying to appeal to international human rights organisations, but they didn't react. Human Rights Watch failed to come when we were hoping they would. I got used to bombardments somehow but never could get used to the sirens. After we fled to Sevastopol, there was a parade there and sirens sounded as a part of the performance. I thought I was going to pass out and my dog that came with us from Lugansk died of a stroke on the spot.

Rebels on Retreat, But Fighting On

Sloviansk

The ATO was challenging the rebels more seriously in early summer, but their ranks which started with a few thousands also grew. After over eighty ATO troops were lost, Poroshenko decided to negotiate and on June 20 announced a ceasefire which barely held. Attacks continued and on June 24 rebels shot down a Ukrainian Mi8 helicopter. Kyiv amassed troops and weapons, but was not going ahead with an all-out offensive on Sloviansk. Ukrainian commanders were reluctant to engage in urban warfare with the certainty of heavy casualties and potentially face the Russian paratroopers invented by Strelkov. Destruction remained limited, mostly resulting from erroneous targeting or because some of the rebels' mobile fire positions were in residential areas, which attracted return fire. The Ukrainian tactics appeared to be designed to wear the rebels down so they would either surrender or leave. *Prince* describes his understanding of the situation at the time as he held the frontline:

> Poroshenko wasn't about to demolish the town completely. The fight was to control the heights. The density of fire was very intense, but casualties in Semyonovka were light because we dug in very deeply. What matters was the quality of defence, the way you dug in. It was unclear at the time why the Ukrainian side shelled us mercilessly but then wouldn't launch an attack after the artillery prepared the ground for it.[10]

The significance of Sloviansk was that while it held, it attracted the main brunt of the Ukrainian offensive. Eventually, the Ukrainian military started mining areas around the town and it appeared that the rebels were going to be trapped inside. A local fighter defending a block post recalled a 20-tank-strong attack against his unit which was armed only with machineguns. Chief of staff *Mikhailo* noted that "it was clear that we had to leave." *Prince*, on the contrary, believed that Sloviansk was ready for defense, was no longer bombed from the air and could have been held. But this is not what happened. Feeling abandoned by Russia, Strelkov, at this junction, found himself in charge of a situation which he was not prepared for:

> The special operation finished by the end of May. And then the war started. I never had to supervise large-scale military operations involving different types of armed forces. I was taught military theory but didn't have the relevant experience. My intelligence specialisation was in "frontline and beyond frontline operations."
>
> In general, the experience of small local wars was of little help for full-scale warfare, like in Donbas. It was wholly incomparable. At Yampol [where Ukrainian army launched an offensive on June 19], for example, the rebels were running away under artillery bombardment because they were so frightened. I couldn't blame them because I was scared myself. But I couldn't run like them because I was the commander. In Chechnya, I had the support of the state. I could call artillery or aviation in. Russia was behind me. In this case, the state resources were deployed against me. It was an incommensurably different balance of forces. I was unable to defend the territories any further with such forces and armaments.[11]

On July 1 Poroshenko announced large offensive to defeat the rebels. Ukrainian push included the use of Su-24 bombers and powerful *Smerch* 300 mm multiple launch rocket (MLR) systems although the cities of Sloviansk and Kramatorsk were full of civilian population. On July 2, Kramatorsk was struck with 9M55K antipersonnel cluster munitions, and Tochka and Tochka-U short range ballistic missiles were shortly used as well.[12] Following that, Strelkov ordered the retreat and on July 5–6 the rebels suddenly left Sloviansk. He gave an impression that, like in the battle for Stalingrad, he personally was going to stand until the last drop of blood. *Prince* recalled that Strelkov said farewell to the withdrawing fighters, and he thought Strelkov would stay, but he withdrew as others did, and the retreat shattered him. Strelkov was not well-received in Donetsk, which by then had its own power-holding.

The city was given up without Ukrainian ground offensive, because, as Wilson expresses, "Ukrainian blood was worth more than Russian treasure."[13] In the end, Sloviansk was not taken by an assault, but achieved by a means of 3-month siege, and Strelkov was allowed to escape. The ATO command missed the sudden retreat which allowed Strelkov to withdraw military vehicles, most of the weapons and hundreds of fighters. The same pattern was applied in the town of Siversk in Luhanska oblast, which the rebels left overnight and the residents woke up in the morning to discover that it was in nobody's hands until the ATO forces moved in after a few hours.

There were bitter recriminations between the former combatants whether Sloviansk could have held further without Russian direct military help, and Strelkov's argument was that it could not. In his interview he maintained that he had been fully convinced that he could count only on himself and own forces, and retreating at the right moment saved them from destruction. There were some rebels who maintained that Strelkov should have died fighting in Sloviansk, that his death should have become a tragic symbol of resistance and an inspiration for the future fighters for the *Russian World* cause. Another criticism was that he did not warn all rebel units of the impeding retreat. There were fighters who did not align themselves with his command and they learnt about it only when Ukrainian forces entered and they had to make individual escapes. It was pointed out that Horlivka was not surrendered by Bezler despite the situation there being very tough. Several of my respondents mentioned that Strelkov was asked [by somebody in Russian officialdom—not clear by whom] why he "surrendered the town without an order when weapons were being supplied to him," but it is not known who was supposed to give this order.

Other Donetsk Theatres

As Sloviansk distracted the main conglomeration of the Ukrainian forces, the areas to the south and east had the time to build their defenses, but, in Strelkov's view, *Vostok*'s operations around Donetsk were pretty disastrous, an opinion which was confirmed by Borodai: "the tactical planning of Marinovka combat was a failure. Khodakovsky's first three operations—Donetsk airport, Marinovka and a Basai base–were rather unfortunate. We took the base, but the arsenal which was our target, blew up." In Strelkov's view, *Oplot* was fighting slightly better, but Zakharchenko and Khodakovsky were not the military geniuses and had a limited talent for war.

Vostok's attack in May 2014 to capture Donetsk airport was ill prepared with poor reconnaissance, as a result of which the enemy's strength was underestimated. The battalion had no means for air defense and was vulnerable to the strikes of Ukrainian bombers when they came. Worst of all, it shot down a truckload of rebel fighters who died in friendly fire and *Vostok*, to their horror, discovered that those whom they thought were the enemy, wore St. George's ribbons. The rebels lost fifty people, quite a few of them were volunteer combatants from Russia who arrived just the day before. The next attack on June 5 on Marinovka checkpoint south of Savur Mohyla was aimed at clearing a corridor to the border from Donetsk. However, *Vostok* failed to do this when the fighters were a mile away from the border and the Russians offered no support from the other side. Marynivka failure was painful for *Vostok* after a recent unsuccessful offensive at Donetsk airport. After that, a share of its fighters went to Russia where they underwent military training.

The war was slowly but surely arriving on the doorstep of previously tranquil areas and the retreat from Sloviansk drove the point home. Still, the war was not yet total and civilian life continued alongside fighting. When 2,000 hungry and battered troops of the Sloviansk brigade entered Donetsk on July 5 and discovered a peaceful megapolis with open restaurants and functional public transport, they drank and looted for a week until the military command put a stop to it.

The government troops were gaining more ground moving onto Donetsk and Makiivka. Strelkov surrendered Karlivka (in Ukrainian, Karlovka in Russian) on his retreat from the north which allowed the Ukrainian side to capture Piski (in Ukrainian, Peski in Russian) and Avdiivka, and opened the road onto Donetsk. *Vostok* had to retreat from the flanks and came under heavy artillery fire as a result. Strelkov believed that the DNR-held areas throughout the oblast were not ready for defense. He ordered most of his battalions to redeploy from Donetsk to Snizhne, Shakhtarsk, Mospyne (in Ukrainian, Mospino in Russian) and Ilovaisk to strengthen their defenses, but there was no overall command and control, and relations between commanders were complicated, with Bezler playing his own fiddle. In early summer the Ukrainian side was in a better shape: it succeeded in preparing for the offensive and mobilized troops and weaponry, and did not suffer many setbacks. The rebel forces on the contrary were in a deep material crisis. Their firepower was nowhere near that of the ATO. They only started to be supplied in modest quantities from Russia and waged war mostly with the weapons and military vehicles seized from the enemy. Training camps for the rebels at the grounds in Rostov oblast in Russia and in Donbas were set up in the summer. Still, many trainees started from zero and although the training was very intense, it took time to prepare combat-ready fighters while the war was in a full swing. After the training, the units were equipped by the weapons seized from the Ukrainian depots in Crimea and sent to the battlefields. It is unsurprising that Russia was the place from where the rebels got help, but it did not mean that they always had what they wanted. There were other forces and opportunities that came from the region itself, from elsewhere in Ukraine and from the world outside.

Moscow hesitated for a long time about supplying weapons to the rebels beyond those seized in Crimea. It did not know whom it could trust, because it was hard to be sure which of the no-name warlords apart from Strelkov and Borodai were reliable, could handle complex weaponry and were not outright bandits. It eventually identified a number of commanders such as Mozgovoi and Bezler who appeared more coherent and they were brought to Moscow for "consultations," but the task was not an easy one, as the United States realized when it had to distinguish between "moderate rebels" in Syria from not quite so moderate. From what is possible to conclude from trusted rebel sources, *военторг* (literally "the military supply store," a euphemism for the Russian deliveries of weapons and ammunition) started working in earnest since July. Subsequently, heavy weapons were acquired, such as *Buratino* fuel-air multiple-rocket launcher system which creates fireballs and could be fired at a long range. The Ukrainian side tried to use tanks, but, as Lavrov wrote, "the capabilities of Ukrainian armed forces, the conditions at the combat theatre and the nature of the conflict have not been conducive to the use of tanks for independent mobile warfare operations." Moreover, the Ukrainian armed forces received a delivery of upgraded tanks only in September 2014 which were originally destined for export, such as to the Democratic Republic of Congo.[14]

Retreat in Luhanska Oblast

Fighting in the Luhanska Oblast ignited in the north. The oblast had an advantage of a better access to the Russian border, but there were fewer commanders with military skills. Cossack forces of Pavel Dremov and Alexei Mozgovoi' *Prizrak* occupied the so-called Slavonic Shield—a northern industrialized triangle. It included Lysychansk with its oil refinery, which was Rosneft's main oil processing facility in Ukraine, Sievierodonetsk with its Azot fertilizer producer, and Rubizhne (in Ukrainian, Rubezhnoe in Russian). They proclaimed independent "Lysychansk and Severodonetsk People's Republics," did not want to recognize the "LNR leadership" and aligned themselves with Strelkov. Dremov at first commanded a Stakhanov Cossack self-defense force which evolved into a "Severodonetsk Garrison" with up to 500 fighters.

Before Poroshenko's election as president, the security situation in Luhansk city was not particularly tense. However, the war came in June and soon became very brutal. After June 2 aerial bombardment on the central square, on June 14 a military transport Il-76 MD which was supposed to bring reinforcements to the besieged Ukrainian troops in the Luhansk airport was brought down by a rebel strike, in which forty-nine Ukrainian servicemen died. Since then, the areas surrounding the airport witnessed ferocious fighting because the ATO side aimed to secure air routes. The rebels suffered a defeat when a Ukrainian attack led by the *Aidar* battalion captured the town of Schastia (Happiness) near Luhansk on June 14–15 where the power station was located that supplied electricity to the most of the oblast. Rebel sources reported that the attack was accompanied by heavy shelling, as a result of which about 100 civilians died. On June 16 Russian VGTRK TV channel aired the video, which showed that *Aidar* was committing mass atrocities against civilians in Schastia including extra-judicial killings. The report was rejected by Kyiv.

On June 17 the fighting moved to the Metallist village 10 km away from Luhansk, with *Aidar* in the lead. The VGTRK crew came under mortar fire from the direction where *Aidar*'s positions were located and two Russian journalists were killed. Moscow accused the Ukrainian pilot Nadia Savchenko who reportedly fought at *Aidar* in correlating the fire and deliberate targeting of the clearly identified media crew. Savchenko's defense was that she was abducted by the rebels in Luhansk Oblast and transported to Russia, and her prosecution was illegal. The Russian side claimed that she attempted to cross the border disguised as a refugee and was thus detained.[15] Savchenko spent nearly two years in Russian jail, with the world leaders appealing for her release until she was finally freed in 2016.

In July, the countryside around Luhansk city was falling under the government control. The ATO forces succeeded in cutting off a strategic Luhansk–Krasnyi Luch transport artery and seized Heorhiivka (in Ukrainian, Georgievka in Russian) through the combined strikes of Lviv paratroopers and *Aidar* fighters. The offensive spearheaded by *Aidar* battalion and backed by the armored vehicles attempted to storm the Luhansk airport but it was strongly defended, including by a Serb volunteer squadron. Still, the ATO forces almost surrounded the city, trapping the rebels and civilians inside.

The situation for *Prizrak* and the Cossacks in the northern triangle got tough. The ATO advances to their south posed a risk of their isolation from the main LNR forces and the Russian border. The Ukrainian tactic at Lysychansk was similar to that in Sloviansk, that is, to surround the city and trap the rebels inside. Strelkov ordered Mozgovoi to withdraw from Lysychansk to Alchevsk before it was too late, as, in his view, the city was indefensible. Mozgovoi, he maintained, would have found himself in a worse situation that Strelkov in Sloviansk, and had to fight his way through to the Russian border with heavy losses. On July 18 the Lysychansk oil refinery was set on fire by a Ukrainian artillery strike.[16] Following Strelkov's order, Mozgovoi and Dremov retreated from Lysychansk and Sievierodonetsk on July 22, 2014.

Other rebel commanders and Moscow apparently disagreed on the inevitability of giving up the northern cities. They pointed out that Mozgovoi withdrew without a fight. Indeed, there was no Ukrainian ground offensive, no street fighting or real storm of the cities. Ukrainian artillery continued shelling for a while after the rebels left probably unaware that they were already gone. Reportedly, a senior Russian Presidential Administration member when he met Mozgovoi, inquired why he surrendered Lysychansk, to which the latter replied that he could have been killed. His interlocutor retorted, "And why did you go into war, then?"[17] Retreats from Sloviansk, Kramatorsk, Lysychansk and Sievierodonetsk sealed the first phase of the war which saw the rebels lose several cradles of their uprising, in which the May referenda were organized and from where many fighters originated. Mariupol was already lost in mid-June. The question was how long they could continue.

A War of Total Destruction

Cutting Novorossiya in two

The war intensified in July when both sides used hundreds of armored vehicles and heavier artillery than they did before. At some point the rebels were in a critical condition, but Moscow finally opened the *voentorg* tap and increased its supplies, as a result of which the rebel ranks grew. They could arm more willing people than in May when they had been vastly outgunned. Manpower advantage of the Ukrainian side became less overwhelming and they lost a monopoly on heavy artillery strikes to which the rebels could now respond in kind. Fighting was in earnest, with ground offensives, merciless shelling and a war of total destruction, such as a rebel attack on July 11 on base camp at Zelenopillya (in Ukrainian, Zelenopolie in Russian) in Luhanska oblast, in which 35 Ukrainian troopers were killed and a large number of heavy armory was destroyed.[18] This was markedly different from the earlier period.

The military situation in July was such that no single frontline existed and the eastern part of Donbas was a patchwork of the rebel and ATO forces running into each other. Borderline areas kept changing hands and there was no certainty who held which segment. The Ukrainian command learnt a lesson that a forward-going offensive without securing the flanks and military reconnaissance was a precarious tactic, as the rebels launched unexpected counterattacks. The ATO strategy changed and was aimed at creating a wider surround of the rebel-held territories which should get narrower as the offensive progressed closer to their positions. Relentless attacks on different directions appeared chaotic, but they followed an overall strategy designed by the minister of defense Valeriy Heletey and head of the general chief of staff Viktor Muzhenko to cut off the rebels from Ukraine's border with Russia, push them inside and trap in a gigantic cauldron.

This did not quite work, and the loss of control over the border in July dispirited the Ukrainian command. Their tactics became less ambitious, but more dangerous because the plan was more realistic. Rather than encircling the whole area, the tongs of the ATO offensive were reduced to separate the Donetsk rebels from Luhansk. Cutting Novorossiya into two was possible because they did not form a united territory and large areas in the countryside were no man's land. The immediate goal was to force the DNR to surrender. LNR, which had a more secure access to the Russian border, could have been dealt with later and probably would not have required a massive use of force. The calculation was that the rebels were likely to run away to Russia rather than fight a hopeless battle. Separation of Donetsk from the Russian supplies could have been fatal for Novorossiya rebellion.

Attacks along the whole front continued toward this purpose. The operation at Debaltseve already disrupted important communication lines between the LNR and the DNR. The first part of the strategy was accomplished. The Ukrainian forces almost cut across Novorossiya, and also threatened to block Horlivka where the situation was very difficult. However, the split maneuver was risky because the corridor where the Ukrainian troops were positioned was long and narrow, and vulnerable to a simultaneous attack from the north and the south which could trap them in.

Southern Cauldron: Loss of control over the Russian border

The Ukrainian border troops offered a spirited defense in Donetsk oblast, where *Vostok* failed to take Marynivka in the south and the border remained under the government control. In June, the Ukrainian command sought to secure firm hold over the Russian border which was wobbly after several rebel attacks. On June 18 the ATO launched a ground offensive toward the border by the combined forces drawn from several brigades and territorial battalions. Initially, it proceeded with no problem in the countryside, and Kyiv announced that control had been restored. However, when it moved to the urban settlements of Krasnodon, famous for partisan operations during World War II which lived up to tradition, and Sverdlovsk, the real fighting began. Hundreds of refugees poured into Russia and were hit by gunfire presumably in erroneous targeting; at least three civilians died who already crossed into the Russian territory. On June 21, 80 Ukrainian border guards also crossed escaping heavy shelling. Adjacent Russian borderlands were full of troops. Military airfields were deployed in an open countryside, Grad missile systems stood ready in forested terrain and "polite people" were hiding in the bushes, but their guns were silent and did not gear into action. Eventually, communication lines over Mius river were cut off, and the ATO side could not move military vehicles across this water artery.

The ATO forces pressed on, and in early July Dolzhansky checkpoint was taken. The rebels were struggling to hold on in Chervony Partyzan (in Ukrainian, Krasnyi Partizan in Russian) in the vicinity of the Gukovo and Izvarino checkpoints. Sverdlovsk was destroyed by then, and the Ukrainian army proceeded with the offensive. While public opinion in Ukraine and Russia concentrated on the debacle of Strelkov's retreat from Sloviansk, the rebel fortunes were actually helped by his brigade's arrival in Donetsk. As a "DNR minister of defence," Strelkov knew that they could not afford to lose the border. He took charge, sent commander *Prapor* to strengthen defenses at Savur Mohyla and moved reserves to the border. *Azov* battalion's attack was repelled, and the rebels' counteroffensive started, this time occasionally aided by artillery shelling from across the Russian border. The distance between the rebel units and the border in some places was in hundreds of meters, but neither side could prevail. When the ATO forces almost sealed the border, the rebels attacked from Savur Mohyla from inside Ukrainian territory. Heavy fighting broke out at Marynivka again and Ukrainian forces got trapped in Dyakove to the east.

On July 11, a Southern Cauldron between Savur-Mohyla and Izvarino was closed, in which forces from the 72, 79, and 24 army brigades found themselves trapped. According to eyewitness accounts cited by Norin, this time the rebel offensive was aided by the Russian artillery from across the border. Moscow's justification for the fire was that it had to provide cover for fleeing civilians to let them escape. Rebel sources maintained that the Ukrainian troops had an opportunity to break free from the cauldron, but their unit commanders did not realize that they were being surrounded and no orders to retreat from their high command came until it was too late. On July 15 the rebels occupied Stepanivka village next to Savur Mohyla and on July 16 finally took Marynivka which held on the longest. The last way out of the cauldron was closed. The survived Ukrainian soldiers were crossing *en masse* into Russia, preferring this option to being captured by the brutalized war rebels. Evacuation of the battle wounded was organized on the Russian side, and sometimes Ukrainian troopers and rebel fighters found themselves in the same Russian hospitals. Helicopters of Russian Civil Emergencies Ministry airlifted heavy casualties to medical facilities inside the country.

The rebels secured a firm hold on the border on August 4 when the 72nd Ukrainian brigade's backbone was broken: over 400 of its members abandoned their armored vehicles and crossed into Russia, where a half of them chose to stay. The last troops still trapped in the Southern Cauldron and receiving no orders from their superiors, made a desperate dash out on August 7–8. The blockade was lifted, but the troops were running out of food and fuel, and were completely exhausted. The loss of the border control was a debacle for Kyiv and a gain for the rebels. In Norin's assessment, successful operation of the Southern Cauldron was due to Strelkov's military planning.[19]

Tragedy in the Air

The death toll was in hundreds, although hard to establish with any certainty at the time.[20] People were internally displaced in Ukraine and, according to

UN High Commissioner for Refugees (UNHCR), reached 140,000 in mid-August.[21] This was a considerable underestimate because as of February 2016, the number of registered IDPs in Ukraine totaled 1.63 million, according to the Ministry of Social Policy.[22] Refugees were also fleeing into Russia and 4.3 million of Ukraine's citizens crossed the Russian border in 2014. Out of them, 3 million returned and in 2016 1.3 million stayed in Russia.[23] Neither side covered themselves in glory as far as civilian life was concerned. On July 23, the International Committee of the Red Cross (ICRC) issued a News Release calling the fighting in eastern Ukraine a "non-international armed conflict and urging all parties to comply with international humanitarian law.[24]

Human Rights Watch documented human rights abuses by the Ukrainian government in Donbas for the first time in May 2014, such as the use of mortars and other weapons in and around populated areas. It issued an open letter to the president stating that "criminal conduct by the insurgents does not relieve the Ukrainian forces of their obligations to act in accordance with international law."[25] The war pattern reminded that of Chechnya under Yeltsin when residential areas were indiscriminately bombed from ground and air by the Russian military. As the war intensified, the rebels were locating their military assets in the densely populated areas and "both armed insurgents and government forces violated laws of war by using weaponry indiscriminately, including unguided rockets in civilian areas. Both sides fired salvos of Grad rockets."[26] Altogether, fourteen proven cases of ballistic missile strikes by the ATO were documented.[27] Human Rights Watch confirmed the use of cluster munitions which the rebels had been alleging: "Ukrainian government forces used cluster munitions in populated areas in Donetsk city,"[28] stating that this may amount to war crimes. However, the alleged use of white phosphorus was not independently confirmed.

The government held a military advantage in that it could bomb the rebels from the air and civilian casualties were sustained in air raids. IDPs from Sloviansk described to the UN Human Rights Monitoring Mission (HRMM) that the air force was shelling the city and bombed a kindergarten.[29] Air raids intensified in July. On July 2, Stanitsa Luhanska was shelled twice by air strikes and over ten civilians were killed, eleven wounded and buildings were destroyed. At least eleven people were killed by shrapnel and eight were wounded in an air strike on Snizhne on July 15, and a civilian was killed in the air strike near Gorlovka on July 11. On July 13, two civilians were killed in Krasnohorivka in the Donetsk Oblast in similar circumstances. On July 15, the Luhansk mayor announced that seventeen civilians had been killed in residential areas during July 14 attacks and seventy-three people received wounds.[30]

The rebels tried to protect the areas they held by all possible means and their efforts to acquire air defense systems were not unusual in the circumstances. In spring, Mozgovoi's *Prizrak* seized two MANPADS-equipped vehicles from the Ukrainian troops which were then used to shoot the first aircraft in Luhansk Oblast. *Strela* and *Igla* complexes were apprehended by Strelkov's forces in Sloviansk where the first downing of a Ukrainian aircraft happened in April. Altogether, ten helicopters, nine fighter jets and three military transport planes were lost in the period of active fighting, according to the Ukrainian air force representative.[31] There were other measures including using Ukrainian war prisoners as human shields. On June 14, after two people were killed and eight injured during an airstrike in Horlivka, Bezler's group threatened to place detainees on the roof of a city municipal building, who included five servicemen from the Kirovograd region and two 25th army brigade officers.[32] After the rebels' air defense capabilities strengthened and some twenty fixed-wing aircraft and military helicopters were lost by the Ukrainians, the air raids mostly stopped.[33]

This was the backdrop against which on July 17, 2014, the Malaysian Airlines flight MH17, en route from Amsterdam to Kuala Lumpur, was downed in the war-torn eastern Ukraine killing all 298 people on board. This tragedy occurred in a senseless, devastating war in which as much as 50,000 could have died (civilians and servicemen)[34] and continued to do so. There was a glimpse of hope that the scale of the disaster was such that the sides would be shocked by inhumanity of the war, come to their senses, stop fighting and start talking. This did not happen, and instead the incident led to a sharp rise in tensions between Russia and the West.

The investigation by the Dutch Safety Board (DSB) in October 2015 found that the plane crashed after being hit by a Russian-made *Buk* missile which exploded above the cockpit, causing the plane to break up in mid-air. The board criticized Ukraine's government for leaving its airspace open to civilian traffic. In September 2016, the Joint Investigation Team (JIT)[35] from the Netherlands, Australia, Belgium, Malaysia and Ukraine reported on the interim findings. It said that the evidence showed the *Buk* missile system had been brought in from Russian territory and was fired from a field controlled by pro-Russian fighters. The crash was caused by the detonation of a Russian-made 9N314M-type warhead carried on the 9M38M1 missile, launched from an area of about 320 sq km in the eastern part of Ukraine. The JIT said that it had been able to track the course of the missile trailer from Russia to the launch site and back into Russian territory following the downing of the plane. It did not state who fired the missile and for what purpose.

The Russian reaction was to reject the findings. The Kremlin said that Russian MoD radar data from Rostov Oblast showed no evidence of a missile flying from the direction the JIT investigation pointed at.[36] Almaz-Antey, the

Russian *BUK* manufacturer, argued that the prosecutors' findings were not supported by technical evidence and ignored the damage to the port engine. The hit sustained by the Boeing did not match the likely damage which would have been inflicted by the type of a missile upon which the international investigators modeled their findings. The older-generation missile which hit the plane was no longer in use in the Russian army and could not have been fired from the modern system they had, but the Ukrainian army still had those old Buk missile systems. Almaz-Antey version was that the missile had been launched from Zaroshenske which was under Kyiv rather than rebel-held Pervomais'ke village near Snizhne.

The rebels admitted that they had a *Buk* launch system, but maintained that it was in Donetsk at the time where they paraded it in full view.[37] By mid-July, the rebels had inflicted damage on the Ukrainian air force, but Kyiv still had six SU-25 bombers and military helicopters in working order which continued with the air raids. The desire of the rebels to acquire a *Buk* had its logic in this context. Aerial bombardments significantly decreased after the fatal shooting, explained Alexander Rahr.[38] The context was that ill-trained rebel forces had been under aerial bombardment for some time and may have been under high level aerial surveillance pinpointing their positions. Forces under this sort of pressure were likely to make mistakes in identifying aircraft targets if not properly trained and particularly if they observed an aircraft flying at a high altitude with a similar profile to a sur-veillance aircraft.

The investigation was aimed to finalize in 2018 but the interim findings did not produce an effect of establishing the truth yet. In May 2017 jour-nalistic investigation in Russia uncovered evidence putting the whole story in a completely new light, but it has not been independently confirmed.[39] If the JIT had included not only Ukrainian, but Russian experts, the "truth gap" could have been overcome, but the distrust appeared unbridgeable. The problem was that the sides did not respond to each other's arguments, but pursued their own lines, leaving an impression that everybody had things to hide. The Russian side changed the story several times which did not add to its credibility. Moscow and Washington took two years to release their radar and satellite data. Ukrainians did not provide information on the whereabouts of their Buk missile systems or transcripts of their military and air traffic control radio calls. Rebels might have had another Buk in addition to the one identified. What the public believed depended on their attitudes toward the warring parties and interpreted the findings in that light. Those who were convinced that Russia was the culprit remained that way, while the rebels and their sympathizers casted doubt on the report as politically biased and one-sided.[40] Those who did not know what to believe continued to be at a loss.

Savur Mohyla

One of the key battles of the campaign was for Savur-Mohyla (in Ukrainian; in Russian, Saur-Mogila), a strategic height in the Donets upland, located five kilometers from the Russian border in Shakhtarsk district in Donetsk Oblast. Originally a tumulus, Savur-Mohyla offered excellent visibility over enemy movements on the barren terrain stretching for dozens of kilometers and, for those armed with mortars, provided an ideal position for shelling across the whole space stretching to the border. Moreover, Savur Mohyla overhung the main highway at Snizhne and Torez, strategically positioned on the way to Donetsk. This is when fascination with the military history of the rebel commanders came useful because this is where the battle resembling the World War II repeated itself. In summer 1943 the Soviet Mius Front command considered that it was vital to wrest control over Savur Mohyla from the German troops. The offensive witnessed several unsuccessful attempts to storm it which was associated with great losses, and was finally taken in August 1943, paving the way to a major Soviet advance westwards. Mindful of its strategic significance and of history lessons, the rebels moved to occupy the empty tumulus on June 7 to prevent it from falling into the enemy hands and to protect their defense lines to the east of Donetsk. They also deployed fighters at Snizhne to secure the rear, thus reducing their vulnerability.

The Ukrainian 79th airmobile brigade had tried unsuccessfully to storm Savur Mohyla since mid-June. On July 6 DNR rebels were attacked by the Azov battalion, but fought off. Azov fighters were weakened because many were bitten by snakes when they got into Khomutovska Steppe nature reserve and lacked remedy against snake poison.[41] However, their efforts intensified against the backdrop of a massive ATO offensive along the whole front in July. The engagement required pulling considerable resources on both sides which was harder on the outnumbered rebels, but they could not afford to relax their grip on the height. Their fortunes were helped when they shot down two Ukrainian SU-25 ground-attack aircraft on July 23. Ukrainian attempts to reinforce their trapped troops, so they can break out of their encirclement and replenish the stocks of their trapped troops by airdrop operations halted after one transport plane and one SU-25 ground-attack aircraft were shot. Presidential Office declared that the elevated height was in Ukrainian hands on July 28, but had to withdraw the statement. What happened was this: an army unit drove to the top but concluded that it was not possible to deploy on its barren ground and being surrounded by the enemy's artillery. Facing a mortal danger, the commander decided to withdraw and saved the lives of his troops. He was put on trial as his actions caused embarrassment to Kyiv.

The ATO troops finally took Savur Mohyla on August 12, thus opening the way on Donetsk which could threaten the survival of the rebellion. A small, but capable detachment of Ukrainian 8th Spetznaz regiment who previously fought at Sloviansk, Kramatorsk, and at Schastia, deployed there. After Savur Mohyla fell, Ukrainian forces received an opportunity to launch an offensive toward the Russian border, but did not use it. They were exhausted, suffered heavy losses, and were running out of supplies as their communication lines were overextended. Some troops were trapped in a cauldron at Shakhtarsk. The battle for Ilovaisk was coming. Later on, after the ceasefire was agreed, the rebels and Ukrainian volunteers were engaged together in a cleanup operation at Savur Mohyla. In the midst of scotched earth, they were finding the remains of their slain fighters and those of the Soviet soldiers who had been killed in 1943 and buried them together. In the words of one rebel who took part in it, "Saur Mogila was a mixture of ordnance, metal and torn-out body parts."[42]

Ilovaisk

The ATO tactics became to encircle each city one by one, lay siege to it, and then storm it when the moment was ripe. When the Southern Cauldron was closed, efforts were made to surround smaller cities of Snizhne, Torez, Krasnyi Luch, and Shakhtarsk where heavy fighting went on, and the ATO forces attacked Miusynsk from the South. Ukrainian army tried to seize some of the cities to turn them into a launchpad for further attacks, but the assaults were repelled, such as the attempted storm of Shakhtarsk on July 31 when twenty-one men were lost, and none was taken. An attempt to attack Horlivka from the east was made from Debaltseve, to where fifteen ATO tanks broke into, which threatened to get to Donetsk and block it. Holding on to Debaltseve was important for the rebels given that it is a major transportation knot, but it was lost on July 28.

The rebel command was determined to prevent the loss of Ilovaisk because the town was strategically positioned for their defenses. Its capture would have enabled the ATO forces to gain control over the H21 highway at Khartsyzsk and Zugres which connected Donetsk with the rest of the rebel-held territory to the east and eventually to threaten Donetsk. The Ukrainian tactic was to cut off the town from the western direction. The rebel fighters began evacuation of the remaining residents and making preparations to resist the coming attack. It began on August 10, in which several territorial battalions participated, such as Zakarpattia (Ivano-Frankivsk), Dnipro–1, Shakhtarsk, Kherson, Svityaz', Azov, Mirotvorets (Peacekeeper), Donbas, and Krivbas, aided by heavy artillery of the military.

Ilovaisk was defended by a battle-hardened *Somali* battalion under *Givi*'s command who originated from the town and included some experienced fighters from the "Slavyansk Brigade." As the battle progressed, fresh units from *Vostok* and *Oplot* were moved in and launched counterstrikes, while the Ukrainian artillery shelled the town. Soon the rebels were joined by

Motorola's *Sparta* squadron which acted as a crisis response unit rushing to different battles where the going was tough. *Givi* desperately tried to hold on, moving his resources around, which gave an illusion that the rebels were more numerous than they really were when they kept suddenly appearing at different places.

On August 18, an intensive Ukrainian shelling and deployment of army reinforcements led to an advance, Ilovaisk was encircled and part of it taken; street fighting broke out. Intensity of fire and smoke was such that metal was melting. Neither side knew who was in control in each place and their units often got mixed up. As a Ukrainian trooper later recalled, "in the Second World War, it was clear who were 'ours' (кто были наши) and who the enemy was—they spoke and looked German, had uniforms. Everybody looked the same in this situation, spoke Russian and was dressed in all sorts of gear. It was a total confusion."[43] Still, neither side could overpower the other and win the overall battle. The ATO weakness was that its rear was only protected by the Zakarpattia battalion and several smaller units manning block posts, which turned to their disadvantage later.

Holding on by a Thread

In August, when the frontline moved to the main urban agglomerations in the west, positional warfare began. The Ukrainian side was unable to storm major cities and instead shelled them with heavy artillery from outside, to which the rebels responded with fire. The rebels mostly held cities and towns, but the surrounding countryside was often occupied by the government's troops or was changing hands. Borodai maintained that they successfully defended Horlivka, Makiivka, and Donetsk and retreated only when there was an overwhelming superiority in men and firepower: "when a block post of 20 men is attacked by 20 tanks, what can you do?" In the end, numerically stronger and better armed Ukrainian side seized several towns and villages from the rebels. ATO forces occupied Karlivka and Pervomais'ke in Donetsk Oblast, but an attempted storm of Horlivka failed and a Ukrainian tank was destroyed in the attack. The city continued to hold. The ATO forces tried to encircle Luhansk from the east to cut it from the Russian border and from the west via Lutuhyne (in Ukrainian, Lutugino in Russian) and Luhansk airport, where another cauldron was created. This strategy was almost accomplished.

In August Kyiv proclaimed that a military victory was days away. The ATO forces seized settlements on the strategic communication lines cutting off different groups of rebels from each other. This further undermined their ability to move around and send reinforcements where they were most needed. By August 10 the Ukrainians blocked the approaches to Donetsk–Makiivka–Horlivka agglomeration, where they were met with ferocious resistance and unable to move forward. The LNR was in a really bad shape by then. The ATO troops laid a siege on Luhansk and seized some ground inside the city on August 18; they were also completing their maneuver to isolate and block Alchevsk defended by *Prizrak*, and occupied the villages nearby. Rebels still fought for Luhansk and Stanitsa Luhanska under an unrelenting artillery fire.

However, the Ukrainian side sustained heavy casualties in several failed attacks and more armored vehicles were seized by the rebel groups: in the week of August 16–23 reportedly seventy-nine T-64 tanks, ninety-four Armored Infantry Fighting Vehicles (AIFV), fifty-seven armored personnel carriers (APC), and twenty-four "Grad" artillery systems were captured.[44] The rebel resistance continued: they fought back at Ilovaisk and on August 19 the ATO troops were forced on retreat at Stanitsa Luhanska. A counteroffensive was launched at Torez and Snizhne. Ukrainian *Shakhtarsk* battalion continued to be trapped in a cauldron and the rebels still had control over most of the border.

While their troops were fighting, the commanders had to decide if they would continue to hold on and, if so, for how long they could do it. Decisive help from Russia was not coming, despite weapons' and ammunition supplies. Combatants got calls from their parents urging them to come home before they were all killed. Strelkov issued an order to withdraw from Donetsk, but Antiufeev dismissed the order, and the local commanders—Zakharchenko, Khodakovsky, and Alexei Dikiy, a former Donetsk police chief—refused to give up the city. It was Strelkov who was given up in the end—on August 14 he resigned as the DNR "minister of defence." In *Prince*'s view,

> The rebels were in such grave situation through their own fault because people were badly organised. Military conscript points in each town were answerable to their own field commanders and did not send individuals with appropriate military experience to where they were needed. Preparation and intelligence collection were non-existent.[45]

In August, the senior leaders who knew the true state of affairs felt that they were fighting a losing battle and faced annihilation. *Prince* expressed that "We thought that we would separate in the woods and dig down there in small groups." Strelkov recalls the lowest point of the rebellion, when he felt it was hitting the bottom:

> At the beginning of August, the only hope was for a miracle. The rebels' spirits were very high, but I was aware of the overall situation and didn't know how to get out of it. Retreat is the most difficult technical moment in military planning. I thought that we'd have to prepare for street fighting in Donetsk and then make a corridor to Russia's border in order to withdraw with the fighters, their families and our supporters.[46]

Both Borodai and Strelkov felt sure that they faced death. Borodai reflected on his time at DNR:

> As a sober-minded person, I thought most of the time that the chances of getting out of the situation alive were almost nil. The hope was that even if all of us die for the right cause, this is also a happy end. I approach everything with a sense of humour, it is kind of *noir*, and some people don't appreciate that.[47]

The Northern Wind

The mood at the Independence Day parade in Kyiv on August 24 was jubilant, with pro-war public enthusiasm flying high and armed troops marching toward a sure triumph at the front. At that very moment, the *Northern Wind* blew: Russian forces were already crossing the border, but eyewitness reports of the Ukrainian ground commanders were ignored by their superiors.[48] Although Kyiv had been making public statements about a massive Russian army presence since the outbreak of Donbas troubles, in reality it did not behave as if it believed that an intervention from across the border would come. The border in the South was not secured even along the sections which had always been under Ukrainian control. Kyiv was not prepared that the military convoys from Russia would bluntly drive across the border and engage in combat. Between 2,000 and 4,000, according to different accounts,[49] Russian paratroopers were deployed to aid the rebels who faced a 50,000-strong Ukrainian army,[50] and the tables were turned in a matter of days. Vladimir Putin indirectly acknowledged the involvement of Russian servicemen in Donbas, saying that,

> We've never said there are no people there dealing with certain matters, including in the military arena, but this doesn't mean that regular Russian troops are present there. Appreciate the difference.[51]

Apparently, only a tight circle of trusted confidants was let into the plan, but not the middle-ranking commanders. They were not ordered into any special preparations. According to *Prince*,

> The counter-offensive was kept a deep secret, we knew nothing. It came suddenly. One minute Blagodatnoye and Novoazovsk were taken, and the next, the units were already approaching Mariupol. We never saw the Russian forces and didn't have any joint operations with them, but could see that something was going on. The artillery shelled precisely on target and then we attacked, but we didn't realise that this was a part of a plan. Orders were given from time to time to attack here and there, but who was giving them and why wasn't clear. Everybody was surprised, wondering who could have organised this, because rebel detachments were disconnected and a lot of them didn't know each other.[52]

The Russian contribution was not only in troops, but crucial for designing the military strategy. The MoD General Chief of Staff's hand was evident in collecting and processing intelligence, and strategic and operational planning when each unit commander was set an individual task depending on their fighting capabilities, terrain and the enemy forces they were likely to face. Disparate actions of the LNR and DNR battalions had to be coordinated across a large theatre and timed appropriately, so that their simultaneous attacks from different directions made an overall strategic sense. The rebel commanders did not have the skills of that level.

The August counteroffensive resulted in a disastrous defeat for the government side, with several battalions trapped in cauldrons. The *Northern Wind* blew in two directions—in the north and south, while the rebel counteroffensive also developed on two fronts: westwards from their position near the Russian border at Uspenka and southwards from Donetsk and Mospyne at the time when the main concentration of the Ukrainian forces was in the north. Savur Mohyla found itself at the southern tong of the offensive aimed at encirclement of the Ukrainian group of forces at Ilovaisk. The Russians surrounded the height and moved further, making continuation of its defence lacking any sense. Still, the ATO troops did not surrender but attempted a breakthrough on August 24 which succeeded at first, but then its participants got into a worse nightmare of fighting at Ilovaisk.

There, the Russian paratroopers quickly crushed through the Ukrainian defence lines around the town and moved to attack its gear which had not been secured. The rebels clashed inside the town with now surrounded Ukrainian forces and lifted the siege on their own units in the Ukrainian-held parts of the town. Colonel Gordiychuk, who commanded the Ukrainian breakthrough out of Savur Mohyla and led his troops into Ilovaisk, got wounded and taken prisoner with his surviving soldiers, and was exchanged later.[53] In three days, it was all over: on August 27 the Ilovaisk cauldron was completely sealed off and left behind. This was the key battle which altered the course of the confrontation between Kyiv and Donbas.[54] On August 29 President Putin publicly appealed to the rebel command to provide safe passage for the trapped Ukrainian troops. Such passage in return for armored vehicles worked in several places and the Starobesheve cauldron set a pattern of the surrender of military vehicles in exchange for safe passage out. Vehicles, weapons and equipment have been apprehended by smaller, but determined, rebel armed groups.

However, there were arguments over whether Ukrainian servicemen should be allowed to keep their armory and duty weapons, which some commanders allowed to happen and were criticized later for. The passage out of Ilovaisk turned into a tragedy and the Ukrainian troops suffered losses when Russian tanks and armor strafed them as they retreated through the corridor.[55]

According to the rebel version, the deal was agreed with the Ukrainian Lt. general Ruslan Khomchak, which he confirmed later, that his troops would be allowed to exit in exchange for the captives the Ukrainians held, as well as surrender of their armored vehicles and weapons. The Ukrainian side was reluctant to give up the armory and formed two convoys totaling a thousand men each. The Russian commanders asked for a pause in order to consult their superiors on which action to take and how a passage of two large and fully armed convoys would be organized.

Khomchak's nerves apparently gave way. He decided not to wait and ordered a dash out of the besieged situation. The Ukrainian forces moved and opened fire. Yurii Lysenko, an acting company commander of the 39th territorial battalion, recalled that "Khomchak said 'I have no time to wait. This is the order—engage in combat. We'll dash through and attack the Russians.' The first machine went on an attack. Russians returned fire. Our battalions were half disarmed as most of the ammunition was packed away for transportation and they only had their machineguns." Lysenko cited the words of a Russian officer who eventually took him prisoner: "You suddenly got into your vehicles and went on attack. We had no choice but to defend ourselves."[56]

A slaughter unfolded. The Ukrainian troops were on an open plain in a full view of the adversary deployed in forested terrain. They were getting no orders as their officers were equally lost, did not know the land and were disoriented which direction to run to. They were seeing "Chechens" (possibly, Caucasian-looking rebels or just those with beards) whom they feared more than anything and tried to surrender to the Russian units where they had better chances to survive. General Khomchak together with several commanders managed to escape, but the majority was less lucky.[57] Several battalions and army regiments were almost annihilated. Altogether, Ondryi Senchenko, the head of the interim parliamentary investigation commission on the Ilovaisk disaster estimated the Ukrainian losses as up to 3,500 dead, although the Ukrainian MoD gave much lower figures. The MoD figures were rejected by the territorial battalion commanders who had fairly accurate records of their losses.

The *Northern Wind* also blew in Luhansk oblast where the rebels' counteroffensive commenced on August 19 and in several days was reinforced by the Russian troops. Luhansk airport was the scene of the most intense fighting on August 31. The next day the Ukrainian forces withdrew after all-night clashes with the rebels aided by Russian paratroopers. Things were moving very quickly. An attack toward the Azov Sea led to the capture of Novoazovsk and provided the rebels with a seaport access. Advance forces were already reaching Volnovakha and Mariupol. The tables have turned, and the Ukrainian forces went from victorious to retreating in a matter of days, and their spirits were down. Rebels, in their turn, received a morale boost and were determined to go forward to retake the lands they originally controlled. They were however ordered to stop, and battlefront stabilized. The summer campaign when the main military actions happened was over, but both sides were dissatisfied with their positions.

NOTES

1. UN OHCHR, "Report on the human rights situation in Ukraine," 16 February to 15 May 2017, June 2017, 2.

2. Field observation in Sloviansk in August 2014 showed the pattern of destruction consistent with the use of such systems.

3. Rid and Hecker, *War 2.0*, 215.

4. Alexander Juchkovsky, author's interview, May 2017, via Skype.

5. Office of the UN High Commissioner for Human Rights, "Report on the human rights situation in Ukraine," 15 July 2014, 4.

6. Human Rights Watch, "Chechnya: Report to the 1996 OSCE Review Conference," 1 November 1996, D816, http://www.refworld.org/docid/3ae6a7d214.html, "Russian Federation: Armed Conflict in the Chechen Republic: Seeds of Human Rights Violations Sown in Peacetime," 31 March 1995: EUR 46/010/1995.

7. CNN own investigation confirmed by the OSCE SMM, see Diana Magnay and Tim Lister, "Air attack on pro-Russian separatists in Luhansk kills 8, stuns residents," CNN June 3, 2014. http://edition.cnn.com/2014/06/03/world/europe/ukraine-luhansk-building-attack

8. http://riafan.ru/355913-za-chto-pogibla-gorlovskaya-madonna

9. Local rebels interviewed by Alexei Tokarev in Donbas, information conveyed by Tokarev in an interview with the author.

10. Prince, author's interview, Moscow, May 2016.

11. Igor Strelkov, author's interview, Moscow, May 2016.

12. Lavrov, "Civil War," 216.

13. Wilson, *Ukraine Crisis*, 139.

14. Lavrov, "Civil War," 239–240.

15. Tom Parfitt, "Russia charges female Ukrainian pilot over journalists' deaths," July 9, 2014, http://www.telegraph.co.uk/news/worldnews/europe/russia/10957438/Russia-charges-female-Ukrainian-pilot-over-journalists-deaths.html

16. *ITAR-TASS*, 18 July 2014.

17. Author's interview with a Kremlin-close analyst, Moscow, May 2016.

18. http://colonelcassad.livejournal.com/1660462.html

19. Yevgenii Norin, "Звезда и смерть Южного котла ВСУ," (Moscow: Sputnik i Pogrom, 2014).

20. UN OHCHR figure for April–August death toll was over 2,220, but that was very conservative, in its own admission.

21. UN OHCHR, "Report on the human rights situation in Ukraine," 17 August 2014.

22. Published in "The Number of Registered IDPs Decreased in 2017," Relief Web, 6 March 2017, http://reliefweb.int/report/ukraine/number-registered-idps-decreased-2017

23. http://www.migration-patent.ru/index/razdel3/chislo-bezhencev-iz-ukrainy-v-rossiyu

24. ICRC, "Ukraine: ICRC calls on all sides to respect international humanitarian law," News Release, 14/12523 August 2014, https://www.icrc.org/eng/resources/documents/news-release/2014/07-23-ukraine-kiev-call-respect-ihl-repatriate-bodies-malaysian-airlines.htm

25. Human Rights Watch, "Ukraine: Human Rights Watch Letter to Acting President Turchynov and President-Elect Poroshenko," 6 June 2014, https://www.hrw.org/news/2014/06/06/ukraine-human-rights-watch-letter-acting-president-turchynov-and-president-elect

26. Human Rights Watch, "World Report 2015: Ukraine Events of 2014," https://www.hrw.org/world-report/2015/country-chapters/ukraine#f8c745

27. Tsyganok, "Neokonchennaya Voina," 421.

28. Human Rights Watch, "Ukraine: Widespread Use of Cluster Munitions. Government Responsible for Cluster Attacks on Donetsk," 14 October 2014, https://www.hrw.org/news/2014/10/20/ukraine-widespread-use-cluster-munitions; further examination see in Human Rights Watch, "Technical Briefing Note: Cluster Munitions' Use in Ukraine," June 2015, https://www.hrw.org/sites/default/files/supporting_resources/ukraine_clusters_briefing_note_final.pdf

29. UN OHCHR, "Report on the human rights situation in Ukraine," 15 June 2014.

30. UN OHCHR, "Report on the human rights situation in Ukraine," 15 July 2014.

31. "10 вертолётов, девять боевых самолётов и три транспортных самолёта. Представитель ВВС Украины Рассказал В Лондоне О Потерях И Перспективах Военной Авиации Страны," November 20, 2014 http://www.militaryparitet.com/ttp/data/ic_ttp/7092/

32. UN OHCHR, "Report on the human rights situation in Ukraine," 15 July 2014.

33. Reuben R. Johnson, "Lack of Funding Undermines Ukraine Air Power," 12 June 2015 https://www.ainonline.com/aviation-news/defense/2015-06-12/lack-funding-undermines-ukraine-air-power. According to Lavrov, the loss of at least 21 aircrafts: 13 planes and 8 helicopters, are confirmed by evidence, in Anton Lavrov, "Aircraft, Tanks and the Artillery in the Donbas," 228–249, in *Brothers Armed*, 228.

34. According to the German intelligence service estimates, the real losses in the Ukrainian civil war at 50,000 dead, cited in https://www.rt.com/news/230363-ukraine-real-losses-german-intelligence 8 February 2015.

35. For updates and progress reports see the investigation website https://www.om.nl/onderwerpen/mh17-crash/

36. "Malaysian flight MH17 downed by Russian-made missile: Prosecutors," 28 September 2016, http://www.reuters.com/article/us-ukraine-crisis-mh-idUSKCN11Y0WN

37. Borodai, author's interview.

38. https://www.gazeta.ru/politics/2016/09/28_a_10220129.shtml#page5

39. Alexei Chelnokov, Sergei Sokolov, "Уничтожить факты проведения специальной операции," 22 May 2017, *Sovershenno Sekretno* weekly, http://www.sovsekretno.ru/articles/id/5703/

40. For an overview of conspiracy theories on the Russian side see Tsyganok, *Neokonchennaya Voina*, 455–462.

41. Tsyganok, 358.

42. Cited in Norin, "Звезда и смерть Южного Котла ВСУ, 2014" (Moscow: Sputnik i Pogrom, 2015).

43. Cited in Norin, "День, когда Украина дрогнула: Иловайская мясорубка, часть первая," (Moscow: Sputnik i Pogrom, 2015).

44. *TASS*. 28 August 2014. East Ukraine militias seize large amount of Ukrainian armor—Kiev's hacked data. http://tass.ru/en/world/747032

45. Prince, author's interview, Moscow, May 2016.

46. Igor Strelkov, author's interview, May 2916.

47. Alexander Borodai, author's interview, Moscow, May 2016.

48. http://voennizdat.com/news2/?mark=1&model=25

49. Author's interviews with *Prince*, Chalenko, Dergachoff, Barabanov, Norin.

50. According to the then Prime-Minister Arsenii Yatseniuk, "В АТО на востоке Украины принимают участие 50 тысяч украинских мужчин,–Яценюк,"August 11, 2014, http://zik.ua/ru/news/2014/08/11/v_ato_na_vostoke_ukrayni_prynymayut_uchastye_50_tisyach_ukraynskyh_muzhchyn__yatsenyuk_513604.

51. Vladimir Putin's Annual News Conference. 17 December 2015. *President's of Russia Website*. Moscow http://en.kremlin.ru/events/president/transcripts/press_conferences/50971

52. Prince, author's interview, May 2016.

53. Yevgenii Norin, "Сражение года: оборона Саур-Могилы," (Moscow: *Sputnik i Pogrom*, 2015), http://sputnikipogrom.com/russia/26673/battle-of-2014/#.V-zeblQrK70

54. Yevgenii Norin, "День, когда Украина дрогнула: Иловайская мясорубка, часть первая" [*Battle for Ilovaisk*] (Moscow: *Sputnik i Pogrom*, 2015), http://sputnikipogrom.com/ilovaisk/22734/battle-of-ilovaisk/#.V-ztxVQrK70

55. International Crisis Group "Eastern Ukraine: A Dangerous Winter," *Europe Report* 235, December 2014.

56. Cited in Norin, *Battle for Ilovaisk*.

57. Norin, *Battle for Ilovaisk*.

Chapter 8

Consolidation amid the New (Dis)order

The period from September 2014 and into 2015 onwards witnessed the last major battles, a rough shaping of frontlines that became the future "contact lines," separating the NGCAs from the rest of Ukraine, and transformation of warlordist DNR and LNR into proto-state formations. The forces of order gradually overpowered that of disorder, the rebellion became institutionally entrenched, but its final political goal remained elusive.

MINSK AND BEYOND: CEASEFIRES AND KEY BATTLES

The Minsk-1 Protocol brokered on September 5, 2014, under the aegis of the OSCE, was a relief for Kyiv. The army had suffered heavy losses, exceeding the official figures.[1] Desertion,[2] mental disorders, suicides, and self-mutilation were widespread. Some captured soldiers changed sides and joined the rebels. Poor supplies and logistics, the lack of training and coordination resulted in setbacks and a loss of life. Although in western regions patriotic feelings were rife and men wished to join the army, mobilization resource throughout the country was at near exhaustion. President Poroshenko stated that around 65 percent of military vehicles had been lost.[3]

The memorandum of September 19 specified the Protocol's provisions, notably on force deployment, although the sides reneged on and off on their implementation at different stages later. Many rebel commanders disapproved of Minsk and were willing to continue fighting. Moscow had to exercise pressure: it curbed anti-Minsk rhetoric and put the Novorossiya project on hold because it contradicted the provision on the special status for the territories stipulated in the Agreement.[4] The uprising's leaders who had come from Russia were already taken out and the hard-liner Antiufeyev was encouraged to leave in September. The ceasefire shaped the new territorial configuration. It prevented the seizure of Mariupol which was within rebels' reach and calmed the situation down. Zakharchenko explained an abrupt halting of the offensive on the city when their forces were already entering the suburbs as the rebels' own decision: they had insufficient manpower to back up the frontline troops as 2,300 men were needed which the rebels did not have, and they also experienced fuel shortages. Ukrainian command threatened to block the water flow of Siverskyi (in Ukrainian, Seversky in Russian) Donets–Donbas canal, which would have left the rebel territories without any supply.[5] There are other explanations, such as the strength of the ATO defenses, and conspiracy theories of oligarchic collusion.[6] All in all, Mariupol remained under the government control.

The inter-Minsk period witnessed transformation of the guerrillas into a more organized fighting force, thanks to the Russian instruction and internal consolidation. Territorial units and task forces were introduced and former "Somali pirates" acquired boots and night vision goggles. Still, the rebels remember the time of hardship when they stayed in dug-outs on the frontline in winter, otherwise used schools, nurseries and other public buildings, and only had summertime uniforms in winter. Food was scarce and a pool of buckwheat with a can of beef for a whole squad was a common meal.[7] Some areas had no electricity, although Luhansk and the environs had a supply from Schastia power station which was under Kyiv, and were sending the LNR-produced coal in exchange. Attempts to make peace directly rather than through the international mediators were not abandoned. However, the October 2014 talks by Mozgovoi, which brought together a wider group of participants from both sides, did not produce the same hope of reversing the course of the conflict as his earlier effort in summer did, according to a Russian volunteer combatant who took part in both talks. The war went too far by then and the fighters were brutalized by it. Peacemaking aspiration was largely not shared by the rebel movement frustrated that the ceasefire prevented further advances and left a sense that the aims of the rebellion were not fulfilled.

Shelling and firefights continued after the ceasefire, but, according to Norin, "the war in autumn assumed a different character reminiscent of a First World War scenario." The front moved very slowly while being saturated with weapons. Typically, a company would be dashing in and out of the neutral zone supported by Grad artillery, howitzers, everything on earth they had.[8] Violations were driven by attempts to create a defensible separation line, with both sides seeking to improve their positions. The rebel objectives were to capture Donetsk airport to stop shelling of the city, Volnovakha, Debaltseve, where the frontline dipped deep into their territory, and Schastia, with its power generation capacity. Mariupol came under the rebel shelling in January 2015, with thirty people killed. They also staged subversive acts to disrupt the Ukrainian army's supplies and communication lines, while the ATO forces fired at their positions. Heavy fighting broke out at the 32nd blockpost where the ATO troopers were ambushed and thirty-five of them killed. It resulted in losing twenty military vehicles, for which Ukrainian commanding officers were blamed by their superiors.[9]

Government-held Donetsk airport and Debaltseve were vulnerable from the start and, from a military point of view, holding them only made sense if they were to be used as launch pads for a future offensive. The rebels were determined not to let this happen. According to the Minsk-1, Donetsk airport to the north of the city was supposed to be handed over to the DNR in exchange for territorial concessions elsewhere, but Kyiv was unwilling to do so. The rebels were also not exactly taking Minsk as a guide to action on the ground, and were not good at keeping their side of the bargain. The Ukrainian troops shelled the city from the airport's tower inflicting casualties in Donetsk residential areas, thus creating an imperative to put a stop to this. The airport was not the biggest battle of Donbas conflict, but the most destructive and uncompromising. The terrain was difficult for an attack as it had to be staged in plain view of the adversary who had a network of underground shelters to provide cover. The rebels discovered that the Ukrainian army could be a strong and dangerous enemy when its operations were well organized. The airport defenders who held on for a long time were nicknamed "cyborgs" for their "superhuman" fighting qualities.

The rebel forces were comprised of *Somali* commanded by *Givi*, Motorola's *Sparta* and *Vostok* battalions. However, the rebels were still irregulars who this time were faced with a proper army. Their inherited problems such as a lack of coordination and an uneven level of skills and resilience came out. Communications between *Somali*, *Vostok*, and artillery that was backing them broke down in the November 2014 attack, while inexperienced Cossack forces proved unreliable and many were killed, although the Ilovaisk veterans who took part in the offensive all survived.[10] *Motorola*, in a goodwill gesture, allowed a passage of food and water supplies to the Ukrainian troops inside the airport for "humanitarian reasons." He was criticized by Strelkov, now publicly commenting on the military developments from Moscow, that this was a dumb thing to do. It would have been in everybody's interest, he maintained, not to prolong the battle but drive the point across that the Ukrainians should stop resistance and leave or surrender. The battle for the airport lasted for eight months, and it was finally taken on January 22, 2015, but ATO positions remained dangerously close to it. There were disagreements whether the airport had such strategic significance to justify enormous human cost sustained on both sides.

The war's last major battle was coming. Debaltseve was on the prime target list, because it was the main railway hub, also located on the strategic

Donetsk–Luhansk highway and occupying a heightened ground, from which the ATO artillery shelled the rebel-held positions along the wedge between the LNR and DNR. Strategic position of Debaltseve explains the hard battle fought for it, in which several hundred troops on both sides were killed within a month. The attack by the combined LNR and DNR forces started in January 2015 from two opposite directions and was pointed inside the wedge. Alexander Zakharchenko came to personally supervise the offensive and lift the morale. The rebels were not as outnumbered and outgunned as they were in the summer campaign, because *voentorg* by then filled the gaps in rebel capabilities with weapons and ammunition, and their combined forces totaled about 6,000 against 8,000 ATO troops.

However, they absorbed many new locals, for whom this was the first real battle. One DNR officer recalled that an exodus of a half of fresh recruits after the first combat was a typical occurrence. Local infantrymen were brave, but unskilled and undisciplined, as a result of which some operations collapsed because groups would not advance to a designated position. A fighter from the *Hooligan* rebel battalion (commanded by Denis Kudrin) recalled an occasion when they were supposed to be backed by a tank, but it simply chose not to show up. Eventually, many among recently formed "regular" regiments quickly disintegrated into small fighting groups with mind of their own. Some individuals waged their own wars. Such was a man from Donetsk who by then was demobilized from the DNR forces but went to Debaltseve to observe the action. He saw that things were in bad shape, went back to collect his armaments and fought where he chose using the arms he had.[11]

The rebel forces struggled with the offensive. Unlike in August 2014, the Ukrainian army succeeded in establishing frontline defenses and was ready to resist the attack. The January 25 tank battle at Sanjarovka was one of the most severe episodes, when a group of Novorossiya tanks inflicted sudden and horrendous damage on a Ukrainian position, but could not hold the height because it lacked infantry support. Vuhlehirsk (in Ukrainian, Uglegorsk in Russian) was the weakest point of the ATO and their defenses were poorly organized, in which the regular army and territorial battalions both participated. *Donbas* commander Semenchenko ordered his troops into action without prior reconnaissance and some of them were shot in friendly fire. Rebels also suffered gigantic losses. The battle for Debaltseve was the first time when they had to shell residential areas, and many expressed their dissatisfaction with this, because they saw themselves as the source of "good" and practiced local recruitment. Rebel sources complained that not the best military advisers were sent from Russia, that the operation was badly planned with separate companies launching their own attacks and that equipment, coordination and communication were failing. Fighters were dying in friendly fire. Internal recriminations continued and a strict chain of command was absent.

After these frustrated efforts, the *Northern Wind* blew again. Russian soldiers appeared at the end of January, not as a single squad, but in small teams of three. They were not aware which of the teams went where. According to *Kommersant* journalist Ilya Barabanov who interviewed the troopers, they all submitted their resignation letters before being sent to Donbas. Only those were sent who really could fight. They were told where they were going, went willingly and there was more enthusiasm to go than available places. The troopers were dispersed through different units of the DNR army which needed a helping hand the most. They typically would solve the task set out for them and made themselves scarce, while the local rebels would finish the job and secure the gained ground.[12] In Norin's account, *polite people* appeared at a late stage when the rebels already took Lohvynove (in Ukrainian, Logvinovo in Russian), when they were reinforced by a company from the 5th Russian tank brigade stationed near Ulan-Ude, and were nicknamed "Fighting Buryats" after that. They numbered between 200 and 300 men and had around 30 tanks.[13] *Novaya Gazeta* published an interview with a tank trooper who was among these Russian forces, although the date when he claimed he was wounded in combat (February 19) was implausible because operations were over by then.[14]

While the troops were fighting, Merkel, Holland, Putin and Poroshenko arrived in Minsk on February 11 for the talks in the "Normandy format" where they were joined by DNR and LNR "premiers" Zakharchenko and Plotnitsky. The parties signed the Minsk-2 agreement on February 12, 2015, which committed them to a ceasefire from February 15, separation of forces and redeployment of heavy weapons away from the frontlines. Unlike Minsk-1, when fighting stopped at 6 pm on the dot after signing, this one made no immediate impact. Mozgovoi wrote that "characters who went to Minsk, lost the authority over the troops in action, both on the Ukrainian side and in our republics. Do these people who signed the agreement actually understand, that they are just nil?"[15] Hostilities not only did not cease but escalated. Zakharchenko who just signed the ceasefire agreement, went straight to the frontline where he was wounded while taking part in combat with a machinegun in his hands. The Ukrainian forces were eventually surrounded and suffered a defeat, and a large number of tanks and military vehicles was apprehended. On February 18 Debaltseve was taken and the frontline evened out. *Prince* who fought at Debaltseve recalled that they found 22 wounded Ukrainian soldiers trapped in a Ural heavy lorry who were allegedly abandoned by their officers when they realized that they were surrounded and could not escape with the wounded. One soldier survived, was given first aid and transferred to the Ukrainian side, but died there. Rebels suspected that his death was not accidental but prevented the release of the story.

Military actions at Debaltseve spelt the end of the Minsk-1, and Minsk-2 stipulated the territorial gains as the new *status quo*, which has not greatly changed since then. The second ceasefire enabled the reduction of shelling of Donetsk, but from April 10 bombardments and sporadic firefights affected Piski, Karlivka and Avdiivka settlements in close proximity to the city. In February 2015 *Azov* battalion launched an attack in the south at Shyrokyne (in Ukrainian, Shirokino in Russian) to distract the DNR forces from Debaltseve, although the settlement was located in a buffer zone and an attack on a neutral territory violated the Minsk-1 agreement, as was the rebel offensive on Debaltseve. Fighting went on until Shyrokyne was given up by the rebels on July 2. The Minsk-2 ceasefire lasted for 4 months, less than Minsk-1, when heavy fighting erupted in late May in the vicinity of Donetsk airport, Mar'inka, Krasnohorivka, Bakhmut, Dzerzhynsk (renamed Toretsk in 2016) in Donetsk oblast, and at Schastia and Stanitsa Luhanska in Luhansk, with Moscow in the background halting the insurgents' appetites. Mar'inka in particular was a badly planned and executed initiative by Zakharchenko in which 30 rebel fighters lost their lives and a hundred were wounded.[16] Rebel sources claim that they almost captured it, but were told to let go, as it was hard to hold and taking it did not make a strategic sense.

At first, the rebels did not take their obligations under Minsk very seriously until Moscow got firmer in enforcing them, and the ATO side appeared to share the logic. The ceasefire was disrupted by bigger and smaller incidents, and the sides spoke several times as if a new war was imminent, although escalation was not in strategic interests of Kyiv or Moscow. Deployment of the OSCE Special Monitoring Mission (SMM)[17] in 2014 also helped considerably in reduction of hostilities because, as put by an observer, "their ice cream vans are everywhere and an OSCE rep is sitting under every bush." The scale of shelling had gone down, but residential areas continued to come under fire. The distance between the trenches was as short as 50 meters in some places, which meant that fighting often broke out by accident rather than through any kind of planning, but the sides blamed each other. They staged unnecessary provocations, such as an engagement at Yasynuvata (in Ukrainian, Yasinovataya in Russian) when Zakharchenko took a decision to move a checkpoint 50 meters into government-controlled territory.

Fighting in Avdiivka in January–February 2017 was the latest episode of military escalation and a culmination of the Ukrainian "creeping offensive." Radio Free Europe reported that since mid-December 2016 the ATO forces kept step-by-step advances into parts of the neutral territory near the towns of Avdiivka, Debaltseve, Dokuchaievsk, Horlivka and Mariupol, reducing the distances between the sides. Finally, on January 26 the troops advanced onto Novoluhanske concealed in farm trucks, taking the rebels by surprise, and it took hours for the latter to engage. Alexander Hug, the deputy OSCE

SMM chief monitor said the direct result of forward moves was escalation in tension, which turned into violence. As a result, both sides positioned large-caliber artillery, including towed howitzers, main battle tanks, and multiple-launch rocket systems banned under the Minsk deal "in the open with impunity."[18] However, although fighting was ferocious, the frontline has not altered much, and it appeared that the rebel defenses withstood a battle test. In a rebel's admission, their air defense have capabilities strengthened and "now protect fairly reliably. Two Tochka-U [SS-21 Scarab] ballistic missiles, launched by the ATO forces at Avdiivka, have been intercepted over Donetsk. Weapon systems that we have are also of good quality."[19]

REINING THE DISORDER IN

Chaotic situation rich on internal conflicts was rampant after the initial idealism subsided and values suffered reduction to reality. Guerrillas periodically locked each other in dungeons. Commanders competed against each other in how many block posts they had. Each field commander had his security system, which he enforced by erecting block posts and introducing "passage permits." A volunteer recalled how a cortege of "polite people" was not let through the territory controlled by a local warlord. The situation at the LNR was worse than at the DNR which had a semblance of an integrated military and political structure. Corruption and asset grabbing flourished in Luhansk: reportedly, "Vice-Premier" Vassily Nikitin nearly lost his job in August 2014 because of embezzlement of Russian humanitarian aid. He was believed to bribe Gennady Tsypkalov, the head of the "LNR Council of Ministers" at the time by handing over two apprehended mansions in order to keep his place. Alexei Karyakin, chairman of the National Council, managed to buy a house reportedly worth US$29 million in Moscow city area for his family. One new minister moved into the house of a senior Luhansk judge Leonid Fesenko who fled, and his family was seen wearing Fesenko family's clothes.[20]

The LNR had seven separate battalions and other smaller groups. Eventually, these unruly regiments had to be brought in line, sometimes by coercive means when attempts to make them comply failed.[21] Cossack units were the biggest challenge as they resisted disarmament and reintegration. The line was to disperse the Cossacks into different regiments, but there were too many of them and they were unwilling to be separated from each other. Cossack sources maintained that they were thrown into Debaltseve combat as a cannon folder where they have to go on attack with no prior reconnaissance and were running into Ukrainian forces, who fired on them.

The exodus of the Cossack ataman Kozitsyn to Russia, orchestrated by Moscow, left many of his former fighters facing the new forces of "law and order." A colorful ataman *Kosogor* in Krasnyi Luch who proclaimed his own "Cossack republic," dismissed an LNR-loyal city mayor and set up his own TV station, instilled trepidation into the locals. When his Cossack warriors were chased out, it was a great relief for many. Brutal incidents of the internal infighting determined to instill a monopoly on violence included murders of Cossacks in Krasnyi Luch, disarmament of "Odessa" detachment in Krasnodon and arrest of its commander Alexei Fomichev (*Foma* call sign) who was finally allowed to leave for Moscow after a long time spent in a Luhansk dungeon. *Oplot*'s action against a Chechen stronghold at Khartsyzk which was reputed to be a nest of crime was also welcomed by the local population.

Efforts to rein in the "wild battalions" were formalized by the order adopted on March 30, 2015, stipulating that those who did not belong to a formal armed structure had to forfeit all their weaponry or face criminal charges as members of illegal gangs.[22] Still, disarmament was a long and painful process, and took over a year to complete. Combatant volunteer *Strannik* who was one of the people in charge of transforming the disorder into some semblance of normality explains:

> The republics required authoritative institutions which had to be built. Disparate regiments had to fall into a regular army structure. This caused resistance. Each commander had his own combat experience behind them and would refuse to integrate with others whom he didn't respect or who were his opponents. There were some regiments which bluntly refused to disarm. I also had to sack volunteers who came from Russia where they had dropped everything, lost their jobs, families, homes. This was very hard.[23]

Assassinations went hand in hand with stabilization process. High-profile murders of autonomous commanders who were also known to oppose the Minsk agreement took place throughout 2015. They were more typical for the LNR. The physical elimination of uncontrollable figures was not the first choice option—they were given opportunities to change their ways and some did, especially in the DNR which had fewer such incidents. *Mirage* battalion commander Roman Voznik (call sign *Tsygan*) was assassinated in Donetsk on March 26, 2015 and there were several non-fatal attempts on prominent commanders, such as *Givi* and Zakharchenko. The LNR commanders were said to refuse to listen when they were told that they were not untouchable and tended to overestimate their significance, as rebel interlocutors indicated. *Prince* recalls the conversations that went on at the time:

> All these guys didn't want to fall into line. They believed that they were all war heroes. Now they were told that "guys, the times have changed and you should join the corps. We'll of course hang some medals round your necks, but

you must obey." But all of them overrated themselves. "So and so supports me, such people speak to me. They won't dare touch Me" (меня не посмеют) All these commanders all the time wanted to go and "mop up" Lugansk. It was all not serious.[24]

Strannik adds that Cossacks in the end lacked the political will to turn on Luhansk and depose Plotnitsky, with whom they had serious disagreements and justified grievances. The year started with gunning down of *Batman* (Alexander Bednov), a champion of Luhansk city defense, in January 2015, for which the LNR leadership felt it could take responsibility, as his reputation for criminality was well-known: "*Batman* was a bandit, who raided businesses and grabbed houses."[25] In *Prince's* assessment,

Bednov was a splinter from Mozgovoi. Initially they were together. At first he was a committed rebel who was fighting for a cause, but then it all went as usual. He didn't take much part in active combat and had no frontline of his own, thus his authority among commanders wasn't great. Bednov wasn't a figure who could influence the situation. That's why the LNR authorities could openly state that they had liquidated him. A Russian volunteer call sign Kot (Cat) died in that shooting.[26]

Yevgenii Ishenko (Malysh), mayor of Pervomaisk and a Cossack Guard commander, who served two prison sentences before the war in Russia, one for murder, was killed on January 23.[27] 2015 ended with a professionally executed assassination of Pavel Dremov the day after his wedding, cruel even by the LNR standards. *Novaya Gazeta* pointed at Igor Plotnitsky who was apprehensive of compromising files which Dremov had on him.[28] Dremov reportedly held too much *kompromat* on the others and could not be relied upon in his quest for territorial control, power and money.[29] It is believed that the murders were ordered by Tsypkalov and Karyakin who eventually fell on their sword. In September 2016 Tsypkalov was accused of treason and plotting a coup, was detained and, according to the LNR "officials," hung himself in his cell. Karyakin was accused of committing serious crimes and involvement in the coup.[30] The most salient was the assassination of Alexei Mozgovoi on May 23, 2015, following previous failed attempts as the commander was not an easy target. Although an obscure Ukrainian group took responsibility, this occurred so deep into the rebel-held territory that it appeared improbable that Ukrainian operatives could penetrate that far, the rebels maintained. Mozgovoi seemed to anticipate his forthcoming death and wrote a poem beginning with:

How good it is to die in May,
Lay in a moist springtime terrain.[31]

Mozgovoi was the only one widely grieved and remembered. He was believed to have conflicted with the LNR over the control of income from the Alchevsk metal works located in the town he was in charge of, but the main reasons were likely to be politics rather than business. Those who knew him stressed that he seemed to genuinely believe in Minsk as a road to power-sharing and registered his organisation in Ukraine.[32] "Mozgovoi was seeking a transition from a warlord to a politician and paid a price for it."[33] It was obvious that Mozgovoi and Dremov emerged as nuisance figures, who made plenty of noise. Mozgovoi wrote letters to the Kremlin and had independent political ties, such as with the Communist Party. Many international volunteers fought at *Prizrak* attracted by his charisma and popularity. Mozgovoi was killed a few days after he, together with Dremov, sent an open letter to the Russian Federal Assembly stating that politicians did not pay sufficient attention to the problem of "Russians as divided people" (русский народ), deprived them of legal protection and denied their own subjectivity. They called on the legislators to support the "Russian Project" launched by a group of intellectuals in Russia and start with setting up a Commission on Problems of the Russian people at the Federal Assembly. The letter stated that "time has shown that only with a national project and consolidation of the Russian people is it possible to respond to modern threats."[34] Just like the *Russian Spring*, Mozgovoi and Dremov were heading toward risky terrain.

Life expectancy among prominent commanders was rather short. This was aided by the situation that the SBU improved their capabilities, and operations of Ukrainian reconnaissance-saboteur groups could inflict losses inside the NGCAs, as rebels maintain. *Motorola*, one of the rebellion's symbols, was killed in Donetsk on October 16, 2016. *Motorola*'s funeral brought 50,000 mourners to the city streets and turned into an outpour of grief well beyond Donbas.[35] *Givi* was killed when a rocket was fired into his headquarters on February 8, 2017. Their assassinations were believed by the rebels to be SBU-masterminded and carried out by people on the inside. There were other victims among important military commanders, but as they did not have a media profile, their deaths went unnoticed by outsiders. SBU was said not to let the rebels relax by frequently staging subversive acts, explosions, assassinations and knife attacks. Women were reported also to be used for this purpose, as they would lure officers and then attack them or lead into harm's way.[36]

At the same time, a new strategy of military consolidation was gradually taking root. It was launched in late November 2014 after the elections into the *de facto* authority structures. Building up the military organization got underway, conducted under supervision of the Russian advisers with the locals at the front. International Crisis Group (ICG) noted that the rebels were "moving steadily—with substantial, probably growing, Russian command input—toward creation of a functional army."[37] This was aided by defections of senior Ukrainian officers which took place in 2015 in addition to the rank-and-file soldiers changing sides. In June Alexei and Yuri Miroshnichenko brothers, the officers of Ukraine's external intelligence agency, defected to the LNR, as well as Oleg Belousov, the head of Luhansk customs inspectorate. DNR gained Alexander Kolomiyets, the chief military analyst and former aide to Ukraine's minister of defense, and another seven senior officers who changed sides. In December an SBU general-major Alexander Tretyak switched his loyalty to DNR, and Yuri Davydov of the MoI joined the LNR ranks. Less prominent defections continued. Apart from giving morale boost, this provided the rebels with a better insight into capabilities of their adversary.

The battalions were transformed into two corps. In DNR, Kononov held a political appointment of the "defence minister," but the identity of the corps' commander was not known.[38] Corps command-level salaries were reported to be *on par* with those in Russia, and lower ranks drew pay according to a local scale. Russian military got a double pay and troops used to receive top-up payments for combat operations (боевые), but this practice stopped after the involvement in Syria in 2015 on account of cash shortages in the Russian budget.[39] According to *Novaya Gazeta*, the corps numbered 32,000, out of whom 30,000 were Ukrainian citizens.[40]

NASCENT POLITICS

The initial political goals of the movement were diffused, as it represented a release of collective emotions which culminated in Novorossiya idea. It was not precisely politically shaped. Some figures behind it, such as Khodakovsky and Tsaryov, supported the idea of a united and pro-Russian Ukraine, into which Donbas could fit in.[41] Tsaryov still maintained in 2017 that he remains a Ukrainian opposition politician who stands for a different kind of Ukraine, which is more friendly to its Russophone population and which Donbas can rejoin. *Strannik* noted that "the idea was to build Novorossiya, but it was discredited by Strelkov and Tsaryov. Russia made some correction to it, and DNR and LNR emerged. Novorossiya is a frozen project." However, it made little sense to pursue it as a political project in the circumstances. In Tsaryov's recollection of the events, "[it was implied] that Novorossiya contradicts the Minsk-1 agreement and should be put on hold. I assembled the deputies and told them so. However, some of them still run their parliamentary surgeries as Novorossiya deputies."[42] There was no more role for Tsaryov who was an outsider from Dnipro after Donbas indigenous leadership took the center stage. He became an opposition figure relocated to Russia. Other figures among the rebels were skeptical that the option of a Russia-friendly Ukraine was viable, feeling that a pro-Russian constituency in mainland Ukraine had diminished, while negative feelings toward Russia had gripped hearts and minds.[43] Some rebels were saying that they were not interested in Russia's geopolitical projects, but in Donbas's future. Some seasoned fighters who later were offered to go to Syria, refused.

While development of *Novorossiya* stalled, things were shaping up on the ground through a bottom up process. The uprising unleashed creativity which transpired in romanticized designs, for example, derived from the reconstruction of a pre-Soviet past. At LNR, projects of a Cossack People's Republic or a Republic of Don Army (Войско) were flying around, reflecting Luhansk's Cossack legacy. These were of course not Cossacks in any real historical sense, but what Derlyugian and Cipko call "Neo-Cossacks" in relation to Kuban.[44] It is interesting to see what happens when a leaderless militancy succeeds. The structure of the movement remained horizontal and non-hierarchical until the republics organized elections. Already at that time, differences between more industrialized and urbanized DNR and more disparate LNR influenced how their respective power-holding shaped. Despite identity and ideological commonality, DNR and LNR did not aspire to integrate into a single territorial and political unit, but established their own governing arrangements.

Gradually, the "republics" became more limited in the remit of their autonomous action on the domestic front, in which Moscow started to get more involved. The first sign of it was the move to withdraw Strelkov who was the symbol of the rebellion and a leader with an overall vision and authority. When the rebels were left to manage on their own, they ceded the initiative. The local commanders have only themselves to blame for a lost opportunity to claim more ground because they were unable to establish a common platform and form a united military structure. When Mozgovoi attempted to call a Military Council in 2014 and set up a single Novorossiya Army, the other commanders largely ignored it. The situation of different groups fighting their own wars reminiscent of the White armies during the Russian Civil War who unlike Trotsky, could not establish a single command-and-control system, created a power vacuum. It was subsequently filled by Donbas curators from Russia who promoted pliant figures into politics and took out nonconformists.[45] Commanders had to integrate into the system not on their own terms and the rules of the game were determined elsewhere. Those who were prepared to accept, survived and gained appointments.

War was a superfast social lift that skyrocketed field commanders to the prime positions. Moscow decided to rely on the most coherent leaders with proven war credentials, such as Khodakovsky and Zakharchenko at the DNR, and set out on building their capacities for them to evolve into political figures: "Moscow put its stakes on Zakharchenko—a straight guy, courageous, charismatic, easy to manage and women like him."[46] Observers characterize the DNR premier—who was a mining electrician before the conflict, – as a figure who is easy to get along with, but not a Moscow puppet. Moscow appears happy with the choice, as explained by a Moscow academic with access to the ruling circles: "it is good that the local leaders are simple guys—they are easier to manage."[47] Independent observers are less convinced. As put by Andrei Purgin, "revolution is a too rapid social lift, and some get sick out of gravitational acceleration."[48] Another view is that Zakharchenko is a situational leader, suitable for the moment but with no strategic vision. He is being crudely promoted with T-shirts, and magnets bearing his face and his motto "Responsible for the republic" (в ответе за республику) is everywhere.[49] It must be noted that despite starting from a low base, potential of individuals such as Zakharchenko should not be underestimated. As Karabakh experience in Armenia showed, the warrior elite were capable of becoming very tough political actors when they learnt the new game.

On November 2, 2014, the elections were held and Moscow had a hand in their script. In the absence of its own parties and given a break with the established all-Ukraine polity, local legislatures were elected by direct vote from among competing public associations. In DNR, 16-year-olds were legible to vote, a new provision inspired by the Scottish referendum, while the age stayed at 18 in LNR. Over a million people were reported to have voted in DNR, 104,000 of them remotely, and 700,000 in LNR, including volunteer fighters from outside. Three polling stations for refugees were organized in Russia. DNR elected 100 deputies and LNR 50 to their councils. Two electoral blocs crossed a 5 percent barrier in each republic and got in (*Donetskaya Respublica* with 68.3 percent and *Free Donbas* with 31.7 percent in DNR, and *Peace to Luganshina* with 70 percent and *Lugansk Economic Union* with 22 percent in LNR).[50]

Elections of the republics' heads turned into confidence votes for Zakharchenko (79 percent) and Plotnitsky (63 percent). Bezler who tried to enter the race, was lured out of DNR and kept in Russia. LNR experienced tensions with commanders being blocked from participation: one electoral list was registered only after a tank was brought in and took an aim at an electoral commission. Although wartime elections could hardly be free and fair, they conveyed internal legitimacy to Donbas leadership and facilitated their political transition. Kyiv's and Western governments subjected the elections to severe criticism. Consequently, Donbas elections were legitimate in the eyes of some, but illegitimate for others, for whom the question of legitimacy became a barrier rather than an enabling factor.

In the view of Ilya Barabanov, "military-policing regimes" were formed on the territories. Some popular warlords and politicos were marginalized, so that they would not engage in an independent game. A middle line shaped up and the opinions that deviated too much from it got discouraged. Khodakovsky, who initially was a consistent adherent of "Donbas in friendly Ukraine" and subsequently – a believer that the Transnistria variant was the most viable option for Donbas, got demoted in February 2016,[51] as well as hard-liner Alexander Kofman, the former DNR "minister of foreign affairs." Pavel Gubarev and Andrei Purgin, the uprising's original ideologues, did not find themselves among the new power-holders. Purgin was sidelined, became a mere deputy of the local legislature, and gradually moved into oblivion: in a June 2016 poll 59 percent of respondents were unable to recognize who he was. Denis Pushilin was the only one who made it into power from among the early political activists. He used to be an MMM pyramid scheme promoter in Donbas before the conflict and became the speaker of DNR parliament (People's Council). Pushilin serves as the representative at Minsk negotiations. Pushilin popularity was limited (17 percent support rating in June 2016)[52] and was alleged to be implicated in corrupt schemes, but was rewarded for his loyalty and willingness to take instruction.

Proto-statehood was formed in the conditions of uncertainty. Self-governing arrangements got rooted and new systems started functioning, even if their legality was not recognized and managerial elite was weak. Justice and security institutions were established, including much feared security "ministries" recruited out of the former fighters and retired personnel from their SBU predecessor. UN OHCHR noted in 2015 that NGCAs started to behave in a state-like fashion: "more centralised civilian administrative structures" and "procedures" developed in the DNR and LNR. These included the "legislature," "judiciary system," "ministries" and "law enforcement." The "republics" began issuing passports to residents. Among other "laws," "legislative bodies" of the DNR and LNR adopted "legislative acts" governing criminal prosecution in the territories under their control.[53] Republics' internal documents in 2017 were recognized for travel to Russia.

Attitudes toward the leaders who came on the top were not uniform, but it was hard to deny them support. Poll data points this way, although polls in wartime conditions may be far from accurate. According to a poll conducted in DNR in October 2015, 65 percent fully or partially trusted Zakharchenko and over 50 percent fully or partially trusted the Donetsk mayor Martynov.[54] A poll by a different company in June 2016 showed that 22 percent of DNR residents trusted Zakharchenko and 25 percent positively assessed his activity, a decrease from 36 percent in July 2015 taken by the same group. What did not appear to change was his "anti-rating"—the rate of DNR premier's disapproval stayed at 34 percent. The proto-state institutions enjoyed a dismal trust level, with security agencies faring better than civilian bodies. The military were the most trusted (an increase from 8 percent to 18 percent in six months) due to a purge from dubious elements, improved behavior of rebel fighters and their "time-proven integrity and devotion to their cause." The ministry of state security, with 17 percent, was the next most trusted institution.[55]

Thus, the proto-statehood was invented and installed. Some local rebels perceive what has happened as a "revolution" as it radically redefined political order, in which they used to live. It was no longer an imperfect democracy of Ukraine of the period of independence, but a military government relying on security provision as its main claim for legitimacy. Juchkovsky, speaking from the midst of action on the ground, reflects on how political trajectory has evolved:

> volunteers presented a movement of idealists, and then politicians intercepted the process. In the end, all turns out not as was hoped before. But local people say that this vector is still preferable to returning to Ukraine. They are grateful to Russia and to the rebels that they defended them. But what it used to be at the beginning, the Novorossiya idea—it is not here, and this is sad.[56]

This is a view from the rebel milieu and may not reflect what everyone in the local society thinks. Diversity of views held by ordinary residents will be addressed in chapter 11.

The new de facto authorities subsequently started co-opting segments of the old elite, but now the power equation was not in favor of the former oligarchy. Wealth no longer translated into power over politics and security, and it did not determine the rules. Big business was allowed to operate as long as it adapted to the new realities and knew its place. Spy mania and a search for the fifth column ran high in the wartime situation. The atmosphere smelled of danger. Those suspected of spying or dissident "coloured revolution" activities were frequently locked up, so public expression of political opposition became limited.[57] The number of respondents at DNR who considered that functioning opposition was needed decreased from 69 percent in January 2016 to 62 percent in June.[58]

LNR fared worse with respect of an indigenous cadre available to fill senior positions. Moscow researcher Ivan Loshkariov characterized LNR as a "warlordist—bureaucratic" regime, which is an interesting combination of terms. An international observer with experience of both NGCAs noted greater confidence of the Donetsk *de facto* authorities: "in LNR, they are more the servants of the system, while Zakharchenko and his people appear to have more of a mind of their own."[59] Plotnitsky's appointment halted a centrifugal tendency in the territory, but his administration brought back many of the same people who served under the old governor Yefremov, which was not what was hoped for. Plotnitsky with a weak influence over the state of affairs was hardly an impressive figure, and the efforts to increase his visibility through billboards in public places appeared as a compensatory measure for his lack of charisma. They served to remind the public of his presence against the background of high prices, low wages and decline in living standards. In August 2016 he was nearly killed in an assassination attempt, declared that a coup against him was plotted, and both of his parents shortly died out of mushroom poisoning.

In Borodai's recollection, the two oblasts had their own rivalry.

Donetsk and Lugansk were different oblasts and had a separate existence in Ukraine before the war. Lugansk elite was apprehensive of the Donetsk one which was richer, more numerous and more charismatic. As a result, the idea of unification was immediately rejected on the Lugansk initiative out of the fear that they will be overpowered by Donetsk. This also transpired in popular sentiments.[60]

Subsequently, instead of pulling forces together, the "republics" created borders between each other. Reportedly, Russian presidential administration suggested to Zakharchenko on a few occasions that LNR and DNR can form one unit, with him as the leader. The Russian military were advising to at least integrate the armies into a single structure which could be vital if a war resumes. But the clients not always listen to their patrons, and this is not happening because

Those who are making money out of it, have a different opinion. All have their own mafia, criminal power-holding, tough guys who control assets and resources. Plotnitsky also tries to control stuff. There are more internal disputes and murders of commanders at LNR. Even Russian curators are not up to scratch there. There are checkpoints on main roads, customs inspections. Cargo has to be declared and duties paid. Population at LNR wants to unite with DNR. They are very angry and say: "they built a 'border'—what kind of raving madness is that?" So, the issue is postponed, and also depends on which way the question of war and peace would go.[61]

HOSTAGES OF THE SITUATION: WHERE NEXT?

After years of separate existence, the rebels were not where they started in spring 2014. A distinct movement crystallized out of amorphous aspirations and dreams, and acquired political identity and a degree of popular support. Perhaps several hundred volunteers who came from Russia and elsewhere decided to stay and now perceived Donbas as their home. They understand that not everything is perfect, but are quite happy and do not wish to leave as they enjoy constantly changing dynamic, things happening all the time and the atmosphere of excitement of struggle for the cause. Some accepted downshifting as one Moscow upper-middle-class man who went to Donbas when the war broke out to serve as a company commander in Luhansk. He stayed on after he demobilized from the "LNR" army. A young Moscow pub waitress woman also was happy to stay. A man from Russia's Lipetsk became a lieutenant in DNR artillery forces and enjoys it. Combatants from other parts of Ukraine, who lost their careers and businesses there, and who unlike most of Russian volunteers had been at war nonstop since 2014, such as a tank trooper from Kharkiv and a fighter from Odesa, are believed to be the most irreconcilable. They do not want to make peace, but express that they wish to "return home in tanks" and are determined for this to happen.[62]

Majority of Russian combatants went back, but did not lose touch with their former comrades-in-arms in the region, keep up their networks, arms and trainings bases, and as put by Norin, "will gallop back" if something start happening. "Everybody understands, that if a war re-starts, the current brigades and corps will shrink down a lot, and the war will be waged by those who really want and can do something." Many rebels who demobilized feel the same. They returned to civilian life and became reservists who would move to the frontlines if the NGCAs come under a ground offensive. They carried their weapons home before forced disarmament took place: a pistol in a bedside table and a machinegun in a wardrobe was a standard occurrence. One rebel kept an anti-tank gun in his wardrobe and a bunch of *Shmels* under the bed.[63]

Old altruism subsided and people started counting money again, including in defence duties. A fighter in the army was getting 15,000 roubles which was not much, but it mattered in the conditions of high unemployment. Many spirited middle class fighters left the ranks as they had jobs to go to, or had transferrable skills to be able to find one, and were replaced by a less educated cohort, for whom soldiering was just a job. However, a caliber of such "15-rouble soldier" is low. "The LNR and DNR rebels are different now. These are former miners. They wish to be paid for the service, while the volunteers only wanted food and cigarettes."[64]

This is inevitable because the conflict remains "hot" rather than "frozen." The relevant question is how much land the rebels wished to take before they decided that the war was over. The situation on the ground was such that both the Ukrainian military and the rebels were not satisfied by the war outcomes and believed that they could win a victory. As long as shelling of populated areas by Ukrainian army was possible, incentives for war prevailed. Zakharchenko and Eduard Basurin, deputy commander of DNR military corps, promised more than once to "have the rebel tanks in Kyiv," but qualified these statements by "in case the Ukrainian side starts a new offensive." Certainly, any offensive ambitions must be measured against improved fighting capabilities of the Ukrainian armed forces and the effort they had invested in fortified defenses against the line of contact. For example, the rebels tried to seize Piski and Avdiivka, but the Ukrainian side resisted and the attack failed. However, a decision to supply lethal weapons to Kyiv, if taken by Western powers, is likely to prompt attempts at territorial acquisition before this happened. In this logic, offensive operations would need to be completed and a new frontline line established conducive to the rebels' defense needs before these weapons were deployed, as this would be harder to do so afterwards.

The resumption of war remained a major preoccupation for society, with the resultant pressure on the *de facto* authorities to push the Ukrainian army away from those positions that allowed the shelling of civilian areas. UN OHCHR shows that far more fatalities occurred in the NGCAs than in the GCAs, and in early 2017 42 percent of casualties were sustained as a result of shelling.[65] Data from an October 2015 poll showed that around 80 percent of Donetsk city residents perceived a very high degree of probability that military hostilities would resume.[66] A pragmatic argument, in which some commanders believed, was that advances much further beyond the current positions would not be to the rebels' advantage. Populations further westwards may not welcome them as liberators, but treat them as oppressors. In case of a mass offensive, the rebel forces will have to shell civilian areas which will turn people away from them. They should stop the fight at the point where a viable defence frontier could be established and rebel-held cities were out of Ukrainian artillery range. There were strong disincentives for capturing Mariupol which was used as a seaport for legal exports from the NGCAs until 2017. Moreover, it is a big city which would need to be supplied and could be a burden for DNR's fragile economy.

At the same time, there was a political argument that the areas formerly under the rebel control as of May 2014 where the population voted "yes" in May 2014 referenda were the part of the same polity and should be joined in. Irrespective of nonrecognition of the referenda, their results provided a coherent foundation for the rebel narrative. The vote gave the rebels a claim to legitimacy in the eyes of their supporters in the NGCAs and beyond as people there, in their line of argumentation, expressed their will, and Kyiv was holding them by force. In this logic, these lands should be retaken, including Sloviansk, Kramatorsk, Mariupol, Sievierodonetsk, and Lysychansk. Many fighters originated from there, cherished the dream of "liberation" and returning home. Moreover, these cities had industrial capabilities, useful for expanding the economic base for the NGCAs. General Sergei Petrovsky (Khmuryi *Gloomy, Bad Soldier*), formerly head of DNR military intelligence, noted that 30–40 percent of fighters thought this way, while he and the others considered the administrative boundaries of Donetsk oblast a viable target.[67]

Taking the territories back which the rebels originally controlled inspires the fighters and is a big grudge against their political leaderships who would not order the offensive: "The 'republics' included much larger lands. We are on the stump of the territories which proclaimed independence three years ago."[68] Only then their desire for territorial gains would be saturated and the will for a lasting ceasefire would be genuine rather than forced inducing them to freeze the conflict and concentrate on rebuilding civilian life. Moscow's lack of green signal for such offensive remained an obstacle to the spread of the conflict. Can this last? Juchkovsky does not think so, as the situation is constantly on the brink:

> Frontline is next to cities, it doesn't change although fighting continues. I think that military hostilities are inevitable and that the logic of the process leads this way. It does not even matter who will start. When there is a frontline with a huge amount of people and armaments, when nobody is trying to separate these forces and does not agree on any compromises, when none of the provisions of the peace agreement are implemented, it is inevitable that something will flare up. This is a powder keg, and neither side wishes to solve the crisis. This knot can be cut only by some decisive act, and this can be a military operation. Population also wants an offensive, however strange this might sound, so that something changes towards resolution. "Let it get worse if war resumes, but this will bring some concrete result," they say. This state of uncertainty is the most awful thing. People all the time are expecting either our or their offensive. This barbaric shelling, destruction is unbearable. The USSR produced enough arms for a long war with the West, and all this stuff is firing and firing now.[69]

Thus, preoccupation was to ensure continuous survival rather than conquer great new vistas. A dash beyond Donbas did not appear on anybody's cards and opening of a second front amounted to not more than a wild fantasy. When I asked a former rebel fighter from Kharkiv whether he believed that the city should be taken, he replied in the negative: it would have to be heavily bombarded and was too beautiful to be destroyed. He was unwilling to see this happen. The idea of a greater Novorossiya defined in historical terms of Catherine the Great epoch was not entirely gone, but was rather floated in politicized circles than among fighters. The Donbas movement although rooted in its local context, was not confined to narrow geographic boundaries, because its ideology was not based on an ethnic homeland and was not territorially bound. So, where would it end? As put by Akhra Avidzba, *Pyatnashka* battalion commander, "Who knows: maybe, the end will come when we will be removing the American Statue of Liberty, like Lenin, from its pedestal stone?"[70]

To conclude, the rebels in three years after the uprising were not quite where they wanted to be. Whether the glass is half-empty or half-full, depends on the perspective. On the downside, Russia did not take them in. Security situation calmed down, but not stabilized and casualties occurred on an almost daily basis. A threat of a major government offensive could not be ruled out. Political direction was that of duality: internally, a movement was gaining momentum as toward building of "independent republics," and externally—as a line for reintegration with the rest of Ukraine. This left the end goals free to interpretation. At the same time, the NGCAs did not implode and a nascent political order was installed. New elites emerged out of field commanders. Criminal situation was reined in and defence forces became a major pillar of "statebuilding." Economy took a hit, but did not collapse and many of Donbas's productive capacities remained. Importantly, the experience of war, resistance and survival gave birth to a new quality in people who went through it, and their identity was now based on more than just historical and cultural closeness to Russia. The NGCAs were preparing for a long haul of uncertainty, waiting for big players to act, but in the meantime were consolidating internally. Little dramatic change was expected as the tectonic shift which prompted them into existence had already occurred.

NOTES

1. Alexei Miroshnichenko, an intelligence officer of SBU 5th Department who defected to LNR, named 2,600 dead in Ilovaisk and 6–7,000 dead at Debaltseve, press conference in Luhansk on 15 June, *Colonel Cassad*. http://colonelcassad.livejournal.com/ Also International Crisis Group 2015 briefing. *ATO Memory Book* officially records losses, but the Ukrainian military had released some statements giving higher numbers.

2. "Kyiv May Now Have As Many as 16,000 Armed Deserters on Its Hands," October 5, 2015. *SputnikNews*. http://sputniknews.com/military/20151005/1028034616/ukraine-army-deserters.html

3. "Poroshenko: army lost 65% of armour in fighting in eastern Ukraine," *Russia Today* September 22, 2014, http://russian.rt.com/inotv/2014-09-22/Poroshenko-V-boyah-na-vostoke

4. As put by Alexander Kofman in May 2015 when Russian-Ukrainian relations began to normalize, "the Novorossiya project is temporary suspended."

5. Alexander Zakharchenko in conversation with Alexander Chalenko, who conveyed this information to the author in an interview.

6. Interview respondents, irrespective of their political orientations, pointed to the role of Rinat Akhmetov who allegedly was in cahoots with somebody who had the power to halt the offensive, but no evidence was available to support this theory, while interlocutors stressed that what they heard were "rumors" or offered their own readings of the situation.

7. Author interview with a rebel from Lysychansk.

8. Yevgenii Norin, author's interview.

9. "Боец: Командиры знали, что 32-й блокпост находится в окружении, и нас отправляли прямо в засады," November 21, 2017, https://112.ua/statji/boec-komandiry-znali-chto-32-y-blokpost-nahoditsya-v-okruzhenii-i-nas-otpravlyali-pryamo-v-zasady-149093.html

10. Yevgenii Norin, *Fall of Donetsk Airport* (Moscow: Sputnik-i-Pogrom, 2015).

11. Cited in Yevgenii Norin, *Battle of the Year: Seizure of Debaltseve* (Moscow: Sputnik i Pogrom, 2015). http://sputnikipogrom.com/2015-in-review/48901/battle-of-2015/#.V_jJlFQrK70

12. Ilya Barabanov, "В пампасах Донбасса," *Kommersant*, February 19, 2015, http://kommersant.ru/doc/2671088

13. Norin, "Battle of the Year."

14. Elena Kostyuchenko, "Мы все знали, на что идем и что может быть," March 2, 2015, *Novaya Gazeta*, https://www.novayagazeta.ru/articles/2015/03/02/63264-171-my-vse-znali-na-chto-idem-i-chto-mozhet-byt-187

15. Cited in Norin, "Battle of the Year."

16. Valery Shiryaev, "Это — война," *Novaya Gazeta*, August 8, 2016, https://www.novayagazeta.ru/articles/2016/08/08/69482-eto-voyna

17. http://www.osce.org/special-monitoring-mission-to-ukraine

18. "Anxious Ukraine Risks Escalation In "Creeping Offensive," January 30, 2017, *Radio Free Europe/ Radio Liberty*, https://www.rferl.org/a/ukraine-russia-creeping-offensive-escalation-fighting/28268104.html

19. Alexander Juchkovsky, author's interview. On missile launch see https://sputniknews.com/europe/201702131050611355-ukraine-tactical-missiles/

20. Tsyganok, "Neokonchennaya Voina," 443.

21. "Боевики «ЛНР» осуществили принудительное разоружение «казаков» в Петровском, Красном Луче и Лутугино,"*Ostrov*, 3 April 2015,http://www.ostro.org/general/society/news/467734/

22. UN OHCHR 2015b.

23. Strannik, author's interview, Moscow, May 2016.

24. Prince, author's interview.

25. Alexander Chalenko, author's interview.

26. Prince, author's interview.

27. Alexander Chalenko, author's interview.

28. Yulia Polukhina, "Как устраняли командиров, нелояльных главе ЛНР," *Novaya Gazeta*, December 16, 2015, http://www.novayagazeta.ru/inquests/71182.html

29. Vladimir Dergachoff, author's interview.

30. 24 сентября 2016 http://www.novorosinform.org/news/61054

31. Alexei Mozgovoi, poem published in 2013, https://www.stihi.ru/2013/06/01/8015

32. Alexander Chalenko, author's interview.

33. Alexander Borodai, author's interview.

34. "Командиры ЛНР попросили Госдуму РФ поддержать «Русский проект»," *Regnum*, May 20, 2015 https://regnum.ru/news/1926116.html

35. Dmitrii Kirillov, "Моторолу проводили как символ," Gazeta.ru, October 19, 2016 https://www.gazeta.ru/politics/2016/10/19_a_10259765.shtml#page2

36. Alexander Juchkovsky, author's interview.

37. International Crisis Group, "The Ukraine Crisis: Risks of Renewed Military Conflict after Minsk II," Europe Briefing 73, April 1, 2015, 2.

38. Ilya Barabanov, author's interview.

39. Author's interview with an informed political observer, Moscow, May 2016.

40. Valery Shiryaev, "Это — война," *Novaya Gazeta*, August 8, 2016, https://www.novayagazeta.ru/articles/2016/08/08/69482-eto-voyna

41. See, for example, Oleg Tsaryov's interview "Новороссии нужен мир." September 19, 2014. *Russkaya Vesna* http://rusvesna.su/news/1411037873

42. Oleg Tsaryov, author's interview.

43. "Павел Губарев: Наша цель — новая страна, страна мечты," 30 September 2014, http://rusrand.ru/events/pavel-gubarev

44. Georgi M. Derluguian and Serge Cipko, "The Politics of Identity in a Russian Borderland Province: The Kuban Neo-Cossack Movement, 1989–1996," *Europe-Asia Studies* 49, no. 8 (1997): 1485–1500.

45. Boris Rozhin in *Colonel Cassad*, 18 December 2015. http://colonelcassad.livejournal.com

46. Alexander Chalenko, author's interview.

47. Vladimir Zharikhin, author's interview.

48. Quoted by Alexei Tokarev "Андрей Пургин: Не Надо Делать Из Донбасса Мордор!" 12 May 2016 https://defendingrussia.ru/a/andrej_purgin_ne_mordor-5889/

49. Alexei Tokarev, author's interview.

50. *RIA Novosti*. November 3, 2014. http://ria.ru/infografika/20141103/1031547731.html

51. February 19, 2016, https://regnum.ru/news/polit/2083009.html

52. Poll quoted by Gazeta.ru on August 4, 2016, http://www.gazeta.ru/politics/2016/08/03_a_9747233.shtml#!photo=0

53. UN OHCHR 2015c.

54. RIA Novosti Ukraine. November 30, 2015 http://rian.com.ua/interview/20151130/1001245689.html

55. Research was conducted by independent social scientists commissioned by "DNR Entrepreneurs" Association based in Donetsk, cited by Gazeta.ru, August 4, 2016, http://www.gazeta.ru/politics/2016/08/03_a_9747233.shtml#!photo=0

56. Alexander Juchkovsky, author's interview.

57. Dmitrii Kirillov, Vladimir Dergachoff, "МГБ приходит ночью" January 30, 2016, https://www.gazeta.ru/politics/2016/01/30_a_8048999.shtml

58. Vladimir Dergachoff, Dmitrii Kirillov, "Хорошего мало, зато нет «бандеров»," August 4, 2016 http://www.gazeta.ru/politics/2016/08/03_a_9747233.shtml#!photo=0

59. International Kyiv-based humanitarian worker, author's interview.

60. Alexander Borodai, author's interview.

61. Alexander Juchkovsky, author's interview.

62. Yevgenii Norin, author's interview.

63. *Shmel* is a rocket-propelled infantry flamethrower known in Afghanistan as Shaitan-tube.

64. Prince, author's interview.

65. See map of "Civilian casualties along the contact line, 16 February–15 May 2017" in 18th UN OHCHR report.

66. "Yevgen Kopat'ko: На Донбассе с трудом представляют, как жить вместе с теми, кто воевал против них," interview by Kirill Vyshinkii, RIA Novosti Ukraine, November 30, 2015, http://rian.com.ua/interview/20151130/1001245689.html

67. "Большое интервью генерала Петровского, или так говорит 'Хмурый,'" December 12, 2014. http://www.ukraina.ru/interview/20141226/1011633098.html

68. Alexander Juchkovsky, author's interview.

69. Alexander Juchkovsky, author's interview.

70. Avidzba interviewed by Alexei Tokarev in "Героизм Показывать Можно, Но Нельзя Страдать Тупостью," March 14, 2016, https://defendingrussia.ru/a/ahra_avidzba_intervju-5361/

Chapter 9

New Symbolism in the Digital Era

This is not going to be an action chapter. This chapter will deal with a cultural and semantic side of things—the images of self and the other which trigger emotions, symbols, and meanings that help to transmit feelings into action, and the ways of their communicating so that they acquire a power of their own. Images and symbols enable people to come to terms with who is "us" and "them" in the circumstances when "them" until recently had been "ones of us." Warring parties around the world try to create an inspiration for "rallying around the flag," but this flag has to be produced in the cases when it was not supplied by historical circumstances. When new symbols and messages are created and are transmitted, they turn into tools to draw more people in, and assume an autonomous existence. The chapter traces the process of how the rebels have done this, and is a crossover between culture, politics, and communication, all essential ingredients to make the rebellion a real, full-blooded thing, which are not less important than building up the fighting capabilities. It seeks to represent perspectives of the conflict participants through their own cultural expression. It does not apply a test of plausibility, whereas the members of *Somali* battalion were not black, this does not mean that they could not call themselves *Somalis*.

The rebellion can be framed in terms of a social movement, that is, when groups of actors adopt the same symbols, values, and beliefs, and create networks of shared meanings with the intention of changing some aspect of the social structure.[1] The movement requires some symbolism to foster a sense of a collective cultural identity that can carry a powerful emotional and moral resonance. Sacrifice and myths of war are particularly effective in creating identity consciousness and sentiments of mutual dependence and exclusivity which reinforce this shared culture.[2] The social process of conflict was a tremendous opportunity for creativity on an individual and group levels as it was opening the doors into the new world and making a break with the old one. This was a bottom-up process which sprung up in different places simultaneously and brought their colors to it. The revolutionary spirit it unleashed produced its discourses and images which the collapse of the communist system and transition to the Western-style liberal democracy failed to do. Post-communism transformation essentially meant an application of imported concepts and *know-how* to the local context and left little room for indigenous creativity. The struggle for Donbas was different as it energized own powers and resources.

The improvised and anarchic nature of the insurgency that characterized Donbas conflict transpired not only in its military and political aspects, but also in the construction of a new "imagined community" that allowed people to develop a sense of who they were and where they were going. The conflict emerged in an absence of pre-manufactured beliefs and clear-cut identities because of its largely non-ethnic character, which otherwise would have supplied it with a narrative justifying a claim to a homeland. At the same time, history was important for extracting the new ideas and meanings. The conflict can be seen both as conventional, in a sense, timeless, and very postmodern. "Old" in the sense that people were prepared to die for such signifiers as language, land, and a "community of my people," but postmodern as well, combining anti-westernism, the glory of God, challenge to the liberal world order, and antifascism. The main themes were assertion of indigenous culture and values, claim to have own voice heard, expression of shared bonds of solidarity and sacrifice, and the war of "non-West" against the "West," with the use of "Western" tools against the "West." The conflict actors interpreted the faultlines that divided them from the "Other" as a non-Western civilization asserting itself against it. The efforts of the West as they saw it, to promote its values of liberalism as universal, which were embodied by the new authorities in Kyiv, came against a countering response.[3]

The war was fought in the information space, as well as on the battlefield. However, insurgencies' initial ideas typically present a release of pent-up emotions and latent ambitions before they could evolve into a narrative of some kind as a semiological way of constructing shared reality.[4] The rebellion narrative and subculture which went with it gradually evolved out of the ingredients at hand and became effective as it managed to create its own discursive community. This subculture presented a cherry-picked combination of symbols that the rebels claimed, ranging from the uptake of old signifiers, such as the Russian Orthodox Church which peacefully coexisted with godless Lenin, to the views on the Scottish referendum happening at the same time in 2014 and the immersion into modern western pop culture.[5] It is easy to dismiss these beliefs and their expressions as a mishmash of gibberish which does not fit into a rational discourse, but if it had a pull of attraction, then it was real. The rebels were projecting their worldview, no matter how incoherent and contradictory it was: if they could get the audiences to buy into it and start reproducing, then it worked, as it co-opted more followers.

Recognizing that conflict was played out in the global and local media space, the insurgents tried to use the weight of the media against the media to counteract it. Communications directed at support and adversary bases were seeking to evoke emotions as social movements do by sowing distrust, reappropriating anger, countering fear and showing contempt through the use of satire.[6] Modern technology made it possible to spread the word and post an image, quickly claiming the "truth space" as soon as an event happened. Development of media resources from below not only helped to get information into the public domain, but also facilitated refining of the narrative out of the early cacophony of beliefs and emotions.

WHAT IS MY NAME?

The rebellion came about very quickly and could not identify itself with a claim to a territory, material culture, myth of Golden Age or blood bonds. However, the conflict participants had to draw the lines of self-identification somehow. They molded different cultural elements of individual and collective senses of self into a melting pot, and were drawing on local and global references in the process. Some of the references were rooted in the region's past, such as its Cossack heritage, while others were distant, but the insurgents felt they had an affinity in the spirit and values with them. Cultural associations were far from inward-looking. On the contrary, Donbas movement regarded itself as a chain in a liberation struggle of other peoples around the world. The references to political events and heroic characters from European and world history reflected that, such as the Risorgimento, Garibaldi's liberation war in Italy, Spanish International Brigades, Jeanne d'Arc, and Che Guevara. Novorossiya's original design referred to the Italian Lega Nord. Connections were also made to the former Yugoslavia and the historical Slavic brotherhood that left its imprint in Donbas. For example, the town of Slavyanoserbsk in Luhanska oblast was named after the Serbian officers who were there in the service of Russia's Empress Elizabeth in mid-eighteenth century.

Cultural expressions manifested in different forms, such as fighters' radio call signs, names of battalions and the invention of new paraphernalia. The whole affair had an element of theatricality with the conflict participants becoming actors on a gigantic stage and populating it with characters and decorations, against which the plot unfolded. Anybody could play a role and become a director, a costume designer or a star, especially if they had such photogenic looks as the commander *Givi*. New individual identities were expressed in radio call signs which the insurgents invented and by which they communicated, such as Demon, Shaman, Lynx, Gypsy, Contra, Padre, and Bodkin. *Douchman*, for example, was a popular call sign and is an Afghan word for "enemy." As the Soviet Union fought the war in Afghanistan in 1979–1989, it influenced vocabulary of the *Russian World* and the term entered its folklore. These designations reflected the spirit of defiance and a developing free guerrilla army. One can call oneself some name and then live into the role. People would enact different fictional characters in this real-life performance, such as commander *Batman* (Alexander Bednov) who set up a battalion of the same name. A similar process was underway in Ukrainian territorial battalions. Numbered call signs appeared much later when a command-and-control structure emerged. Strelkov's call sign was "First" and, as put by Norin, "in truth, he was the Number One."[7]

Call signs served as an image booster when the fighters could project themselves as more powerful individuals than the reality perhaps was. For example, there were plenty of Tsars (Kings)—there were seven of them in Sloviansk alone. The first volunteer commanders in Sloviansk were Prince, Viking, and Cap (shortened from Captain). Russian combatants were said to be more creative and attuned to globalized culture. For example, there was a *Kiba*, a young man from Russia who named himself after a popular character a *shinobi* fond of his dog, from a Japanese anime Naruto. Members of reconnaissance units favored animal call signs, such as Spider, Fox, Cobra, Opossum, and Owl, as they associated their missions with clandestine nighttime activities which required predatory qualities. Nice and fluffy animals were a domain of women's call signs, such as *Kiska* (female kitten) and sometimes more voracious, as *Tigra* (Tigress), as there were women in active combat duties. Call signs could express menace toward the adversary and fortitude of their bearers: a young man in one DNR's reconnaissance team called himself *Palach* (Executioner). Self-images could reflect certain pessimism, such as Khmuryi (Solemn, call sign of general Petrovsky, one of the top DNR commanders). On the sunny side, there were a *Dobryi* (Kind, who was a deputy brigade commander), *Svyatoi* (Saint), and *Zolotoi* (Golden).

At the same time, my interlocutors noted a scarcity of fantasy in inventing individual self-designations. A rebel told the story of a man who was asked when he came to enlist what was his call sign. He shrugged his shoulders and replied *Liuboi* (Any) and ended up with the *Any* call sign. There were a lot of *Batyas* (colloquial for Dad). The other common signs were Kaban (Wild Boar), Ded (Granddad), and Starik (Old Man) or Staryi (Old) which did not necessarily signify the advanced years of their bearers but were chosen as self-mockery. A rebel remarked that "there was always confusion with call signs. Several people often would answer a radio call all at once." The right of ownership could have fatal consequences: one Boar shot down the other at a Donetsk petrol station when their dispute over which of them was the real one turned into a fit of rage.

Naming of battalions reflected myth-making for internal consumption as the fighters had to create some group coherence. Subsequently, their catchy names got famous among their support base thanks to prolific social media activity. Several set up their own websites, accepted donations through the internet and developed a dedicated network of followers. Some names were geographic and were related to the space which the rebels claimed to represent, such as the Army of the South-East, *Vostok* (East), or *Kalmius* named after a Donbas River. Others were referenced in time, for example, battalion August which was named after the month it was set up. They could carry a protective message such as *Oplot* (Stronghold) projecting reliability and solidarity for its supporters, or directed against the adversary, such as the Chechen battalion *Smert'* (Death). *Prizrak*[8] (Avenging Ghost) combined menace that was set on revenge with invisibility and mystical qualities of a "life after death." The battalion got its name because it outwitted death: the original rebel group survived a bombing, in which the Ukrainian media reported them killed; thus they disappeared as full-blooded fighters and became "ghosts." *Sparta* battalion was named after Sparta in ancient Greece whose 300 warriors defended Thermopylae Pass against a superior Persian army, in parallel to Donbas fighting, in which the rebel forces were vastly outnumbered.

Circumstances of conception explain some names. *Somali* battalion got its name from the first line up. When the fighters first came together and the weather was hot, they were dressed in all manner of civilian clothes, such as shorts, trainers and granddad's uniforms. They laughed at themselves because they did not look like a proper combat force, and decided that they more resembled Somali pirates rather than regular troops; hence they became *Somali*. *Pyatnashka* (Fifteen) "international brigade," commanded by the Abkhaz combatants Akhra Avidzba and Stavros Baratelia, got its dashing name after the number of its founding members- volunteers from Abkhazia, Russia, and other CIS countries. Its insignia included the flag of unrecognized Republic of Abkhazia and 15 stars, one of them black to commemorate its fallen founder Irakli Adleiba.[9]

WHO ARE "THEY"? IMAGES OF THE OTHER

In many ways, people on both sides of the conflict were and continued to feel close, and experienced short social distances from each other. The insurgents and members of pro-government forces sometimes knew each other in previous life or got connected on social media when the war started. As a local rebel said to me: "we could be lambasting each other and trading accusations on internet, and then something'll come up to which we'll both react the same. A photo of a little girl holding a kitten. And we both put 'Like' to it. What was neutral, still connected us a lot." However, the need to draw the lines and define "us" and "them" was of crucial importance for the new identity construction. The emergent "friend" and "foe" paradigms were called to mark a dividing line in the society where divisions traditionally had mostly been soft and barriers were fluid. The process has already started at Euromaidan which brought rapid linguistic innovation when new catch-phrases were born. It eventually moved from relatively benign nicknames into a more dangerous territory when the "villain," against whom the struggle was pursued, became designated in tangible and graphic terms. This process involved practices and language of "othering" to denigrate and de-humanize the opponents and reduce them to objects.

The term *Moskaly* meaning Russians and pro-Russian Ukrainians was in long use to name "the Other": in 1838, Ukrainian poet Taras Shevchenko wrote a poem "Kateryna" that reads "Fall in love, O dark-browed maidens, but not with the Moskaly."[10] *Moskaly* was used by Euromaidan supporters in attribution to their fellow countrymen who were not enthusiastic about Euroassociation. Starting from a widespread social label, it acquired a darker connotation when it began to appear in threatening contexts. It not only featured in badges and fridge magnets that could be found at the Andriyivskyy Uzviz tourist market in Kyiv, such as "God bless that I am not a Moskal," but also appeared in menacing sloganeering to describe those who should be dealt with. *Moskalyaku na gillyaku* (literally "Moskals on a branch" or Russians to hang) became a much watched video during a wave of anger provoked by Russia's actions in Crimea, although it was shot during the Euromaidan days in 2013 when Yanukovych was still in power.[11]

When the protest rallies in the Southeastern Ukraine broke out, the Maidan participants labeled their pro-Russian opponents *vatniks* literally meaning *bodywarmers* in reference to a military-style padded jacket worn by the Soviet soldiers. Its further derivative was *vata* (literally cotton wool), a meme that turned the enemy into an object and an amorphous mass devoid of any power of thought. At first, *vatniks* were pro-Russian citizens, in the view of some, Sovietized lumpenproletariat,[12] who supported the separation of Crimea and close ties with Russia for Southeastern Ukraine, but who were not prepared to fight for it and preferred more passive forms of protest.[13] It was later applied to the rebel fighters as well.

The other derogatory label that emerged was *colorad* (Colorado beetle) meant to reduce the enemy to a parasite insect. Pop singer Alexander Marchall summarized it by applying the label to himself: "I am a Russian *colorad* who loves vodka and parade." The meme featured in the commentary on social media on the Odesa massacre, in which *"colodary* burnt," and was applied to the World War II veterans who publicly displayed the St. George black and orange ribbon. The ribbon was introduced under Catherine the Great in 1769 together with the order of St. George, the patron saint of Russia, after whom the highest military award was named. The ribbon was revived in a Russian newspaper campaign in 2005, timed to mark the war victory, and people were encouraged to wear the ribbon on that day as a mark of remembrance. It then took on a wider significance that hinted at a symbol of "Russian greatness" linking it with the Soviet legacy. The ribbon was banned by law in Ukraine in June 2017 after Ukrainian nationalists burnt St. George ribbons during the celebrations, marking the anniversary of the victory over Nazi Germany in World War II in Kyiv on May 9.[14] As the fighting in Donbas progressed, the term *separ* (shortened from "separatist") appeared in application to the rebel fighters and their supporters, and was often used in street talk and in social media. The official designation of Donbas rebels as "terrorists" and the fighting – as the Anti-Terrorist Operation quickly became a popular one, mostly used in a combination with "Russian," that is, "Russian terrorists."[15] The rebel-controlled areas of Luhansk oblast came to be known as "Luganda" or "Lugandon" to symbolize chaos and lawlessness in reference to African countries as they were seen by the pro-Maidan supporters.

Russian armed forces, by contrast, possessed human qualities. The two terms born out of the Crimea crisis were *zelenye chelovechki* (little green men) in relation to unidentified gunmen who appeared in February on the peninsula. The Ukrainian response to the *little green men* catchphrase became *little black men* to describe members of territorial battalions. *Vejlivye liudi* (polite people) were those who "politely" interacted during the takeover forcing a peaceful surrender. The ironic term was used both in Ukrainian and Russian discourse. It was invented by Boris Rozhin, a Russian blogger from Sevastopol who first mentioned it in his Live Journal post on February 28, 2014.[16] The meme *polite people* became popular in the Russian-speaking world. Putin mentioned it in March 2014, and it was applied by the rebels themselves in relation to the Russians sent by the state on special missions. Rozhin explained that he decided not to claim a copyright, although one could buy jackets at Moscow street markets with a *polite people* tag.

Several labels appeared among pro-Russian constituencies as a direct reaction to the Euromaidan. They identified the opponents as mentally disturbed or temporarily possessed by a craze, and the word play between Maidan and Down (syndrome) was used to characterize them as such: *Maidowns* or *Maidanutye* (temporary insane through the Maidan experience), while one territorial battalion commander was labeled a *Downhouse*. The term *Pravoseki*, shortened from Pravyi (Right) Sector, was applied to the members of the group of the same name. The Right Sector's Euromaidan reputation supplied the term with a notorious connotation, as their actions drove radicalization of the protests and clashes with the police. The other terminology was rooted in Ukraine's divided history and centered on Stepan Bandera. *Banderovtsy* (supporters of Bandera) was a Soviet-era nickname for Western Ukrainians which was the opposite stereotype of *Moskaly*. It characterized its bearers as nationalists, who waged a partisan warfare against the Soviet rule into the 1950s and believed to harbor anti-Russian feelings ever since. Banderovtsy, Bandery, or Banderlogy, a meme from Rudyard Kipling's the *Jungle Book* to describe the monkeys of the Seeonee jungle, came to refer to pro-Europe, pro-Western Ukrainians who supported Maidan and opposed Yanukovych's presidency. The Nazi symbolism of some Maidan territorial battalions is well documented by Western journalists.[17] It resulted in anti-fascism becoming a crucially important theme in the developing narrative of the rebellion. The *Telegraph* wrote in 2014 that "the Azov men use the neo-Nazi Wolfsangel (Wolf's Hook) symbol on their banner and members of the battalion are openly white supremacists, or anti-Semites."[18] Fascist symbols of pro-Maidan groups,[19] such as the swastika,[20] as well as references by *Svoboda* (Freedom) political party, which was represented in the parliament, to their World War II roots, that included the history of punitive operations to enforce Nazi rule in Ukraine[21] fostered an anti-fascist discourse and imagery. As fascist symbols were displayed by the members of territorial battalions,[22] they started to be called *Naziki* (Nazis), the term also applied to the National Guard.

In the vein of anti-fascist symbolism, the word *junta* (pronounced as *khunta*)[23] was used in the rebel world to characterize the new power-holders in Kyiv per association with Latin American "fascist" coups such as the one that brought Pinochet to power in Chile. It briefly featured on the Russian TV channels following the Yanukovych ouster, but was removed when holding of the new presidential elections in Ukraine was announced. Poroshenko was recognized by Moscow as a legitimate president rather than a *junta* leader, which caused outrage among anti-Maidan activists in Ukraine. As put by Tatiana Montyan, Kyiv-based human rights defender, in her barrage against Moscow policy: "Who made you recognize *khuntyat'* (*junt-lings*), dear Russia?"[24] Banned from Russian national TV, the term *junta* continued to live on in folklore and on social media, and inspired further Russified derivatives.

The Donbas war supplemented the new vocabulary with warrior neologisms, although it must be stressed that they reflect the rhetoric of the active conflict participants. They were not necessarily shared by everybody in Donbas where many in society blamed the conflict on the Kyiv government and its western backers rather than on the ordinary Ukrainians or even members of the Ukrainian armed forces who responded to calls for mobilization. As the fighting broke out, the popular battlefield words in the rebel camp to designate the adversary became *Ukr* (shortened from Ukrainian) or *ukrop*, a wordplay on "Ukrainian," which literally means *dill*, used as an equivalent to the term *separ* applied on Kyiv side. The *Ukrop* label placed the adversary into herbal kingdom depriving it of human features and *Ukropia* (dill-country) came to mean Ukraine. In response, an UKROP political party abbreviated from Ukrainian Assembly of Patriots was established by right-wing Euromaidan activists. The Dill label became popular in Ukraine after artist Andrei Yermolenko designed a chevron which featured it and put out free on internet. It was used by ATO fighters, volunteers and ordinary people.

REBELS CRAFT SYMBOLS

Traditionally, the symbolism of *Kyivan Rus* was of importance for Russians,[25] as it represented the roots of Christian Orthodoxy and was perceived as being at the heart of the formation of Russian civilization.[26] This legacy was revived in the rebel narrative in its strong connectedness to religious spirituality. Faith was meant to lift fighting spirits and overcome fear as many rebels were believers. The rebel movement richly drew upon the Russian Orthodox religious signifiers. Yet, they coexisted with Islamic beliefs quite harmoniously, while numerous combatants from Muslim groups, such as North Caucasians, Azeris, Tajiks and Kazakhs joined *Novorossiya* movement and there was even an Islamic battalion. It can be said that the rebellion was in a sense an inter-faith movement to defend own culture, faith and uniqueness of communities against the forces of secularizing global liberalism, which tries to make everybody look the same. Prince showed me a photo of a slogan of Dagestani fighters at the time: "From Orthodox Muslims to Orthodox Christians" [православным от правоверных].This was another face of a popular improvisation. As Vladislav Mal'tsev wrote at the time, "groups which failed to find their place in the conditions of peace and in the framework of legitimate public institutions found their relevance in the regions of Ukraine where the armed conflict was unfolding."[27] Initially, the rebels were using Christian Orthodox symbols without being blessed by the official Church of the Moscow Patriarchate which expressed its opposition to participation of the faithful in the armed combat and to the use of religious means for political ends. This did not dissuade the adherents from their convictions and the ways to promote them, as religion was important on an individual level and the local priests were largely with the rebellion.

Russian Orthodox symbols were meant to strengthen spiritual resistance, provide comfort and a sense of belonging to a community of believers. They also had a protective function. They were noticeable in posters carried by demonstrators and in the names of some rebel groups who felt that God was with them. Old Believers blessed the *Russian Spring* movement and gave their ancient crosses to Russian volunteers leaving for Donbas, which they carried with them trusting their protective power. Icons often featured at cordons and barricades as protective signs. Flags bearing Mandylion that revived an old Russian warrior tradition were placed on tanks and became battalion banners. Old Cyrillic fonts typically used only by the Church appeared on the rebel insignia.[28] Banners of the *Russian Orthodox Army* were seen flying at checkpoints in Sloviansk, Makiivka, Donetsk, and other areas. Its headquarters featured a prayer house and were richly decorated with icons. Another Christian battalion bore an exotic name of the *Russian Orthodox Sunrise*. Some religious symbolic which the rebel groups in Donbas used were derived not from the present time, but from an early historic period of sixteenth to seventeenth century and referred to the pre-Schism (*Raskol*) tradition closer to Russian folk core. It was suppressed in the Soviet era and neglected by the modern Russian state, which modeled its revival on the continuity with the later historical period. Old Russian state symbols were also resurrected. For example, Alexander Zakharchenko chose to be inaugurated in November 2014 to the march of the Preobrajensky Regiment, from the era of Peter the Great.

Religious motives were also instrumental in construction of the enemy images. Non-Orthodox credentials of pro-Maidan forces with roots in Western Ukraine with its Catholic and Protestant congregations were often stressed by the pro-Russian camp, even if they did not constitute a majority among their opponents. The symbolic based on dark Gothic motives, fonts and red-and-black color combinations characteristic of Western Ukraine allowed picturing their opponents as the "forces of darkness" while the rebels presented themselves as the "forces of light." Oliksandr Turchinov, an adherent of a Word of Life Baptist church who ordered the ATO was nicknamed as a Bloody Pastor.

The rebellious "republics" decided fairly early on that the introduction of some "state" symbols was important for internal consumption in order to provide graphic expressions of the Self. "Official" flags and coats of arms were adopted which expressed Donbas's distinctiveness and combined the most important elements of the local context—the region's Cossack, agricultural and industrial make up. Some grounds have been laid already, upon which they could build. Visionary *Novorossiya* had been developing its symbolic over a period of time.[29] In the 1990 Donetsk journalists Vladimir and Dmitry Kornilovs revived the flag of *Donetsko—Krivorojskaya Respublika* as a symbol of their *Interdvijenie* movement. The battle flag of Novorossiya became the most famous when it started appearing in frontline news in 2014, and the rebel forces fought under it. It combines red color as a symbol of World War

II victory with a blue St. Andrew's cross against a white background refer-ring to Russia's naval jack. The label reads "Free Will and Labour" (Volya i Trud). Although the flag bears a strong resemblance to that of the Confeder-ate States of America's navy jack and battle flag, its creators claimed a local ancestry.[30] According to it, a crimson flag with St. Andrew's cross was given to the Cossacks of the Black Sea region by the Russian Emperor Alexander the Great, while red, crimson or mauve flags was already used by the Cos-sacks before and were associated with a local folk hero.[31]

The history of how the flag emerged was as follows. On December 4, 2013, three Ukrainian intellectuals—Chalenko, Alexander Vassiliyev, a historian from Odesa, and Mikhail Pavliv—got together to design the *Novorossiya* flag. Chalenko insisted at that meeting that the flag should include a double-headed eagle in its coat of arms. Pavel Gubarev's wife Ekaterina designed the insignia and the Gubarevs couple engaged in promotion of the symbols on social media. Reaction on pro-Ukrainian sites and on Facebook was at first stormy, then dismissive in a vein like "leave these fantasists alone," they are a kind of Tolkien fandom. Chalenko later told me that "when I watched Ukrai-nian tanks being destroyed under this flag in a few months" time, I thought that symbols had become the reality."[32]

This is what the DNR and LNR designers came up with to produce their "state" symbols. DNR had a head start. Its black, red and blue flag was conceived by the *Donetskaya Respublica* organization in 2005 and signifies the colors of mining, blood and sea, respectively. Religiosity featured in heraldry, such as in its coat of arms which contains a double-headed eagle (with no legs) and Archangel Michael with a sword and a beard. The LNR flag had no prior history and was designed from scratch. Communism-era references were important at the LNR, and its symbolic reflected that, while the place of religion was low-key. Its flag prominently featured the five-point star relating the new "republic" to its Soviet heritage supplemented by a small eight-point Orthodox star in its coats of arms. This is a *Rus'* or a Virgin star meaning eternal life, which appears in Andrei Pervozvannyi old Russian military award.

Russian volunteer leaders, including Borodai and Strelkov, were not aware of the existing symbols and myths, and they were not in the center of their attention. Strelkov, being a Monarchist and modeling himself on a White Army officer, tried to revive features dating to the period of Russian nobil-ity, such as in uniforms and titles of military ranks, which he attempted to introduce in Sloviansk. His theatrical personality, – Strelkov's hobby was in reconstruction of costumized historic military battles, – left its imprint. Still, he felt that the rebel leaders did not invest much into paraphernalia and there was no time for this, although he said to me in reflection symbolism was important for the local people. It's somehow connected to the South, to their mentality. But we did very little of that. Gubarev designed the Novorossiya insignia. I introduced military awards and the ranks of poruchik (lieutenant) and podporuchik (second lieutenant),[33] which Zakharchenko—a black bone—later abolished."[34]

Borodai was more aloof on the subject. He critically assessed Strelkov's attempts at constructivism: "they establish an entire political department in Slavyansk which was busy discussing titles of ranks, designs of uniforms and insignia. There was no time for that. What we needed was to fight the war."[35] He reflected that while some collective symbols were no doubt needed, it was not clear what could make sense in the circumstances. The context was too eclectic even in its graphic incarnations to be plausibly presented as "local." Borodai was saying to me that

> The Donetsk city insignia, for example, was a palm tree.[36] "Donetsk People's Banana Republic," we used to joke. The symbol of *Oplot* was a rhino, also hardly a Donbas native. So we were all over the place on this.[37]

The characters described in this book eventually found their images represented by a Russian sculptor Timur Zamilov, who started to produce handmade metallic toy soldiers modeled on them. His creations feature Motorola, Strelkov and a colorful Cossack warrior Babay which became big sale hits.[38] On a sober note, the conflict produced some real-life characters that inspired a popular appeal, became "heroes" in the eyes of their followers and emerged as new role models. If in the 1990s the models for young Russian males revolved around a "cool bandit" image,[39] they became replaced by patriotic characters of the *Russian Spring*.

COMMUNICATIONS: SPREADING THE WORD, POSTING AN IMAGE

Volumes are written about "Russian hybrid warfare."[40] The role of Russian national media which pumped emotional messaging since the beginning of 2014 must be acknowledged, but it is also worth remembering that it is not a magic powder which turns everything into ashes. Exploration of insurgents' media contests representation of the conflict as a plot masterminded in some underground brain cellar in Moscow. It is in fact akin to the belief held by Soviet public about anti-Soviet political jokes which they thought were designed by the CIA and planted into the USSR to undermine it from inside. When Communism fell, these people realized that the CIA did not have a sense of humor.

In 2014, fifteen Russian channels were banned by Ukraine's Television National Council in a move aimed at diminishing Russia's cultural presence in public space. This changed the media scene, although 18 percent of viewing audience in 2015 still managed to watch Russian TV.[41] However, Russian channels were not the only information source with sympathetic coverage of Donbas rebellion. Moreover, the Russian TV reported on Donbas from an officially sanctioned line and did not go into many local details. The rebels were not always happy with the mainstream Russian channels either which were, in their view, too cautious and did not give sufficient prominence to the negative trends during Euromaidan at first. An interviewed Russian volunteer combatant who in 2013 used to work as a journalist at the NTV channel in Moscow was dissatisfied with how the network covered the events in Ukraine. He felt that their reporting contained little analysis on the depth of the crisis and there was no sense of urgency that things might turn up badly wrong. He was saying to me that

> we used to cover the events in different regions of Ukraine together with local journalists, but then some Ukrainian colleagues started declining to cooperate with us. NTV was not raising the alarm early enough. They did not listen to me in 2013 when I was talking about a threat to the *Russian World*.

Mass communications do not have to solely rely on state outlets because trust can be established online thanks to a declining price of connectivity. The novelty of the twenty-first-century warfare is that "irregular movements started using commoditised information technologies as an extended platform."[42] Unlike the earlier post-Soviet conflicts, where the recognized states had a considerable advantage, Donbas unfolded in the digital era when nobody had an information monopoly. It was possible to supply alternative viewpoints which eventually created the demand for them. The rebels benefitted from the recent trends which work in favor of modern insurgents, because information becomes more social and less state-owned, nobody has a monopoly on it, the costs of global telecommunications decrease and target audiences are increasingly more diverse.[43]

The rebels were pursuing their communication campaigns alongside fighting, as they were trying to put their point across. The significance of external communication was recognized early on, just as it was in the conflict in Abkhazia, where one of the first things that the Abkhaz *de facto* authorities did was to establish their Apsny-Press news agency in 1995. Dismissed as illegitimate at first, its materials became recognized as the main source of news on the state of affairs in Abkhazia. From the onset, the rebels established their information channels on internet, such as digital TV and websites, and used electronic media, for example, Live Journal or VKontakte social networking site to put their side of the story out. These allowed them to reach out to population directly. LNR Cossack commanders were establishing their TV stations as a matter of priority in the areas they controlled. The rebels were aided by foreigners in speaking to global audiences who joined their cause. They made their contribution by filming and distributing the video material, such as Margarita Seidler from Germany who was by Strelkov's side in Sloviansk[44] and a man from Poland who was in charge of communications in Donetsk.[45]

As with any communication in the conditions of warfare, the rebel outputs were aimed at a particular construction of reality, favorable to their cause. It included ideological, emotional and, at times, religious connotations. Communication was geared in two directions: adversary and supporter outreach. The latter was based on the premise that people trust the news with which they have "frame alignment," that is, the convergence between the narrative and the views and beliefs they already hold. In supporter outreach, victimhood, such as civilian casualties, was emphasized to invoke a feeling of indignation, but also a focus was put on large costs and the price paid by the ATO forces in Donbas. The "real-life" tales of heroism and focussing attention on the cruelty of the adversary bring out gloomy and sometimes hard-to-watch scenes, although viewers were warned in advance (*zhest"*) before starting a video.

The rebel channels, although obviously reflecting their ideological positions, posted fairly accurate news often confirmed by video or other evidence.[46] They also shed light on disagreements within their own ranks, especially during the active phase of the conflict when political and personal rivalries between field commanders were acute or when opposition to the Minsk agreement was strong. As a result, they came to be viewed as credible and appealing both to the Russian-speaking and international audiences due to their creative use of imagery, punchy humour, candid narrative and insights into differences within the rebel camp. These sites and channels continued to have an audience in the rest of Ukraine because the internet it is much harder to ban than TV.

The war was fought in the conditions when the population of Donbas was heavily connected to the internet and knew how to use it. Anybody could become a newsmaker, a producer, a journalist or a photographer if they had a story to tell that the public wanted to hear. New media resources for the first time showed fighting as it was, through high quality, wide ranging video footage uploaded on YouTube with astonishing speed. It was possible to see a lot of scenes shot from different cameras/ angles which made it easier to distinguish fakes, which were also used by the rebels for disinformation purposes, for example, by Bezler and Strelkov. As Bolt writes, "pictures speak louder than words. Rather they speak viscerally and emotively. They depend both on what revelation the image brings to the viewer, and what pre-knowledge the viewer delivers to the image."[47]

Prevailing content was fairly optimistic, in the same vein as Winter describes in his work on the ISIS, and built a "coherent narrative that is at once positive and alternative." The media outlets played the role of a morale booster and inspired a new kind of digital solidarity. They helped to construct icons and images when it was hard to tell in the end who was doing the fighting and who was better in creating the right look. A Kyiv-based international observer remarked to me,

> I felt at the time that the information warfare was won by the rebels on the Russian side. Smiling and upfront people were DNR and LNR. I thought in 2014 that they will win.

To be fair, *Givi*'s photogenic looks often featured and brought him fame perhaps beyond his wildest dreams, such as in the video of fighting for Donetsk airport,[48] on which the BBC filmmakers modeled an episode of their "World War Three: Inside the War Room" film, albeit without *Givi* and the rebels' authorship. The rebels when I was speaking to them soon after the film was released, were irritated about it, but did not know how to react.

The internet played a major role in crowdsourcing of funding. The initiative started already during the Crimea crisis, but did not go very far as the Russian state arrived. However, money was required for Donbas to finance a dispatch of volunteers of different kinds, and procure humanitarian and "non-humanitarian" aid. Prince explained that "people are charitable. When they see that the situation is bad, they are ready to help those in need. They trusted us because we were on the ground." He recalled that their effort used to collect 5–7 million roubles per day in the most turbulent months of 2014. Many Russians from abroad including from the United States, United Kingdom, Germany, Australia etc., sent their life savings of $50,000–$100,000 to procure what the rebels needed. *Babushkas* contributed their funeral savings. A donation point was opened, to which people brought cash, uniforms, flak jackets, etc. They came not only from Russia—for example, a retired general from Kazakhstan called to offer 4000 elite tactical vests which they had spare. The new media outlets were relevant for forming the public opinion and keeping the interest going, but my respondents dismissed their significance for mobilization of volunteer combatants from Russia for fighting in Donbas. In the words of Borodai, "they played some role, but minimal. Somehow these people found each other when they went to Transnistria before. They already know other like-minded people and find ways to get in touch when a need arises."

None of the rebel media resources could be described as "mass" but they were hardly "niche" either, because they had a sizeable following and came to shape the relevant segment of public opinion. One prominent rebel resource which sprang to life was *Novorossiya News—Strelkov's Briefs* ("Новости Новороссии — сводки от Стрелкова" novorosinform.org) which was the most conspicuous project and quickly acquired a half million users. The coverage was brief, with little pontificating, but fast. The administrators, their location unknown succeeded in establishing a network of contributors throughout Donbas and published their reports very quickly with only slight editing. Afterwards, the publication described itself as an information agency of a "Greater Russia" which was started in 2014 owing to the events in Crimea and Donbas. Its initial mission was to cover military developments in the region, but as it became more established, it moved to report on the developments in the *Russian World* and some global events. The agency praised itself that it raised subjects that mainstream media silenced.

RussVesna (Russian Spring rusvesna.su/news) started in March 2014 and since then became a fairly professional resource with English, French, German and Arab versions, in addition to the main Russian site. It covered the NGCAs internal news, developments in Ukraine, Russian policy and international relations presented from a Russia-friendly point of view. It had a good journalistic team including Andrei Babitsky, the famous Radio Free Europe war correspondent. Babitsky covered the Russian campaigns in Chechnya where in 2000 he was detained by the federal security forces, swapped for Russian war prisoners and handed over to Chechen warlords with whom he was believed to be in complicity. He was well known for his oppositionist stance against the Russian military intervention and for the interview with Shamil Basaev in 2005 after the Beslan school siege. Despite his hard-earned credentials, Babitsky was asked to leave the RFE because the agency disputed his reportage of the murders of civilians by *Aidar* battalion in Donbas. Such incidents were later independently reported by *Amnesty International*.[49] He brought his professional passion to Donetsk where he found himself after Prague.[50]

War journalism that scaled down after the end of active military operations in Chechnya in the early 2000s, was in demand again, but this time anybody could participate without being a professional. Donbas got connected to other war theatres such as Syria and Libya. Existing media resources which had been hardly known before sprung into prominence, such as Anna.news-info registered in Abkhazia in 2011. *Anna News* specialized in quite daring coverage of war zones such as Libya and Syria which are prominent in Russian discourse as examples of the West's disastrous impact on the world and was known for publishing footage recorded directly from Syrian Army tanks. Strelkov in his time as a journalist cooperated with it. *Anna News* posted numerous live video reports and interviews from Donbas at the height of the conflict that were reposted on other sites. In April 2016, its website was defaced by a group of Ukrainian hackers.

The sheer volume of the new sites was prolific—communication was regular, proactive, with variation in characteristics and different voices sending the same messages with a plausible flexibility. They apparently could find sufficient receptive audiences to consume the content. Another feature was wide-ranging, rejection-based counter-speech aimed to dispel the story from the Ukrainian and Western media.[51] The rebel websites saw their mission in "information resistance," offering military updates and reports on civilian and military casualties inflicted as a result of ceasefire violations by the ATO. In the rebel view, the facts on the ground were not adequately reported by the OSCE SMM[52] which sought to attribute the blame equally so that no side was evidenced as breaching the ceasefire more than the other. Thus, SMM was nicknamed as a "Society of the Deaf and Dumb" when rebels were pointing out to the glaring episodes which happened in its full view, but did not find their way into the publicly available reports. The other preoccupation was exposing fakes from the Ukrainian side, a mirror image of Stop Fake website from Kyiv (http://www.stopfake.org) dedicated to identifying fakes in the Russian coverage.

An interesting blog was *Colonel Cassad: a Mouthpiece of Totalitarian Propaganda*, a Live Journal blog by Boris Rozhin of the Centre of Military—Political Journalism (cigr.net) in Sevastopol, which he started in 2009. *Cassad*'s design pulls a sarcastic joy from mixing Stalinist-era symbols with global trash manifested in cartoons and icons of the regular contributors. The central figure of Colonel Cassad is an evil-looking cartoon character dressed in a combination of Wehrmacht and Stalinist apparel. Several other icons include a vicious *matryoshka* with a two-pronged tongue sticking out of its mouth ready to bite with words, a slightly mad Dostoevsky, Spanish Commandore and Tyrion Lannister of the Game of Thrones. The archive section of the site is entitled "NKVD[53] archives," the military history section is called The Bloody Past, while "Red Resources" are the links to like-minded sites. "Totalitarian statistics" said that in mid-2016 Cassad had nearly 270,000 page views, social capital of 14,000 and was the 3rd most popular in Cyrillic site in the Live Journal user ratings.

Before Crimea, *Cassad* was a fairly unremarkable affair, dedicated to military history and occasionally commenting on politics. However, the change happened overnight with the Yanukovych ouster when Sevastopol rose and *Cassad*, prompted by his followers' questions, started reporting on the events around him. The reportage attracted attention and mobilization of resources followed suit. Well-wishers wanted to send money to the anti-Maidan protesters, but did not know where to, as pro-Russia demonstrators did not have any organized capacity at the time. *Cassad* played a role in crowdsourcing funding because he was on the ground and was not tarnished by association with the authorities. *Cassad* was a highly opinionated journalism which did not pretend to be objective, and expressed authoritative positions on the developments in the field during the war which seldom proved wrong. On occasion, it entered polemics with prominent field commanders and Novorossiya leaders who were sensitive to its views and felt the need to respond to Cassad's criticism. It published many direct entries from rank-and-file rebels, as well as reposted writings of their Ukrainian counterparts who fought against them. This was making the reader see a great deal of commonality in the ordinary people's experiences and the absurdity of a fratricidal war.

"Patriotic" outlets, such as *Novorossiya Briefs*, *Anna-news*, publicists Alexander Juchkovsky of *Sputnik i Pogrom* (*S&P*) and Boris Rozhin of *Colonel Cassad* helped to turn Strelkov into a media personality and maintained his profile when he was "switched off" from the Russian federal channels. *Sputnik i Pogrom,* a significant resource, did not emerge out of Donbas, but was established in 2012 and is the largest independent media outlet on politics, history and culture in Russia which is solely financed by subscription and donations from private supporters with a minimal reliance on advertising. *S&P* is not a news site, but an analytical publication of conservative, patriotic and Slavophile orientation with in-depth historical content and some talented journalists writing for it who share this worldview. It is an intellectual resource of Russian "patriotism," and played a big role in forming public opinion among the *Russian World* on the situation in Ukraine and the developments in Donbas. *S&P* is a critic of Putin's political system from a nationalist perspective, and, as put by Solovei, "it is engaged in messaging and propaganda in quite concrete ways and for concrete political purposes."[54]

To conclude, the rebellion created a certain cultural identity allowing it to claim a distinct community, a subculture assembled from different elements, which generated appeal among its followers in and beyond Donbas, and a way of communicating strategically to its support base. It gave names and meanings to emotions the rebels experienced and helped to turn them into actions, as well as supplied them with graphic symbols. The process showed that sub-state actors could construct an imagined reality with the tools they had, and not necessarily have to rely for a state to prop them up. It appears that the insurgents took a leaf out of IS "media enterprise" whose key features were innovation and experimentation, credibility of facts on the ground, of course, – reported from their perspective, – theatrics and short distances between propaganda and action, when the role of the media was to inspire people to act.[55] Donbas also produced its influence onto the Russian cultural space, created new expressions and heroic figures that generated admiration and an emotional resonance.

Religion turned into a more important factor than could have been expected in a previously atheistic society, because it lived on a popular level and came out in spiritual force when the moment called. This subculture would continue its existence, even if political conditions change, as it became internalized. Moreover, social communications allow cultivating digital strategic depth. When battlefield movement is minimal and little happens, the intensity of social media postings scales down. However, as virtual connections have been established, they can be reactivated to serve the cause again, in Ukraine or elsewhere.

NOTES

1. Bolt, *Violent Image*, xviii.
2. Smith, *Ethno-symbolism and Nationalism*, 28.
3. Huntington, *Clash.*
4. Bolt, *Violent Image*, xvi.
5. On general tendencies see Jason Dittmer, *Popular Culture, Geopolitics, and Identity* (Lanham, MD: Rowman and Littlefield, 2010).
6. Flam, "Emotions' map."
7. Yevgenii Norin, author's interview.
8. http://mozgovoy.info/
9. http://www.dialog.ua/news/78762_1455621232
10. Taras Shevchenko, "Kateryna," translated by Mary Skpypnyk (Toronto: 1960), http://sites.utoronto.ca/elul/English/248/Shevchenko-Kateryna-Skrypnyk-trans.pdf
11. Появилось видео, как подростки кричат "москаляку на гиляку" March 15, 2014, http://korrespondent.net/ukraine/3320021-poiavylos-vydeo-kak-podrostky-krychat-moskaliaku-na-hyliaku
12. The German word is normally shortened to "lumpen," and this is how it entered the Russian and Ukrainian languages.
13. Some labels analyzed in this section are described in a Korrespondent.net article "Колорады vs Укропы. Какие слова подарили Украине Майдан и война" June 6, 2014, http://korrespondent.net/ukraine/politics/3374179-kolorady-vs-ukropy-kakye-slova-podaryly-ukrayne-maidan-y-voina
14. "Ukraine Bans Russian St. George Ribbon," *Radio Free Europe*, June 12, 2017, https://www.rferl.org/a/ukraine-bans-russian-st-george-ribbon/28542973.html
15. On "terrorist" references see Driscoll, "Alternative Facts."
16. http://colonelcassad.livejournal.com/1440088.html
17. http://www.abc.net.au/news/2015-03-13/inside-the-mariupol-base-of-ukraine's-azov-battalion/6306242. For analysis of later developments see Joshua Cohen, "Ukraine's ultra-right militias are challenging the government to a showdown," June 15, 2017, *The Washington Post*, https://www.washingtonpost.com/news/democracy-post/wp/2017/06/15/ukraines-ultra-right-militias-are-challenging-the-government-to-a-showdown/?utm_term=.dcdd9f36213f
18. Tom Parfitt, "Ukraine crisis: the neo-Nazi brigade fighting pro-Russian separatists," August 12, 2014, http://www.telegraph.co.uk/news/worldnews/europe/

ukraine/11025137/Ukraine-crisis-the-neo-Nazi-brigade-fighting-pro-Russian-separatists.html

19. For an outline, see Nicolas Kozloff, "Ukraine: Nationalist Flags, Insignia and Curious Symbolism," January 16, 2015, http://www.huffingtonpost.com/nikolaskozloff/ukraine-nationalist-flags_b_6489988.html

20. "German TV Shows Nazi Symbols on Helmets of Ukraine Soldiers," September 12, 2014, https://ukraineantifascistsolidarity.wordpress.com/2014/09/12/german-tv-shows-nazi-symbols-on-helmets-of-ukraine-soldiers/

21. Michael Goldbarf, "Party's followers honour the veterans of the Waffen-SS's local Halychyna brigade, formed in 1943 to fight the Soviets," *The Guardian*, June 2, 2012, https://www.theguardian.com/world/2012/jun/02/euro-2012-antisemitic-football

22. Shaun Walker, "Azov fighters are Ukraine's greatest weapon and may be its greatest threat," *The Guardian*, September 10, 2014, https://www.theguardian.com/world/2014/sep/10/azov-far-right-fighters-ukraine-neo-nazis

23. The word "junta" is of Spanish origin and means a military rule. It is pronounced "khunta" in the Russian language.

24. Tetyana Montyan in interview to Pravda.ru, May 2016, http://youtu.be/4UGcCTxG_Ok

25. Victoria Hudson, "'Forced to Friendship'? Russian (Mis-)Understandings of Soft Power and the Implications for Audience Attraction in Ukraine," *Politics*, 35, no. 3–4 (2015): 330–346.

26. Ekaterina Turkina, "Russia-Ukraine Crisis: Value-Based and Generational Perspective," *Studies in Ethnicity and Nationalism* 15, no. 1 (2015).

27. Vladislav Mal'tsev, "Бригады освобождения Новороссии," *NG-Religions*, July 2, 2014, http://www.ng.ru/ng_religii/2014-07-02/5_novorossia.html

28. Nina Kouprianova, "Beyond Left and Right, Beyond Red and White: Framing the Liberation War in Donbas," March 14, 2015, https://ninabyzantina.com/2015/03/14/beyond-left-and-right-beyond-red-and-white-framing-the-liberation-war-in-Donbas/

29. Maxim Edwards, "Symbolism of the Donetsk People's Republic," Open Democracy, 9 June 2014.

30. Alexander Chalenko, author's interview.

31. http://actualcomment.ru/novaya_simvolika_novorossii.html

32. Alexander Chalenko, author's interview.

33. Both terms originate from the military ranks of the Russian Empire and were abolished by the Bolsheviks after the 1917 Revolution. They were associated with the monarchy and never used in the Soviet and new Russian army.

34. Igor Strelkov, author's interview.

35. Alexander Borodai, author's interview.

36. The palm was created by smith mason Alexei Mertsalov for the 1990 Paris Industrial Fair where it received a Grand-Prix.

37. Alexander Borodai, author's interview, Moscow, May 2016.

38. "Стрелков, Моторола, «вежливые люди» и бойцы Беркута стали прототипами для фигур игрушечных воинов" May 21, 2015, http://rusvesna.su/news/1432209695

39. Svetlana Stephenson, *Gangs of Russia: From Streets to Corridors of Power* (Ithaca: Cornell University Press, 2015).

40. Michael Kofman, "Russian Hybrid Warfare and Other Dark Arts" 11 March 2016, *War on the Rocks*, http://warontherocks.com/2016/03/russian-hybrid-warfare-and-other-dark-arts, Keir Giles, "The Next Phase of Russian Information Warfare," NATO Strategic Communication Centre of Excellence, http://www.stratcomcoe.org/next-phase-russian-information-warfare-keir-giles, undated

41. "Почти 20% украинцев смотрят новости на российских каналах," June 30, 2015, http://zn.ua/UKRAINE/pochti-20-ukraincev-smotryat-novosti-na-rossiyskih-kanalah-181033_.html

42. Rid and Hecker, *War 2.0*, 13, 32.

43. Rid and Hecker, *War 2.0*.

44. Alexei Ovchinnikov, "The German Woman in Novorossiya: Margarita Seidler," *Komsomol's kaya Pravda*, August 11, 2014, http://www.kp.ru/daily/26267.5/3145047/; November 14, 2015, http://unitedarmedforcesofnovorossiya2014.blogspot.co.uk/2015/11/the-german-woman-in-novorossiya.html

45. "Pole investigated for joining pro-Russian rebels in Ukraine," *Radio Poland*, December 8, 2016, http://www.thenews.pl/1/10/Artykul/189812,Pole-investigated-for-joining-proRussian-rebels-in-Ukraine

46. International Crisis Group, "The Ukraine Crisis: Risks of Renewed Military Conflict after Minsk II," Crisis Group Europe Briefing 73, April 1, 2015, 8.

47. Bolt, *Violent Image*, 130.

48. https://www.youtube.com/watch?v=msHBV3Cg_mU

49. Amnesty International, "Ukraine: abuses and war crimes by the Aidar volunteer battalion in the north Luhansk region," 8 September 2014, index number: EUR 50/040/2014.

50. Babitsky explains his transformation in an interview to *Komsomolskaya Pravda*, "Андрей Бабицкий: «Как я стал агентом ФСБ»" August 10, 2015, http://www.msk.kp.ru/daily/26417.5/3290904/

51. Winter draws these conclusions from his study of the IS media operations. Charlie Winter "Media Jihad: The Islamic State's Doctrine for Information Warfare," The International Centre for the Study of Radicalisation and Political Violence, London: Centre for Strategic Dialogue, 2017.

52. The SMM made an unprecedented decision to make their reports publicly available, which increased transparency, but made them more open to criticism.

53. NKVD was KGB's predecessor of the 1920s.

54. Valerii Solovei in testimony on the Sputnik I Pogrom website.

55. Whiteside, "Lightening the Path."

Chapter 10

Power of the State, Power of Ideas

This chapter seeks to interpret the *Russian Spring*, how the Russian state reacted to it, and what happened to it in the aftermath. It tries to extract its credo and the ideas which underpinned it, and explain how they had an ability to pull people from near and far away to mobilize for the defense of the *Russian World*. It also sheds the light on Donbas "foreign fighters," that is, those combatants who joined from the non-Soviet world.

By mid-August 2014, the situation in Donbas presented Moscow with a difficult choice. As the rebels, determined to fight till the bitter end, were facing a prospect of a very bloody defeat with disastrous consequences for the population, Moscow had to confront whether it would allow this to happen. A defeat risked damaging the leadership's reputation as protector of the *Russian World*. If the *Russian World* became a shambles, the legitimacy of Vladimir Putin's presidency would suffer. The question from the public would have been: "if so much went into strengthening the Russian state, where was the state when the *Russian World* needed it most?" Stamping out of the pro-Russia rebellion in Donbas threatened to turn the *Russian Spring* into a domestic protest movement which could create a far more credible challenge to the ruling regime than the urbanite anti-corruption protests led by Alexei Navalny. Strelkov's popularity was at its height[1] and could unleash unpredictable consequences as he was getting a handle on leadership. Even if Strelkov died as a martyr, he would have remained an inspirational figure for his followers. A defeated *Russian Spring* would have provoked a dangerous emotional resonance which could be hard to contain and its cause had its sympathizers within the ruling elite.

The Kremlin saved the situation by taking control over the uprising. It squared the dilemma by rescuing and strangling the *Russian Spring* in one blow. August 2014 witnessed the removal of Strelkov, reportedly against his will, facilitated by Alexander Borodai, followed by Borodai himself vacating his post. Local man Vladimir Kononov (call sign *Tzar*) took over as the DNR defense minister. The dawn of improvisation, in which the field commanders played prominent and independent roles, was heading toward sunset. As put by *Prince*, "the politicians win over the field commanders, they are more cunning and don't dash reckless." The *Russian Spring* was at its end, and politics was coming into play now.

AUTUMN AFTER THE *RUSSIAN SPRING*

The effect of the August counteroffensive was that it reversed the tables and forced Kyiv for the first time to negotiate seriously. The ceasefire deal signed on September 5 stopped further advances, although the insurgents who were riding a wave of success, were keen to proceed, but Moscow resolutely held their appetites back. The main job was done by then. The message from the state was clear: the *Russian Spring* played a commendable role when the decisive moment came, but this role was over and, from now on, the state would take responsibility for Donbas's fate. As put by a Kyiv-based international observer, "Novorossiya might have been a strong idealist project with a strong army. But the state killed it."[2] Those volunteer combatants who accepted the new rules of the game were welcome to stay, but the ensuing peace negotiations did not presuppose the participation of Russian citizens in key roles representing people of Donbas. The Russian volunteers were unenthusiastic about remaining through the transition anyhow as their goals had not been met. Several commanders left of their own volition, either fatigued by war and unable to take danger and atrocities anymore or because of disagreements with local guerrillas. Borodai who visited Donetsk once in October 2014, maintained that he left because his mission was accomplished and the role he set himself to play came to an end:

> Essentially, I left when everything was done. I put the top team together and the rest joined by themselves. Some had to be purged later. A state of sorts was built and could be transferred to the locals. I suggested Zakharchenko to succeed me. I appreciated that the negotiation process would kick into action. That meant that Donbas would be forced by Russia and Kyiv—by the West into talking. The talks were inevitable and presence of strange characters with Moscow *propiska* (registered address) would have been funny. [Denis] Pushilin-type figures were needed for that.[3]

Since then, the Kremlin exercised a certain influence on the internal politics in Donbas, and while Moscow's role was not the key but it was enough to show to the insurgents that it would not let them sink. Control was projected through the supplies of humanitarian and "non-humanitarian" aid, provision of training, pointed management interventions, when the locals were not coping with civilian functions, and bringing in the main figures to Russia for "consultations" and political education. Efforts were made by Moscow to help the promising commanders to evolve into political figures, soften the stance of radical warlords who could act as spoilers, and take them out of Donbas, if necessary. The tap of military supplies switched on and off for the individual commanders, depending on whether they fell in line. Moscow also tried to oversee the financial side of its assistance.

Nonconformist commanders who were not prepared to play at the new politics were pushed out. Igor Bezler was lured to Moscow, prevented from returning and subsequently relocated to Crimea, but had good sense not to resist when purges of field commanders began. Bezler was not a figure of any political significance—unlike Strelkov, whose popularity in Donbas and Russia was growing exponentially. Strelkov was blacklisted from crossing the border from the Russian side and, in early 2015, Malofeev was discouraged from providing further sponsorship. Still, Strelkov did not fall victim to an assassination, although assassinations were widespread at the time. He was an ex-security serviceman and the services' corporate ethic dictates not to give up their own. The DNR former commanders were confined to respectable, but narrowly defined roles which carried the benefits of cooperation but implied disincentives from developing activities and profiles deemed too independent. Strelkov and "Novorossiya" disappeared from the federal TV channels. Alexander Dugin, a founder of the "Eurasianism doctrine"[4] hardly known outside narrow conservative circles before, and Sergei Kurginyan, a controversial TV host show and commentator, were given public prominence to counterbalance and discredit the *Russian Spring* actors with genuine political capital. Dugin and Kurginyan soon turned in to a liability and their rhetoric had to be toned down.

Most of the volunteer combatants left after the battle for Debaltseve in early 2015 as the task was largely solved and an order came to persuade them to return, although those who wanted, stayed. Funding from their private benefactors subsided.[5] Some were not happy because they did not think that the mission was accomplished. Strelkov remained a popular figure among the DNR rebels who fought in the conflict, but general public in the "republic" started to forget him. His approval rating decreased from 60 percent in January 2015 to 33 percent in June 2016, but it was still greater than of any of Donbas own politicians included in the same poll. He was characterized by respondents as "a decent man, the kind you don't find in the DNR anymore."[6]

Ex-combatants faced social consequences of reentry on return. Some could not reintegrate into their civilian lives, such as a biker from Sakhalin who dropped everything to go to fight in Donbas. Others overstayed their leave of absence and lost jobs or businesses as a result. Some took to drinking and there were several suicides. Some families could not understand why their men chose to go to the war which they did not have to and avoided talking about the subject, creating a depressing silence around their husbands and sons. Others were abandoned by their wives during their absence and left their apartments to estranged families, themselves becoming homeless as a result.[7] Ukrainian citizens who were not from Donbas could not return to their original homes. Sometimes they had no valid documents to allow them to seek legal employment in Russia, as the state programs only applied to the former residents of NGCAs.[8] The state did not provide Donbas veterans with any special status like the veterans of the Afghanistan war had, but they hoped that this would change.[9] Two veteran organizations—Novorossiya Movement[10] chaired by Strelkov and the Union of Donbas Volunteers by Borodai—provided assistance to those in need and families of the slain fighters.

Looking back, the contribution made by the volunteer combatants to Donbas uprising was assessed by its actors as "organisational, ideological (идейный) and demonstrating support of the Russian people (Borodai)." A Donetsk rebel explains that "we had the will, and volunteers from Russia brought the fighting experience and survival skills at war. They taught us how to conduct a war, and they raised our fighting spirit." *Strannik* concludes, "If the Russian volunteer movement hadn't happened, the resulting uprising and resistance wouldn't have survived."

The significance of the *Russian Spring* as a distinct phenomenon was the greatest in the early weeks of the rebellion and subsided when the locals got more used to their new roles. Although many Russian combatants stayed after September 2014, and some continued in commanding positions, they blended into the mainstream rebel milieu and became more at one with them. The *Russian Spring* did not create Donbas rebellion, but was crucial to its development in three respects. It brought in people with experience in guerrilla warfare who were also sufficiently battle-hardened to withstand the strength of the first Ukrainian offensives. It installed a political organization which allowed for the formation of nascent authority structures and the development of political personalities in the new "republics." Importantly, the volunteer movement conveyed a sense of solidarity and empowerment, that those who associated themselves with the *Russian World* were not alone in the time of troubles. In the words of a female resident, "I was heartened to see that so many people were prepared to defend the *Russian World*." However, in a bigger sense, as expressed by Strelkov, "the values of the *Russian Spring* remained unrealised." Prosvirnin, speaking for the Russian nationalist spectrum, adds that "by participating in the events in Donbas, we hoped that they will lead, at minimum, to destruction of structures of power in Ukraine, and, at maximum, in Russia. But we overestimated their fragility."[11]

The *Russian Spring* had a limited opportunity to manifest itself since the exodus from Donbas, but it may be dormant rather than gone. In Strelkov's words, when I asked him about how he interpreted the outcomes,

[Moscow] tried to ruin the Novorossiya project, but it didn't succeed. What we've achieved is irreversible. The territories [in Donbas] became a hostage of the situation. The Russian Spring has been postponed for a certain period, but it will turn into an internal crisis [in Russia]. It will be directed inwards.[12]

However, the role which the *Russian Spring* supporters hoped he would play, did not materialize and frustrated those who were prepared to rally around him. In the view of one field commander,

Strelkov has re-appeared, but he isn't doing the kind of work which makes it worth it. He could have become president, but he doesn't seem to get the reality. You can't just sit and wait for something to start here so you can be on top again. Times have changed. He should do something interesting rather than just waiting for something to happen.[13]

Still, Strelkov seemed to have found his role, at least in the interim. He remained an enigmatic and influential figure on the Russian nationalist socket, proactively launching statements and initiatives. His *Novorossiya Movement* continued to serve as a locus for supporters and sympathizers. Like many among the fighters, Strelkov found personal happiness in Donbas. In December 2014, Strelkov married Miroslava Reginskaya, whom he first met as a young man in Transnistria, to where she volunteered as a nurse. Their paths crossed again in Sloviansk, when they both arrived there. The wedding photo of handsome Strelkov with beautiful Miroslava featured in his office during our interview, softening an otherwise severe atmosphere of the Novorossiya movement reminiscent of Hemingway's "Men Without Women" collection of stories. The caption said: "Heart to the Beloved, Honour—to No One" (Сердце—Любимой, а Честь—Никому). But he is not a leader with a larger mission anymore, at least for now.

POWER OF IDEAS: WHAT THE *RUSSIAN SPRING* STOOD FOR

If we are to understand what impact the events in Donbas had on the *Russian World*, we have to acknowledge that the Ukraine crisis brought to life emotions of indignation, solidarity and moral duty in the face of collective danger, and activated deep-hidden identity layers in the society which have been dormant since the World War II. I argue that the forces it unleashed can be more challenging to the political order of the President

Putin than Western sanctions and liberal criticism, because their bearers are driven by strong core values, upon which they do not compromise, and these values touch upon identity chords in wider society. Moreover, the *Russian Spring* actors gained fighting experience and organizational capabilities through Donbas. The conflict gave a huge boost to the *Russian World* which for the first time acquired a large emotional resonance and got its first "heroes," as characters such as Strelkov and *Motorola* were in the eyes of their followers. It exacerbated the perceived values gap between the West and Russia, yet it claimed that Russia occupied the higher moral ground by defending its core values of honor in the context of the unique historical, religious, and cultural bonds with Ukraine.[14] "National pride of Greater Russians," which Lenin was critical of in 1914 as World War I broke out,[15] showed a century ago that it was not entirely confined to the "dustbin of history."

Here we take a look at the rebellion's collective beliefs and ideals beyond individual motivations. Isaiah Berlin stresses that ideas, convictions, and reasoning on "who we are" and "where we are going" have always been of crucial importance for the "vanguard of Russian society," even if they let to unpalatable conclusions.[16] Whether the *Russian Spring* actors are indeed a "vanguard" can be arguable, – and many would claim exactly the opposite, – but as they were activists and many belonged to the thinking class, ideas were of importance for them.

In the rebel narrative, the fall of the USSR is regarded not as a failure of the Soviet system, but as a spiritual and tragic rupture within the *Russian World*, a momentous event which artificially separated the people united by common values, culture, and historic tradition. In this view, the *Russian World* is not a challenger to the West, but has a sense of its natural borders, and people within it should enjoy protection if they come under attack. It is not interested in what does not belong to it and lays no claims on the world outside it.[17] Given Russian involvement in Syria, a reader may disagree, but a distinction between the *Russian World* and how the Russian state understands its global interests has to be kept in mind.

Despite placing a material burden, Donbas, if interpreted in larger historical terms from the *Russian Spring* perspective, was an accomplishment: it unequivocally demonstrated that those seeking protection of the *Russian World* would receive it and that this protection means serious business. This myth-making reconnected contemporary Russia with that of the Tsars when Russian protection was given to the Christian people who wished to escape the embrace of the Ottoman Empire and were turning their loyalty to Moscow. In this paradigm, the events of the 1990s in the Balkans would not have happened if Russia instead of pursuing the policy of acquiescence under Yeltsin, lived up to its historical role. As put by *Prince*, ''Russia is the kind of empire which is prepared to help its adepts in other countries. It's returning to the club of great powers which get involved in others' affairs." Although reconfiguration of values and a pivot toward a claim for a distinct civilizational identity were present in Russian political discourse for a long time already,[18] it was Donbas that brought these amorphous ideas into focus by putting them in action.

There is an argument that the views of the *Russian Spring* actors were so eclectic that they did not make up any coherent set of ideas: Tsyganok in his book on Donbas war states that although Russia has a great deal of so-to-speak "monarchists," they made no concerted push in this direction during their time in Novorossiya.[19] More accurate is perhaps Norin's view that "the war united all those who had a political position of some sort, does not matter which one. There were pathetic alliances between communists and monarchists, a crowd of National-Bolsheviks, and there were a plenty of Russian nationalists in *Rusich* and communists in *Prizrak*. All with patriotic orientations flocked to Donbass." It would be wrong to say that all ideas came from Russia, as Donbas produced its own thinkers. Pavel Gubarev, for example, instead of positioning himself as a Russian nationalist, offers an alternative made up of Eurasianism, "cosmism," and "non-dogmatic" socialism, based on a mixed economic system and direct democracy. His *Novorossiya* movement established on May 22, 2014, in Donetsk by over a thousand delegates was meant to promote a new model of statehood, free of the "evils" of modern Russia and Ukraine.[20]

Nevertheless, although the *Russian Spring* actors had different ideological credentials from monarchism to Bolshevism to anarchism, they had a common core. Borodai in our interview outlined the philosophy of the *Russian Spring* as a distinct movement:

The ideology of the Russian people doesn't need to be invented. It's simple and easy to explain. The Russian people were artificially divided by the fall of the Soviet Union. The borders were administrative and the state was in fact unitary. The Russian people wanted re-unification, but there were opponents who wanted to suppress that. Such opponents took power in Kyiv through an armed coup. Of course, the Russian people couldn't miss this opportunity, so they conducted a reunification operation for those who wanted to re-join Russia.

The Russian Spring is a natural phenomenon, an ordinary Russian people's (*narodnoye*). Russians were not regarded as a *narod* (people) in the Soviet times. They were a population mass of some kind. Their distinctness didn't exist. It's as if they didn't have their own pains, dreams and historical memories. This stereotype to an extent was inherited by the bureaucrats in the Russian state. As the year 2014 demonstrated, this premise was false. In reality, the Russian people exist. They have their mental paradigms, their cultural stereotypes, their own historical memories and their own visions of the future, and their dreams.

The Russian Spring brought the Russian identity back to life—it hadn't been entirely dead before, but it had been swept under the rug(загнана под спуд) and no one had to deal with it much. Now it has to be dealt with.

In large measure, the Russian Spring achieved its goals. Not only because it managed to return Crimea to Russia and defended Donbas republics, but also because it succeeded in demonstrating to the world and the elite of the Russian Federation that Russian people exist and can act out of their own free will, without approval from the top. This is somewhat dangerous for the elite because the elite started to realize that these people have their own goals and capacities and can act without the bosses' orders. However, this doesn't have to be dangerous because, if the elite were oriented towards state-building and the strengthening of the state, then the ideas, then the aspirations and dreams of the Russian people and the elite would coincide. But if the elite's interests are different from the interests of the state, then it is dangerous. But why should there be such a schism? Their interests should be the same. Today's elite is largely de-nationalized: it is not statist, or imperial, it is mostly cosmopolitan and political-economic. You can see this in their materialism as they move between Monaco, London, and New York and back.

The Russian people are a state-forming nation. For them, statehood is an essential feature. It differs from an ethnos in this way. Russian nationalism is exclusively of a statist character, it has nothing to do with ethnicity. I had all sorts of Russian nationalists [among the rebel ranks]—Ossetians, Tatars and others. They didn't become Russian. Abkhaz Akhra, a *Pyatnashka* commander, remembers that he is Abkhaz. But there is a difference between a nation which is capable of state-building and an ethnic group which is built upon blood ties. A nation like the Russians, or the Romans in their time, do not think of horizontal ties of blood and kin, but the vertical connections along "a man and a state" line become dominant. They are not concerned about your bloodline. You can even be Chinese, but if you feel yourself Russian, and believe that Russia is your state, then, even if you look Mongoloid, you are Russian all the same.

Crimea and Donbas are substantial achievements of the Russian people in territorial and spiritual-ideological senses. The state elite became more patriotic compared to comprador one of the 1990s. A revival of the Russian state and Russian people had already been taking place in the 2000s under Putin. However, [in relation to the *Russian Spring*] the state tries to control any powerful social movements because the state is apprehensive of anarchy. Because the state is about regulation and control, and armed anarchy (стихийность) is not welcome. If somebody breaks the state monopoly on violence, even for the good of the country, they potentially become a problem and should be brought under control. This is the natural process.

The Russian Spring will develop further. It will be slower at times and faster at others, but it will move. This movement isn't always noticeable. Sometimes there are high points, but there are also low points and steps backwards. Still, you can clearly trace its way forward.[21]

Borodai is essentially raising a problem of a majority group lost in a multiethnic state. While minority groups are allowed expressions of their distinctiveness, if the majority does the same, this is typically regarded as crude nationalism. For example, the Scots and the Irish in the UK can set up their nationalist parties and have own parliaments, but when Nigel Farage, the former UK Independence Party (UKIP) leader, talks that the English might want the same, this is perceived as being in bad taste. Saying that "I am English" is a far more loaded statement than "I am Welsh." Russians experienced the same in the USSR when distinct "Russianness" was discouraged in favor of the Soviet unity of people, while minorities were allowed more of their ethnocultural expression. This does not mean that Russian sentiment was not felt and shared. Does this make Borodai an ethno-nationalist? Surely not, because the *Russian Spring*'s definition of its "community" is emphatically non-ethnic. An important pillar is the concept of "state-ism" (государственность): centrality of the state and vertical ties within it, and the notion of a civic nation along a Russian model. These views may be more accurately described as "patriotic," but then it has an oppositionist streak and its support to the Russian leadership is conditional rather than absolute, and nowhere near loyalty to a tsar.

Those who belong to the "Russian nationalism" socket, such as Juchkovsky, would like more primacy to be given to ethnic Russians as a defensive mechanism against nationalisms of other groups. However, the main claims of Borodai narrative—centrality of civilizational identity and subjectivity of the Russian people, moral values, and a sense of a community within its "natural" historical borders – are fairly representative of the common ground, upon which diverse actors of the *Russian Spring* agreed. In this sense, as Smith writes, nationalism can fulfill some useful function such as legitimization of community and solidarity bonds, ideal of popular sovereignty and collective mobilization.[22] However, the term "Russian nationalism" may be misleading because, as Sakwa explains, "nationalism" as such is alien to the Russian tradition where historically the focus has been on maintaining the state. Ethnic nationalism has been rather weak, and national cohesion was based on Orthodox Church and cultural traditions that transcended ethnic divisions. The main features of political identity have been more statist and civilizational. In this paradigm, a strong Russian state is the central feature of the very existence of the Russian people. The definition through a common history is more inclusive as it allows rising above narrower signifiers, such as language, ethnicity or religion.[23]

Borodai belongs to the school of thought which concentrated around Prokhanov's *Zavtra* paper, and Strelkov occasionally wrote for it in the past—so-called *gosudarstvenniki* (state-ists) who assume that the Russian multinational state was engaged for centuries in a struggle to defend "the

Russian idea" against the forces of cosmopolitanism. *Gosudarstvenniki*
are rooted in the nineteenth-century tradition of Slavophilism. They stress
the existence of a historically constituted supra-national community on
the Eurasian land mass, in which various peoples were broadly able to
pursue their own destinies even when incorporated into the Russian state.
They imply a social definition of nationhood which includes Russian
diasporas.[24]

Marlene Laurelle who researched the concept of Novorossiya, identifies
three themes in it: first, "post-Soviet," meaning reformulation of Russia's
great-powerness and messianism; second, Tsarist nostalgia and the reactiva-
tion of ultraconservative Orthodox circles; and third—paradoxically—fascist.
Data from primary sources support only the first theme in its different facets. Religion, although important on individual level, was not extrapolated
as a basis for future political and social order of *Novorossiya*. Faith-based
combatant groups existed and were making references to waging an "Orthodox *jihad*," but did not appear in any mood to build a Christian state on the
rebel-held territories. Communism, leftist socialism and anarchism were also
pronounced themes, which would have prevented Novorossiya from taking a
religiously explicit route.

Data from the rebel sources (interviews, websites, symbolic) are opposite to Laurelle's view: anti-fascism was an important theme for joining
the movement. Her framing of the Russian Spring as "fascist" rests on two
points. The first point is that "it sublimates violence, filling the Russian
nationalist Internet and social media world with images of volunteers in
khaki uniforms, proudly displaying their weapons and posing in macho
ways around tanks or destroyed military equipment. The narrative—and
the nationalist hard rock music—that accompanies these images promotes
violence, sacrifice."[25] This is normal insurgents' behavior and we should
not expect anything different from them. In fact, irregular fighters in the
war theaters where they have an access to internet—territorial battalions in
Ukraine, Kurdish *peshmerga*, *jihadi* fighters in Syria, and South Sudanese
rebels—do exactly the same: they picture themselves as macho victorious
warriors, while death of fallen comrades is treated as a sacrifice for the
right cause. Second point is that the elderly leader of the Russian National
Unity (RNU) Alexander Barkashov was involved in sending volunteer
combatants to Donbas. This is true, but so did many other and by far more
prominent figures. Exotic RNU's claim to fame dates back to 1993, and
the organization was looked down as marginal and chauvinist even in Russian nationalist circles. As put by Juchkovsky, "we always thought of such
people as freaks. We avoided all sorts of national-socialists, Hitler admirers
and other 'sub-culturists' whom we did not consider a part of the 'Russian
movement.'"[26]

FIGHTERS FROM FAR AWAY: GLOBAL SOLIDARITY MOVEMENT

Donbas is a twenty-first-century conflict and carries its hallmarks, of which transnational activism is a distinct feature. Ease of travel and communication facilitated arrival of this force into Donbas. It was the second conflict in the post-Soviet space which attracted significant numbers of foreign fighters, and ideological elements in both were the key. The wars in Chechnya brought in highly motivated Arab warriors who fought in other theaters against the West and USSR in Afghanistan before coming to the North Caucasus.[27] They brought *jihadi* ideology and fighting skills to the region and provided the indigenous resistance with supply channels to access money, weapons and global Islamist solidarity.[28] Their input fell on fertile soil and elevated the national liberation struggle to a wholly new level.

Ideological elements, albeit of a different kind, have also been salient in the appeal of Donbas for transnational activism. Some arrivals were Russophones who considered that people were attacked for their pro-Russia position and the *Russian World* was in need of protection. They included almost forgotten Baltic Russians and other citizens of the former Soviet countries who irrespective of their own ethnicity emphasized with Russia. It turned out that the Russian legacy in the post-Soviet world was still persistent and withstood the regional and global influences, explaining why Central Asians such as Kazakhs and Tajiks fought for *Novorossiya*. However, fighters from the Caucasus and Belarus, as well as Russian nationalists, could be found on both sides of the conflict divide, depending on their individual convictions.[29] They at times faced their ethnic kin on the battlefield.[30] Although most Georgians were with Kyiv, there were well-known Georgian fighters among the rebels, and even one who fought in Zviadist troops against Eduard Shevardnadze's forces in Western Georgia in the early 1990s.[31] Volunteer combatants from the post-Soviet countries do not easily lend themselves to be described as "foreign fighters" as per Hegghammer's definition, because they still came from the same historical and linguistic milieu, and experienced a fictive sense of kinship. Donbas was not a foreign war for them, although many were not ethnic Ukrainian or Russian.

There was another cohort, less related to the shared history and culture. No pattern can be traced in terms of their national representation, as foreign fighters came from all over the world. The Serbs felt the urge predictably fought for the rebel cause as they believed that they were one people with the Russians (один народ). A handful of Russian fighters had participated in the ex-Yugoslavia wars and they felt the urge to reciprocate. The first Serb battalion "Yovan Shevic" numbered 45 fighters in Luhansk oblast. Then right-wing Serbs from *Cetnik* movement arrived in July 2014, numbering 205, and were commanded by Bratislav Zivkovic who founded a Slavic Squadron out of Serbs, Bulgarians and Russians.[32] They were known to have fought for Luhansk airport.[33] Other Serbs, according to a Serb fighter Dejan Beric, joined the 1st interbrigade which had Chechen, Azeri and other fighters from post-Soviet countries, as well as Spanish, Slovak, French and one Kosovo Albanian.[34]

Rebel websites reported and posted video footage of a great diversity of the international fighters, for example, people from Brazil, Poland, Portugal, Greece, France, Italy, Spain, Germany, Switzerland, Israel, India, the United States, and the United Kingdom.[35] In *Prince*'s recollection, the first arrivals were from Latvia and Western Ukraine, but then there were many Greeks and French Leftists. The French formed perhaps the largest contingent after the Serbs among the fighters from outside the post-Soviet world. Some had Russian ancestry, but not all. Victor Alfonso Lenta, a former French corporal in the Third Marine Infantry Paratroops Regiment who served in Afghanistan, Ivory Coast, and Chad was one of the main recruiters in France for Donbas. He trained the local guerrillas in urban warfare in Donetsk oblast. Idealism, giving to others, and solidarity spirit brought to the fighting zone not only fighters but also activists who assumed a range of civilian and support duties. The French, for example, were not all fighters, but doctors as well who treated battlefield and civilian casualties.[36] There were also many Greeks, some of whom had local roots because of a large historical community of Pontiac Greeks in Azov and Black Sea lowlands, and in Kuban and Donbas. Interestingly, according to the Italian Interior Ministry figures, there were more Italian nationals fighting in Donbas than in the Middle East although the total numbers were quite small.[37] Germans numbered about a hundred, but most of the identified cases were born in the USSR or in its successive states, and were recent immigrants in Germany.[38]

Numbers are hard to assess. Former field commander Oleg Melnikov says, "there were about 1500 foreign volunteers apart from those from Russia, and about 300 Serbs among them."[39] By far not all spent long periods in Donbas and foreign fighter presence has been reducing since 2015. Many concealed their identities and did not advertise participation as they were apprehensive of prosecution at home. Six EU countries criminalized joining fighting abroad without state authorization, even if money was not the reason, which was perhaps a reaction to a surge of foreign fighters in Syria, at its peak at the time, rather than because of the war in Ukraine. Most foreign fighters outside of the former Soviet Union did not speak the language, apart from the Serbs and other Slavs who could quickly adapt and some French with a Russian ancestry. This did not seem to affect their motivation and the ability to fight, as long as they learnt the basic words and commands.

The reality of frontline existence was so severe and risks to life so high that it is unlikely that mercenarism could be common, and ideological and emotional considerations were a major driver, as participants recalled. Borodai said that "as there was no money to be made, people with convictions and adventurists came."[40] Prospective foreign fighters were thoroughly interrogated on their arrival about their ideological credentials as the rebels were beware of spies and did not want to take on board unreliable adventurists. The flow of foreign fighters did not completely stop after the Minsk agreement. A fighter from Chile spent four months in Luhansk to where he arrived in late 2015. He explained to me that he was strongly motivated by anti-imperialist and anti-hegemonic values. He spoke no Russian and very little English. This was his first war, although he had military training with FARC guerrillas in Columbia. He was expecting a second volunteer—his friend from Chile to join him. He was not thinking how he was going to go back or when.

The conditions in the field he described were dire: the barrack where the rebel fighters slept in winter had a room temperature of minus six degrees while it was minus fourteen outside. The room was heated by an electric heater which worked only because power supply from the Schastia station had not been cut off by the Ukrainian authorities. There were no flush toilets or hot water showers. The fighters were paid 15,000 roubles a month ($230), out of which they contributed 10,000 Rb to a communal fund to buy food and cover expenses, and had 5,000 Rb ($77) to spend. He said that because they were in frontline trenches, there was no need for spent cash, and combatants use the money for cigarettes, chocolates, haircuts, and other little necessities. Nobody particularly cared about money. There were other foreign fighters serving, he explained, but they were intermixed with local rebels. The author observed two fighters from *Prizrak* who were from Finland. There are also celebrity figures from the West who did not fight but expressed their solidarity with Donbas, such as American Jeff Monson, a Mixed Martial Arts fighter and political activist who acquired a Russian citizenship in 2015[41] and went to set up his martial arts school in LNR in September 2016,[42] producing a morale boost for the locals.

KYIV'S FOREIGN FIGHTERS

Kyiv also had its fair share of ideologically driven foreign fighters, either motivated by the ideals of Ukraine's independence, replaying own rivalries with Russia and some were inspired by national-socialist or extreme right-wing values.[43] The countries with large Ukrainian diasporas such as Canada and historically related Poland sent fighters mostly to fight for Kyiv, and there was also a noticeable presence of the Swedes and Georgians.[44] A few Russian radical nationalists fought on the Kyiv's side. Those from Russia were not considered war prisoners by the rebels and treated very cruelly if captured.

Some neo-Nazis from the EU countries have joined the Ukrainian territorial battalions, and anti-Russian attitudes presented a strong incentive for some. The numbers are hard to judge. Rebel *Nemets*: "I never saw live or dead foreign fighters from the Ukrainian side, but my comrades had. What I saw were foreign bank cards with non-Ukrainian names, kit and food rations that Ukrainian army could not have. We would take food and cash. I had my estranged family in Kharkiv and needed the money to make child maintenance payments, but we as volunteers were not paid. So, it was lucky when we came across something like this."

Not everybody was aware that they were doing something which might be illegal and assumed that international organizations would be on their side. For example, an armed group of Swedes dressed in black military-style fatigues made its way into Kharkiv where it astonished an international staff with a request to supply them with shields so they could "fight the Russians" better. Otherwise they were fully equipped they said. The shocked staff advised them to leave the country immediately.[45] A recruitment network to fight for Kyiv was organized by Issa Munaev from the Netherlands, recruiting volunteers in Chechnya and from Chechen diaspora before Munaev was killed in fighting at Debaltseve in 2015. More recently, according to *Novaya Gazeta*, four Islamic battalions were set up, one of them included only Chechens. Private military companies were also used, mostly staffed by 300–400 Poles. Even black people were noticed at frontlines, but these were singular occasions.[46]

Some of those who fought with territorial battalions were unable to return to their homelands, especially to Russia and Belarus where they would surely be prosecuted. They found themselves of little value for the country they fought for. Although they were promised Ukrainian citizenship by the President, it was granted in single cases and several hundred individuals were left abandoned, with no state assistance available for them, despite their battalion commanders' appeals to the presidency. Some lost documents, were ill or left with permanent injuries with no means of supporting themselves apart from assistance from their former battalions. However, some battalions were disbanded and ceased to exist. Other former fighters went into hiding, fearing immigration officials who could deport them.[47]

The warring parties and their proxies accused each other of using mercenaries, but no proven cases of participation of private military professionals from outside Russia are known. There have been no prosecutions for the crime of mercenarism in Ukraine. The authorities identified at least 176 foreigners who served with DNR and LNR, but this figure includes those from Russia. In March 2016 the UN Working Group on Mercenaries, which conducted a fact-finding mission to Ukraine including to the NGCAs, concluded that the lack of coherent information on payments and the motivations of fighters makes it difficult to ascertain which fighters were mercenaries.[48]

DONBAS CALLING

The question is why somebody from a position of comfort in the West would do such extraordinary thing as to go and fight in a foreign war, when a possibility of getting killed was real. Experience of the Spanish Civil War provides some answers. Donbas combatants described their motivations much in the same terms as testimonies of American veterans who fought in International Brigades cited in David Malet's book. Both argued that they had a "duty as an antifascist": "Antifascism became established as a transnational identity that lined disparate individuals who did not otherwise share historical, linguistic or sectarian ties, and it was furthermore established as an identity under an attack that required the defence of its members."[49] Malet characterizes Spanish civil war as a non-ethnic intrastate war in which the foreign fighters were non-coethnic with the local Spanish insurgents. Both sides had foreign fighters. They were true believers who viewed the local civil conflict as just one front in a larger transnational struggle in defense of their group. This transnational identity defined itself against a counterpart ideological group. They believed that their worlds faced an existential threat at the hands of the other. Theirs was a defensive mobilization against an existential adversary, and recruitment happened through a panoply of identity organizations. "The constant *causes belli* used to recruit foreign fighters is . . . the necessary defence of their transnational identity communities."[50] Stradling, in his study of the Spanish Civil War, delineated three categories of foreign fighters in Spain: (1) the ideologically solid, (2) the superficial idealists who experienced an emotional surge to fight for the "good," and (3) selfish opportunists for whom abstract ideas were meaningless.[51] In Donbas, first two motivational groups apparently prevailed, although there were some adventurists on both sides who merely wanted to gain a thrill of war, but most did not stay long.

The volunteer movement of Leftist *Drygaia Rossia* (Different Russia) set up by the Russian writer Eduard Limonov (real name Savenko; originally from Ukraine) claimed to be the heir of Spanish International Brigades. It used the term "Interbrigades" as self-designation. They drew parallels because both Spanish Civil War and Donbas inspired ideological motivations. They started as chaotic uprisings in which foreign fighters played a key role in supplying the momentum and spirit to the indigenous protests. As the wars progressed, foreigners were gradually replaced by local insurgents. Both movements saw their struggles as "anti-fascist," which influenced their rhetoric and imagery, while romanticism of resistance brought cultural and creative figures into the guerrilla ranks. Many foreign fighters in both war theaters were civilians and had to master combat skills on the spot. Military advisers from the USSR/ Russia had been present in both cases, and conservative Western media wrote about a large presence of the Soviet troops in Spain at the time, which was repudiated by archive data released later.[52]

Many foreign fighters were driven as they saw it, by responsibility to protect the civilian population, because the Ukrainian government backed by the West deployed "the army against its own population," a standard Western justification for interventions in Kosovo, Iraq, Libya, and Syria.[53] In contrast to the prevailing US and EU narrative, they viewed Ukraine, not Russia, as a "fascist aggressor." In the words of a French fighter from Toulouse, "I fight in Donbas against imperialist expansion and western capitalism. I could not fail to go and came, in the first instance, to protect the population."[54] He stated that:

> This is our war. It touches upon all of us, Europeans. These are citizens' militias, they are not mercenaries or professional soldiers, they are highly motivated, but need training. It is very important to show that there are people in the West who are ready to go against the wrong actions of their governments and to enter the war risking their lives to defend that other world. Europe is now in a precarious situation when the power-holders are at a loss on what to do in a situation when young Europeans go to fight against their ally. We are not mercenaries, we are not paid. We are not terrorists. Our following is growing. There is a "Unité Continentale" brigade which brings together volunteers from western countries.[55]

The "clash of civilisations" narrative was fundamental in framing the rebellion and elevated it from a local fight to a different level. Rather than interpreting the conflict as a crisis of center-periphery relations in Ukraine that turned violent, this ideology emphasized such concepts as the "antifascism" and resistance to a global advance of Euroatlanticism. It provided Donbas movement with a larger claim, which connected it with globalized postmodern culture. The "civilisational" aspect of the war seen as non-West showing the limits to the West on its power and expansion[56] meant that it had resonance beyond Ukraine and Russia as a US-Russia proxy war,[57] in which Ukraine came to symbolize a contestation of globalized identities. The Donbas conflict, unlike the ethno-nationalist wars in the South Caucasus and the Balkans of the 1990s amounted to far more than a struggle for an ethnic homeland. Its open-endedness created a solidarity appeal for foreign fighters from around the world who were motivated by ideological causes, which they saw as anti-Atlanticism, resentment of western hypocrisy, double standards and a righteous sense of moral superiority. *The Guardian* cites, for example, a desire "to stand against western imperialist aggression."[58] The key messages included a rejection of global capitalism which only cares about power, understanding of the world through the prism of geopolitical rivalries and rallying around an anti-Western pole. Stopping the spread of colored revolutions epitomized by the Euromaidan that could be repeated elsewhere, especially in Russia, presented a worthy cause.

The conviction that Russia was the only country which could oppose the US global advance was shared among the foreign fighters. A volunteer from Finland who fought with *Prizrak* for seven months explained that what drove him was anti-fascism and the duty to stop an outbreak of a major European war propelled by the United States: "If such war starts, it will affect Finland, not the United States. By defending Donbas, I am protecting my own country." Like many among foreign fighters, he had a high human rights' motivation which played a significant emotive role. The fighter described witnessing Ukrainian army bombardments in violation of the Minsk agreement at the LNR, where he was based. In his view, deliberate targeting of residential areas by the ATO was determined to cause panic.[59] The other theme was of hypocrisy: international organizations and Western human rights groups, instead of upholding values irrespective of geopolitics, largely ignored suffering of Donbas civilians because of the latter's loyalty to Russia. "Indivisible" human rights agenda got sacrificed to serve the masters of global capitalism.

Anti-fascist theme was particularly resonant among the foreign fighters from the countries which had their own histories of struggle against fascism, such as Spain, Italy, and Latin America. Appearance of fascist symbolic in the hands of some Maidan activists and their violent sloganeering triggered their response emotions.[60] *Black Lenin* (Aijo Beness), a Latvian citizen, a son of a Russian mother and a Ugandan father, and a member of Leftist *Drugaya Rossia* party in Russia and of the Communist Party of Great Britain (Marxist–Leninist), explains the events in Ukraine from the position of anti-fascism intertwined with the anti-capitalism. If the below argument sounds absurd, the industrial decline in Ukraine after Euromaidan supplies evidence to his thesis for a receptive audience:

Western Europe supports the actions of a fascist Ukrainian junta in Donbas because the West financed a Euro-Nazi coup in February in Kyiv, as a result of which the most reactionary forces backed by big business came to power. The West for a long time sought to tear Ukraine away from Russia and turn it into a bread basket of Europe so that Ukrainian labourers work the fields and the industry is liquidated.[61]

Foreign fighters mostly held political beliefs or belonged to some movement in their own countries. Those from Italy were largely members of leftist groups, but one Italian citizen turned out to be a supporter of Lega Nord. Western Europeans were mostly Leftists, but there were many right-wing Serbs and some from France were also on the right of political spectrum. Left and right-wing orientations were irrelevant in a transnational identity movement, as long as the fighters were clear what they were fighting against, and this did not prevent them from getting along with each other and the local rebels. Their convictions might have mattered if foreign fighters were to influence a construction of the new political system, but that was not their role as they were solidarity soldiers rather than revolution exporters. What they had in common were frustrated identities dissatisfied with the modern state and its political order, and disappointed with liberal values. Quest for justice for the people of Donbas, and emotional resonance of equality and fraternity of the resistance united them. Rękawek finds their beliefs too contradictory to find a common thread in the messy conglomeration of illiberalism and anti-Europeanness. Yet, stripped from conspiracy theories and personal prejudices, the common agenda is possible to grasp. It rests upon four main notions which together form a worldview and in which traditional right and left distinctions are not really relevant:

1. Rejection of the dominant ideology of liberalism shared by Western ruling elites that the present democratic system works for all and that capitalism is fair, and if an individual did not succeed in it, it is their own fault;
2. Reaction against unequivocal support given to Ukraine for opposing Russia which dares to speak up to the West, irrespective of the illegality of the forced power change in Kyiv and violent actions of pro-EU activists. This support is seen as a cog in Euroatlantic expansionism determined to conquer more ground further East which must be stopped, and the war in Donbas is the moment to do so;
3. Humanitarian and human rights considerations that became powerful when civilian casualties mounted and women were crying on camera: "We do not want to go into Europe. Please, please, do not bomb us into Europe."[62] The same way as NATO exercised a "responsibility to protect" in the interests of Albanians in Kosovo, a popular anti-NATO mobilized to protect civilians in Donbas;
4. Anti-fascism: Maidan gave prominence to pro-fascist groups, unleashed their appeal, and increased the visibility of its symbolic, which triggered a counter-reaction.

IN THE AFTERMATH

Prosecutions of foreign fighters returning from Donbas who fought with the rebels, took place in Kazakhstan where the most severe punishments were handed; also at least eight people were prosecuted in Serbia, and some were in Latvia and Poland.[63] Estonia handed over its citizen to the Ukrainian authorities to be prosecuted there. Spain attempted to prosecute Sergio

Becerra Vasquez and several other men who fought for the rebels for the "actions which might influence the country's neutrality," but it was inconclusive and they were left off the hook in the end.[64] As some foreign fighters felt unable or unwilling to return, in 2016 the de facto authorities announced that they would grant LNR and DNR "passports" to their foreign fighters who were welcome to stay.

International solidarity generated by fighting in Donbas did not evaporate even when active hostilities subsided. The Union of Donbas Volunteers tried to institutionalize these international links around a concept of "volunteerism." Borodai stated in his address at the Union conference, which involved foreign participation, that "the essence of volunteerism is self-sacrifice. People are alive as long as volunteerism, giving oneself up for an idea, exists. Volunteers can be humanitarian and with arms in their hands." The movement has members from Europe and beyond, such as an MP from Belgium, and enjoys following in Italy (Coordinamento Solidale per il Donbas, Fronte Europeo Sociale, Speranza), Sweden (Donbassföreningen Malmö), Belgium (Euro-Rus), Germany (International Bloggers Association), Spain, Finland, and others. It brings together groups of various political persuasions, for whom "Russia is a source of justice and honour," both right and left wings. One of the colors is that of a Slavic unity and solidarity with Serbs, pledging that the "defeat in the Balkans" would not be allowed to be repeated in the post-Soviet space. Serbs (Union of Serbian Veterans and Volunteers) and Kurds (federal national—cultural Kurdish autonomy in the Russian Federation) are among active participants. There are also people from western Ukraine who oppose the Kyiv government.[65] The movement is no *Komintern*, but still reflects a wider calling. The identity that glues these factions and individuals together includes such elements as reaction against bias in Western media and politicized approach to Donbas conflict, sympathy for the rebellion, interest in Russia and an anti-Western sense of geopolitics. This is not to say that all are Putin's fans and that they are in pay of the Russian government.

It does not appear that returnees from Donbas pose a threat to their own societies in the same way as *jihadi* fighters coming back from the Middle East do, apart from individual personal traumas suffered through participation in combat. All they seek is to lead private lives rather than start a clandestine movement. However, it is one of the faces of opposition to the dominant unilateral global order with its remarkable blindness to collective emotions that do not fit into it. The pull of Donbas is part of the same process of polarization of identities in Europe and beyond that led to Brexit vote: resurgence against the global liberal elite, which gives the air of "knowing better," the belief in the triumph of capitalism and the spread of a US-led "democratisation project" which was destined to create a backlash.

NOTES

1. According to *Ekho Moskvy* radio station poll on August 5, 2014, Strelkov would have been a preferable winner of the 2018 election rather than Vladimir Putin, "Игорь Стрелков был бы более желательным победителем на президентских выборах 2018 года, чем Владимир Путин," http://echo.msk.ru/news/1373384-echo.html

2. Author's interview with a Kyiv-based international observer.

3. Alexander Borodai, author's interview, Moscow, May 2016.

4. Ray Silvius, "The Russian State, Eurasianism, and Civilisations in the Contemporary Global Political Economy," *Journal of Global Faultlines*, 2, no. 1 (2014): 44–69, 54.

5. Valery Shiryaev, "Это — война," August 8, 2016, *Novaya Gazeta*, https://www.novayagazeta.ru/articles/2016/08/08/69482-eto-voyna

6. Poll cited by Gazeta.ru on August 4, 2016.

7. Interviews at the Union of Donbas Volunteers with those who tried to support their former comrades-in-arms, February 2016.

8. Vladimir Dergachoff, "Батю гривны погубили," March 20, 2016 https://www.gazeta.ru/politics/2016/03/20_a_8130713.shtml

9. Interviews at the Union of Donbas Volunteers, February 2016, Moscow.

10. http://novorossia.pro

11. Prosvirnin in correspondence with the author, May 2017.

12. Igor Strelkov, author's interview, Moscow, May 2016.

13. Interview with a field commander who fought in DNR alongside Strelkov, May 2016, Moscow.

14. David C. Speedie, ""Soft Power": The Values that Shape Russian Foreign Policy," *U.S. Global Engagement*, July 30, 2015.

15. Vladimir Lenin, "О Национальной Гордости Великороссов," *Social Democrat* newspaper no. 35, December 12, 1914.

16. Isaiah Berlin, *The Power of Ideas* (Princeton, NJ: Princeton University Press, 2002), 72.

17. Borodai speaking at the International Conference of the Union of Donbas Volunteers, February 27, 2016, Moscow.

18. Silvius, "The Russian State."

19. Anatolii Tsyganok, *Donbass: Neokonchennaya Voina*, 311.

20. Gubarev, *Torch*, 201–211.

21. Alexander Borodai, author's interview.

22. Smith, *National Identity*.

23. Sakwa, *Russian Politics*, 214, 219.

24. Richard Sakwa, "Russian Nationalism and Democratic Development," in *Russia After the Cold War* eds. Michael Bowker and Cameron Ross (Harlow, Addison Wesley Longman, 1999): 199–220, 213, 215.

25. Marlene Laruelle, "The three colors of Novorossiya, or the Russian nationalist mythmaking of the Ukrainian crisis," *Post-Soviet Affairs*, 32, no.1, (2016): 55–74, 67. DOI: 10.1080/1060586X.2015.1023004

26. Alexander Juchkovsky in review of Gubarev's *Torch of Novorossiya*, 13 November 2015, https://sputnikipogrom.com/review/46747/the-torch-of-novorossiya/

27. Cerwyn Moore, "Foreign Bodies: Transnational Activism, the Insurgency in the North Caucasus and "Beyond,'" *Terrorism and Political Violence* (2015): DOI: 10.1080/09546553.2015.1032035

28. Author's research in the North Caucasus, 1996–2003, also Gordon M. Hahn, *Russia's Islamic Threat* (New Haven and London: Yale University Press, 2007), 36–39, Richard H. Jr. Schultz and Andrea J. Dew, *Insurgents, Terrorists and Militias* (New York: Columbia University Press, 2009), 144–145.

29. Natalia Yudina, Vera Al'perovich, "Затишье перед бурей? Ксенофобия и ра дикальный национализм и противодействие им в 2014 году в России," (Moscow: Sova Centre, 2015).

30. Shaun Walker, "We like partisan warfare, Chechens fighting in Ukraine–on both sides," *The Guardian*, July 24, 2015, http://www.theguardian.com/world/2015/sep/24/ukraine-conflict-Donbas-russia-rebels-foreigners-fighting

31. Yevgenii Norin, author's interview, May 2017.

32. http://arhiva.alo.rs/vesti/aktuelno/cetnicki-komandant-bratislav-zivkovic-u-donjecku/58287

33. Sergei Dmitriev, "«Добровольцы» Донбасса: кто и за кого сражается на востоке Украины," July 23, 2014, http://ru.rfi.fr/ukraina/20140722-dnr-lnr-dobro-voltsy-donbassa-kto-i-za-kogo-srazhaetsya-na-vostoke-ukrainy

34. *Colonel Cassad*, July 21, 2015, http://colonelcassad.livejournal.com/2297517.html

35. Main sites are *Coloned Cassad, Rusvesna.su, Life News*; also see reports by state Russian news agencies, for example, "Ряды ополченцев Донбасса пополняют иностранные добровольцы," August 30, 2014, https://russian.rt.com/article/47712, "Когда нельзя остаться в стороне: почему иностранцы воюют в рядах ополчения ДНР," March 6, 2015, http://www.vesti.ru/doc.html?id=2403295

36. Regnum. Ru, February 23, 2015, https://regnum.ru/news/polit/1898296.html

37. Emanuele Scimia, "The Multi-Faceted Reality of Italian Foreign Fighters in Ukraine," *Jamestown Foundation* Eurasia Daily Monitor 12, no. 187, October 16, 2015.

38. "DW: на стороне ополченцев в Донбассе воюют около сотни немцев," April 25, 2015, https://www.gazeta.ru/social/news/2015/04/25/n_7142845.shtml

39. Vladimir Dergachoff, Alexander Braterskyi "Донбасская «интербригада» пойдет под суд" February 27, 2015 http://www.gazeta.ru/politics/2015/02/27_a_6429433.shtml

40. Borodai, author's interview.

41. "Jeff Monson: Why I Became A Russian Citizen," *Newsweek*, April 1, 2016, http://europe.newsweek.com/jeff-monson-why-i-became-russian-citizen-411315?rm=eu

42. "Джефф Монсон лично подбирает тренеров и помещение для открытия своей школы единоборств в ЛНР," September 10, 2016, http://www.novorosin-form.org/news/60355

43. Alexander Clapp, "Why American Right-Wingers Are Going to War in Ukraine," *Vice Magazine*, June 20, 2016, http://www.vice.com/read/nationalist-interest-v23n4

44. "ДНР: иностранные наемники сражаются в Донбассе на стороне силовиков," *RIA Novosti*, May 21, 2015, http://ria.ru/world/20150521/1065716403.html, "ДНР: ополчение на 10-15 процентов состоит из иностранных добровольцев," September 10, 2014, http://ria.ru/world/20140910/1023574083.html

45. Interview with an international organisation's staff, Kharkiv.

46. Valery Shiryaev, "Это — война," 8 August 2016, https://www.novayagazeta.ru/articles/2016/08/08/69482-eto-voyna

47. Maria Antonova, "They Came to Fight for Ukraine. Now They're Stuck in No Man's Land," *Foreign Policy*, http://foreignpolicy.com/2015/10/19/ukraines-abandoned-soldiers-russian-belarusian-volunteers

48. "Foreign armed actors: UN expert group urges accountability for human rights violations," UN OHCHR, March 22, 2016 http://www.ohchr.org/en/NewsEvents/Pages/DisplayNews.aspx?NewsID=18511&LangID=E#sthash.6tvEZpVW.dpuf

49. Malet, *Foreign Fighters*, 124.

50. Malet, *Foreign Fighters*, 198.

51. Robert Stradling, *History and Legend: Writing the International Brigade* (Cardiff: University of Wales Press 2003), 106.

52. Alexei Blumminov, «Интербригады»: Как это было в Испании и как это есть на Донбассе. Politnavigator, September 7, 2015, http://www.politnavigator.net/interbrigady-kak-ehto-bylo-v-ispanii-i-kak-ehto-est-na-donbasse.html

53. Pepe Escobar, "From Minsk to Wales, Germany is Key," RT, August 28, 2014.

54. 11 December 2014, https://politconservatism.ru/interview/inostrannye-dobrovoltsy-novorossii-protiv-amerikantcev

55. "Ряды ополченцев Донбасса пополняют иностранные добровольцы," August 30, 2014, https://russian.rt.com/article/47712

56. Huntington, "The Clash of Civilizations?"

57. See Rękawek, "Neither "NATO's Foreign Legion" Nor the "Donbas International Brigades": (Where Are All the) Foreign Fighters in Ukraine?" *PISM Policy Paper* 108, no. 6 (Kacper, 2015) Rękawek cites anti-Americanism, anti-liberalism, extreme nationalism and rejection of European integration as common ideological values.

58. Shaun Walker, "We are preventing a third world war": the foreigners fighting with Ukrainian rebels. Eastern Ukraine has become a hub for those who believe the Russia-backed rebels are the last line of defence against fascism," *The Guardian*, September 24, 2015. http://www.theguardian.com/world/2015/sep/24/ukraine-conflict-Donbas-russia-rebels-foreigners-fighting

59. Personal observation, February 27, 2016, Moscow.

60. See for example, interviews with Prizrak foreign fighters, February 14, 2016 at "Иностранные добровольцы бригады «Призрак» — второй год в бою," http://ukraina.ru/opinions/20160214/1015604881.html

61. "Донбасская «интербригада»"

62. See, for example, this video "Gorlovka–Uglegorsk 'Donbas under fire: The Roads of War," January 2015, https://www.youtube.com/watch?v=woeAVg5M80w&feature=youtu.be

63. Polina Matveeva, Alexander Braterskyi "Ополченец Донбасса под польским судом," December 8, 2014, http://www.gazeta.ru/politics/2014/12/08_a_6333149.shtml

64. Mirren Gidda, "Disbanded Brothers," Newsweek, November 4, 2015, http://europe.newsweek.com/disbanded-brothers-what-happens-when-ukraines-foreign-fighters-return-home-335906

65. Personal observation, February 27, 2016, Moscow.

Chapter 11

Rebellion in Ukrainian Context

Inviting in or Shutting the Door?

CHALLENGE FROM THE EAST: KYIV'S RESPONSE

The initial conflict in Donbas could be interpreted as a crisis in the center-periphery relations triggered by the violent government shake-up in Kyiv and framed in the terms of power devolution. Such approach may have helped to resolve it at its beginning, if the region's cultural concerns were addressed and fears were alleviated. However, federalization idea was rejected by Kyiv outright as it was coming from Russia with no discussion on substance, although power devolution could have offered a way out of the developing tensions. This was because the new Kyiv rulers were influenced by the loss of Crimea whose autonomy was used as a springboard for the separation bid. Consequently, Kyiv insisted on the unitary state structure apprehensive that more regions would break away.

High-level diplomacy geared into action as violence was breaking out. Four-partite talks in Geneva between the foreign ministers of the United States, the European Union, Ukraine, and Russia on April 17, 2014, pledged the commitment to steps to de-escalate the crisis and to "inclusivity," but made little impact.[1] Although the Ukrainian government signed up to a statement in Geneva which called for negotiations between the authorities and the representatives of Donbas to find a settlement, those negotiations never happened.[2] In May Poroshenko's election brought hopes as many in Ukraine welcomed the new president as the answer to the split along the regional lines and hoped that his policies would be inclusive. He personified the quest for unity, because society was apprehensive that internal divisions could tear the country apart, and his declared priorities of peace as a pre-condition for reforms found a popular resonance.

Reforms started and many things happened in a relatively short period, but some drove away from resolution of the conflict. A radical shake-up of managerial and security elite, although logical from the perspective of the Ukrainian politics, focused on renewal, marginalized forces who could have bridged to the East. It exacerbated a misbalance within the ruling elite, undermined a possible peace constituency and with it—the prospects for peace. The Law on "Purification of the Government" (Lustration Law) adopted on September 16, 2014, banned persons associated with Yanukovych's administration from holding public office.[3] It eliminated many advocates of the East from official positions and had an effect upon the senior officer corps; for example, about 20 percent of the Ukraine's SBU officers fell under the Law and had to vacate their jobs. 5,000 officials were banned from holding posts in the law enforcement and 925 were fired.[4] Some civilian administrators left without waiting for the ban to come into force. There were also economic changes, in which Donbas was a likely loser. Much of Ukraine's industrial heritage was considered obsolete and in need of restructuring. Economic value of the East diminished, and disruption of the ties with Russia made an outlook for Donbas unattractive.

Popular expectations that the new president would bring a quick peace so that the country could move forward with reforms did not come true. In 2014, opportunities were missed at critical moments in summer. The first was when Poroshenko came to power and before support for the rebel cause in Donbas got entrenched. Instead, the army reinforcements and heavy weapons were sent in. Informal political talks were also half-hearted. They were organized between Moscow and Kyiv under the auspices of the Trilateral Contact Group on Ukraine, which was created after a meeting of heads of states in Normandy on June 6, 2014, and included representatives of Ukraine, Russia, and the OSCE. The Group was chaired by the OSCE special representative, Swiss diplomat Heidi Tagliavini.

On June 20, 2014, Poroshenko announced a ceasefire and a peace plan, according to which the rebels were to lay down their arms and either surrender or leave for Russia within a week. After that, the government would restore control over the border with Russia where a 10 km buffer zone would be established. In return, the president guaranteed language rights for the South-East and pre-term local elections. Putin responded that negotiations should include the rebel representatives. On June rebels who were in no mood for surrender, promised to honor the ceasefire if they participated in talks, which took place in Donetsk. Kyiv requested Leonid Kuchma to represent it, and the talks also included Russian ambassador Mikhail Zurabov, Ukrainian politicians Viktor Medvedchuk and Nestor Shufrych, and the rebel leaders Zakharchenko and Borodai. Kuchma, the main face of Ukrainian peacemaking, was unpopular in Donbas. He neither carried a convincing aura of "citizens' diplomacy" around him, nor had a formal government role, as Kyiv did not wish to attribute an official status to the talks. Participation of Medvedchuk as a mediator was backed by Angela Merkel. The rebels released the OSCE observers that were held hostage as a goodwill gesture. However, Borodai recalled that neither side had much faith in negotiations as a road to peace:

> Some very clever (хитромудные) people kept coming from Kyiv, MPs, Jewish community leaders; they waved fingers and hinted at some multimillion bribes. Medvedchuk, Shufrych and "eternal Ukrainian president" Kuchma came. I could see the pointlessness of all that, but had to keep up the airs, engage in negotiations, attend conciliation commission meetings, although I thought of it as an empty talk. Kuchma was saying: "Ukraine is indivisible and you are criminals, surrender." Medvedchuk looked clever and chuckled sceptically. Heidi was the only person who genuinely wanted to achieve results. I was sorry for her—she was creating the conditions, but we had nothing to talk about. We wanted to go to war. The positions of the sides were: "you should die—no, we will live, but it is better if you die." Each side was saying to the other—go out and shoot yourselves.[5]

It was clear that the June ceasefire was too short and the attached conditions unrealistic. Kyiv unilaterally ended it and began the offensive on June 30, 2014. The OSCE Contact Group attributed the responsibility for disruption of talks to the rebels and proposed the following way forward: an OSCE-supported monitoring and verification mechanism coming into effect together with the entry into force of the ceasefire, implementation of an effective border monitoring, the release of all hostages; and start of inclusive dialogue.[6] However, these measures were belated as the ground was already moving and a full-scale ATO offensive commenced. On July 2, 2014, the ministers of foreign affairs of Germany, France, Russia and Ukraine agreed in Berlin to resume peace talks, but it took the crash of Malaysian airliner for the group to re-convene. The new round of peace talks was held on July 31, 2014, in Minsk, where Kyiv insisted on the same conditions, and negotiations yielded no results. Then in early August when the rebels were in retreat, lost cities and asked for talks, Kyiv declined.

In September Kyiv for the first time negotiated in earnest after suffering a military defeat. However, the president failed to prepare society for the painful concessions which the peace deal entailed, and could not build an elite consensus around it, let alone rein the battalions in. Faced with politicians from the "patriotic" camp, such as prime minister Arsen Yatseniuk, minister of Interior Arsen Avakov, and the head of the SBU Valentyn Nalyvaichenko, whom he did not wish to turn into his opponents, the president preferred to avoid taking major risks by aggressively pushing a peace agenda. Forthcoming parliamentary elections of October 2014 held amid a surge in patriotic moods were a test whether he could entrench his standing in the national politics.

Focus on the elections superseded the president's peacemaking endeavor, while the new parliament was less conducive to peace than its predecessor. Ukrainian elites have never been a monolith,[7] and rivalries and concerns about future influenced their behavior. Shifts in internal politics, re-division of assets and spheres of influence emerged as major preoccupation, as their stakes were going up and down, and they were unable to elaborate a coherent approach toward peace.

Yet, conciliation was possible. The "party of peace" existed in Ukraine both among the public, more in the East where many wanted to end the armed hostilities, and among the elite. The latter included the remaining PoR figures, moderates in a newly established Bloc of Petro Poroshenko (BPP) presidential party, oligarchs with assets in the East, such as Dmytro Firtash and Rinat Akhmetov, and a number of public intellectuals. Ousted Donbas elites were conscious that they could come back only if a peace deal can soon be made while their assets were still of value, and would have been allies. However, the presidential communication strategy did not follow the drive toward peace. Media was not preparing society for a settlement, and the apprehension of the "hawks" in the government and of patriotic citizens' groups was too great. This was despite the president had a significant leverage over the information sphere since four out of the five main TV channels were controlled by the friendly oligarchs or directly by him.

Poroshenko's approach was characterized by duality. Presidential group, while pursuing its militant rhetoric, simultaneously acted toward peace. It realized that the war was ruining the economy, the army needs were draining resources, and the burden of IDPs was hard to sustain. Steps were taken to keep up the connectors with the NGCAs after Minsk-1 rather than to cut off Donbas from a lifeline. The government maintained transport links where possible, and with improved security after the 2014 ceasefire a railway line to Luhansk reopened. Pensions and benefits to the residents of the NGCAs were paid but they had to obtain them in the GCA. No policy on cutting the rebels from the national currency existed, but there was a problem of moving cash to the territories. Trade in fragile conditions went on. This "push me pull you" situation contained both drivers for war and peace.

A more confrontational approach to the NGCAs has been emerging after the parliamentary elections, in which the hawkish parties showed a strong performance. Rhetoric expressed a gradual hardening of the state line: Donbas Reconstruction Agency set up in September 2014 re-emerged in April 2016 as the Ministry for Temporarily Occupied Territories and IDPs, but it continued to pursue a constructive approach. Still, Kyiv was cutting the connectors and narrowing down a common space. It suspended budget allocations to the NGCAs. Social payments, which had to be obtained in the government-controlled areas, became less accessible when the government stepped up measures to halt "pension tourism."[8] Freedom of movement was limited by Temporary Order of January 21, 2015,[9] and by summer 2015 the legal ways into the NGCAs were a number of official crossing points. Passage was difficult, as it necessitated obtaining a permit sanctioned by the SBU and issued by the ATO command, and crossing the line was dependent on frequent road and checkpoint closures. Exchange with the NGCAs got restricted.

SOCIAL EFFECTS

Politization of society which started with Euromaidan increased civil activism and the capacity for self-organization in Ukraine. When violence broke out in the South-East and thousands of IDPs poured westwards escaping fighting, international humanitarian assistance was slow to arrive. The West demonstrated a conspicuous lack of attention to the developing disaster, while the United Nations and the European Union underplayed the scale of humanitarian crisis, in which by autumn 2014 1.3 million were forcibly displaced from Donbas.[10] The crisis was met by ordinary Ukrainians who in this situation demonstrated a tremendous generosity. They donated clothes and medicine, hosted the displaced in their own homes, and contributed money and time to the relief efforts organized by the citizens' groups, many of whom had no prior experience of charity work. Protestant churches were active humanitarians and quickly put their followers into action. Civil activists conducted rescue operations: for example, Donbas SOS which was set up in March 2014 evacuated 3,788 persons from the areas under fire in summer.[11] As the state help was not coming, volunteers in Kharkiv set up a "Kharkiv Station" group at a flat of one of its members and organized round the clock reception at the railway station, the main gateway out of the ATO zone, to meet traumatized and disoriented arrivals.[12]

Call to arms had a popular resonance in pro-Maidan quarters and was a patriotic morale booster. One view was that while Second Maidan split the society along identity lines, the war united it, as people who had been ambivalent toward the Ukrainian statehood, came out strongly in support of it, including some ethnic Russians.[13] The conflict in Donbas instigated popular participation and sparked pro-war enthusiasm. This manifested in the weapons' procurement by civilians that took place. It is worth noting in this context that Ukraine was a major arms producer and continued with exports.[14] The state arms trader *Ukrspetzexport* advertised a diverse range of defense products and in 2014 participated in arms fairs such as Farnborough, when the hostilities in Donbas were at their height.[15]

The moment fostered security sector reform from below. The bottom-up process cleared some of the old baggage which previous reform efforts could not challenge, and enhanced the pro-war stakes. Territorial battalions acquired political prominence. Social media communications brought increased transparency and mobilizing power. As it appeared that arms were in one place, while fighting was in another, *Help Army* volunteers rushed to close the gap. They collected donations and organized "people's supplies" of anything from helmets and bulletproof vests to tanks and APCs. *Phoenix Wings* group of Yuri Biryukov, an IT entrepreneur, advertised in social media,[16] while its leader not only fought the rebels, but also the MoD until his successful appointment as a ministerial aide for procurement.[17]

The war outbreak changed the life of Donbas which could not join the new-style patriotism. Insecurity and economic deterioration produced a negative impact upon the government-controlled areas which came out as a loser compared to previous well-being. Population felt ostracized as "second class citizens" for Kyiv, downcasts who lost their working class identity of an industrial region which they used to be proud of. The war divided them from their fellow country folk in the NGCAs and among themselves. Split was felt on group and individual levels: some covertly sympathized with the rebellion, others were ardent patriots and many found themselves between a rock and a hard place as they were loyal to their country, but were uncomfortable with the direction it was taking.

It was apparent that rebel sympathizers continued to exist in the cities formerly under their control, such as Sievierodonetsk, Kramatorsk,[18] and Mariupol. In a local expert view, many people in these areas "still do not like Ukraine much and like Russia. They are afraid of the Right Sector and are alienated by the "national idea."[19] Moreover, the rebel partisan movement made its subversive presence felt and did not inspire much trust in allegiance of the residents in Kyiv's eyes. In Bakhmut, for example, a local man together with his sons waged a secret war against the battalions and was bringing the documents of his victims to the DNR command as an evidence of his operations.[20]

Residents, in their turn, had issues with the government. Those who at first welcomed restoration of the government control were disappointed because "we waited for the Ukrainian army, but got battalions instead." The battalions were the worst advertisement for Kyiv's cause. "Men in camouflage" who did not identify themselves, wore masks and were not answerable to an overall command, were their source of grievances. In the words of a five-year-old boy, "the one who is in a uniform, is a bandit." While rebels appropriated cars and raided banks and businesses for cash, they were more often doing it for the cause as they needed to sustain the insurgency. Now violence became random and sometime pointless, without an obvious material benefit, such as firing at a civilian funeral procession in Krasnyanka.[21] Two female shop assistants who requested to pay for goods taken in a shop in Krasnoarmeisk [now Pokrovsk] district were shot.[22]

Aidar in Luhansk oblast was responsible for most of civilian disappearances. In August 2014 it abducted the Sievierodonetsk mayor and three other officials, and kept them in a dig-in hole for 10 days until the detainees parted with their money. Local administrators were harassed in their offices if they were suspected of disloyalty, such as not properly displaying state symbols, or if graffiti expressing support for the rebels was noticed in their towns. Human life became cheap. Illegal detentions of alleged "separatists," and abuse and intimidation by armed men left the residents vulnerable. Robberies were commonplace. Postal services were working at their full capacity, moving the looted goods. "Who won, loots" principle reined.[23] Weapons proliferated and shots were often heard, and *Dnipro* and *Donbas* battalions clashed with each other.

The lack of security, the same as in the NGCAs was the biggest concern. The closer the area was to the line of contact, the more acute was the war fear. IDPs from the conflict zones were fleeing the fighting around the cities, but no state assistance was available and they were left at a mercy of the municipal authorities and citizens' groups who mobilized for help. Many among the authorities were "acting" because previous administrators fled, were dismissed or detained for collaboration, and budgets were in disarray. Lack of communication from Kyiv had a discouraging effect. Nationalist manifestations in Kyiv were interpreted as geared against Donbas, while the region was left with few political resources to oppose the radicals as it lost its voice on the national scene. PoR was in disgrace and no politicians or oligarchs were prepared to stand for the region as they could be seen as "traitors." People with a pro-Russian orientation, or those who had grievances against the new authorities, were apprehensive of expressing their views publicly, afraid of being detained as a separatist and a rebel spy. SBU was apprehending ten people a day on the basis of YouTube video clips posted on social media.

The economy has been changing. Some valuable industrial capacities stayed in the NGCAs, as well as major mines. Machine-building and chemical works were declining due to energy shortages, and disruption of an integrated production cycle with the Russian economy adversely affected the industries, making skilled working force redundant. Donbas feared becoming a buffer zone between the rebels and the rest of the country, and was staring into the prospect of state neglect and lack of investment. Ongoing insecurity, disruption of supply and market chains, as well as of transportation links meant less attractiveness for investors. Restricted border access resulted in the region turning from an industrial hub into a military garrison and a dead end. De-industrialization prospect loomed and with it—a loss of esteem.

The region had its own pro-Ukrainian activists who had received a boost out of the power change in Kyiv, but were in their turn dissatisfied with a too slow pace of change. They demanded prosecution and a purge of disloyal and allegedly corrupt officials associated with the PoR and big business to end the impunity for embezzlement of public funds. They sought to increase public control over appointments to the regional administration and campaigned for transparency of the recruitment process. However, they did not manage to appoint as many of their members into the positions of power as they had hoped for because few had required professional qualifications. Capable and ideologically sound administrators were scarcely left in Donbas. As a result, the groups were strong on criticism of public officials, but weak on finding suitable replacements. A hotly contested sphere of education was another priority for them. Activists demanded sacking of all headmasters who allowed school premises to be used to hold the May 2014 referendum.

Nevertheless, two parts of Donbas preserved certain similarity in the following two years despite living in different information spaces. Several surveys undertaken in both parts in 2016 confirm that. Ukrainian branch of German *IFAK Institut* discovered in June 2016 that common features included strong association with a regional identity and the desire for a paternalistic state, as well as a belief in the need for a strong agency to protect the region's interests.[24] In ZOiS survey, social distances between people did not seem to increase: personal contacts between two parts of Donbas continued, and 14 percent in the government-controlled and 20 percent in NGCAs said that they felt more strongly now that they were "both Ukrainian and Russian," than in 2013. A majority—53 percent in the government-controlled Donbas and 70 percent in the NGCAs—listed Russian as the dominant language spoken at home, and 21 and 17 percent, respectively, said that their main language at home was Russian but that they occasionally spoke Ukrainian.[25] Geopolitical orientations showed uniformity in their negative attitudes toward NATO and the European Union: 72 percent of ZOiS respondents in the government-controlled Donbas and 82 percent in the NGCAs were against Ukraine joining the European Union. Interestingly, 30 percent in government-controlled Donbas thought that the war was the result of Western intervention, while 37 percent blame Russia. A third of *IFAK Institut* respondents did not want Ukraine to enter any alliances (30 percent at DNR and 38 percent in GCAs), and an alliance with Russia was favored by 22 percent at GCAs.[26]

Human interaction with those living across the contact line although disrupted, has not been lost,[27] and many did not perceived them as "enemies," but as those who had bad luck to find themselves in these circumstances. A desire for coming back together existed. In the words of a Kramatorsk civil activist,

anger at those on the other side diminished. Many understand that we should search for peace, and that time for it is now. Everybody is tired. Bad peace is better than a good war. They are our friends and relatives. People were dying in Gorlovka, Makeevka because of shelling—we are very worried about them. Why nobody talks about what happens to them?[28]

NGCAS: MANAGING SURVIVAL

The NGCAs fared worse in how life felt. After Minsk-2, the NGCAs comprised about 30 percent of former Luhansk and 40 percent of Donetsk oblasts. The territories sustained uneven damage. While Donetsk was only destroyed on its western edges, Horlivka took a heavy toll and supplies hardly reached it. An international humanitarian worker recalled that when he first travelled there after the September 2014 ceasefire, the town appeared a ghost. Death and destruction were everywhere, as well as a lack of basic commodities and severe disruption of communal infrastructure. It was one of the worst-affected places in Donbas and a different picture from Donetsk where life continued almost as normal. As access to Horlivka was always a problem, no aid was delivered directly there, and "Donetsk was capturing aid destined to the city." It formed one military theatre with Debaltseve and the frontline town of Vuhlehirsk which was almost totally wiped out in ferocious shelling in January 2015. In Luhansk oblast, the most dreadful humanitarian situation was in the north in heavily bombarded Pervomaisk and Slavyanoserbsk.[29]

The international community tried to use practical issues of mutual concern as a tool for peacemaking outside of the formal political track. OSCE attempted this with demining and maintenance of infrastructural links, Médicine Sans Frontiers (MSF)—with TB and cancer care to make the sides preserve communication channels. However, an involved practitioner concluded that "all this failed. The only real peacemaking tools were business operations, such as smuggling of coal or consumer goods."[30] Government restrictions, far from forcing surrender, had the effect of boosting grey economy networks thriving on petty smuggling. Actors among Ukrainian officials, territorial battalions, rebel commanders, and businesspeople all had a stake in them. Trade trickled through various informal channels, including Western Ukrainians delivering goods from the Russian side.[31] Eventually, foodstuffs from Russia started to prevail over Ukrainian produce.[32] Russia provided essential social payments in the NGCAs.[33] Khodakovsky, the then "DNR Security Council" chair stated that 70 percent of the "republic's" budget expenditure was covered by Moscow in 2015. Juchkovsky estimated that from April to October 2015 Moscow spent 150 billion roubles ($2.42 billion) on civilian aid alone.[34] In 2015, according to German paper *Bild*, Russia was spending US$73 million a month to subsidize public sector, in addition to supplies of gas and electricity.[35]

Economic decline was apparent. Some factories were forced to close, and had their equipment cut and sold for scrap metal. Several coal mines were flooded and shut down. They perhaps died a natural death as they used to be subsidized and their operations made economic sense only when they were integrated into the production cycle that no longer existed.[36] Many buildings were damaged or destroyed, some businesses withdrew and currency problems prevented a banking system to get on its feet for a long time. *Hryvna*, in short supply by then, was getting out of circulation, replaced by the Russian rouble, which became an "official" currency in February 2017. By mid-2016, recovery to an extent has taken place. Rehabilitation of housing was accomplished, apart from the "grey zones" that regularly came under shelling. Businesses started to return and new production was developed, especially in agriculture where the lack of competition from the mainland helped the local farmers.

There was a difference between the situation in so-called "grey zones" near the frontlines and the rest of NGCAs where maintenance of normalcy in wartime produced important psychological effects for keeping population's spirits up. The areas outside of the line of fire were quickly returning to life, with public transport and infrastructure functioning. In early March 2015, the railway connection was restored and Ukrainian press reported that "Terrorists in Debaltseve Repaired a Railway Line." The staff of communal services in Donetsk were praised as "everyday heroes" because they preserved the appearance of normality. International observers in Donetsk stressed that the city was very clean.[37] In the words of sociologist Yevgen Kopat'ko,

I would like to believe that the most difficult times in Donetsk are already over, and a huge number of people remained in the city. I would not like to idealise anything, but today Donetsk is very clean. Communal services work exceptionally well. Of course, the war has laid its imprint on the life in Donetsk, but what immediately meets the eye is that how much people changed. Those who stayed. Because a war brings out the worst filth, but also creates incredible relations among people, new type of solidarity.[38]

IDPs and refugees started to return. This was confirmed by the figures both from Ukraine and Russia, although rebels' own statistics was at variance with those of the Ukrainian government. UN Office for the Coordination of Humanitarian Affairs (OCHA) estimated the remaining population in the NGCAs at 3 million,[39] while according to the DNR department of statistics, by July 1, 2016, 2.3 million lived in the territory against pre-war 3 million and LNR provided the figure of 1.5 million residents, which totals 3.8 million altogether.[40] Russian Federal Migration Service reported that the numbers of refugees from Ukraine decreased from 1 million in February 2015 to 600,000 in a year's time.[41] According to Donetsk mayor Igor Martynov, by 2016 many of the displaced returned and the city population reached 850,000 residents against 1 million before the war. Some moved to Donetsk from heavily bombed settlements in the countryside where they could not sustain livelihood. DNR sources estimated the remaining inhabitants in these areas at 75 percent of pre-war population.[42] The war prompted urbanization and depleted countryside: less than 100,000 lived in rural areas in LNR and 110,000 in DNR.

Improvements in security in the second half of 2015 alleviated the most pressing safety concerns, as shelling reduced.[43] Efforts were put into the restoration of law and order, with vivid effects. Although the curfew held, a visitor to Donetsk observed that while in autumn 2014 many armed rebels were seen in the streets, by the summer of 2015 that was no longer the case. In autumn 2015 LNR police started returning vehicles misappropriated during the chaos of the uprising, to their rightful owners.[44] Crime levels were higher than before the war, but this was consistent with the nationwide trend: statistics showed 1.5 time growth in pre-meditated murders in Donetsk from 2013 to 2015, but the situation in Kyiv was worse with 1,250 such murders in 2015 compared to 470 in 2013.[45] Given massive proliferation of weapons, it is in fact surprising that crime level was not much higher.

Medical staff, teachers, social care workers and prison staff were not paid by Kyiv since July 2014, although many continued with their jobs even without salaries until the rebels organized their payment system. Many people were out of work. One survey assessed that the rate of hidden unemployment went down in DNR from 39 percent in January 2015 to 28 percent in June 2016.[46] Ukrainian "GFK Ukraine" data estimated unemployment at DNR at 20 percent, while only 2 percent were registered with job centers as seeking vacancies.[47] Salaries were low, amid higher commodity prices than in the GCAs where living standards were slightly better, although they had to pay more for housing, transport, and public utilities. The humanitarian situation improved: in June 2016 only a half of the population (54 percent) relied on aid as compared to 69 percent in January 2015.[48]

Life of the NGCAs consisted of plethora of some temporary solutions, short and long-cuts, and indirect ways of going about practical problems. Some people have money to spend: for example, a chic car dealership operates in Luhansk selling luxury cars with Georgian number plates. A travel agency in Donetsk books holidays abroad. Many queue to cross into the GCAs in order to obtain Ukrainian biometric passports for visa-free travel to Schengen countries since liberalization regime for Ukraine was introduced in June 2017. A certain negative adaptation also took place, and a fatigue with constantly being on edge settled in: "some just have this doomed look, like old people who live in frontline villages. They no longer pay attention. Even if a shell explodes 50 meters from them, they won't raise an eyebrow. "We don't want to leave," they say."[49]

A fear of a "colour revolution" through NGOs and civil-minded independent groups grew, especially after an attempt to blow up the Lenin monument in Donetsk in February 2016 which was seen as a symbolic expression of pro-Ukrainian sentiment. This explains a clump down on "Responsible Citizens," an NGO registered in Ukraine, which had been operating in Donetsk oblast, and arrests of public intellectuals such as religious scholar Igor Kozlovskyi.

"Responsible Citizens" did not hide their moderate pro-Ukrainian position and were vulnerable to an accusation of a lack of patriotism. They used to receive support from the international humanitarian community, including Danish Refugee Council, MSF and "Dopomozhem" Foundation, but were more than just aid providers. They explained that "we more than once expressed opinions which contradict the main DNR line, opinions which they consider as "anti-state."[50] Its politically active leader Marina Cherenkova, former Donetsk oblast deputy governor, was detained twice by the "DNR ministry of state security" for alleged "spying" although no formal charges were pressed, and subsequently relocated to Kyiv. An attempt to arrest a pro-Ukrainian activist Maria Oleinik, leader of *Prosvity* NGO was made in January 2016, but she managed to go into hiding.

Obstacles to peace are many. The rebel leaderships are fearful for their safety, do not trust amnesty offer promised under the Minsk Agreement and believed that they would be prosecuted, especially since Kyiv's "terrorist" rhetoric led them to think that this would be the case. Passage of time and gradual disentanglement exacerbates the divide with the rest of Ukraine. Visitors report enthusiasm for the "young republics" and a stronger pro-Russian orientation: "Они все больше ватники" ("they are even more *bodywarmers*.")[51] Aspiration for joining Russia exists, although a public discussion of the subject is discouraged. In the view of my respondents in NGCAs, both local and international, while this generation was alive, the rebellious territories would not be returning to Kyiv. The population's position shifted toward self-rule and away from Ukraine. The residents that suffered the ATO bombardments turned against it in a "Won't forget, won't forgive!" mood as civilian casualties mounted. Anti-Ukrainian narrative persists despite all what people went through under the rebel rule—torture in dungeons, banditry, proliferation of armed militias, and Russia not taking them in. Acquiescence of the de facto situation was shown by returns among the displaced who were prepared to live under the insurgent regime. Donbas moved on, paid the price for survival, created a new elite and its people changed. It would be reluctant to go back at its own will.

The sense that there is no end in sight was the most depressing: "Now we have an in-between period, there are no ends, no logic—everything bears on a pile of accidental factors."[52] Perceptions are held that everybody from Donbas is considered to be a separatist for the rest of Ukrainians, even if they did not initially support the rebellion, and the question was whether they were regarded as "bandits" or fellow citizens. A shadow of separatism would still be hanging over. A doctor in Makiivka said that she received abuse on social media from the other side although she merely carried on as a doctor. There were doubts that Donbas people are welcome and a feeling that Kyiv was only interested in the territorial control to turn the region into a buffer with Russia. One Makiivka resident said that "Kyiv is behaving towards us like an abandoned husband who one day pleads with his wife who left him "please, return, I'll mend my ways," and the next day chases her with an axe. What we should believe?" Moreover, there were doubts that Kyiv had sufficient resources and organizational capacities to truly integrate the NGCAs even if goodwill existed. There were voices who were saying that perhaps in the lieu of solution Russia should buy Donbas from Ukraine as the US government bought Alaska from Russia.

Polls paint a complex picture of what the population might think, although only the cities of Donetsk, Makiivka and Luhansk were polled in NGCAs.[53] Support for re-integration into Ukraine did not disappear, and a range of preferences indicate aspirations for the recognition of the region's special status, either within Ukraine or Russia. 45 percent of ZOiS respondents in the NGCAs "strongly" or "rather" agreed with the principles of the Minsk Agreement.[54] At the same time, 54 percent reported that they felt less like Ukrainian citizens compared to before 2013. The war experience politicized the population, and 53 percent report an increased interest in politics.[55] In *IFAK* poll, support for "DNR as a self-governing entity" increased from 15 to 20 percent in 18 months (January 2015–June 2016), and 18 percent of respondents identified themselves primarily as "DNR citizens." The constituency wishing to reintegrate into Ukraine remained largely stable, up from 13 to 15 percent, in the same period.[56] According to Donetsk-registered *Osobyi Status* (Special Status) sociological center poll, in June 2015, 36 percent of DNR respondents supported the idea of joining Russia, 18 percent favored an imagined *Novorossiya* from Kharkiv to Odesa, 14 percent preferred an "independent state within the united borders of the DNR and LNR," and 10 percent would agree to a special status within Ukraine.[57] Views on the dynamic of change were not exactly optimistic: in June 2016 24 percent DNR respondents stated that wellbeing improved, 33 percent believed the opposite and 44 percent saw no change.[58]

Industrial connections with mainland Ukraine were not wholly disrupted when restrictions were introduced, and business actors on both sides sought to preserve them. All this time Kyiv has been buying and Donbas rebels have been selling coal while Kyiv supplied them with electricity and water. Major enterprises from NGCAs got re-registered in Mariupol and paid taxes to Kyiv, such as Stakhanov ferroalloy works and Alchevsk Iron and Steel Works (AMK) co-owned by Sergei Taruta and a part of the ISD corporation, which have been operating throughout the conflict and exported their produce via Ukraine under its customs stamp. The most prominent belonged to the SCM holding owned by Rinat Akhmetov (8 DTEK and 9 Metinvest enterprises).[59] The rebels did not nationalize them in 2014 when their aspirations for nationalization were replaced by an understanding that if the status quo was preserved, the industries would continue functioning and salaries would be paid, allowing thousands to work and live. Akhmetov had a clear agenda of protecting his material interests in the chaotic conditions, and this was what apparently happened. Since his enterprises were export-oriented, access routes had to be maintained, and their production found a way to do so through mainland Ukraine.[60] The port of Mariupol served as the rebels' offshore zone, allowing legal export from the NGCAs.

Unlike some other oligarchs, Akhmetov remained a relevant figure in Donbas because he was quick to establish a humanitarian agency *Dopomozhem* Foundation, early on and became the main aid provider on both sides throughout the most acute crisis.[61] Some rebels were believed to be on reasonable terms with him. His former associates started to return to positions in the energy sector, and communal and housing services in the NGCAs. The same happened in the government-controlled Donbas where an HR manager at a CSM enterprise became the new mayor of Mariupol. Borodai considered it as a normal process of adaptation to the new conditions:

> A certain revolutionary process took place. The old elite was replaced by a new one, although parts of the old elite now try to return and join the processes that are taking place in Donbas. Some even succeed. It's natural, as it happened after 1917. Akhmetov's cadre still exist as many were connected to him. He was the main oligarch who used to be omnipresent in Donbas where he controlled many social and political spheres before the war. It's obvious that any more or less able person would've come under his spell of attention at some point.[62]

Arrangements for mutually beneficial exchange were disrupted in January 2017 when war veterans and members of patriotic groups, supported by some MPs, laid a blockade on cargo access to the NGCAs. Their aim was to cut off what they termed "trade in blood." The action was fed by frustration with the stalemate, perceived government inaction, including in release of prisoners kept by the rebels and opposition to the Special Status proposal. Some protesters were reportedly paid.[63] The rebels demanded that Kyiv puts a stop to blockade and returns to the previous arrangements, but instead on March 15 the Security and Defense Council announced the suspension of all cargo traffic with the NGCAs.[64] The action was criticized by the Normandy partners—Germany, France, and Russia.

In response, the *de facto* authorities took 54 major companies into "temporary external management."[65] Kyiv's action caused a short-term dip as enterprises were facing closure,[66] but worked to increase the gap with the rest of the country where the process of Ukrainization has accelerated, and forced the NGCAs away from the common space. Re-orientation toward Russia meant that the effect of cutting off old economic ties was not catastrophic. The industry still required ore supplies from Kryvyi Rih (in Ukrainian, Krivoi Rog in Russian),[67] but otherwise was adapting to function outside of Ukraine's production cycle. It was viewed by Juchkovsky as a logical step in separation and achieving self-sufficiency:

Blockade benefitted the "republics." This is a moral shift because for three years a large share of our enterprises was paying taxes into Kyiv's budget and part of this money was going into the ATO. So, some of people's money went into them being shelled here. This is absurd, but this was a transition period, things were complicated, and there were problems with salaries. It was necessary to stop this long time ago, and it's very good that this happened.[68]

PEOPLE AND THE WAR

Ukraine was undergoing a profound political and cultural transformation since Euromaidan. It was becoming a different country to what it used to be at the time when Donbas conflict broke out, and this transformation mattered for the prospects for peace. National vision and who is invited into it was forming. After Maidan, a culture of use-of-force for political ends became more accepted. The conflict in the East provided a useful peg for Kyiv politicians to hang a new national idea on and it became a creation myth with its "heroes" and history in the making. In this paradigm, the outbreak of violence in Donbas was interpreted not as a civil war in Ukraine, or as a counter-insurgency operation which went wrong, but a war between Ukraine and Russia. No expression of dissent was tolerated in liberal circles on such core beliefs as victory over "terrorists" or attitude toward Russia. Large pro-war support emerged among Kyiv middle class and especially among politicized intelligentsia, media, think tanks and universities.[69]

Culture became a war theatre and an assault on culture became a legitimate pursuit. In July 2014, Russian films, including "The White Guard" based on Mikhail Bulgakov's novel and shot in Kyiv before the second Maidan, got banned.[70] As stated by Alexander Roitband, a Ukrainian artist-turn-ideologue, "Russian literature and music should not be banned, but I made a revision of Russian literature for my own sake. I understand that what we encountered is in large part the consequence of Russian culture."[71] A physical expression of this trend was the fall of Lenin monuments (Leninopad) that took place in the aftermath of Maidan when over a hundred were toppled by activists. Lenin struck back in Kharkiv, taking an eye of one of its executioners when a chain collapsed and hit him in the face. It might be surprising that Lenin so passionately mattered after 25 years of independence. The onslaught on Soviet-era symbols was characteristic of the 1990–1991 period in Soviet Russia when many were removed as Communism was ending, but not in Ukraine where statues of Lenin mostly stayed in the south-east. The reason for the demolition of monuments after Maidan can be regarded as a disguised attempt to distance from the cultural past shared with Russia, identified with Sovietism, and reflected substitution of "Soviet" for "Russian."

These symbolic actions caused resentment in Donbas which felt no urgency to part with its heritage. At first, statues of Lenin survived in its major cities. Later on, when military hostilities were in full swing, one of the first things the Ukrainian forces did when they regained control over cities was to demolish the statues. In Sievierodonetsk, the Ukrainian Radical Party leader Oleh Lyashko removed the monument in one swift move, before the public had time to object, and Lenin also fell in Lysychansk. The argument about the statue in Kramatorsk assumed an existential character in autumn 2014 because of the strengths of feelings pro- and against demolition. Redefining history and social consciousness emanated from the center: in May 2015 the law was adopted ordering to dismantle the remaining Soviet monuments within six months and wipe out Communist-era public place names. Over 20 cities and thousands of settlements were to be renamed.[72] The process of identity-formation on an anti-Russian basis and patriotism linked to the past struggle against the Russian/Soviet Empire intensified. As expressed by a political analyst Ihor Semyvolos,

> The process of destruction of a Soviet identity is happening as a destruction of the Russian one and deconstruction of "Russianness." Cultural ties with Russia are disrupted, not only political ones. Russians inflicted a great humiliation upon us, and we should have satisfaction.[73]

Atmosphere became less tolerant.[74] As Ukrainian and international peace-building activists expressed, "the notion of diversity and plurality of political ideas is politically charged, and many are not ready to acknowledge this as a reality. . . . Political discourse mostly promotes nationalist positions and marginalises voices that do not fit into the views that dominate the media."[75] Acceptance of identity differences became a problem, and some identities were not viewed as legitimate. As pro-Russians were associated with the political Left, it became discredited and barely had a voice in public discourse. In December 2015 the Communist Party was banned by a court order. Emotive and aggressive public rhetoric meant that voices of dissent were silenced not as much by the state, but by society activists. Mikhail Pogrebinskii, director of Political and Conflict Studies Centre, lamented that Elena Bondarenko, an ex-PoR MP who tried to campaign for peace, was hounded on live TV when a *Svodoba Slova* (Freedom of Expression) program gave her airtime: "they are representatives of civil society. Do they have any arguments, or only hysterical insults? And all of these are civic-minded activists, our civil society."[76] Bondarenko received death threats and was assigned armed protection by the Ministry of Interior in April 2015.[77]

Changes in public atmosphere meant that the eastern regions including Donbas lost influence on the national scene. Even the word combination

"Eastern Partnership" [with the European Union] was unpopular because of the "East" word.[78] Vouching for an Eastern identity could be dangerous. In January–April 2015 eight former officials with pro-Eastern leanings committed suicide under dubious circumstances. Oleg Kalashnikov, a former MP from the PoR, was gunned down at the same time in Kyiv, as well as a journalist Oles' Busina, who was critical of the military campaign.[79] Sergei Sukhobok was another journalist found dead. The most prominent political murder was of *Ukrainska Pravda* editor Pavel Sheremet in July 2016. Then in September 2016 the offices of the *Inter* TV channel were set on fire twice by former Ukrainian military personnel who disapproved of its editorial policy, and the attackers left an anti-tank mine behind. In 2015 forty-one foreign journalists were banned from Ukraine, most of them Russian, and further seventeen were added in 2016, despite an outcry from international rights" organizations.[80] Gradually, some prominent figures among Kyiv intelligentsia who adhered to an "Eastern" orientation, chose to leave.

Religion joined the battleground. At first the Ukrainian Orthodox Church (the Church) under the Moscow Patriarchate abstained from an involvement in politics, but it still faced a reputational challenge after Maidan. Although it gave its spiritual support to the Ukrainian army, it pursued a politically neutral stance, called for peace, reconciliation and prevention of violence, but the calls did not resonate and the Church was vulnerable to accusation of being insufficiently patriotic. Shift from neutrality happened in spring 2015 when the senior clergy remained seated while the ATO fallen troops were commemorated.[81] The tone was set by Patriarch Kirill, the Head of the Moscow Patriarchate, who stated in reference to Ukraine that "when godlessness becomes state ideology, and people die and churches are ruined as a result, this is more than ideology."[82] The Church was losing parishioners and parishes, when sixty-five transferred to Kyiv Patriarchy by the end of 2016, but some reportedly were harassed by the Right Sector militants into doing so. Priests who opposed collections in churches for the ATO needs were deposed in a number of cases. Churches were vandalized, subjected to arson attacks, and it is believed that there were some murders.[83] Some churches switched to service in Ukrainian instead of old Slavonic. Nevertheless, the Church still had a large influence in society. Some clerics, but not all, followed Russian narrative, but there was no evidence of direct instrumentalization and leveraging of the Church by the Russian government.[84] The head of Church Mitropolite Onuphrii personally facilitated prisoner release from the DNR captivity in 2016.

Society's views on the conflict showed great diversity. Minsk Agreement inspired conflictual attitudes: while some viewed it as a greater compromise than the country should accept, others did not wish re-integration with the people they felt nothing in common with. In a poll by Razumkov Centre in

December 2015, 35 percent of respondents negatively assessed the progress of the Minsk process, 56.4 percent did not support the Special Status provision, while 23.8 percent were in favor.[85] War enthusiasm was not evenly shared in society, with hawkish segment active against the backdrop of an ambivalent milieu. In September 2014 the majority wanted peace, with 27.8 percent respondents supporting it at any cost and further 22.6 percent believed that serious concessions could be made for it (50.4 percent). Only 15.8 percent considered that continuation of military hostilities was preferable to compromises.[86]

After two years, many in society were tired of war. Opinion surveys by different research groups paint a picture of a society divided on Donbas issue. In July 2016, 53 percent did not support continuation of the ATO in Donbas against 33 percent who did; 65 percent supported resolution of the conflict through peace negotiations in the Minsk format, while 21 percent were in favor of the use of force by the government to resolve the crisis. 50 percent of the respondents said that they generally followed the news on peace talks while 43 percent did not.[87] In July 2016 only 27 percent of respondents said that they would help territorial battalions in an event of a conflict with Russia, while 38.7 percent would support those who advocate stopping the war. 24.7 percent stated that they would do nothing. Only 22.8 percent were in favor of active military operations until a full control of the territories was regained, even if this meant a direct confrontation with Russia. A quarter of respondents was in favor of reintegration of NGCAs on the basis of a "special status" or a wide autonomy, while 18 percent considered that the NGCAs should be just cut off and live as they like. Only 7.4 percent were ready to recognize their independence. It was symptomatic that over a quarter of surveyed respondents could not choose any answer.[88]

During my interviews, many expressed that Donbas was not worth painful sacrifices for: its people were different and the war-torn territory was not of a particular value; it was better to cut the losses and move on. Although bitterness toward Russia remained strong, not everybody was willing to pay a price for the war. Questions were raised whether the country would make a better progress toward its European future without a hostile and devastated region, and its warlordist elite. European prospects and economic realities came to dominate the public mind, sidelining the war in the South-East and undermining the resolve to settle the issue in definitive terms.

The war only added to a negative image of Donbas. The arguments against holding on were that social change in the region was profound: many among professional class left, those who stayed were low-educated, unskilled masses with the values alien to that of modern Ukraine, and their society was incompatible with the country's European choice.[89] Moreover, retired people in Donbas constituted pressure on the social security, while the devastated territories with damaged industry and infrastructure would require a colossal revival package which the country could not afford.[90] Such views were held even by those who originated from the NGCAs, but threw their loyalty with Kyiv: "I am no longer interested in their return. Ukraine does not need Donbas economically: industry has died and agriculture is hard-going there because of no tradition for it. Most importantly, lots of blood has been spilt, and it would be impossible to breach it."[91] The most sober view perhaps was that "in fact, nobody knows what to do with Donbas now."[92]

Accommodation of society to the conflict to certain extent happened. Since August 2014, all employed people and enterprises contributed 1.5 percent of their income to the ATO needs. Men could be mobilized to the battlefield, but in big cities it was possible to avoid being drafted. Although casualties were mounting,[93] their true scale was probably withheld and, dispersed around the country of over 40 million, they were not immediately felt. Families of the ATO troops staged protests for better military procurement, healthcare for the wounded and prisoner release, but not on a pro-peace agenda. A sizeable but passive constituency in favor of "cutting the cancer off" did not transpire into an active peace support, as such moods seldom found a political articulation. A collective "victim" identity started to emerge which blamed the country's misfortunes on outsiders, most notably on Russia, but some were unhappy with the West as well. Widespread cynicism toward politicians fed the notion that the current government would not get the country a good deal, so it is perhaps better to wait until more trusted leaders emerge.

The questions of whether *it is worth it* and *when enough is enough* are legitimate ones to ask. Russia's example can be telling: Moscow reconquered Chechnya at an enormous price of two wars, only to arrive at a popular desire to exclude it from the Federation for "bad behaviour" ten years later. The public came to see it as a locus of *jihadi* militancy, banditry, unjust and cruel governing practices incompatible with the Russian norm, and was worried about the costs of subsidies to the federal budget and immigration from the North Caucasus into major Russian cities. In this line of argument, "we were stupid to stop them when they wanted to leave. Now they no longer want it, and we are stuck."[94]

DEALING WITH THE PAST

One provision of the Minsk Agreement which was seemingly to the advantage of both sides was prisoner exchange. This touched upon other aspects of Dealing with the Past, such as compilation of the full lists of the dead and missing persons, investigations of the circumstances of their death or how they went missing, identification of human remains and compensations to the victims. However, even prisoner exchange has been problematic, although the number of captives held in the NGCAs was fairly low. The government urged the release of 121 individuals, while the NGCAs admitted to holding of only 47, and campaigned for release of 771 persons from their side. The government said that thirty of them had no connection to the conflict, sixty were charged with grave crimes and were not legible for amnesty and several hundred did not wish to return to Donbas.[95] Throughout the conflict, torture in captivity was a problem. In 2017, UN OHCHR stated that it "is deeply troubled by allegations indicating the systematic use of torture and ill-treatment by the SBU against conflict-related detainees in order to extract confessions."[96]

The Ukrainian side established a mechanism for prisoner exchanges with the NGCAs, but in Russia, there was no state help for the relatives of Russian citizens who went missing in Donbas. Oleg Melnikov, head of "Alternativa" NGO, set up a non-governmental prisoners' exchange committee in Moscow. He considered that both sides were failing to fulfill the Minsk provision on the prisoner exchanges, although the example of his committee showed that it was possible: "I actively help Ukrainian citizens, keep in touch with the embassy, consulate, the SBU on people's trafficking and exchanges."[97] Relatives in Russia hoped to find their family members who volunteered for the conflict among unaccounted captives who were lost in Ukraine in chaotic conditions of 2014. They may be hoping for a miracle. A source on the Ukrainian side explained that by 2016 it was not probable that such prisoners remained in a private captivity and were not handed over to the SBU. The reason for keeping private prisons has been that battalion commanders sought to exchange the captives for their own fighters detained on the other side rather than for any Ukrainian troopers or to sell them to families. With "wild battalions" becoming the thing of the past and a reinforced command structure, this was no longer possible. Holding on to prisoners did not make sense, unless they were high-profile cases who could be put on trial such as Russian servicemen or Sloviansk mayor Shtepa.

Dynamism was introduced by the release of an MP Nadia Savchenko from Russian captivity who was swapped for two Russian servicemen in May 2016. After a celebrity welcome in May, Savchenko turned herself into an uncomfortable figure for the authorities in a space of three months. The former pilot decided that she should take responsibility for peace as she did for war. The first step was humanitarian—to return the war prisoners home. Savchenko, an action woman with strong beliefs and energy, set herself to liberate other Ukrainian detainees, but soon discovered that the problems stemmed not only from the rebels, but also from inaction, bureaucratic inertia and indifference of the authorities in Kyiv toward the plight of the law-abiding citizens who answered the mobilization call and ended up in captivity. "Why our President does not talk to Zakharchenko and Plotnitsky directly to bring our guys back?" she publicly inquired. In August 2016 she and her sister with their symbolic names of Vera (Faith) and Nadia (Hope) called a rally under a slogan "Don't leave our own" (Не бросай своих), after which Savchenko accused the president of inaction and went on a hunger strike.[98]

In October she went to Moscow to attend a trial of two Ukrainian citizens accused of involvement in fighting in Chechnya, causing a painful reaction in Kyiv.[99]

Her escapades produced an effect: the LNR authorities established a working group on prisoner exchanges and said that they were ready to talk directly. In September 2016 LNR reached an agreement with Medvedchuk, appointed as a Ukrainian representative for prisoner exchanges, and two Ukrainian soldiers were handed over to Kyiv in exchange for their people. Encouragingly, Ol'ga Kobtseva, the Working Group Chair, announced that the LNR was ready to "discuss proposals, reach consensus and set people free." The exchange formula—"how many of ours for how many of them"—was a bone of contention because both sides tried to impress their domestic publics that "our" people were more valuable than "theirs." An agreement to exchange "all for all" was reached, but remained on paper. LNR declared that it was giving away 47 persons to Kyiv and receiving 618 back,[100] but while the talks were underway, DNR captured another 7 Ukrainian servicemen.

WHAT DOES IT TAKE FOR PEACE?

Formal peace process has been underway since September 2014 Minsk-I ceasefire when an implementation mechanism for the Protocol and the Memorandum was established and the Joint Centre for Control and Coordination was set up. The Centre consisted of Ukrainian and Russian military officers and dealt with separation of forces, resolution of disputes and moving forward with the peace plan, while OSCE SMM monitored its work. The mechanism proved largely ineffective and did not prevent violence on the ground. Ukrainian military command changed when Heletey resigned as a minister of defense on October 12, 2014. Still, the ceasefire allowed space for concentrating on a political framework with assistance of international mediators. As the impasse appeared too great, Minsk process sought to reduce it by cutting the problem into pieces. This way, each piece appeared manageable and the problem did not seem as overwhelming as a result. The sides negotiated on the basis of Ukraine's territorial integrity, which the rebel leaders acknowledged under Moscow pressure.

The main pillars of the Minsk Agreement were cessation of hostilities, exchange of all prisoners, and a deal on the distribution of powers between the center and the "special status regions," with a permission for them to maintain their own police force in exchange for the center's prerogative to appoint judges and prosecutors. Other key issue for the rebels was legitimization of their leadership through a recognized election, whereas Kyiv insisted on the local elections according to the Ukrainian law and under its supervision. Constitutional guarantees of the country's non-accession to rival blocs, such as NATO, presented one of the rebels' demands.[101] The main stumbling blocks were a constitutionally guaranteed Special Status for Donbas and a return of control over the Russian-Ukrainian border to Kyiv.[102]

The peace process which started as a crisis response and enabled scaling down of hostilities, settled in for a long haul. Were these measures put into practice in September 2014 as designed, they had a fighting chance to succeed. Later on, they did not lose relevance, but implementing them was becoming more difficult as the conflict got entrenched and the sides mastered the art of driving a hard bargain. Kyiv refused to engage with the rebels as negotiation partners,[103] and their negotiators had no official status. Those on the Kyiv side were former government officials acting in personal capacity. Rare calls by Ukrainian intellectuals to hold direct talks with the rebels went into void. As Andrei Yermolayev, director of *New Ukraine* Institute argued, "refusal to nego tiate with the representatives of DNR and LNR only accelerates the process of statebuilding in these 'republics.' A *de facto* border between us has been erected already, and new processes of consolidation at DNR and LNR are in effect state formation processes."[104] Discouragement of direct talks at the time when they could have been a game change was at odds with West's own position of dealing with unrecognized leaders elsewhere. As Sakwa argues,

> The fundamental inability of Kyiv and its Western allies to understand that this was . . . a genuine revolt against a particular type of statehood . . . meant that they could not recognise the political subjectivity of the rebellion as a force with which there should be dialogue.[105]

Kyiv did not signal a great willingness for embracing the "republics" as "lost souls" who were still welcome at home. No internal grounds were set in motion to enable society to accept a solution which would convey a certain respectable role for the other party. Although Minsk process forced to engage with the rebel representatives, Kyiv's rhetoric remained viral. It was hard to see how the mental gap would be bridged if the insurgents would have to be welcomed as partners in a peace deal and a power-sharing. Function of the conflict for Ukrainian domestic politics was not lost on the rebels:

> Kyiv has got incentives for internal consumption for the war. Its rhetoric is geared towards the fight against the *Russian World* which Donbas is the fore post of. If this rhetoric subsides, legitimisation of the present Ukrainian regime would be problematic: how it would explain what people at the front were dying for?[106]

Duality in the approach to peace persisted: Kyiv was simultaneously participating in the internationally sponsored talks and shelling the NGCAs. This made its opponent doubt sincerity of the government's negotiation effort, the same as Kyiv was not sure about the rebels' commitment to Ukraine's territorial integrity. The faith in a military solution had not been abandoned in Kyiv. The government came to believe that its capabilities improved and a battlefield victory was feasible. The army, starting from a low base, got better and the territorial battalions were brought under the line of command, purged of unruly elements and became more disciplined forces. Western military training and supplies of ammunition from Poland and Lithuania[107] beefed up the army's capabilities when the US, UK and Canadian troops were deployed to train and build capabilities of the Ukrainian military "to address Ukrainian fundamental security challenges."[108]

It did not look like Kyiv had a coherent policy toward Donbas. While positive inclusion was preferable by the international community, this approach encountered resistance in Ukraine where the meaning of "peace" became contested and unpopular, and equated with an acceptance of defeat. The liberal consensus was that the ceasefires were not a road to peace, but a lull in fighting to better prepare to win the next round. International staff in Ukraine were observing widespread negative conception of "peace" and a lack of local ownership outside of the government controlled Donbas. "The negative perception of the peace process by large sectors of Ukrainian society which sees it as capitulation" has been a significant constraint.[109]

Time was working against re-integration, as positions hardened. Peace process lacked an elite buy-in, as there were fewer forces who were prepared to work toward peace than in 2014. The former managerial elite lost its credentials and surviving oligarchs and industrialists of Yanukovych era struggled for self-preservation and had little bargaining power. Special Status Law had weak advocates and strong opponents. Political class was not in the mood for decisive compromises, and the sense of national honor was so strong that it was blocking a substantive discussion on the Special Status bill. The legal change had to pass through the parliament which included the battalion commanders and politicians elected on the patriotic wave. The 2014 Rada had less representation from the East and few among the existing MPs speaking for its interests were influential. It emerged as a peace spoiler, "with different actors within it using opposition to the peace process as an opportunity to increase their political capital."[110] Radical parties campaigned hard and brutal against the bill to introduce the Special Status,[111] because it looked like to them as a "Putin's win." Drafts of an alternative Law on Occupied Territories prepared by *Bat'kivshina* and *Samopomich'* political parties, and non-aligned MPs appeared,[112] but were criticized by the president: "Such law will destroy the Minsk process. It will bury international sanctions against Russia, as they are tied to 'Minsk.' The OSCE mission will leave Donbas. We will remain alone."[113] However, in October 2017 he introduced the law in the parliament that defined the NGCAs as "temporarily occupied" as a result of the "Russian aggression against Ukraine" and would give the president the right to use force to regain Kyiv's control over Donbas. This law would constitute a major step away from the Minsk agreement, signifying a break with the previous policy, which had Minsk at its heart.[114]

Patriotic moods and significance of the conflict for the new nationhood worked against a solution which would appear as an acceptance a defeat, even if a temporary one, and a loss of face for the president who was vulnerable to personal criticism. Special Status would in fact mean federalization, which Kyiv viewed with an apprehension, as having risky implications for the center-periphery relations because some other regions might demand the same rights. The leadership did not appear to have much appetite for absorbing the rebellious territories and letting the battle-hardened Donbas with its embittered society, leftist and anti-oligarch aspirations and a "Trojan horse" of pro-Russian sympathies into fragile Ukrainian polity. The Special Status ran into a political impasse.

No public peace process was in evidence because the public was believed to reject the idea of compromise. Civil society, commonly assumed to be on the side of peace, can actually act to prevent peacebuilding if it contradicts its strongly held beliefs. In the words of Ihor Semyvolos, "Minsk Agreement is an additional factor of conflict for the country. Its implementation would not change the basic premise of the war between Russia and Ukraine. The war is not over, and Russia will be weakened; therefore, it is not in Ukraine's interests to give up too much ground in the Minsk process now. Time is working in Ukraine's favour."[115] Civil activists formed a vocal anti-Minsk lobby and some went a great length to ban participants from NGCA, even a Ukraine-registered NGO,[116] from the events abroad. As a result, "the voices of organisations working in the east and in NGCAs are not being heard in the capital or internationally."[117]

Certainly, not all parts of Ukrainian society are unified in opposing compromises or in holding a narrow perspective on the conflict. Non-organized voices from different parts of the country exist, but they have no legitimate opportunity for expression. They are dispersed, and suffer from a fear of retribution and psychological depression. International dialogue forums usually do not consider these views when looking into promoting inclusion. Civil society is polarized as much as society in general, as tensions within the country remain, and the internal conflict dynamics between different sections of society stays in place.[118] Low-key peace dialogues between civic organizations from both parts of Donbas take place, but participants from the NGCAs increasingly have problems with entering government-controlled territory. Beyond that, civil society dialogue barely happens because facilitators who arrive to the region from Kyiv, themselves often hold distinct nationalist positions and this discourages expression of dissenting views.[119]

To conclude, the Minsk framework was so far apart from the parties' aspirations that it was hard to see it as a basis for a settlement. Kyiv wished a unitary state, facing away from Russia. The rebels seek the opposite at the least. The war trauma was huge. People in Donbas could hardly imagine how they were going to live together with those who were warring against them. Developing feeling of victimization in Ukraine was affecting society's ability to move forward. It could be argued that in an absence of a political will for a resolution, freezing the conflict and installing a genuine cease re along a mutually agreed Contact Line could be in Kyiv's pragmatic interests as it would allow it to move on with its European Association Agenda. However, the dynamic in the country was the opposite and political momentum was not in favour of cutting losses. It was making Kyiv less flexible; therefore, a strategy of waiting until the tables reverse and Ukraine strengthens its position vis-à-vis Russia was implicitly employed. This was precarious because an opposite scenario was also possible, and a weakened Moscow would not necessarily be more conducive to settlement; in fact, it might be to the contrary. As a reminder, Azerbaijan's economic and military might vis-à-vis Armenia brought no progress in Karabakh settlement, but instead increased insecurity along the contact line.

The alternative to Minsk was to enter direct negotiations, but Kyiv did not wish to take this route and had no option, but to stay with the process. It has put hopes into its western allies, but its foreign policy objective of keeping and deepening Western sanctions on Russia conflicted with the other, that is, to reintegrate Donbas, which could not be done without Moscow cooperation. The questions were which one was more important, how serious it was about resolving the conflict, and what price it was prepared to pay. Moreover, if Kyiv wanted its Western allies to maintain pressure, it could not be seen as non-cooperative in implementation of the Minsk Agreement. The circle was increasingly difficult to square.

NOTES

1. "Ukraine crisis: Deal to 'de-escalate' agreed in Geneva," BBC, April 17, 2014, http://www.bbc.co.uk/news/world-europe-27072351

2. Oleg Tsaryov, author's interview.

3. The law inspired controversy among political actors in Ukraine. See Georgi Gotev "Ukraine brings its lustration controversy to Brussels," March 24, 2015, https://www.euractiv.com/section/europe-s-east/news/ukraine-brings-its-lustration-controversy-to-brussels/

4. Viktoria Zhuhan, "This is how Ukraine's old regime battles lustration," June 2, 2016, http://euromaidanpress.com/2016/06/02/yanukovych-regime-aims-to-recover-wages-war-on-ukraines-lustration/

5. Alexander Borodai, author's interview, Moscow May 2016.

6. Press statement by the Trilateral Contact Group, July 15, 2014, http://www.osce.org/home/121317

7. Oliver Bullough, *Looting Ukraine: How East and West Teamed up to Steal a Country* (London: Legatum Institute, 2014); Wilson, *Ukraine Crisis*.

8. Tadeusz Iwański, "Still together, but apart? Kyiv's policy towards the Donbas" OSW Commentary, Centre for Eastern Studies, no. 160, February 6, 2015. Since 2016, Ministry of Social Protection stopped payments to nearly 400,000 persons from Donbas who were found by SBU as fictively registered in GCAs, but in reality living in the NGCAs, in Dmitrii Kirillov, "Донбасс возьмут блокадой," 29 December 2016, gazeta.ru.

9. UN OHCHR 2015a.

10. Ekaterina Stepanova, Chapter 22 "Russia," in *The Oxford Handbook of the Responsibility to Protect*, eds. Alex Bellamy, Tim Dunne (Oxford: Oxford University Press, 2016).

11. http://Donbassos.org/about_ru/

12. Galina Kozhedubova, "Харьковские чиновники советуют переселенцам: "Звоните волонтерам. Они вам все сделают" *Fakty,* August 19, 2014, http://fakty.ua/186575-harkovskie-chinovniki-sovetuyut-pereselencam-zvonite-volonteram-oni-vam-vse-sdelayut

13. Ihor Semyvolos, author's interview.

14. Rumer Eugene, "Sending Weapons to Ukraine Won't Help," *Defense One*, June 2, 2014.

15. Presented at the Agency's website http://www.ukrspecexport.com

16. http://wings-phoenix.org.ua/

17. Founder of the volunteer organization "Wings of the Phoenix" appointed assistant of Minister of Defense, October 6, 2016, http://euromaidanpress.com/2014/10/06/founder-of-the-volunteer-organization-wings-of-the-phoenix-appointed-assistant-of-minister-of-defense/

18. Personal travel in Donbas in 2014, Donbas expert interviews, 2014–2015.

19. Alexei Kachan, author's interview.

20. Alexander Borodai, author's interview.

21. Donbas resident, author's interview.

22. Donbas resident, author's interview.

23. Kostyantynivka, author's interview, Donetsk Oblast.

24. The survey was commissioned by analytical centre *Thought Factory Donbas*, and conducted by the Ukrainian office of international research agency IFAK Institut GmbH & Co. in June 2016 http://www.ifak.com.ua/ru/research/osobennosti_soznanija_i_identi4nosti_jiteley_podkontrolnyx_i_nepodkontrolnyx_ukraine_territoriy_doneckoy_oblasti1/

25. Gwendolyn Sasse, "The Donbas—Two parts, or still one? The experience of war through the eyes of the regional population," ZOiS Report 1/2017, https://www.zoisberlin.de/fileadmin/media/Dateien/ZOiS_Reports/ZOiS_Report_2_2017.pdf

26. Poll cited by Vladimir Dergachoff, Dmitrii Kirillov, in "Хорошего мало, зато нет «бандеров»," *Gazeta.ru,* August 4, 2016, http://www.gazeta.ru/politics/2016/08/03_a_9747233.shtml#!photo=0

27. "Ukraine—The Human Face of the Eastern Conflict," Summary of Brussels conference, January 23, 2017, organised by ACF, DDG, DRC, PiN and NRC.

28. Civil Society Dialogue Network Meeting, "How to make the peace processes in Ukraine more inclusive?" EPLO meeting report, February 28, 2017, Vienna, Austria.

29. Author's interview with an international humanitarian worker, November, Kyiv, 2015.

30. International Kyiv-based practitioner, author's interview.

31. *Left Bank.* http://society.lb.ua/war/2015/06/10/307826_boeviki_zablokirovali_edinstvenniy.html

32. *Colonel Cassad.* 7 June 2015. http://colonelcassad.livejournal.com/2015/06/07/

33. International Crisis Group, "Russia and the Separatistsin Eastern Ukraine," *Europe and Central Asia Briefing* 79 (February 5, 2016): 5.

34. Georgii Alexandrov, "Воевать нельзя мириться," *The New Times*, 41, December 7, 2015.

35. Cited in Boyd-Barrett, *Western mainstream media*, chapter 6.

36. Alexei Kachan, author's interview.

37. Author's interviews with international humanitarian practitioners based in Kyiv with access to the NGCAs, November 2015.

38. Kopat'ko, "На Донбассе с трудом."

39. Cited by Vadym Chernysh, Ukrainian Minister for Temporary Occupied Territories and IDPs, in interview with Dmitrii Kirillov, "Донбасс можно вернуть только дипломатией," 19 January 2017, gazeta.ru, see also at https://www.humanitarianresponse.info/en/operations/ukraine

40. "Зарплата в 10 тысяч рублей!" http://www.gazeta.ru/politics/2016/08/09_a_10112825.shtml, also Chernysh above interview.

41. Cited in Vladimir Dergachoff, Dmitrii Kirillov «Зарплата в 10 тысяч рублей в ДНР очень хорошая!» August 12, 2016, http://www.gazeta.ru/politics/2016/08/09_a_10112825.shtml

42. «Зарплата в 10 тысяч рублей!» http://www.gazeta.ru/politics/2016/08/09_a_10112825.shtml

43. Alexei Kachan, author's interview, Kyiv, November 2015. A graph on reduction in civilian casualties by month is in UN OHCHR 18th Report, June 2017.

44. Alexei Kachan, interview.

45. Cited in http://www.gazeta.ru/politics/2016/08/09_a_10112825.shtml

46. Poll in gazeta.ru, August 4, 2016.

47. http://www.gazeta.ru/politics/2016/08/09_a_10112825.shtml

48. Gazeta.ru, August 4, 2016.

49. Juchkovsky interview.

50. Yulia Nikitina, "Донецк без ответственных," *Fontanka*, February 9, 2016, http://www.fontanka.ru/2016/02/09/138/

51. Kopat'ko, interviews with international staff with humanitarian access to the NGCAs, also Kachan, Kyiv, November 2015.

52. Resident of Donetsk, author's interview via Skype.

53. It is not clear how representative was the sample or whether the people were contacted who were already known to researchers.

54. Sasse, ZOiS, 11.

55. Sasse, ZOiS.

56. Poll cited by Gazeta.ru, August 4, 2016.

57. Conducted in Donetsk and Makiivka, 1000 respondents interviewed face to face.

58. Poll cited by Gazeta.ru, August 4, 2016.

59. http://www.scmholding.com/

60. Vladimir Dergachoff, "Год хаоса и независимости: Как прошел год самопровозглашенной ДНР," *Gazeta.ru,* April 8, 2015, http://www.gazeta.ru/politics/2015/04/07_a_6630201.shtml

61. For details see Rinat Akhmetov Foundation's website http://www.fdu.org.ua/en

62. Alexander Borodai, author's interview, Moscow, May 2016.

63. *UNIAN*, March 14, 2017, https://www.unian.info/politics/1821672-donbas-blockade-activist-admits-getting-paid-for-participation.html

64. "Ukraine Announces Suspension Of Cargo Traffic With Separatist-Held Areas," *Radio Free Europe*, March 15, 2017, https://www.rferl.org/a/ukraine-suspension-cargo-traffic-separatists/28371097.html

65. *Bloomberg*, March 22, 2017, https://www.bloomberg.com/news/articles/2017-03-22/industry-revival-fizzles-out-as-ukraine-counts-cost-of-blockade

66. Ilya Barabanov, "Донбасские заводы вырабатывают стратегию," March 9, 2017, http://www.kommersant.ru/doc/3236732

67. "На пальцах. Почему ДНР-ЛНР не могут быть экономически состоятельным," May 28, 2015, http://www.ostro.org/general/economics/articles/471428/

68. Alexander Juchkovsky, author's interview.

69. Keith Gessen, "Why Not Kill Them All?" *London Review of Books* 36, no. 17 (September 11, 2014), 18–22.

70. *BBC Russian Service*, "Госкино Украины запретило" "Белую гвардию" и "Поддубного" July 29, 2014, http://www.bbc.com/russian/international/2014/07/140729_ukraine_russia_cinema

71. "Украинская культура — это не только Тарас Шевченко." May 21, 2015. Alexandr Roitburd interviewed by Ilya Asar, https://meduza.io/feature/2015/05/21/ukrainskaya-kultura-eto-ne-tolko-taras-shevchenko

72. *Radio Free Europe*. June 12, 2015, http://www.rferl.org/content/ukraine-decommunization-dnipropetrovsk/27064346.html

73. Ihor Semyvolos, author's interview, Kyiv, November 25, 2015.

74. Gordon Hahn, A Day in the Life of "Ukrainian Democracy," July 14, 2015, http://www.russiaotherpointsofview.com/2015/07/ukrainian-democracy-by-gordon-hahn.html

75. EPLO Vienna conference report, 7–8.

76. *RIA Novosti Ukraine,* "Власть надолго запустили механизм дискредитации гражданского актива—эксперт," November 4, 2015, http://rian.com.ua/politics/20151104/376379855.html

77. *RIA Novosti*, "Милиция Украины выделяет охрану экс-депутату Бондаренко из-за угроз," April 17, 2015, http://ria.ru/world/20150417/1059276533.html

78. Presentation at Chatham House workshop "The EU as a regional power: the Eastern Neighbourhood," (London: RIIA, December 2, 2015).

79. The fatalities were as follows. Nikolay Sergienko, ex-deputy director of Ukrainian State Railway Company, died on 26 January. Other suicide victims were Alexei Kolesnik, ex-chair of Kharkiv oblast council, Sergei Walter, Melitopol ex-mayor, Alexander Bordug, Melitopol ex-police chief, Mikhail Chechetov and Stanislav Melnik, ex-Party of Regions MPs, Alexander Peklushenko, Zaporojie ex-governor, and Sergei Melnichuk, former Odessa prosecutor. In April's spat of killings Kolesnikov, Buzina and Sukhobok were murdered; observers believe that they are related http://ru.tsn.ua/politika/komu-vygodny-gromkie-ubiystva-kalashnikova-i-buziny-i-kogo-mogut-zachistit-sleduyuschim-421368.html

80. *Human Rights Watch*, "Ukraine: 17 Russian Journalists Banned," June 1, 2016, https://www.hrw.org/news/2016/06/01/ukraine-17-russian-journalists-banned

81. *Left Bank*, May 8, 2015, http://society.lb.ua/war/2015/05/08/304358_pred-staviteli_upts_mp_vstali.html

82. *TASS*, March 24, 2015, http://tass.ru/mezhdunarodnaya-panorama/1991140

83. According to Maxim Vilkov in presentation at the OSCE Human Dimension Implementation meeting 2016, Vienna, September 2016, reported in "Нападения на УПЦ в Украине: избиение священников, убийства и поджоги храмов," September 29, 2016, http://comitet.su/item/napadeniya-na-upc-v-ukraine-izbienie-svyashhen nikov-ubijstva-i-podzhogi-hramov.html. Also see "Metropolitan Onufriy called Avakov to objectively investigate the murder of the UOC (MP) priest and nun," *RISU*, August 12, 2015, https://risu.org.ua/en/index/all_news/state/church_state_relations/60796/

84. Hudson, "The Ukrainian Orthodox Church of the Moscow Patriarchate as a Potential "Tool" of Russian Soft Power in the Wake of Ukraine's 2013 Euromaidan," *Europe-Asia Studies*, 70, 2018 (forthcoming).

85. Sociological Service of Razumkov Centre, December 2015, conducted among 2000 respondents in Ukraine apart from Crimea and NGCAs.

86. The poll conducted September 12–21, 2014 in the GCAs. See "Majority of Ukrainians are ready to make serious concessions to Russia and DPR and LPR leaders in exchange for establishment of peace," October 9, 2014, *Ilko Kucheriv Democratic Initiatives Foundation,* http://dif.org.ua/en/events/majhment-of-peace.htm

87. Poll by Research & Branding Group among 1795 respondents in Ukraine apart from Crimea and NGCAs, July 2016.

88. "Війна і мир: питання національної безпеки в дзеркалі громадської думки," Sofia Sociological Research Centre, July 2016, http://sofia.com.ua/page174.html

89. Ihor Semyvolos, author's interview, Kyiv, November 25, 2015.

90. Alexei Kachan, author's interview, Kyiv, November 26, 2015.

91. Alexei Kachan, author's interview, Kyiv.

92. Volodymyr Prytula, author's interview, Kyiv, November 2015.

93. Data from June 2016. According to the Anatoly Matios, the Deputy Prosecutor General of Ukraine and the Chief Military Prosecutor, nearly 3,000 Ukrainian soldiers were killed during two years of war in eastern Ukraine. The non-combat death toll is extremely high standing at 1,294 servicemen. "Shocking statistics of

non-battle casualties of Ukraine's army," June 11, 2016, http://uatoday.tv/society/shocking-statistics-of-non-battle-casualties-of-ukraine-s-army-670993.html

94. Anna Matveeva, "The north-eastern Caucasus: moving away from Russia," in *Fire from Below: How the Caucasus Shaped Russian Politics since 1980s*, ed. Robert Bruce Ware (New York: Bloomsbury, 2013), 253–282.

95. RIA Novosti Ukraine, http://rian.com.ua/society/20170513/1024001245.html

96. UN OHCHR 18th Report, 2.

97. Oleg Melnikov, author's interview, Moscow, May 2016.

98. "Савченко назвала условие прекращения голодовки," September 8, 2016, *Korrespondent.Net*, http://korrespondent.net/ukraine/3742305-savchenko-nazvala-uslovye-prekraschenyia-holodovky

99. "Зачем Надежда Савченко приехала в Москву," October 26, 2016, *Kommersant*, http://kommersant.ru/doc/3126407?&utm_campaign=push&utm_source=kommersant

100. According to Ol'ga Kobtseva, "ДНР и ЛНР договорились с Киевом об обмене всех пленных," September 22, 2016, https://lenta.ru/news/2016/09/22/prisoners

101. Ilya Barabanov, "Авторы поправок, очевидно, ставили перед собой цель составить документ максимально приемлемый для Киева," *Kommersant*, June 9, 2015, http://www.kommersant.ru/doc/2744603

102. For examination of Minsk process from the Russian perspective see "Бесконечный Тупик. Состояние И Перспективы Процесса Политического Урегулирования Конфликта Между Украиной И Республиками Донбасса. К Первой Годовщине Минских Соглашений," Analytical Report (Moscow: Centre for Current Politics, February 11, 2016).

103. Premier Yatseniuk speaking in Washington: "My government will never talk to terrorists until they are 'behind bars or sitting in a prison cell,'" quoted in "Ukrainian PM Blasts Separatists: 'We Will Never Talk to Terrorists.'" *Foreign Policy* June 10, 2015. https://foreignpolicy.com/2015/06/10/ukrainian-pm-blasts-russian-separatists-we-will-never-talk-to-terrorists/

104. Author's interview with Andrei Yermolayev, March 2017, also see Yermolayev, "Москва переиграла Киев, нужно срочно договариваться с Донбассом," August 14, 2015, *Politobzor*. http://politobzor.net/show-61904-andrey-ermolaev-moskva-pereigrala-Kyiv-nuzhno-srochno-dogovarivatsya-s-Donbasom.html

105. Sakwa, *Frontline Ukraine*, 181.

106. Alexander Borodai, author's interview.

107. Will Ponomarenko, "Ukraine to tighten border rules for Russians, boost spending on cyber security and defense," *Kyiv Post*, July 11, 2017, https://www.kyivpost.com/ukraine-politics/ukraine-tighten-border-rules-russians-boost-spending-cyber-security-defense.html

108. Lee Berthiaume, "Ottawa Quietly Eases Restrictions on Canadian Military Mission in Ukraine," *Canadian Press*, June 14, 2017, https://tgam.ca/2tHjlcF. Ben Watson, "In Ukraine, the US Trains an Army in the West to Fight in the East," October 5, 2017, http://www.defenseone.com/threats/2017/10/ukraine-us-trains-army-west-fight-east/141577/

109. Vienna EPLO meeting report, 5.

110. Vienna EPLO meeting report.

111. *Kyiv Post*, "Third serviceman dies from Rada grenade attack," September 1, 2015. The incident occurred amidst protests organised by the Radical Party and *Svoboda* party to oppose the bill.

112. Several versions were prepared. MP Nataliya Veselova from Samopomich faction submitted the draft law No. 6400-1 "On temporary occupied territories by the Russian Federation and being beyond Ukrainian control due to the armed conflict with terrorist groups." Mustafa Nayyem of BPP faction submitted the draft law No. 6400-2 "On temporary occupied territories by the Russian Federation." Both of these draft laws are alternative to the Draft Law No. 3593-d "On the Temporarily Occupied Territory of Ukraine," which was submitted by the Rada Deputy Chairwoman Oksana Syroid and 10 other MPs, http://radaprogram.org/en/content/two-bills-temporary-occupied-territories-registered-vr

113. Cited on 15 March 2017 by UNIAN: https://www.unian.info/politics/1824186-poroshenko-passing-law-on-occupied-territories-to-destroy-minsk-process.html

114. Radio Free Europe, "Amid Scuffles And Smoke, Bills On East Ukraine Conflict Advance In Parliament," October 6, 2017, https://www.rferl.org/a/ukraine-parliament-donetsk-luhansk-bill-debate-scuffles/28777537.html

115. Ihor Semyvolos, author's interview.

116. Donetsk NGO interview, Brussels, January 2017, and an interview with staff of an international organisation, December 2016.

117. EPLO meeting report, 6.

118. For overview see Puri, "Human Security."

119. EPLO meeting report.

Chapter 12

What Is Donbas for Russia?

Much has been written by scholars about Russian policy over the crisis in Ukraine explaining it from the perspective of European and global security governance and challenges presented by Moscow to an international rules-based system.[1] John Mearsheimer explains the crisis from a realist perspective stressing that liberal order provides a poor interpretive framework for how states behave when seriously challenged.[2] However, neither realist nor liberal theory adequately explains the international dimension of the crisis. Michael Aleprete argues that unfolding events forced Moscow to react quickly rather than pursue a preconceived strategy.[3] The result, as Michael Slobodchikoff states, was that while Russia has been isolated by the Ukrainian crisis, "even more fundamentally, the crisis has ensured that Russia is dissatisfied with the global order"[4] and is likely to act influenced by the consequences of this dissatisfaction. Elizabeth Wood in her study of Russia's actions concludes that the crisis bears the hallmarks of a tangle of justifications and causes that were not easily divided in the justified and unjustifiable.[5]

What is there left to say? The book however would not be complete if it ignored the role of the Russian government. Most of the discourse in academic and policy literature is based on the Russian official statements, and inevitably centers on the president Putin. But I said at the beginning that this was not going to be a Putin book. This is because I cannot offer a particular insight into "what Putin really thinks" and dare say that it is not that important. Faced with a Donbas-type challenge, another Russian leader would have acted along similar lines. Russia has core elite, who think sufficiently alike to make policymaking and execution easy, and this creates an impression of an omnipresent and omnipotent Putin ruling single-handedly. I argue that the Ukrainian crisis was events-driven and dynamic, and Moscow was dragged into the situation in Donbas by the local insurgency, its supporters in Russia, its sympathetic elite members, the *Russian World* ideology, and by the actions of the Ukrainian side, which employed violence. Within Russia's own belief system and mind-set, it could not fail to act in the circumstances it was in, given the historical, cultural, and kinship relationship to the people in Donbas. As Huntington reasoned, it is natural to rally support from the members of own civilization when under threat and Russia did not think it could absolve itself from the insurgency. It had the desire, the will, and the resources to shape the conflict. Since the end of communism, Russia remained a torn country between "pro-Western" and "self-sufficiency" directions, but Donbas helped it to resolve the century-old question of whether it was part of the West or the leader of its own distinct civilization.[6] Although Russia got embroiled in Donbas by default rather than design, and the conflict turned into liability for Moscow, it cannot turn itself away because the conflict transformed Russia, shaped its identity, and Moscow has reasons to worry about its domestic implications. If the events were to be repeated, it would have acted faster and more coherently, but largely in the same way.

The chapter is based on interviews with experts and analysts in Moscow who were close to decision-making circles, journalists who covered the conflict, ex-combatant leaders, and Russian liberal intellectuals, on observations made in Ukraine during the time of the crisis, as well as on secondary sources. It explains some of the mechanics of support to the rebellion, what happened in the aftermath, and how Moscow approaches the peace process. It seeks to bring fresh insights into the little-known aspects of the crisis from the Russian side and explain the logic of Moscow's behavior rather than justify it. Understanding the other side is relevant because if the conflict is to be resolved, it is not unimportant to know what they may think.

DORMANT RUSSIAN WORLD

Before the crisis, Moscow's role in Ukraine was not particularly active. Russia's projection of power was pursued by such instruments, as energy prices, cheap loans, publications in Russian media on the status of the Russian language in Ukraine, and the application of economic carrots and bureaucratic sticks to persuade Kyiv to join the Customs Union. This did not stretch to attempts to control government appointments, influence composition of state budget or manipulate legislature. Moscow put its stakes on getting into power a Russia-friendly president which Yanukovych seemed to be at the time. Loyalty was considered the quality Moscow valued in Yanukovych most. Russian political advisers worked on his 2010 electoral campaign and also on securing electoral outcomes in the ARC's parliamentary elections. Moscow did not support any independent activism of a pro-Russia nature in Ukraine.

Vladimir Zharikhin, deputy director of the CIS Institute in Moscow, told me that "pro-Russia forces in Ukraine had no organized political expression and it was unclear whom to support, if anybody."[7] The *Russian World* concept was hardly applied in Ukraine in any political sense before the Euromaidan. Alexei Tokarev of MGIMO remarked that "while the West articulated its ideas clearly, and its adherents knew what they were vouching for, nobody explained what the *Russian World* meant. As Yanukovych sought to be a president of all-Ukraine, he was not interested in promoting this narrative."[8]

Pro-Russia intellectuals and observers in Kyiv later lamented that Moscow did not get sufficiently engaged with Ukraine's society, and found itself with few soft power instruments at its disposal when destabilization loomed. They, as well as their counterparts in Russia, saw a Western hand as it had "the money, time and experience to groom a constituency oriented at them."[9] Former Russian diplomat based in Kyiv, Sergei Pinchuk, lamented in his tellingly entitled article "Pushkin Offers No Defence Against the Right Sector" the deficiencies of Russia's approach:

> The informational war over Ukraine was lost ten years ago after the first Maidan. Russian diplomats put their stakes not with working with civil society and young people, but with the "agents of influence"—businesspeople, popular writers and select politicians such as Petro Poroshenko who was a frequent visitor at the Russian Embassy receptions at Kyiv's luxury Intercontinental Hotel Ballroom. The embassy used chamber culture tools: literary books, poetry readings and film screenings. This was not what was needed.
>
> Russia's discourse pursued the archaic line of the "unbreakable friendship" of the Slavic people which didn't resonate among youth, could not convey any appeal of Russian civilization, and the communication was often outdated and clumsy. Young Ukrainians, meanwhile, had ample supply of alternative discourse of the nationalist kind, stressing that "Russians are alien," "they are inherently 'Asian'" (NDLR, meaning backwards or Barbaric) and had a propensity to slavery. Russia failed to mobilise its loyalists to organise themselves. It created a network of coordination councils of Russian loyalists, but this was over before it even had begun, and the movement played no role during the crucial events. The loyalists did not become a powerful lobby, like Asians are in the US; they could not promote their representatives into big business or political appointments. They began to resemble a forever-persecuted people who could only appeal to Mother Russia for protection.[10]

This rapidly altered when the idea of the *Russian World* supplied the missing content. The term *Russkyi Mir* (Russian World), before it gained prominence after Crimea, had been used to mean different things to do with Russia, such as a bookstore in London or a restaurant in Milan. Formally, the *Russkyi Mir* foundation modeled on the British Council was established in June 2007 as a joint project of the Ministry of Foreign Affairs and the Ministry of Education, for the purpose of "promoting the Russian language, Russia's national heritage and a significant aspect of Russian and world culture."[11] The Foundation was active in the countries with a substantial interest in Russia. Initially, "the policy toward compatriots and the concept of the *Russian World* were conceived as tools to allow Moscow to simultaneously honor post-Soviet borders and address the concerns of those who did not perceive them as fully legitimate."[12] Eventually, Moscow began to use the *Russian World* concept in more political terms moving it beyond the cultural definition so that it would rival the Western normative discourse. It started to stress a challenge to unipolarity and the "end of history" ideology, expose contradictions in Western societies, and project its interpretation of international affairs presented in culturally familiar terms. "Until spring 2014, discussions about the new Russian national identity, including the *Russian World* concept, did not have much to do with Russia's foreign policy and national security agenda. The revolution in Ukraine allowed Russia to securitize the question of identity; that is, to make it one of the issues critical for the survival of the Russian nation and statehood."[13] The *Russian World* includes the Russian Orthodox Church as an essential part. According to Petro, the term *Russkyi Mir* was employed differently by the state and the Church. "Where the state uses it as a tool for expanding Russia's cultural and political influence, the Church views it as a spiritual concept linked to God's objective for the rebuilding of a Holy Rus. The relationship between the two provides a popular and definable framework for Russian foreign policy."[14]

LOCKING HORNS OVER EUROMAIDAN

In 2013, Moscow did not foresee the upheavals coming despite its geographical proximity and cultural closeness, and the Russian intelligence failed to detect or manage events in Ukraine early on. It turned out that it did not understand well Ukraine's dynamic and motivations of its political and societal actors. It simply did not know whom to deal with when the government machine started cracking and responded reactively when the crisis unfolded. Russia and the United States acted as mirror images in their conviction that the events were masterminded by the other. The US role in Maidan was overestimated by Moscow and, worse, there was a belief that Washington had a clear hand in writing the script. The impression of American authorship was reinforced by the leaked Nuland's telephone transcript in which she and the US Ambassador to Ukraine Geoffrey Pyatt were designing Ukraine's post-Yanukovych future despite the fact that the president was still in office.[15] There were other less high-profile examples.[16]

Moscow made two errors of judgment over Euromaidan. Firstly, it assumed that Brussels would seek to find a compromise between the two association options and communicate to Kyiv's political elite that the two associations were not mutually exclusive. Secondly, it overestimated Yanukovych's statesmanship capacity leaving him to manage the growing crisis. Preoccupied with the prestigious project of hosting the Winter Olympics, Putin focused on Ukraine fairly late. Moscow did not send any *little green men* to rescue struggling Yanukovych when he felt threatened and offered no physical protection to keep him in power. According to informed observers in Moscow, this option was not even considered.

Two turning points over Euromaidan increased the distrust of the European Union in the Russian eyes.[17] Firstly, Brussels only deplored the violence of pro-Russian supporters in the south-east, but did not do it with the same determination when the pro-EU activists used force. This led Moscow to accuse the West of double standards and a selective vision.[18] Secondly, the European Union's guarantees given to the Ukrainian president when the power-sharing deal with the opposition leaders was signed in February 2014, were not backed by any power instruments and proved futile. Yanukovych was ousted on February 21, 2014, the day after he signed the agreement. The European powers failed to influence their support base in Ukraine, nor did they condemn the violation of the agreement to which they were a party, even if they were disappointed that it did not work. The lesson that Russia drew was that EU security guarantees and words of honor could not be trusted in an hour of need, while Moscow would offer a safe haven to deposed rulers.

After the ousting, the fear that NATO would use an opportune moment to quickly absorb Ukraine into the bloc, and that US military vessels would be stationed in Crimea instead of Russia's Black Sea fleet was one of the policy drivers for the action Moscow took. Public pressure in Russia expressing concern over the fate of the pro-Russia constituency on the peninsula set an emotional chord. Moscow's essentially reactive policy of 2013 changed with the annexation of the peninsula, but this was a unique development. The way the Kremlin acted appeared that Moscow had plans only for Crimea, but not for Donbas. "Glaziev files"—Sergei Glaziev's leaked conversations with pro-Russian activists in southeastern Ukraine held in February 2014—suggested—if they are true—that Moscow was supportive of public expression of pro-Russian sentiment in these cities, but took few practical steps to organize any rigorous protest action.[19] One idea floating in Moscow after Euromaidan was to continue to recognize Yanukovych as the legitimate president of Ukraine. In this case, pro-Russian forces in Kyiv, Odesa, Dnipro, and Kharkiv could have been supported in low-level provocations in a bid to put pressure on the new power-holders, so that they re-programmed Ukraine toward geopolitical neutrality and a greater autonomy for the south-east. This scenario was not employed, as Moscow had no knowledge of the local actors and was at a loss as of whom to deal with after the PoR showed its futility.[20] Dergachoff added that the Kremlin might have overestimated the strength of pro-Russian sentiment in Kharkiv. Its elite hesitated, while the existing pro-Russian forces were unable to organize themselves to challenge Kyiv into concessions.

As a result, Moscow's moves in spring were inconclusive and brought no resolution, although its federalization proposal was sensible and similar to the European Union's stance in Macedonia, but did not find sympathetic audience in the West, which was exasperated by Crimea which impacted upon the West's perception of Moscow. Many in the West feared that the Ukraine scenario could be repeated in the Baltic states, which were already in NATO and the European Union. Armstrong argued that when Ukraine plunged into a crisis over its politicized identities in 2013, Moscow should have been an ally in resolving it, but this did not happen.[21] As put by Alexander Mercoulis, "the Russians have always sought a negotiated solution to the Ukrainian conflict. In fact, they had a plan of what to do in the South-East, proposing federalisation."[22] *Prince* expressed to me with hindsight that in his view Moscow should have acted earlier when the Ukrainian president showed his true worth: "Russia lost this geopolitical game. It should have gone ahead and removed Yanukovych itself and not have his whole government relocate to Moscow after Maidan."

MOSCOW GEARS IN

While Ukrainian and Western press wrote in spring about "Kremlin invasion" in Donbas,[23] this was not how it felt on the other side. Grassroots actions unseen before in the region, about which relatively little was known, took Moscow by surprise. The rebel leaders maintain that the Kremlin was slow to believe that Donbas uprising was a genuine thing and could not grasp significance of the *Russian Spring*. The Kremlin's cognitive frame was geared toward statist and elite-driven interpretations of events, which in its view were masterminded by capitals of friend or foe countries, and to believe that society could be an actor with its own autonomous will was too much of a step out of an established mind frame. Borodai who tried to act as a go-between from rebels to Moscow recollects that

> For a long time, the bureaucratic structure in Moscow couldn't comprehend what was going on. At the beginning, when I was meeting high level officials, they were completely astonished. "What? What is this—the people are uprising? For Russia? That's amazing." They seemed to have gotten used to situations

where popular uprisings could only be against Russia. And here we had a patriotic, pro-state movement—not an orange revolution. So there was a cognitive dissonance. They didn't know how to react—whether to welcome or condemn us. It seemed like they were thinking, "these are our guys"—they stand for us, for Russia—but how to deal with them? What about the international community? What about sanctions? Maybe just leave them to themselves? This is what Moscow was thinking.[24]

Despite inflammatory public rhetoric, Moscow tried to build bridges with new Ukrainian authorities through informal contacts and in April an agreement was reached that all Ukrainian military hardware from Crimea would be returned to Kyiv. A total of 3,502 units were handed over and some of these weapons were subsequently used against the insurgents.[25] The political equation started to alter in favor of the rebellion, but Moscow placed its expectations to settle the matter with the forthcoming President Poroshenko whose electoral victory seemed assured, and support to the rebels was very limited. The Kremlin recognized Poroshenko's electoral victory already on May 26 which was a blow to the insurgents who went to a great length to prevent the elections from happening.[26] However, Poroshenko's first move was to step up the military effort and fighting escalated. Putin called the Ukrainian president on June 12, 2014, but this failed to improve prospects for peace. On June 16 Russia suspended handover of military hardware from Crimea in response to *Aidar*'s attack on Schastia.[27] Moscow started to get more involved when the expectations of deal with Poroshenko faltered. In July, Donbas informal curators such as Malofeev and Aksyonov, newly installed in Crimea, were sidelined and political oversight was moved to the Presidential Administration, with Presidential Aide Vladislav Surkov in charge of Donbas affairs.

Subsequently, one action on the ground led to another, the insurgency grew, sucking the state in, to the dismay of the liberals in the government and big business who had invested into integration with the West and could see their efforts ruined. Tensions between hawkish and dovish responses explained the zigzags in Moscow's early policy toward Donbas, such as its tacit approval of the referenda followed by an attempt to halt them. The opposition between "westernisers" and "patriots"[28] resulted in elusive and at times contradictory strategies, but it seemed that in the run-up to Minsk-1 the liberals in the ruling circles were gaining an upper hand. Intense consultations were going on between the Russian and Ukrainian Presidential Administrations. However, the liberal forces had no support from the West which instead announced sanctions[29] on Russian officials in September 2014, four days after the Minsk peace deal was agreed. Moscow interpreted that its efforts to secure the deal were "rewarded" by sanctions, which undermined its incentives for cooperation with the West over the crisis. The EU and the US sanctions levied in

2014 and their prolongation were welcomed by the Russian nationalist circles because they strengthened their hand and precluded the Russian leadership from a pivot to the West. It was obvious, as the argument went, that the West always meant Russia harm, and now showed its real intentions. Strelkov wrote in his blog in reaction to the US decision to add new sanctions in September 2016 to emphasize its solidarity with Kyiv: "[welcome], more sanctions, good and varied" (больше санкций, хороших и разных).[30]

Based on the rebel and witness accounts, the involvement of the Russian troops in Donbas was minimal and before the August 2014 counteroffensive, there was a great reluctance to send the army. Regular troops were used for combat operations twice—in August 2014 when eight battalion-tactical groups were deployed and in February 2015. These two offensives resulted in the political outcomes of Minsk-1 and Minsk-2. Outside of that, small military reconnaissance units dashed in and out of Donbas throughout the active phase of the conflict, as evidenced by instances when members of the Russian military were captured, claiming to have "lost their way." Mobile teams were deployed on occasion to secure the main highways leading to the Russian border, for example, at Ilovaisk which was important given its location on the direct road to Luhansk.

According to the Ukrainian MoD in response to *Novaya Gazeta*, 13,000 regular Russian troops were stationed in the NGCAs (the earlier statements of Ukrainian military and politicians put the numbers at 90,000 which were reproduced in the West).[31] Western sources later claimed between 10,000 and 12,000 regular troops in Ukraine, but the evidence was inconclusive,[32] and a fair amount of what was presented as "evidence" was later refuted by security professionals.[33] *Novaya*'s own investigation revealed that although different battalion-tactical groups had been deployed in the vicinity of the border (from where they could in theory cross in and out of Donbas), these deployments happened at different times and at different segments, and the troops' numbers never exceeded 4,500 at any one time at the maximum. Troops of the Southern Military District had been deployed there during Yushchenko's and Yanukovych's presidencies as well.[34] Accounts gathered for this book imply that the numbers were not anywhere near tens of thousands. Moreover, most did not stay longer beyond their mission which was to back the August counteroffensive and the final push on Debaltseve. Nemtsov's report "Putin War" puts the number of dead among Russian troops by early 2015 as 200.[35] All reasonably verified information on the Russian contract soldiers who died participating in 2014 operations was collected by the *RBK*,[36] and although it does not give a total figure, the numbers are in their dozens. Some Western publications make tenfold higher claims.[37]

Russian military and civilian advisers appeared in Donbas after Minsk-1 when the state pulled the plug on the *Russian Spring*. However, many of them had done their military service in Chechnya and were not familiar with the local context. The terrain was different, and Donbas situation required different skills. For example, the advisers had no experience in how to launch an attack under persistent *Grad* shelling because the Chechen rebels did not have heavy artillery.[38] Subsequently, state-sponsored "volunteers" for jobs which required considerable technical skills were recruited from the Russian provinces through *voenkomaty* (military recruitment offices) from among former paratroopers and similar forces, positions believed to be paid 50,000 ($775)–60,000 ($930) roubles a month.[39] However, there was no sufficient interest for the posts and a private security company was used at a later stage.

There was no domestic law in Russia on the registration and licensing of private security companies. Russian nationals interested in this line of work had to set up companies abroad or use foreign ones as a vehicle, such as Moran Security Group registered in Belize, but with a license to operate in Russia and an office in Moscow.[40] One such company Slavyanskii Korpus (*Slavonic Corps Limited*) was established through the Moran Security and took part in maritime operations to accompany vessels through insecure foreign waters in the 2000s. It was registered in Hong Kong, but by 2012 ceased to exist, until it resurrected in Donbas and some combatants were recruited in this way.

A mysterious and scary *Wagner* (believed to be Dmitrii Utkin)[41] was thought to be at the heart of the resurrection. This was a call sign of the commander of a private security company of the same name. *Wagner* served in the Moran Security before and was later active in Luhansk Oblast, to where he brought his old war comrades from *Slavonic Corps*. Apparently, there was some link to the state, although the company was private. According to *Fontanka*'s investigation, the *Wagner* group had its training ground next to the 10th brigade of GRU spetznaz in Mol'kino in Krasnodar *krai*. Earlier in his career, Utkin himself used to be a GRU spetznaz squad commander at the 2nd brigade.[42] *Fontanka* reported that several of his fighters received Russian military awards sanctioned by Putin.[43] It was thought that *Wagner* group was used for the covert security tasks at the frontline, such as countering enemy reconnaissance and saboteur units which the rebels could not perform. Rebel sources believed that the assassinations in the LNR in 2015 were the work of *Wagner* group, but others said that there was nothing particularly monstrous about them.[44] Shortly after that, *Wagner* was reported dead by the media in 2016, but in reality he was alive.

DONBAS MANAGEMENT

The post-Minsk period witnessed an emergence of a greater elite consensus and a structure for overseeing Donbas affairs was put in place. Moscow felt that it had to assume humanitarian and recovery responsibilities for the region, but got more and more dragged into the local politics and power-holding by doing so. It never admitted its role in order not to add fuel to naming it as a party to the conflict, but in reality Moscow influenced the *de facto* governing arrangements. Efforts were aimed at the integration of governing structures, streamlining a power hierarchy and setting up new bureaucracies. Although it would have been easier to manage one entity rather than two, Moscow did not force the DNR and LNR into a merger. In this foggy situation, the politics of the "republics" presented interplay between local actors and their Russian curators: Moscow set a general line, but local elites ruled.[45] The rebellion has been tamed by Moscow. The NGCAs economy and politics grew to be tied up with Russia, and this process has been gaining momentum after Kyiv halted commercial exchanges with the NGCAs in 2017.

As the reintegration of the territories into Ukraine seemed more distant, interim arrangements for a remote control over Donbas affairs were set up. The division of responsibilities was as follows: General Chief of Staff of the MoD and FSB were responsible for the military-security sphere, and the team of the Presidential Aide Vladislav Surkov at the Presidential Administration was the main locus of political decision-making and policy-setting. Deputy Prime Minister Dmitry Kozak (born in Kirovograd oblast in Ukraine) oversaw socioeconomic issues together with Emercom, the international arm of the Civil Emergencies Ministry which responds to humanitarian emergencies abroad and is active in Donbas. There were Russian officers, serving and retired, deployed in the region. This Russian infrastructure largely avoided contact with the international community present in Donbas. Politicians associated with the conservative Izborsky Club such as Sergei Glaziev, Russian presidential adviser on regional economic integration (who was born in Ukraine), and Deputy Premier Dmitrii Rogozin provided an ideological vector to the region which replaced an earlier diversity of ideas. The public face of Russian liaison with the NGCAs was the Committee on Public Support to the Residents of the Southeastern Ukraine at the Federation Council, the upper house of the Russian parliament, and chaired by the Council's deputy speaker.

In practical terms, Donbas turned into a liability for Moscow as the "republics" were unable to function without the Russian lifeline. Some cash transfers were organized through Abkhazia and South Ossetia which recognized "DNR" and "LNR" and allowed "legal" transfers through these entities.[46] However, some of the dilemmas rehearsed in Transnistria and other breakaways resurfaced, for example, on who would pay for the Russian gas to the NGCAs and compensate losses to Gazprom.The government was concerned over safety of Russia's adjacent border regions. In summer 2014, people with guns were openly voyaging in Rostov oblast, much to despair of local traffic police. Existence of a large territory with loosely controlled weapons and proliferation of citizens' militias produced impacts on crime levels in Rostov oblast: statistics of weapons' seizure available at the MoI website said that in 2015, 14,108 illegal weapons were apprehended by the Rostov police.[47] Novoazovsk port in Donbas provided a clandestine sea access which could be used for contraband. In 2015, Moscow sought to bring the criminal situation in the NGCAs under control and oversaw the sphere of law and order ever since. Because Russian law does not allow FSB to work in Donbas, at least overtly, they had to manage the situation remotely through the often unsatisfactory local cadre, so that disorder did not overspill into Russia. FSB in Rostov oblast reportedly worked hard to curb smuggling of weapons and other undesirable commodities.[48]

An idea was floated at the Presidential Administration to issue Russian internal passports to Donbas residents, although in Russia bearing internal documents does not equate to citizenship. This was strongly opposed by the Ministry of Foreign Affairs.[49] In February 2017, after the cutting cargo traffic to Donbas by Kyiv, Moscow responded by announcing that the "DNR" and "LNR" internal documents would be recognized for travel to Russia. Kyiv and Western policy makers condemned the decision,[50] but Kyiv's position was inconsistent. Since 1992, it has been allowing cars with unrecognized Transnistria's number plates into Ukraine and facilitated its EU exports via Odessa port, providing the breakaway region with a lifeline.

MOSCOW AT THE PEACE NEGOTIATIONS

After Minsk-2, Moscow was unwilling to sanction any further offensive of scale. Kyiv was apparently thinking in similar terms, because the risks of escalation were high for both of them. The parties were preparing for a long-haul "no war, no peace" situation keeping roughly to the 2015 configuration, and the practical arrangements they were making reflected this. Peace negotiations continued in the Normandy format. Moscow's fundamental stance did not change. In Putin's words, "we need a stable, prosperous Ukraine. We very much hope that this will come true,"[51] but this inspired no trust in the West. Surkov's team was given the task to facilitate the reintegration of Donbas back into Ukraine on some decent political terms and reliable security guarantees.[52] This became colloquially known as a *sliv* policy (selling someone down the river), implying that the Kremlin chose its geopolitical stakes with the West over the interests of Donbas people and was prepared to betray them to avoid being an international pariah. The next years were spent proving to the domestic constituency that no *sliv* was planned, and that Moscow would not give up the region without a mutually agreed peace deal.

The Minsk Agreement was a vital step in mending fences with the European states, but it was a provision for a ceasefire rather than a peace accord which was far from sight. Negotiations in the Normandy format were difficult. The atmosphere was such that the West was not prepared to treat Russia as a fair and reasonable partner which was interested in finding a solution to the conflict. The Kremlin felt that its Western partners did not appreciate its efforts in forcing the DNR and LNR, as well as their support base in Russia into adherence to an agreed line, be it on postponing of the local elections which the "republics" wanted to hold independently of Kyiv, suppressing Novorossiya project or halting down the rebels' appetites for a further offensive. Still, the letter of Minsk was fairly close to Russia's original design signed in September 2014, and it continued with it. Gradually, the Minsk process turned into a routine similar to Geneva talks over South Ossetia, with endless rounds of technical consultations with commitments and concessions, and little breakthrough. Moscow successfully resisted the revision of the Agreement in substance, such as the attempts to change sequencing or to reduce the phased implementation to a single package. Its bottom line was that it would not hand over the control over the Ukrainian–Russian border to Kyiv before all other issues were settled, but might provide it to OSCE's peace monitoring force, if an agreement on the composition with Moscow was reached.

Eventually, Minsk process came to be regarded as in the interests of Moscow, Berlin and Paris because it allowed international players to preserve a semblance of diplomacy and claim progress. Following the Normandy group meeting in November 2015, Russian foreign minister Sergei Lavrov noted that full implementation of Minsk agreement, scheduled for the end of 2015, would extend well into 2016, but the following years brought little change. Politicians and analysts called for a reform of the Minsk process, both institutionally and in terms of complementing it with a more targeted agenda, also to widen the circle of participating states.[53] This was clearly unrealistic because the agreement signed in Minsk had the Russian government signatory to it, and was linked to the OSCE, also which includes Russia. Moscow had no reason to agree to an alternative format, and resolution of the conflict without its participation was equally improbable. With everybody's consent, the sides got drawn into a process blessed with international legitimacy, but which was likely to consume the product of a political solution. Alexander Chalenko concluded that Minsk-2 became a "trap for Kyiv. The opponent raised the stakes after Kyiv agreed to it."[54]

Moscow's ultimate goal was to either make Kyiv admit that it did not wish Donbas back or stay with the process as long as this took to accomplish all the stipulated conditions for re-integration. In this paradigm, Minsk process pushed Kyiv into a corner where a winning option was not to play. Moscow assumed that time worked in its favor. It successfully deployed legalistic tools in pointing to the deficiencies in Kyiv's negotiating position. One bone of contention was the holding of local elections in the NGCAs. Kyiv proposed to hold them according to the single mandate principle which deviated from its own mixed system (a combination of the party lists and single mandate constituencies). Moreover, the closed electoral lists proposed by Kyiv contradicted the OSCE norms. This option was put on the table because most of Ukraine's national parties could hardly operate in the NGCAs, while Kyiv was reluctant to accept the participation of the region's new political forces and faces as legitimate. The "republics," in their turn, felt threatened by a prospect of radical activists and associated media arriving into Donbas, who they thought might wreak havoc, stage provocations and disrupt the elections, and open the door for a new wave of turmoil. There was no movement on the electoral front as a result.

Other examples of legal tools, which had their fair points, included the premise that the Special Status law would have no legal force unless the Constitution was amended accordingly. This was said in a response to the one-time Ukrainian proposal that a temporary special status could be given for an interim period of three years. If the Special Status were to be endorsed, the legislatures of the NGCAs could have more say in the adoption of new national laws if they touch upon their interests, a situation disfavored by Kyiv. A Russian expert close to the negotiations remarked that Ukrainian lawyers attempted to introduce modifications to the Minsk-2 agreement which contradicted their own legislation.[55] The sides also traded accusations that decisions of their respective parliaments were illegitimate. In Moscow's narrative, Donbas was not adequately represented in the 2014 Rada because elections there either were not held or took place amid fear and intimidation, and could not be considered free and fair. Kyiv's reaction was that the 2016 Russian Duma was illegitimate because it included MPs from an illegally occupied Crimea.

In the meantime, France and Germany, two Normandy Four members, became more demanding, putting pressure on Kyiv to make progress on Minsk implementation. In September 2016, a European push toward the conflict settlement came from the main Western actors. Jean-Marc Ayrault, French Minister of Foreign Affairs, and his German counterpart, Frank-Walter Steinmeier unveiled the stage-by-stage peace plan which was broadly in line with Moscow's original proposal. Ayrault outlined the three phases. The first stage included the cessation of hostilities and signing an agreement on disengagement, first to be implemented in the three "pilot security areas" along the line of contact, and also the elaboration of the bills on local elections in Donbas and on the Special Status, but not their adoption. The second stage consisted of the adoption of these bills by the parliament, an extension of the pilot disengagement zones from three to eight, withdrawal and storage of heavy weapons, suspension of mine laying and military exercises, full access for the OSCE SMM monitors to Donbas and deployment of OSCE forward patrol bases. The last pillar was for the Rada to set the date for the local elections in the special status districts, adopt constitutional amendments on provisions for decentralization and grant amnesty to all those who took part in hostilities. In parallel, changes were to take place in security sphere, such as disengagement along the front line, establishment of new crossing points, freeing of all prisoners and detainees, and, as a final step—the arrival of observers at the Russian-Ukrainian border.[56] President Putin launched a proposal in October 2017 on deployment of UN peacekeepers, but it is unlikely to get traction because of substantial differences in opinion over the mandate of such operation and Kyiv's insistence that such force must not include peacekeepers from Russia.[57]

Bilateral Russian–Ukrainian relations continued to deteriorate and the train of disentanglement picked up speed. In October 2015 Kyiv banned Russian air carriers from Ukraine, and Moscow closed its airspace in retaliation. On January 1, 2016, Ukraine's DCFTA with the European Union entered into force triggering introduction of the EEU customs duties, and a food embargo was levied because Ukraine joined Western sanctions against Russia. As a result of the loss of the Russian markets, economic damage to Ukraine amounted to US$15 billion at minimum, according to the president Poroshenko's September 2016 Annual Address to the Rada. The volume of Ukrainian exports to Russia declined five times, and Russian share in Ukrainian exports was only 9 percent and going down further.[58] Gazprom intended to significantly reduce supplies and transit through Ukraine after the agreement regulating gas deliveries was to expire in 2019.[59]

At the same time, bilateral informal diplomacy went on. Although president Poroshenko radicalized his stance, throwing his allegiance with the West and reducing his room for maneuver with Moscow, consultations behind closed doors continued, which the Ukrainian side was not keen to make public.[60] Still, the gap was widening. Moscow had fewer interlocutors in Kyiv than at the beginning of Poroshenko's term. As the Ukrainian president moved closer to the United States, his value as a negotiation partner for Moscow diminished and previously intense contacts scaled down.[61] However, despite mutual frustrations, Putin and Poroshenko officially remained "partners" who spoke on the phone.[62] An absence of a politically shaped peace constituency in Ukraine coupled with an exodus of much of the Russia-oriented elite meant that interlocutors were scarce while public atmosphere for cultivating the new elite was not in Russia's favor. Moscow did not seem to comprehend that Ukrainians, irrespective of their positions on Maidan, would be aggrieved by the loss of Crimea and the manner in which it was done, and that the relationship would not be mended without an acknowledgment of these feelings of resentment and bitterness, and offers of material and political compensation, even if Moscow was not considering giving the peninsula back as an option.

INTERNAL EFFECTS

The conflict produced multiple effects on the Russian society and exposed facets which were barely known. It inspired a great deal of civil activism. Humanitarian relief effort was organized by grassroots civil groups. As Ekaterina Stepanova wrote, this self-generating and self-organized societal phenomenon took the government by surprise and demonstrated the enormous potential for civil activism in Russian society.[63] A charitable spirit of Russians was more prominent than was commonly assumed. According to Charity Aid Foundation (CAF) Russia, when violence broke out, 50 percent of the adult population or 44.5 million made monetary contributions and even more gave in-kind donations.[64] Despite its own economic downturn, in 2015 Russia was rated eighth and was included in the top ten countries in the contributions-to-GDP ratio in the *CAF World Giving Index*.[65]

Perspectives on the events in Ukraine bitterly split the liberal world, and political disagreements turned into personal animosities. There was dissent against Russia's actions in Crimea and Donbas, and expressions of solidarity with the Ukrainian cause, to which the authorities reacted with a mixture of lenience and repression. Representatives of liberal circles set up a "Congress of intelligentsia against war, Russia's self-isolation and restoration of totalitarianism" chaired by human rights defender Lev Ponomarev which organized meetings, street gatherings and media publications.[66] Several protest marches in Moscow and other major cities took place, as well as incidents such as a display of the Ukrainian flag on a Moscow bridge on the country's Independence Day and hacking into prime minister's Medvedev Twitter account.[67] The largest anti-war demonstration was organized in Moscow by the liberal opposition parties, such as *Yabloko*, *Solidarity* and *Parnas*, as well as the group of anti-corruption campaigner Alexei Navalny, and brought to the street between 5,000 and 26,000 protesters in September 2014.[68] However, they were not met with a reciprocal anti-war wave in Kyiv, out of which a sustained peace campaign could have emerged, and quickly died out.

The crisis also provoked reactionary politics in Russia. In 2014 nationalist opposition was coming out of the woods, establishing contacts and networks which could propel it into a more serious political force than it had been before. An imperial narrative with its historical reconstructivism became fashionable, taking the public away from pro-Western liberalism. However, the world of Russian nationalism was also split. The main fault line among nationalists was the attitude toward the political regime in Russia: "nobody could imagine that such a tightly-knit, fraternal group could be broken, but the Ukraine question dramatically divided it."[69] Some chose to rally around the government, while others opposed Putin and the Kremlin policy of Minsk, *sliv* and soft suppression of the *Russian Spring*.

The events in Ukraine increased the significance of security and ideational considerations in Russian policy and evolution of identity of its people. Nationalist discourse became more noticeable. Unlike the liberals who concentrated on personal attacks on Putin, the nationalist narrative treated the Russian president with respect, but did not forget his earlier ties with Yeltsin and Berezovsky who brought him to power and his "cosmopolitanism." Nationalists and patriots posed a challenging question of how the ruling elite would square anti-Westernism it unleashed with their own material and cultural immersion into the West. It nailed down an Achilles heel of the Russian leadership. The nationalists' pro-state, but anti-elite sentiment dwelt upon the awkward tension in that many among the Russian rulers were personally integrated with the West as far as their assets, habits and cultural orientations were concerned. Their children were settled in Western Europe. This was true, for example, with respect of the Foreign Minister Lavrov, Russian premier Medvedev and allegedly Putin himself. Strelkov while speaking to me, pointed to a contradiction between public demeanor and personal life, illustrating it with Surkov's example whose child is believed to live abroad: "OK, a wife may be an ex, but the children are never exes. How is this is possible?"[70] The ruling elite could only hope that their nationalist opponents were sufficiently placated so that they would not raise this awkward point too publicly. Those who like Hilary Clinton called Putin "the grand godfather of this global brand of extreme nationalism"[71] did not appear to sufficiently appreciate either the dynamic of Russian politics, or what a face of a Russian nationalist looked like.

CONCLUSIONS AND IMPLICATIONS

Russia does not have a universalist approach to the conflicts in the former Soviet space. The tendency to group ethnic and non-ethnic conflicts together as Russia's projection of dominance in its former empire overshadows their indigenous trajectories and precludes understanding of the differences in Russia's response. It did not intervene, for example, into the Kyrgyz–Uzbek interethnic clashes in Kyrgyzstan in 2010 despite urgent calls by Kyrgyzstan's president Roza Otunbayeva and Uzbek community leaders.[72] The conflicts in Transnistria and Donbas where the *Russian World* identity was at stake cannot be interpreted in ethnic terms. They were caused by resistance against the attempts to separate from the common political and cultural space they shared with Russia and join them to another "civilization" which they did not wish to belong to, such as Romanian in Moldova's case and the European Union for Ukraine. Only they generated a popular appeal in Russia and created waves of solidarity. Although there were volunteer combatants from Russia in Abkhazia in 1993–1994, the most prominent and numerous among them were North Caucasians who went there out of a sense of pan-Caucasian solidarity with the Abkhaz.[73]

Russia paid a big price for the conflict in Donbas, whose ramifications were much greater than of the other post-Soviet conflicts. It was not exactly a foreign policy asset. Russia had committed itself to subsidize the region for as long as it took. Donbas was also closely related to its domestic situation and had a common border with Russia, so that possible effects at home of societal actors who had been involved in Ukraine worry the Russian authorities. Still, Moscow had strong disincentives to give up Donbas, whereas the advantages of handing it over to Kyiv were not obvious. If Donbas was "betrayed," it was likely to cause political consequences, because it would be seen by a significant segment of society not just as surrender, but as complete defeat, as if Russia's rulers abandoned the people who put their trust in it. Although the conflict turned into a liability for Moscow, its ability to open a tap on its resolution should not be exaggerated. It had fewer incentives to press the rebels much further beyond what it had already done, as hostile relations with the West were acknowledged as the new reality. Moreover, Moscow felt that leaving Donbas would not solve the problem Russia had with the West, because its attention would then move to focus on the Crimea question. As predicted by Huntington in 1993, when Russians rejected liberal democracy and began behaving like Russians, the relations between Russia and the West became distant and conflictual.[74]

Looking into the future, what Moscow ideally wanted in Ukraine was for it to remain an independent but Russia-friendly country. Firstly, it had to accept the loss of Crimea, in response for which economic and social concessions would be offered to Ukraine on the peninsula. Secondly, Kyiv would have to allocate a wider autonomy to Donbas and agree on the region's preservation of close links with Russia. Thirdly, Ukraine should preferably participate in the Russia-led regional cooperation or at least adhere to geopolitical neutrality, in return for which various economic incentives would be provided.

There are different schools of thought on viability of such scenario. The prevalent one says that it would never happen and the obstacles are formidable. Bridges with Russia were burnt for the decades to come. The Ukrainian government took the course of integration into Euro-Atlantic structures and there was no significant domestic political force which could challenge this orientation. Ukrainians would be embittered by anti-Russian attitudes for at least a generation after Crimea and Donbas. Dominant public rhetoric was anti-Russian and affected hearts and minds. The other school points out that Ukrainian politics was always characterized by a pendulum movement whose amplitude was going more and more extreme, and at some point the movement would be reversed in Russia's favor.[75] Economic and social problems would gain the pride of place and supersede geopolitical ambitions and European hopes. Russia-friendly forces, in disarray after the PoR's disgraceful end, would consolidate around a more genuine political agenda and new leaders. The West would not provide an unconditional support to Kyiv indefinitely, and its intrusive "big brother" role would generate a push back. This would necessitate restoration of a relationship with Russia in the economic and social spheres at least.

What Moscow was offering to Kyiv was not the best deal, because Minsk provided wide powers of autonomy to the rebellious territories and backing by Russian security guarantees. But it was a deal which was allowing restoring unity and moving ahead with development. The West could not get Ukraine a better deal because the expectations that "fragile Putin's regime" would collapse proved to be wishful thinking. Sometimes what looks like a bad deal is better than no deal because what is on offer at present may not be possible several years later, but clocks do not go back. Russia has more permanent interests in Ukraine as the West does, and its leadership was determined to exercise strategic patience waiting until Ukraine transformed from an existential battleground between Russia and the West into a developing country in a need of international assistance. Geographic position contributes to its power.[76] Eventually, if the inability of making Ukraine a prosperous, stable, well-governed, and EU-loyal state would be on the horizon, Western governments could declare the mission accomplished.[77] Their interest would wane down, leaving middle-level staff to manage the relationship. Then Moscow's goal of having a direct dialogue with Kyiv without the West constantly breathing behind its shoulder may come true. In the short term, there was little Moscow felt it could do to influence Ukraine, until the internal dynamic in the country altered and Russia's power could find an opening again.

NOTES

1. Richard Sakwa, "The death of Europe? Continental fates after Ukraine," *International Affairs* 91, no. 3 (2015): 553–579, Sakwa, *Frontline Ukraine*, Derek Averre, "The Ukraine Conflict: Russia's Challenge to European Security Governance," *Europe–Asia Studies*, 68, no. 44 (2016): 699–725, R. Allison, "Russian "Deniable" Intervention in Ukraine," Dmitri Trenin, *The Ukraine Crisis and the Resumption of Great-Power Rivalry* (Moscow: Carnegie Moscow Center, 2014).

2. John J. Mearsheimer, "Moscow's Choice," *Foreign Affairs* 93, no. 6 (2014) and John J. Mearsheimer "Why the Ukraine Crisis Is the West's Fault: The Liberal Delusions That Provoked Putin," *Foreign Affairs* 93, 5 (2014).

3. Michael E. Aleprete Jr., "Minimizing Loss: Explaining Russian Policy Choices during the Ukrainian Crisis," *The Soviet and Post-Soviet Review* 44 (2017): 53–75.

4. Michael O. Slobodchikoff, "Challenging US Hegemony: The Ukrainian Crisis and Russian Regional Order," *The Soviet and Post-Soviet Review* 44 (2017): 76–95.

5. Elizabeth A. Wood, "Roots of Russia's War in Ukraine."

6. Huntington, "The Clash of Civilizations?"

7. Vladimir Zharikhin, author's interview, February 2016, Moscow.

8. Alexei Tokarev, author's interview, Moscow, May 2016.

9. Zharikhin, Sergei Volkov, author's interviews.

10. Сергей Пинчук, "Пушкиным от "Правого сектора" не отобьешься," February 27, 2014, http://www.gazeta.ru/comments/2014/02/26_x_5928581.shtml

11. *Russkiy Mir* Foundation website http://russkiymir.ru/en/fund/index.php

12. Igor Zevelev, "The Russian World in Moscow's Strategy," CSIS, August 22, 2016, https://www.csis.org/analysis/russian-world-moscows-strategy

13. Igor Zevelev, "The Russian World Boundaries: Russia's National Identity Transformation and New Foreign Policy Doctrine," *Russia in Global Affairs*, June 7, 2014, http://eng.globalaffairs.ru/number/The-Russian-World-Boundaries-16707

14. Nicolai N. Petro, *Russia's Orthodox Soft Power* (Washington, DC: Carnegie Center, 23 March 2015), http://www.carnegiecouncil.org/publications/articles_papers_reports/727

15. "Ukraine crisis: Transcript of leaked Nuland-Pyatt call," February 7, 2014.

16. Alexander Chalenko, author's interview.

17. It can be argued that mutual distrust was accumulated over quite some time, see Dov Lynch, "Europe Faces Russia" Chaillot Paper 60 (Paris: EU Institute for Security Studies, 2003).

18. Putin's interview to *Bild* newspaper, January 11, 2016, http://en.kremlin.ru/events/president/transcripts/statements/51154, "Песков: Запад использует двойные стандарты в вопросе об Украине," March 7, 2014, http://graniru.org/Politics/Russia/President/m.226328.html, "Путин предостерег от опасности политики двойных стандартов," TASS, October 27, 2015, http://tass.ru/politika/1725280

19. The files were published by Ukraine's Prosecutor General's office,"Беседы "Сергея Глазьева" о Крыме и беспорядках на востоке Украины. Расшифровка," August 22, 2014.

20. Interviews with informed observers and Kremlin-close academics, February 2016, Moscow.

21. Patrick Armstrong, "Russian Federation Sitrep," October 22, 2015 http://www.russiaotherpointsofview.com/2015/10/russian-federation-sitrep-1.html

22. Alexander Mercouris, "End Game in Ukraine–Russia Wins," *Russia Insider*, October 12, 2016, http://russia-insider.com/en/politics/end-game-ukraine-russia-wins/ri10390

23. Boyd-Barrett, *Western mainstream media*, chapter 6. State Secretary Kerry urged president Poroshenko "to provide evidence of Russian involvement with separatists with which to confront Russian officials," which apparently was in short

supply, in Peter Baker, "Obama, Seeking Unity on Russia, Meets Obstacles," June 4, 2014, *New York Times*, https://www.nytimes.com/2014/06/05/world/europe/in-show-of-support-obama-meets-with-ukraine-leader.html?ref=world&_r=0

24. Alexander Borodai, author's interview, May 2016.

25. Lavrov, "Civil War in the East," 202–227, *Brothers armed: military aspects of the crisis in Ukraine*, eds. Colby Howard and Ruslan Pukhov, Centre for Analysis of Strategies and Technologies (CAST), Moscow (Minneapolis: East View Press, 2015), 203.

26. Gubarev, "Torch," 216.

27. Anton Lavrov, "Civil War," 211.

28. On substantial plurality of opinion within the political class see Averre, "The Ukraine Conflict," 708–710. DOI: 10.1080/09668136.2016.1176993

29. On sanctions and their politico-economic effects see Richard Connolly, "The Empire Strikes Back: Economic Statecraft and the Securitisation of Political Economy in Russia," *Europe–Asia Studies* 68, no. 4 (2016): 750–773.

30. September 24, 2016, http://novorossia.pro/25yanvarya/2457-igor-strelkov-bolshe-sankciy-horoshih-i-raznyh-.html, Strelkov also hoped for a Clinton's win in the US presidential elections in anticipation that her policy would be more hostile to Russia.

31. Mark Urban, "How many Russians are fighting in Ukraine?" *BBC*, March 10, 2015, http://www.bbc.co.uk/news/world-europe-31794523

32. Sutyagin cites 10,000 troops in December 2014, but does not state his sources, in Igor Sutyagin, *Russian Forces in Ukraine* (London: RUSI, 2015). *Reuters* quoted US General Ben Hodges who said that 12,000 troops were present in February 2015, but did not refer to evidence, in *Reuters*, "Some 12,000 Russian Soldiers in Ukraine Supporting Rebels: U.S. Commander," March 3, 2015.

33. See "Former NATO General Kujat: I don't believe evidence of Russian invasion" https://www.youtube.com/watch?v=l0_yaWyA-1s

34. Valery Shiryaev, Это — война, August 8, 2016, https://www.novayagazeta.ru/articles/2016/08/08/69482-eto-voyna

35. Boris Nemtsov, "Putin. War," (2015) www.4freerussia.org/putin.war

36. Maxim Solopov, "Расследование РБК: откуда на Украине российские солдаты," *RBK*, October 2, 2014, http://www.rbc.ru/politics/02/10/2014/542c0dcfcb b20f5d06c1d87a

37. For example, Taras Kuzio, "Ukraine between a Constrained EU and Assertive Russia," August 24, 2016, DOI: 10.1111/jcms.12447

38. Interviews with ex-combatants who stayed in Donbas in late 2014 and throughout 2015, also coverage in *Colonel Cassad*, 2015.

39. Interview with an informed observer in Moscow, May 2016.

40. http://moran-group.org/en/about/index

41. Wagner, also sometimes called *Compositor* is not a real name. Russian servicemen with "Wagner" surnames should not be associated with Wagner Group.

42. Vladimir Dergachoff, Ekaterina Zgirovskaya, "Российские наемники в боях за Пальмиру," 29 March 2016, https://www.gazeta.ru/politics/2016/03/22_a_8137565. shtml

43. "Сирийские потери "Славянского корпуса" March 29, 2016," http://www.svoboda.org/a/27642396.html

44. Borodai and Norin, author's interviews.

45. International Crisis Group, "Russia and the Separatists," 3.

46. Vladimir Dergachoff, author's interview.

47. "Информационно-аналитическая записка к отчету о результатах деятельности Главного управления МВД России по Ростовской области за 2015 год," Russian Ministry of Interior Rostovo blast office, 2015 data on criminal situation, https://61.mvd.ru/upload/site62/folder_page/007/191/062/informatsionno-analiticheskaya_spravka_o_rezultatakh_deyatelnosti_GU_MVD_Rossii_po_Rostovskoy_oblasti_za_2015.pdf

48. Dergachoff, author's interview.

49. Chalenko, author's interview.

50. "Putin orders Russia to recognize passports issued by Ukrainian Separatists," *The Washington Post*, February 18, 2017.

51. President Putin's Direct Line, April 14, 2016, http://www.1tv.ru/shows/vystupleniya-prezidenta-rossii/pryamaya-liniya-2016/pryamaya-liniya-s-vladimirom-putinym-2016-onlaynreportazh

52. Author's interview with two Kremlin-close observers, Moscow, February 2016.

53. Gwendolyn Sasse, "New Hope in Ukraine Conflict?" 2 ZOIS Spotlight, June 7, 2017.

54. Chalenko, author's interview, Moscow, February 2016.

55. Alexei Chesnakov, director of Centre for Current Politics, author's interview, Moscow, February 2016.

56. "Ukraine–Statements by M. Jean-Marc Ayrault, Minister of Foreign Affairs and International Development, during his joint press conference with his German and Ukrainian counterparts," Official speeches and statements of September 16, 2016, Ministère des Affaires Etrangères, http://basedoc.diplomatie.gouv.fr/exl-doc/France-Diplomatie/PDF/baen2016-09-16.pdf

57. "Envoy welcomes Russian idea for UN troops in eastern Ukraine," *The Guardian*, September 16, 2017, https://www.theguardian.com/world/2017/sep/16/russian-backing-for-un-troops-in-eastern-ukraine-gives-us-more-options-says-envoy

58. "Порошенко: Закрытие российских рынков обошлось Украине в 15 млрд долларов," September 6, 2016, *112 Ukraina* TV channel, https://112.ua/ekonomika/poroshenko-zakrytie-rossiyskih-rynkov-oboshlos-ukraine-v-15-mlrd-dollarov-336567.html

59. Simon Pirani and Katja Yafimava, "Russian Gas Transit Across Ukraine Post-2019: pipeline scenarios, gas flow consequences, and regulatory constraints," *The Oxford Institute for Energy Studies*, OIES paper: NG 105, 2016.

60. Andrei Sushentsov presentation, Chatham House, London, May 2016.

61. Andrei Sushentsov presentation at Chatham House, also leak in Kommersant Daily, « Были вынуждены шутить, чтобы не разругаться », April 28, 2017, http://www.kommersant.ru/doc/3286820?utm_source=kommersant&utm_medium=mir&utm_campaign=four

62. "Порошенко раскрыл подробности последнего разговора с Путиным," *RIA*, May 14, 2017, https://ria.ru/world/20170514/1494268489.html

63. Ekaterina Stepanova, chapter "Russia," in *The Oxford Handbook of the Responsibility to Protect*, eds. Alex Bellamy, Tim Dunne (Oxford: Oxford University Press, 2016).

64. Yulia Khodorova, Maria Chertok, "Russia Giving: Исследование частных пожертвований в России 2014–2015" (Moscow: Charity Aid Foundation Russia), 2015.

65. *CAF World Giving Index* 2015, http://www.cafrussia.ru/news/view/177

66. Danila Gal'perovich, 147 "'Протест был необходим': российская интеллигенция о действиях России против Украины," February 19 (no year), http://www.golos-ameriki.ru/a/russian-intelligensia-maidan-anniversary/3198733.html

67. Katerina Shumilo, "'Остановим войну': как россияне протестуют против действий России на Донбассе," September 8, 2014, http://forbes.net.ua/nation/1378484-ostanovim-vojnu-kak-rossiyane-protestuyut-protiv-dejstvij-rossii-na-Donbase

68. Alec Luhn, "Thousands protest in Moscow over Russia's involvement in Ukraine," *The Guardian*, September 21, 2014, https://www.theguardian.com/world/2014/sep/21/protest-moscow-russia-ukraine

69. Prince, author's interview.

70. Igor Strelkov, author's interview, Moscow, May 2016.

71. Hillary Clinton's alt-right speech, annotated, *The Washington Post*, August 25, 2016, https://www.washingtonpost.com/news/the-fix/wp/2016/08/25/hillary-clintons-alt-right-speech-annotated/

72. Anna Matveeva, "Violence in Kyrgyzstan, vacuum in the region: the case for Russia-EU joint crisis management" (London: London School of Economics, Civil Society & Human Security Research Unit Working Paper, 2011).

73. Author's interviews with respondents in Abkhazia, Georgia, in 1996–1997.

74. Huntington, "Clash," 45.

75. June 2017 KMIS (Kyiv International Institute of Sociology) poll shows that positive views of Russia in Ukraine (44%) outweighed negative views (37%) and that a deep regional divide remained on this issue. Negative views were expressed by the majority of the respondents (56%) in the West, 42% in the Center, compared to 19% in the South and the East. http://kiis.com.ua/?lang=ukr&cat=reports&id=707&page=1, cited by Ivan Katchanovski on his Facebook page.

76. George Friedman, "A Net Assessment of Europe," *Stratfor Geopolitical Weekly*, 26 May 2015.

77. This point was made by Patrick Armstrong in "Ukraine in the Mirror of the Mind," December 6, 2013, http://us-russia.org/1957-ukraine-in-the-mirror-of-the-mind.html and https://patrickarmstrong.ca/2013/12/

Final Thoughts

Imperfect Peace Is Better than a Good War

The book sought to lift some of the fog on the war in Ukraine, although its full history is far from told. The conflict in Donbas did not spring out of nowhere, but had its deep-rooted causes in its history of emergence out of Russian–Ukrainian borderlands, its distinct identity and closeness to Russia, as well as political causes derived from the post-independence development of Ukrainian state, which inspired grievances against it. At the same time, the armed confrontation was not inevitable. As the book demonstrated, "it's all Putin" theory does not adequately explain the conflict, and the Russian government's role is not its only interesting aspect. The reality is richer than any scheme and does not fit into a "plan," but instead unfolds incrementally and incidentally in many improvised ways which could not be predicted or invented before. It gives birth to new stakes and meanings which emerge during the process, and if people are prepared to die for them, they become a new reality. Paraphrasing Leo Tolstoy, the role of personality in history matters, and these personalities may not be presidents, but ordinary people who became actors at the crucial junctions of history. Their individual decisions created a collective will which started pulling in a certain direction and succeeded where resilience of counteracting forces was thin.

The book shows how a conflict can escalate in no time. A chain of collective insecurities in which the action of one side prompted the other to respond with more aggression was what triggered the full-scale war. Arrival of Strelkov and Borodai into Donetsk oblast supplied the nascent uprising with a direction, political and military organization, and a point to rally around, and was interpreted as a signal that Crimea scenario would be repeated in Donbas. In this context, the decision by Turchinov and his ruling group to launch a military operation in response to the amateurish seizures of administrative buildings by no-name protestors proved fatal. Most likely, they would have withdrawn as they had no plan of what to do if they were not challenged by force. Odesa tragedy served as a trigger for many volunteers from abroad to join the fight, and the arrival of Ukrainian territorial battalions produced the same effect on the local rebels. President Poroshenko's decision to escalate into the full-blown hostilities provoked a response in Russia and elsewhere that people in the need of protection should be offered it if they were persecuted for their pro-Russian allegiances, as it was seen in the *Russian World*. The events moved very rapidly, and at no junction there were enough pauses to allow de-escalation. As a reminder, Moscow tried to find accommodation with Chechnya for three years (1991–1994) before ordering troops in. An agreement on a delayed status of Chechnya with its president Aslan Maskhadov provided a chance for peace and Moscow continued interactions with the Chechen government until disorder from the rebellious republic began to destabilize Russia beyond Chechen borders in 1999.

The violent summer of 2014 dramatically changed Donbas. The provisions of Minsk-I, which was concluded in these changed realities, acknowledged them, but the Ukrainian elites and society were not prepared to accept that a possibility to return to the times of Kuchma and Yanukovych was gone; the world had changed since then. Arguably, the Minsk-I provisions were implementable were Kyiv to move quickly and negotiated with the rebel leaderships directly irrespective of whether it accepted their legitimacy or had any respect for them. Moscow did not give up its support to the NGCAs, but it paved the way by drafting the agreement, halted the rebels' offensive, and withdrew too independent political actors who stood in the way of Minsk. The rebel leaderships were internally weak and could have been amenable to being persuaded. They had not yet mastered the levers of power, were disunited and their visions on future were blurred. The population lived in Ukraine long enough to find it hard to imagine a life without it, and many subconsciously expected Kyiv to take the reins again, when it was clear that Moscow was not going to fulfill the aspirations of those who wanted to be a part of Russia.

As time went on, the "republics" grew more confident following Russian assistance in military organization, built up their command-and-control structures, and acquired an unrivalled experience of a modern warfare. A quick victorious offensive along a Croatia-type scenario against Krajina Serbs in 1995[1] would be hard to realize as the rebel positions got entrenched and better defended, and they improved their fighting capabilities. Were Kyiv to pursue an attack, it could not be sure that the *Northern Wind* would not blow again if the rebels were seriously challenged. The risk that a renewed war strengthens the government in Kyiv, but inflicts further territorial losses, was a gamble the president so far was unwilling to take. War talk remained ripe, but little action followed and frustration reigned.

Security incentive scaled down in significance, reducing the "push" factor for peace. Although the rebels were under constant pressure, they did not fear a prospect of a military defeat strongly enough; moreover, were Kyiv to launch an offensive, they could try to use it as an opportunity for a counteroffensive to gain more ground as their appetites were far from satisfied. However, if the war were to resume, the severity of the crisis should not be underestimated. Its ferocity and scale would be worse than in 2014–2015 campaign, because the armies on both sides became better organized and equipped, and were highly motivated. This made the situation more dangerous, because it had a potential to transform Donbas from a local conflict into a regional one.

The story of Donbas war is that of a tragedy which could have been averted and of a conflict which could have been resolved with enough political will and rising above the feelings of hurt and pride. Yet, little movement in this direction happened. Few attempts at peace were made outside of the Normandy format which with all its imperfections remained the main avenue for talks. However, it was a question how sincere were the rebel negotiators in Minsk when they were saying that they accepted the territorial integrity of Ukraine. Zakharchenko, for example, stated in Donetsk on June 15, 2015, that "whatever happens in Minsk, DNR is a self-governing state and will never be a part of Ukraine; blood is between us."[2] This sentiment was repeated by the rebel leaders on more than one occasion.

Kyiv also did not demonstrate much flexibility and continued to reject direct negotiations. The MP Savchenko tried to give citizen's diplomacy a chance, but peace constituency which existed in Ukraine was not organized and politically shaped, and was vulnerable to accusations of a lack of patriotism. Conflict resolution organizations largely were slow to react when the conflict was at its messy height; its actors were angry, but not sure which direction to take and were more prone to be led on the road toward peace. The international peace practitioners were waiting for a mutually hurting stalemate to arrive,[3] a situation when the sides realize that none can win an outright victory and seek compromise, so that the parties become ready for an externally facilitated peace dialogue. What happened instead was the consolidation of the *status quo*. Mutually hurting stalemate was not reached, and with it—a quest for peace. Adaptation to the "new normal" on both sides settled in, with mechanisms and strategies designed for life to go on in the changed circumstances. Even if we assume that Russia and the West acted in good faith in pressurizing their allies into a peace deal, the deal would not last until internal conditions were ripe. By 2016, a sense of a deadlock emerged. Federalization which was what the Special Status actually entailed was disfavored by both sides. It fell way short of rebels' aspirations who fought for an outright independence or joining Russia, and the maximum they could accept was an Aceh-style loose confederation that resolved the conflict in Indonesia, that is, capital's rule in the name but not in substance.

At this junction the events reached the point of no return, having created new realities of warfare, political leadership, internal organization, and ideological narratives which legitimized the actions. A military-political order on the rebellious territories emerged. A new elite cohort developed out of unruly field commanders through a selection process overseen by Moscow which supplied political education and practical guidance. It invested in preventing descent of the NGCAs into bandit formations by helping to build up governing structures and administrative arrangements, and re-orienting supply chains toward Russian market. This does not mean that Moscow ruled them directly or had control over everything that went on, but certain decisions could not be made without its approval. The situation on the ground in the NGCAs underwent a shift toward a relative stabilization. Everyday life got progressively better and some of the displaced returned. Crime and disorder characteristic of the early days of the conflict subsided. Economy shrunk, but did not collapse. Social sector was covered by the Russian subsidies, and the local authorities succeeded in addressing acute vulnerability, reflected in a decrease in reliance on humanitarian aid. All in all, life gradually became manageable. Although living standards were lower than in the rest of Ukraine, the mainland had its own problems and did not appear as a sufficient economic pole of attraction.

If separated parts of Ukraine were to rejoin, they would have to deal with the situation that they became two different animals during the conflict. The country changed considerably, and a "Ukrainian monist" version of identity and the "national idea" dominated the state and public narrative. Dissent was not tolerated lightly and pluralistic identities characteristic of the pre-war Ukraine were not the order of the day. Society that was based on multiculturalism and acceptance of differences was withering away, and what replaced it was unlikely to give returning separatists a warm welcome. In the rebel Donbas, an initial pro-Russian orientation was reinforced by the experience of resistance. It created a new identity based not merely on political and cultural leaning toward Russia, but on a real hell of survival in a devastating war. That is not to say that the obstacles became entirely unbridgeable, but it will take an enormous effort, tolerance and generosity of spirit to overcome this gap.

All parties were dissatisfied with the outcomes, but the most dissatisfied were the rebels themselves, who experienced insecurity and uncertainty about future. Examples of the former Soviet conflicts can provide insights for peace process. Arguably, a window of opportunity for resolution of an internal conflict lasts for a relatively short period of five–six years when either a war (Chechnya: the first war finished in 1996 and the second started in 1999) or peace (Tajikistan: hostilities broke out in 1992 and Peace Accords were signed in 1997) comes in. Tbilisi missed some chances for peace in Abkhazia where hostilities ended in 1993 but not all was lost, while the Abkhaz declared their independence only in 1999. Yeltsin's Moscow was a more amenable conflict resolution partner than it became under Putin, and followed the line on the reintegration of the breakaway republic into Georgia at the time.[4]

The conflict in Donbas renders some important conclusions. Firstly, a leaderless uprising is possible: people will come out when the moment is right. They emerge from different milieus, from inside and outside the region, and there are reasons why people in certain situations participate in a collective violent action. Secondly, the insurgents and their leaderships became a reality and will not wither away. They are likely to grow stronger politically and militarily. The risk of the rebellion's implosion, valid in 2014, was gone in a year's time. Thirdly, the policy line taken by Kyiv not to acknowledge the "people's republics'" political personalities was counterproductive and would have to be reversed, if not by the Poroshenko administration, then by its successor, if negotiations had any chance to succeed. Lastly, the credo of Donbas movement inspired a wider solidarity appeal than ethno-nationalisms of 1990s in the Balkans and the Caucasus which were concerned with their particular grievances. Effect of global culture and communication which amplify identities and significance of values was demonstrated. Emergence of a transnational identity in Europe that challenged Western liberal hegemony of the world order, although marginal, has consequences beyond Donbas.

Eventually, another unresolved conflict was added to the post-Soviet space, this time encompassing a large territory and more than three million people living on it. If the trends continue unabated, which is most likely, Donbas political trajectory will irreversibly move away from the rest of Ukraine. An honest break probably could have been in the interests of both sides before more offensives happened and lives were lost, but taking such step by Kyiv required more courage than the leadership had will for, as it could turn into a political suicide. Where all this would lead Ukraine is uncertain. Looking into the future, either the war can re-start and bring a military resolution, or a frozen conflict would settle in with a gradual reduction in hostilities but no political progress. The option of a deal based on a substantial compromise does not seem viable because neither side have their hearts in it.

Russia found itself in the situation it could not walk away from even if it wanted to. However, the talk of a "failure of Putin's plan" is misleading: it is hard to prove that such plan ever existed, and Moscow's fluctuating actions suggest that perhaps it did not. Moscow reacted each time to the events as they were unfolding. Since Minsk-1, Moscow was pursuing the policy of pushing the NGCAs back into Ukraine on somewhat decent conditions, but this goal became less realizable as the time went on. The "republics" acquired gravitas internally and among their supporters in Russia, so that pushing them into

Kyiv's arms against their will could be done only through substantial coercion, an option which Moscow would not concede. Its policy of recognition of NGCAs as a part of Ukraine however might change if geopolitical context alters, as that of the West's in relation to Kosovo, to where it intervened in 1999 acknowledging the Republic of Yugoslavia's territorial integrity, but in 2008 most Western powers recognized Kosovo as an independent state.

The events in Donbas gave birth to a formative experience of the *Russian Spring* movement which presented a wide societal mobilization in Russia and in the *Russian World* and left its imprint on Russia's own evolution. This book sought to show in which historic circumstances mobilization of volunteer combatants happened. The *Russian Spring* was a solidarity phenomenon when the segment of society felt that the circumstances were such that it must act, and proved that it was capable of autonomous action. Stripped of their opposing ideologies, a similar process was underway in Ukraine, where territorial battalions and *Help Army* movement were formed. The key aspect of the *Russian Spring* was that it came from below as a reaction to an acute political crisis, when people self-organized spontaneously, even if an indirect support of the Russian authorities was provided later. It amounted to far more than an armed movement stirring trouble in the region by Moscow to take another hostage in order to obstruct pro-Western tendencies in its neighborhood. It is hard to predict in what kind of conditions the *Russian Spring* would reappear. Rather than looking for a new foreign battle, its future development might be directed inwards, if and when Russia's internal transformation begins. Further deterioration of the Russia–West relations would give it hope that this transformation goes in the direction it wishes.

Donbas joined the ranks of unrecognized entities which fell out in the process of territorial reconfiguration after the fall of the USSR. Neither Ukrainian nor Western politicians managed to cope with the outbreak of the rebellion that combined indigenous and external combatant elements because their cognitive frame was focused on a "Putin's plan." Although Donbas got stuck in limbo and this was not how it saw its political destiny, the region has moved into the position when survival was possible. In the end, there were no winners in the brutal conflict as both sides inflicted enormous pain on each other and on themselves, and we can only hope that humanity survived in those who went through it. Recalling the Spanish Civil War, we conclude on Hemingway's note, "don't ask for whom the bell tolls. It tolls for you."

NOTES

1. The operation Storm was launched against the self-proclaimed Republic of Serbian Krajina by Croatian army and accomplished victory in three days, gaining

control of the territory as a result. During and after the offensive, about 200,000 Serbs, or nearly the entire Serb population of the area, fled, and crimes were committed against the remaining ones.

2. Video available at http://colonelcassad.livejournal.com/2015/06/15/

3. William Zartmann, "Mutually hurting stalemate and beyond," in *International Conflict Resolution after the Cold War*, eds. Paul C. Stern and Daniel Druckman, Committee on International Conflict Resolution (Washington, D.C.: The National Academies Press, 2000), 225–250.

4. Based on the author's experience of working on resolution of the Georgian–Abkhaz conflict for International Alert (1995–1997), on the conflicts in the Caucasus for Chatham House (1997–2001) and Saferworld (2001–2003).

Appendix A

Interviewees

EX-COMBATANTS ON INSURGENCY SIDE, FACE-TO-FACE INTERVIEWS

1. Igor Strelkov (real name Igor Girkin), from Russia
2. Alexander Borodai, from Russia
3. *Prince*, commander, from Russia
4. Alexander Juchkovsky, recruiter, procurement coordinator, and public communicator, from Russia
5. *Strannik*, commander with Pavel Dremov's Cossack forces, from Russia
6. Commander of *Russian Orthodox Army*, from Russia
7. Roman, middle-level commander, from Russia
8. Fighter from *Viking* battalion, from Russia
9. Cossack fighter, member of Georgievskyi Cossack Humanitarian battalion later, from Russia
10. Fighter originally from Kostiantynivka (26 years old), Ukraine
11. *Nemets*, rank-and-file fighter, originally from Lysychansk (late thirties), first with *Prizrak*, then with Cossack forces of Pavel Dremov, Ukraine
12. Low-level commander, originally from Donetsk (early forties), Ukraine
13. Rank-and-file fighter, originally from Yasynuvata (early thirties), Ukraine
14. *Mikhailo*, Chief of Staff, "Slavyansk Brigade," originally from Azerbaijan
15. Fighter at Luhanska oblast, from Chile

POLITICIANS

16. Oleg Tsaryov, former deputy of Ukrainian parliament, chair of "Novoros-siya parliament"
17. Ukrainian politician, originally from Donbas, who did not participate in the rebellion

DONBAS RESIDENTS (ALL FEMALE)

18. Anastassiya Khmelnitsksya, Donetsk
19. Yulia Gakova, Kramatorsk
20. Inga Zueva, formerly Luhansk
21. Natalia, local authority staff, Kostiantynivka
22. Iryna, businesswoman, Donetsk
23. Marina, civil activist, formerly Donetsk
24. Elena, teacher, Luhansk
25. Halyna, teacher, Rubizhne, Luhanska oblast
26. Anna, doctor, Makiivka

EXPERT INTERVIEWS, UKRAINE

27. Yevgen Kopat'ko, Branding and Research Group, sociologist (originally from Donetsk)
28. Inna Tereshenko, Odesa State University
29. Ihor Semyvolos, director of Middle Eastern Studies Centre, coordinator of Ukrainian Peacebuilding School
30. Yulia Tyshchenko, Head of the Ukrainian Centre of Independent Political Research Board
31. Volodymyr Lupatsy, director of Sofia Social Studies Centre
32. Volodymyr Prytula, editor of *Krym Realii*, Radio Free Europe
33. Andrei Yermolaev, director of "New Ukraine" Centre of Strategic Studies
34. Mikhail Pogrebinsky, Director of the Center of Political Studies and Conflictology
35. Dmytro Vydrin, author and political scientist
36. Yuri Kononenko, Ministry of Education and Science of Ukraine
37. Alexei Kachan, political expert and a head of NGO, formerly a Luhansk city council deputy
38. Sergei Volkov, Kyiv-based political analyst
39. Oleh Protsyk, political scientist and expert on Ukraine (via Skype)

40. Crimea Policy Dialogue participants interviewed in 2012 (in addition to some of the above respondents who were interviewed in 2015): Gulnara Bekirova, Natalya Belitser, Iryna Brunova- Kalisetska, Liliya Budzhurova, Ol'ga Dukhnich, Alexander Formanchuk, Andrii Ivanets, Yusuf Kurkchi, Andrei Mal'gin, Andrei Nikiforov, Yulia Verbitskaya.

EXPERT INTERVIEWS, MOSCOW

41. Valerii Solovei, MGIMO, head of department of public communications
42. Alexei Chesnakov, Centre for Current Politics, director
43. Alexander Chalenko, journalist, *Russia Today*, originally from Donetsk
44. Vladimir Zharikhin, CIS (Diaspora & Integration) Institute, deputy director
45. Vladimir Dergachoff, journalist, *Gazeta.ru*
46. Ilya Barabanov, journalist, *Kommersant*
47. Dmitrii Polikanov, *So-edinenie* society chair
48. Vadim Koziulin, PIR Centre, research associate
49. Sergei Markedonov, Russian State Humanitarian University
50. Yevgenii Norin, military historian, Perm' (via Skype)
51. Alexei Tokarev, MGIMO, senior research fellow
52. Ivan Loshkariov, MGIMO, researcher
53. Yegor Prosvirnin, editor of Sputnik i Pogrom (by correspondence)
54. Sergei Kharlamov, banker

INTERNATIONAL RESPONDENTS

55. Denis Matveev, Crisis Management Initiative (Finland)
56. Natalia Mirimanova, conflict-resolution scholar and practitioner
57. Staff of an international organization, male, interviewed in Moscow
58. Anna Munster, researcher, London
59. Kyiv-based international organization staff, male, interviewed in Kyiv
60. Luhansk-based staff of an international organization, male (via Skype)
61. Kyiv-based international organization's staff, male
62. Kyiv-based international organization's staff, female
63. Kyiv-based international organization's staff, female

Appendix B

Notes on Methodology

Much of the narrative is written on the basis of firsthand material collected through interviews, ongoing conversations, travel and observations taken by the author in Ukraine and Russia, as well as following the coverage of developing stories. It provides the opinions of the key actors, as well as of others who played less prominent but nevertheless crucial roles in the events as they unfolded. This is the first time when the voices of direct participants are heard in Western literature. Interviews were held by the author with 15 ex-combatants (face-to-face interviews) and with two Ukrainian politicians involved in Donbas who did not participate in fighting. Out of combatants, nine were from Russia, four were from Ukraine, one from Azerbaijan, and one from South America. Most of them have higher education, with exception of two individuals, as much as it was possible to conclude from interviews. At least five were history graduates and there were several private businessmen. All ex-combatants were male, ranging from 26 years old to the mid-forties. Two former politicians were older males. Most ex-combatant respondents were eager to share their testimonies and an interview presented an opportunity for condemnation of injustice and for healing of personal trauma. For many of them, participation in the rebellion was the focal point of their lives, a "one-in-lifetime" experience, significance of which they were still processing. Interviewees were not deliberately challenged; rather they were asked to express their stories in their own way. They were not forced into answering questions which could have made them tell direct lies.

It is possible to state that the leadership interviews are fairly representative. Three respondents played the key military leadership roles in the 2014 rebellion. Out of the other prominent figures, five had been assassinated or died before interviews could be arranged, and the *de facto* "premiers" Alexander Zakharchenko and Igor Plotnitsky were not accessible. One prominent commander was not interviewed, but he lives in Crimea since 2015, where research was not conducted. Out of the sample, four were "second-tier" commanders, such as the leader of the *Russian Orthodox Army*, and a few others who rose to larger roles from the pool of the first arrivals. Two interviewees were active recruiters in Russia, and both were participants in Euromaidan protests in Kyiv in December 2013. The respondents from Ukraine (Donbas and non-Donbas) were working class (3) and one—a graduate. More articulate, educated, and politically savvy interviewees provided more coherent narratives and quotes, and their direct speech is preserved where appropriate. Other quotes are used more sparingly or their stories are used cumulatively to reconstruct the events and actions from the participants' accounts.

As a number of key informants held fairly senior positions, supervised people under their command, or stayed in the conflict zone for a long time, they were asked to share their observations on others who participated in the rebellion, locals and outsiders. One, for example, was an active recruiter in St. Petersburg, and organized and sent over 20 teams of combat volunteers to the region in 2014. Commander *Mikhailo* was in charge of personnel records of "Slavyansk Brigade" which totaled up to 2,000 troops at its peak. Two commanders led battalions of 600 and 200 men respectively. Questions were asked about their age, social and educational background, motivations and similar characteristics. Russian military historian Yevgenii Norin, not a combatant himself, who regularly travelled to the region in 2014–2017 and held numerous interviews with local rebels and volunteer combatants, generously shared his data with the author. Although the interviews were conducted independently of each other, they returned similar data on demographics and motivations. This provides the basis for making a more general statement on who and why took part in the armed rebellion, with the caveat that more extensive sampling has to be done inside the region. Triangulation of information was not always possible. No doubt, future studies will enrich, correct and clarify the present narrative.

Collection of primary material was inevitably constrained by the circumstances of the war and ongoing conflict, and access to the informants.[1] It reflects what was possible in the circumstances. For example, no interviews with female ex-combatants were held, although male interviewees and secondary sources provided evidence that they existed. An interview was held with a wife of a local rebel from Donbas, although she personally was only involved in communications' activities. Material could be only collected on how male combatants viewed their female comrades-in-arms, but because no interviews with women were held, this data has not been used in the book as otherwise the gender angle would have been one-sided. Few interviews were held with working class combatants from Donbas, because opportunities to solicit such interviews were limited. The author spent time at two veterans' organizations—"Union of Donbas Volunteers" and "Novorossiya Movement," where observing group conversations and events was possible, which provided insights into the ex-combatants' world.

Use of interviews has several limitations. Firstly, the time lag because time has passed between the interview date and the actual events. The testimonies are retrospective reporting and rely on processed memories which may reflect present interpretations and tend to suppress certain facts, especially if they are traumatic or uncomfortable, and highlight more rewarding experiences.[2] Secondly, individuals can characterize the social process of conflict not how it is, but how it is *ought to* be, arranging their narrative accordingly. All interviewees, not only direct conflict participants, had own political views, and very few managed to rise above them and try to be impartial. The other limitation is that the participants observed the events from different angles and in different places. This can lead to apparent contradictions. For example, some interviewees insisted that no negotiations were held with Kyiv in the earlier conflict period before the OSCE became formally involved, while others maintained that informal talks were going on and off at the time, and continue to this day (spring of 2017). In fact, contradictions in accounts are inevitable and it would be unnatural for everybody to tell the same story. Individuals in extreme circumstances are capable of pursuing inconsistent and seeming mutually exclusive lines of action as they are preparing for different turns of events, not everyone made their final choice and they try to keep their options open.

Interviews, and individual and group conversations with other categories of respondents from Ukraine included ordinary Donbas residents who were not politically involved in the conflict but whose lives have been changed by it, of different leanings, with prevalence of females. Political experts with diverse and sometimes opposing political orientations were interviewed in Kyiv, as well as a scholar and a journalist who were originally from Donbas, but who lived outside the region. Interviews in Moscow were conducted with journalists and bloggers who covered the conflict during its most acute phase. Two of them belonged to Russian liberal media, two to oppositionist patriotic circles, and one was mainstream. This was supplemented by interviews with about ten scholars and political analysts, three of them with ties to Russian officialdom. Several staff of international organizations and humanitarian agencies working in the region were interviewed on a condition of anonymity, because they spoke in their private capacity rather than representatives of their organizations. Many respondents are only identified by general descriptions. Extreme caution was applied with regards to identification of respondents from the region who continue to live in precarious circumstances of insecurity and uncertainty and some of them are in displacement. Only a few of them are put on the interviewees list.

Research for chapter 3 on Crimea was based on interviews and group discussions organized in 2012 with participants of the Crimea Policy Dialogue who represented three different communities of the peninsula. Other respondents in Crimea, most of them Simferopol-based, were interviewed at the time, and follow-up interviews were conducted with some of them in Kyiv in 2015. They were supplemented by communication from a London-based analyst originally from Crimea who witnessed the key events in 2014 firsthand.

Interviews were supplemented by written sources. Where possible, an event reported in an interview was confirmed by published information, and this public source was cited. For some events, publicly available information is too contradictory or non-available. History of the developments on the ground was cross-checked with Pavel Gubarev's account in his *Torch of Novorossiya* book, study of the conflict authored by Russian defense academic Anatolii Tsyganok and with memoirs of ex-combatants.[3] Key events of the military campaign of 2014 were derived and processed from the accounts published by Yevgenii Norin and Alexander Juchkovsky in *Sputnik i Pogrom*, articles by Ilya Barabanov (Kommersant Daily) and Vladimir Dergachoff (gazeta. ru), and journalistic investigations in *Novaya Gazeta*. Ukrainian sources were regularly accessed, such as UNIAN information agency, Ukrainska Pravda, websites such as korrespondent.net, LB.ua, interfax.com.ua, and liga.net, and social media postings were accessed through yandex.ua. Rebel websites and Live Journal postings were regularly consulted, as well as videos uploaded on YouTube. Information was also provided by the "Union of Donbas Volunteers." Western journalists' accounts are referred to, but there are relatively few of them.

The study uses opinion polls, which are illustrative of trends, and allow confirming or denying information from interviews. The word of caution is needed: although sociological research in Ukraine is well-developed, surveys undertaken amid security pressures may not be entirely accurate, and sampling may not adequately reflect the population's composition because population is often on the move. Moreover, research institutions have been also polarized along political lines, and are reputed to be associated with certain positions. Truly "independent" sources simply did not exist and there was no such thing as unbiased reporting. All sides sought to project their version of truth, although some information resources were more reliable than others. Efforts were made to verify where possible, but the book does not claim the last word of truth but rather the best possible approximation.

NOTES

1. On data problems in research on civil wars see Stathys Kalyvas, *The Logic of Violence in Civil Wars* (Cambridge: Cambridge University Press, 2006), 48–51.

2. This phenomenon was encountered by the author while leading the field investigation for the international Kyrgyzstan Inquiry Commission into June 2010 events in the South.

3. Anatolii Tsyganok, *Donbass: Unfinished War. Civil War in Ukraine (2014–2016)* (Moscow: Association of Researchers of Russian Society (AIRO–XXI), 2017), Gennadi Dubovoy, *Rytsari Novorossiyi: Chronicle of a Correspondent* (Moscow: Knizhnyi Mir, 2017).

Bibliography

Aleprete Michael E. Jr., "Minimizing Loss: Explaining Russian Policy Choices during the Ukrainian Crisis," *The Soviet and Post-Soviet Review* 44 (2017): 53–75.

Allison, Roy, "Russian 'deniable' intervention in Ukraine: How and Why Russia Broke the Rules," *International Affairs* 90, no. 6 (2014): 1255–1297.

Amnesty International, "Ukraine: Abuses and War Crimes by the *Aidar* Volunteer Battalion in the north Luhansk region," 8 September 2014.

Amnesty International, "Ukraine: Breaking Bodies: Torture and Summary Killings in Eastern Ukraine," May 22, 2015.

Armstrong, John, *Ukrainian Nationalism*, 2nd edition (New York: Columbia University Press, 1963).

Armstrong, Patrick, Russian Federation Sitrep, October 22, 2015, and "Ukraine in the Mirror of the Mind," December 6, 2013, https://patrickarmstrong.ca/2013/12/

Ashmore, Richard, Jussim, L and Wilder, D., eds. *Social Identity, Intergroup Conflict and Conflict Reduction* (Oxford: Oxford University Press, 2001).

Aspinall, Edward, *Islam and Nation: Separatist Rebellion in Aceh, Indonesia* (Stanford: Stanford University Press, 2009).

Averre, Derek, "The Ukraine Conflict: Russia's Challenge to European Security Governance," *Europe-Asia Studies* 68, no. 44 (2016), 699–725.

Avruch, Kevin, *Culture and Conflict resolution* (Washington, DC: US Institute of Peace Press, 1998).

Avruch, Kevin, "Culture Theory, culture clash, and the practice of conflict resolution," 241–255, in *Handbook of Conflict Analysis and Resolution*, eds. Dennis J. D. Sandole et al. (Abingdon: Routledge, 2008)

Benjamin, Walter, *On the Concept of History* (Frankfurt am Main: GesammelteSchriften I:2. SuhrkampVerlag, 1974), in translation.

Berti, Benedetta, *Armed Political Organisations* (Baltimore: John Hopkins University Press, 2013), 130–175.

Bolt, Neville, *The Violent Image: Insurgent Propaganda and the New Revolutionaries* (New York: Columbia University Press, 2012).

Borum Randy and Fein, Robert, "The Psychology of Foreign Fighters," *Studies in Conflict and Terrorism* 40, no. 3 (2017), 248–266.

Boyd-Barrett, Oliver, *Western mainstream media and the Ukraine Crisis: A Study in Conflict Propaganda* (London: Routledge, 2016)

Boyne, Sean, "Uncovering Irish Republican Army," *Jane's Intelligence Review*, 1 August 1996. http://www.pbs.org/wgbh/pages/frontline/shows/ira/inside/weapons.html

Brass, Paul R. *Theft of an Idol: Text and Context in the Representation of Collective Violence* (Princeton, NJ: Princeton University Press, 1997).

Bremmer, Ian, "The Politics of Ethnicity: Russians in the New Ukraine," *Europe-Asia Studies* 46: 2 (1994).

Brendan O'Duffy, "IRA: Irish Republican Army (Oglaighnah Eireann)" in *Terror, Insurgency, and the State: Ending Protracted Conflicts*, eds. Marianne Heiberg, Brendan O'Leary, and John Tirman (Philadelphia, PA: University of Pennsylvania Press, 2007), 250–284.

Brubaker Rogers and Cooper, Frederick, "Beyond Identity," *Theory and Society* 29, no. 1 (2000): 1–47.

Brunova-Kalisetskaya, Irina and Duhnich, Ol'ga, "Психологические Образы языково -культурных угроз в восприятии городских жителей Крыма," in *Crimea Policy Dialogue* (Moscow: Crimean Policy Dialogue, 2011).

Bullough, Oliver, *Looting Ukraine: How East and West Teamed up to Steal a Country* (London: Legatum Institute, 2014).

Cairns, Ed, *Children and Political Violence* (Cambridge: Blackwell, 1996).

Cairns, Ed, Kenworthy, J., Campbell A., and Hewstone, M., "The role of in-group identification, religious group membership, and intergroup conflict in moderating in-group and out-group affect," *British Journal of Social Psychology* 45 (2006): 701–716.

Chaisty Paul and Whitefield, Stephen, "Support for separatism in southern and eastern Ukraine is lower than you think," The Monkey Cage blog at *Washington Post Online*, February 6, 2015.

Cheng, Christine, "Conflict Capital," British International Studies Association conference paper, June 19, 2015.

Collier Paul and Hoeffler, Anke E., "Greed and Grievance in Civil War." Oxford Economic Papers 56, no. 4 (2004): 563–595.

Collier, George Allen, Lowery, Elizabeth, *Quaratiello 'Basta!: Land and the Zapatista Rebellion in Chiapas* (Oakland, CA: Food First Books, 2005).

Connolly, Richard, "The Empire Strikes Back: Economic Statecraft and the Securitisation of Political Economy in Russia," *Europe-Asia Studies* 68, no. 4 (2016), 750–773.

Costalli, Stefano and Ruggeri, Andrea, "Indignation, Ideologies, and Armed Mobilization Civil War in Italy, 1943–45," *International Security* 40, no. 2 (2015), 119–157.

Czuperski, M., Herbst, J., Higgins, E., Polyakova, A., and Wilson, D., *Hiding in plain sight: Putin's war in Ukraine* (Washington, DC: Atlantic Council, 2015).

d'Anieri, Paul, "Ethnic Tensions and State Strategies: understanding the survival of the Ukrainian state," 25–30, in *Democratic Revolution in Ukraine: from Kuchmagate to Orange Revolution*, ed. Taras Kuzio (Abingdon: Routledge, 2009).

de Figueiredo, Jr. Rui J. P., and Weingast, Barry R., "The rationality of fear: Political opportunism and ethnic conflict," in *Civil Wars, Insecurity, and Intervention*, eds. Walter and Snyder (New York: Columbia University Press, 1999), 261–302.

de Waal, Alex,"Mission without end? Peacekeeping in the African political marketplace," *International Affairs* 85, no. 1 (2008): 99–113.

Dean, James, "Ukraine: Europe's Forgotten Economy," *Challenge*, 43, no. 6 (2000), 93–108.

Deigh, John, "Cognitivism in the Theory of Emotions," *Ethics* 104, no. 4 (2000): 824–854.

Derluguian, Georgi M. and Serge Cipko, "The Politics of Identity in a Russian Borderland Province: The Kuban Neo-Cossack Movement, 1989–1996," *Europe-Asia Studies* 49: 8 (1997): 1485–1500.

DiJohn, Jonathan and Putzel, James, "Political Settlements," GSDRC Issues Paper (Birmingham: University of Birmingham, 2009).

Dittmer, Jason, *Popular Culture, Geopolitics and Identity* (Lanham: Rowman & Littlefield, 2010).

Driscoll, Jesse, "Commitment Problems or Bidding Wars? Rebel Fragmentation as Peace-Building," *Journal of Conflict Resolution* 56, no. 1 (2012): 118–149.

Driscoll, Jesse and Zachary Steinert-Threlkeld, "Alternative Facts: Social Media as Propaganda in Post-Maidan Ukraine" (March 8, 2017), at *SSRN*: https://ssrn.com/abstract=2825452

Dubovoy, Gennadyi, *Rytsari Novorossiyi: Chronicle of a Correspondent* (Moscow: Knizhnyi Mir, 2017).

Dziuba, Ivan, *Internationalism or Russification? A Study in the Soviet Nationalities Problem*, trans. from Ukrainian, edited by M. Davies (London: Weidenfeld and Nicolson, 1968).

Edwards, Maxim, "Symbolism of the Donetsk People's Republic," *Open Democracy*, 9 June 2014.

Elbadawi, Ibrahim, and Sambanis, Nicholas "How Much War Will We See? Explaining the Prevalence of Civil War," *Journal of Conflict Resolution* 46, no. 3 (2002), 307–334.

EPLO, "How to make the peace processes in Ukraine more inclusive?" Civil Society Dialogue Network Meeting report, 28 February 2017, Vienna, Austria.

Escobar, Pepe, "From Minsk to Wales, Germany is Key," *RT*, 28 August 2014.

European External Action Service, "Myths about the Association Agreement—setting the facts straight," http://eeas.europa.eu/archives/delegations/ukraine/documents/myths_aa_en.pdf

Evangelista, Matthew, "Paradoxes of Violence and Self-determination," *Ethnopolitics* 14, no. 5 (2015): 451–460.

Fall, Bernard, "The Theory and Practice of Insurgency and Counterinsurgency," *Naval War College Review* (Winter 1998): 46–57. http://www.au.af.mil/au/awc/awcgate/navy/art5-w98.htm

Fearon, James D. and Laitin, David D., "Violence and the Social Construction of Ethnic Identity," *International Organization* 54, no. 4 (2000): 845–877.

Fearon, James D., and Laitin, David D., "Ethnicity, Insurgency, and Civil War," *American Political Science Review* 97, no. 1 (2003): 75–90.

Ferguson, Jonathan, and Jenzen-Jones, N.R. "An Examination of Arms & Munitions in the Ongoing Conflict in Ukraine." *Armament Research Services Research Report,* no. 3 (2014).

Ferguson, Neil, "The impact of political violence on moral reasoning: Socio-political reasoning in Northern Ireland," in *On behalf of Others: The Morality of Care in a Global World*, eds. S. Scuzzarello, C. Kinnvall and K. Renwick Monroe (Oxford: Oxford University Press, 2009), 233–254.

Ferguson, Neil and McKeown, Shelley, "Social Identity Theory and Intergroup Conflict in Northern Ireland" in *Understanding Peace and Conflict Through Social Identity Theory*, eds. S. McKeown et al. (Peace Psychology Book Series, Springer International Publishing Switzerland 2016).

Flam, Helena, "Emotions' map: a research agenda," 19–40, in *Emotions and Social Movements*, eds. Helena Flam and Debra King (Abingdon: Routledge, 2007).

Fournier, Anna, "Mapping Identities: Russian Resistance to Linguistic Ukrainisation in Central and Eastern Ukraine," *Europe-Asia Studies*, 54, no. 3 (2002), 415–433.

Friedman, George, "A Net Assessment of Europe," *Stratfor Geopolitical Weekly*, 26 May 2015.

Gessen, Keith. "Why Not Kill Them All?" *London Review of Books* 36, no. 17 (September 11, 2014), 18–22.

Glen, Carol M., "Nationalism, Identity and Scotland's Referendum," *Contemporary European Politics* 1 (2015), 5–19.

Giles, Keir, "The Next Phase of Russian Information Warfare," NATO Strategic Communication Centre of Excellence, undated.

Giuliano, Elise, *Constructing Grievance: Ethnic Nationalism in Russia's Republics* (Ithaca: Cornell University Press, 2011).

Giuliano, Elise, "The Social Bases of Support for Self-determination in East Ukraine," *Ethnopolitics* 14, no. 5 (2015): 513–522.

Goldie, Peter, *The Emotions: A Philosophical Exploration* (Oxford: Oxford University Press, 1994).

Gubarev, Pavel, *Факел Новороссии* [Torch of Novorossiya] (St. Petersburg: Piter, 2016).

Halliday, Fred, "The romance of non-state actors," (21–37), 35, in *Non-state Actors in World Politics*, eds. Josselin and Wallace (Basingstoke: Palgrave, 2001).

Hardin, Russell, *One for All: The Logic of Group Conflict* (Princeton: Princeton University Press, 1995).

Haukkala, H. "From Cooperative to Contested Europe? The Conflict in Ukraine as a Culmination of a Long-Term Crisis in EU-Russia Relations," *Journal of Contemporary European Studies* 23, no. 1 (2015): 25–40.

Hegghammer, Thomas, "The Rise of Muslim Foreign Fighters: Islam and the Globalization of Jihad," *International Security* 35, no. 3 (2010–2011), 53–91, annex (unpaged).

Himka, John-Paul. "Western Ukraine in the Interwar Period," *Nationalities Papers* 22, no. 2 (1994): 347–363.

Hobsbawn, Eric and Ranger, Terence, *The Invention of Tradition* (Cambridge: Cambridge University Press, 1992).

Holman, Paul G Jr., "Russo-Ukrainian Relations: The Containment Legacy" in *Ethnic Nationalism and Regional Conflict. The Former Soviet Union and Yugoslavia*, eds. Duncan Raymond W. and Holman Paul G. Jr (Boulder: Westview Press, 1994).

Horowitz, Donald L., *Ethnic Groups in Conflict* (Berkeley: University of California Press, 1985).

Hrytsak, Yaroslav, "National Identities in Post-Soviet Ukraine: The Case of Lviv and Donetsk," *Harvard Ukrainian Studies* 22 (1998): 263–281.

Hudson, Victoria, "Forced to Friendship'? Russian (Mis-)Understandings of Soft Power and the Implications for Audience Attraction in Ukraine," *Politics* 35, no. 3–4 (2015): 330–346.

Hudson, Victoria, "The Ukrainian Orthodox Church of the Moscow Patriarchate as a "Tool" of Russian Soft Power in the Wake of Ukraine's 2013 Euromaidan," *Europe-Asia Studies* 70 (2018).

Huffman, Celia Cook, "The role of identity in conflict," 19–31, in *Handbook of conflict analysis and resolution*, eds. Dennis J. D. Sandole et al. (Abingdon: Routledge, 2008).

Human Rights Watch, "Crimea: Attacks, 'Disappearances' by Illegal Forces. Rein in Units Operating Outside Law" March 14, 2014.

Human Rights Watch, "Ukraine: Human Rights Watch Letter to Acting President Turchynov and President-Elect Poroshenko," 6 June 2014.

Human Rights Watch, "World Report 2015: Ukraine Events of 2014"

Human Rights Watch, "Ukraine: Widespread Use of Cluster Munitions. Government Responsible for Cluster Attacks on Donetsk," 14 October 2014.

Huntington, Samuel P., "The Clash of Civilizations?" *Foreign Affairs* (1993): 22–49.

ICRC, "Ukraine: ICRC calls on all sides to respect international humanitarian law," News Release, 14/12523 August 2014.

International Crisis Group, "Ukraine: Running out of Time" *Europe Report* 231 (2014).

International Crisis Group, "Eastern Ukraine: A Dangerous Winter," *Europe Report* 235 (December 2014).

International Crisis Group. "The Ukraine Crisis: Risks of Renewed Military Conflict after Minsk II," *Crisis Group Europe Briefing* 73 (2015).

International Crisis Group, "Russia and the Separatists in Eastern Ukraine," *Europe Briefing* 79 (5 February 2016).

Josselin, Daphne and Wallace, William, "Non-state actors in World Politics: a Framework," in *Non-State Actors in World Politics*, eds. Josselin and Wallace (Basingstoke: Palgrave, 2001).

Kalyvas, Stathys, *The Logic of Violence in Civil Wars* (Cambridge: Cambridge University Press, 2006).

Kapferer, Bruce, *Legends of People/Myths of State: Violence, Intolerance, and Political Culture in Sri Lanka and Australia* (Washington, DC: Smithsonian Institution Press, 1988).

Karabanova, Viktoriya, "Linguistic Tools for Nation State Building: The Relationship between Ukraine and Its Russian-Speaking Crimea," *Polish Sociological Review*, 144 (2003): 417–433.

Karagiannis, Emmanuel, "Ukrainian volunteer fighters in the eastern front: ideas, political-social norms and emotions as mobilization mechanisms," *Southeast European and Black Sea Studies*, 16, no. 1 (2016): 139–153.

Katchanovski, Ivan "Small Nations but Great Differences: Political Orientations and Cultures of the Crimean Tatars and the Gagauz," *Europe-Asia Studies*, 57, no. 6 (2005): 877–894.

Katchanovski, Ivan "The Separatist War in Donbas: A Violent Break-up of Ukraine?" *European Politics and Society* (2016), 473–489.

Kaufman, Stuart J., *Modern Hatreds: The Symbolic Politics of Ethnic War* (Ithaca, NY: Cornell University Press, 2001).

Kiryukhin, Denys, "Roots and Features of Modern Ukrainian National Identity and Nationalism," in *Ukraine and Russia: People, Politics, Propaganda and Perspectives*, eds. Agnieszka Pikulicka-Wilczewska and Richard Sakwa (E-International Relations: 2015), 57–65.

Kofman, Michael "Russian Hybrid Warfare and Other Dark Arts", *War on the Rocks* March 11, 2016.

Koinova, Maria, "Diasporas and secessionist conflicts: the mobilization of the Armenian, Albanian and Chechen diasporas," *Ethnic and Racial Studies* 34, no. 2 (2011): 333–356. Uppsala Conflict Database.

Kolsoe, Pal, *Russians in the Former Soviet Republics* (London: Hurst & Company, 1995).

Kolstoe, Pal, "National Symbols as Signs of Unity and Division," in *Ethnic and Racial Studies* 29. no. 4 (2006): 676–701.

Korostelina, Carina, "The Multiethnic State-building Dilemma: National and Ethnic Minorities' Identities in the Crimea," *National Identities*, 5 (2003), 141–159.

Kudelia, Serhiy, "The Donbas Rift," *Russian Politics & Law* 54, no. 1 (2016): 5–27.

Kulyk, Volodymyr, "National Identity in Ukraine: Impact of Euromaidan and the War," *Europe-Asia Studies* 68, no. 4 (2016): 588–608.

Kuromiya, Hiroaki, *Freedom and Terror in the Donbas* (Cambridge: Cambridge University Press, 1998).

Kutsenko, Ol'ga, "Тенденции Формирования и Структура Региональной Элиты на Украине," in *Ethnic and Regional Conflicts in Eurasia*, Book 2, Russia, Ukraine, Belarus, eds. Zverev Alexei, Coppiters, Bruno and Trenin, Dmitrii (Moscow: Ves' Mir, 1997), 194–209.

Kuzio, Taras, "Identity and Nation-building in Ukraine: Defining the "Other"', *Ethnicities* 1, no. 3 (2001): 348.

Kuzio, Taras, "The Myth of the Civic State: A Critical Survey of Hans Kohn's Framework for Understanding Nationalism," *Ethnic and Racial Studies* 25, no. 1 (2002), 20–39.

Kuzio, Taras, *Ukraine–Crimea–Russia: Triangle of Conflict* (Stuttgart: Ibidem-Verlag, 2007).

Kuzio, Taras, "Ukraine between a Constrained EU and Assertive Russia," *Journal of Common Markets Studies* 55, no. 1 (2017): 103–120.

Laruelle, Marlene, "The three colors of Novorossiya, or the Russian nationalist myth-making of the Ukrainian crisis," *Post-Soviet Affairs* 32, no. 1 (2016): 55–74.

Lavrov, Anton, "Civil War in the East," 202–227, and "Aircraft, Tanks and the Artillery in the Donbas," 228–249, in *Brothers Armed: Military Aspects of the Crisis in Ukraine*, eds. Colby Howard and Ruslan Pukhov, Centre for Analysis of Strategies and Technologies (CAST), Moscow; (Minneapolis : East View Press, 2015).

Lieven Anatol, *Chechnya: Tombstone of Russian Power* (New Haven and London: Yale University Press, 1998).

Lindemann, Stefan, "Inclusive Elite Bargains and the Dilemma of Unproductive Peace: a Zambian case study," *Third World Quarterly* 32, no. 10 (2011): 1843–1869.

Lipset, Seymour Martin and Rokkan, Stein, *Party Systems and Voter Alignments* (Toronto: Free Press, 1967).

Loshkariov Ivan D. and Andrey A. Sushentsov, "Radicalization of Russians in Ukraine: from 'accidental' diaspora to rebel movement," *Southeast European and Black Sea Studies*, 16, no. 1 (2016): 71–90.

Lynch, Dov, 'Europe Faces Russia', *Chaillot Paper* 60 (Paris: EU Institute for Security Studies, 2003).

Maddens, Bart et al. "The National Consciousness of the Flemings and the Walloons. An Empirical Investigation" in *Nationalism in Belgium: Shifting Identities, 1780–1995*, eds. Kas Deprez and Louis Vos (Basingstoke: Palgrave McMillan, 1998).

Malet, David, *Foreign Fighters: Transnational Identity in Civil Conflicts* (Oxford: Oxford University Press, 2013).

Malet, Michael, *Nestor Makhno in the Russian Civil War* (London: Macmillan, 1982).

Malyarenko, Tetyana "A gradually escalating conflict: Ukraine from the Euromaidan to the war with Russia," The Routledge Handbook of Ethnic Conflict, 2nd edition, eds. Karl Cordell and Stefan Wolff (Abingdon: Routledge Handbooks, 2016).

Malyarenko, Tetyana and Galbreath, David J., "Paramilitary motivation in Ukraine: beyond integration and abolition," *Southeast European and Black Sea Studies*, 16, no. 1 (2016): 113–138.

Malygina, Katerina, "Ukraine as a neo-patrimonial state: understanding political change in Ukraine in 2005–2010," *Journal for Labour and Social Affairs in Eastern Europe* 13, no. 1 (2010): 7–27.

Marianne Heiberg, Brendan O'Leary and John Tirman, eds. *Terror, Insurgency, and the State: Ending Protracted Conflicts* (Philadelphia: University of Pennsylvania Press, 2007).

Marples, David R, "Stepan Bandera: The Resurrection of a Ukrainian National Hero," *Europe-Asia Studies* 58, no. 4 (2006): 555–566.

Matuszak, Slawomir, "The Oligarchic Democracy: The Influence of Business Groups on Ukrainian Politics," OSW Studies no. 42 (Warsaw: Centre for Eastern Studies, 2012).

Matveeva, Anna 'Chechnya: Dynamics of War and Peace', in *Problems of Post-Communism* 54, no. 3 (2007): 3–15.

Matveeva, Anna, "North Eastern Caucasus: Drifting Away From Russia," in *Fire from Below: How the Caucasus Shaped Russian Politics since 1980s*, ed. Robert Bruce Ware (New York: Bloomsbury, 2013), 253–282.

Matveeva, Anna, "Violence in Kyrgyzstan, vacuum in the region: the case for Russia-EU joint crisis management," (London: London School of Economics, Civil Society & Human Security Research Unit Working Paper, 2011).

McFaul, Michael, "Faulty Powers: Who Started the Ukraine Crisis?," *Foreign Affairs* (November/December 2014).

McGarry, John and O'Leary, Brendan, *Explaining Northern Ireland: Broken Images* (Oxford: Blackwell, 1995).

Mearsheimer, John J. 'Moscow's Choice,' *Foreign Affairs* 93, no. 6 (2014), 167–171.

Mearsheimer, John J. "Why the Ukraine Crisis Is the West's Fault: the Liberal Delusions That Provoked Putin," *Foreign Affairs* 93, no. 5 (2014), 1–12.

Memorial Human Rights Centre, Moscow, 30 September 2014, http://www.memo.ru/d/211293.html

Menon, Rajan and Rumer, Eugene B., *Conflict in Ukraine: The Unwinding of the Post–Cold War Order* (Boston: The MIT Press, 2015).

Mercouris, Alexander, "End Game in Ukraine–Russia Wins," *Russia Insider*, 12 October 2016.

Metz, Steven, "Insurgency after the cold war," *Small Wars and Insurgencies* 5 (1994): 63–82.

Moxon-Browne, Edward, "National identity in Northern Ireland," in *Social attitudes in Northern Ireland: The first report*, eds. P. Stringer and G. Robinson (Belfast, Northern Ireland: Blackstaff Press, 1991).

Mufti, Malik, "Elite bargains and the onset of political liberalization in Jordan," *Comparative Political Studies* 32, no. 1 (1999): 100–129.

Münster, Anna, "Transnational Islam in Russia and Crimea," Research Paper (London: Chatham House, 2014).

Mykhnenko, Vlad 'From Exit to Take-Over: The Evolution of the Donbass as an Intentional Community, Paper for Workshop No 20. The Politics of Utopia: Intentional Communities as Social Science Microcosms, Uppsala, 13–18 April 2004

Narvselius, Eleanore, "Polishness as a Site of Memory and Arena for Construction of Multicultural Heritage in L'viv," 84, in *Whose Memory? Whose Future?*, ed. Barbara Tornquist - Plewa (New York: Berghahn Books, 2016).

Nayyem, Mustafa, "Uprising in Ukraine: How It All Began," Open Society Foundation, April 4, 2014.

Nemtsov, Boris, "Putin. War," (Moscow, 2015) www.4freerussia.org/putin.war

Nordlinger, Eric A., *Conflict regulation in divided societies* (Cambridge, Mass: Center for International Affairs, Harvard University, 1972).

Norin, Yevgenii, *Battle of the Year: Seizure of Debaltseve* (Moscow: Sputnik i Pogrom, 2015).

Norin, Yevgenii, "Fall of Donetsk Airport," *Sputnik-i-Pogrom* (Moscow: Sputnik i Pogrom, 2015).

Norin, Yevgenii, "День, когда Украина дрогнула: Иловайская мясорубка," 1st part, [Battle for Ilovaisk] (Moscow: Sputnik i Pogrom, 2015).

Norin, Yevgenii, "Звезда и смерть Южного котла ВСУ," [Star and Death of Ukrainian Armed Forces Southern Cauldron] (Moscow: Sputnik i Pogrom, 2015).

Norin, Yevgenii, "Сражение года: оборона Саур-Могилы," [Battle of the year: defence of Savur-Mohyla] (Moscow: *Sputnik i Pogrom*, 2015).

North, C. Et al. *In the Shadow of Violence: Politics, Economics, and the Problems of Development* (Cambridge: Cambridge University Press, 2013).

O'Loughlin, John, Toal, Gerard and Kolosov, Vladimir, "The rise and fall of "Novorossiya": examining support for a separatist geopolitical imaginary in southeast Ukraine," *Post-Soviet Affairs* 33, no. 2 (2017): 124–144.

"Organisation of Ukrainian Nationalists and the Ukrainian Insurgent Army," (Kyiv: Institute of Ukrainian History, Academy of Sciences of Ukraine, 1978): 385–386.

O'Reilly, Tim, "What is Web 2.0?" http://www.oreilly.com/pub/a/web2/archive/what-is-web-20.html

Office of the United Nations High Commissioner for Human Rights, "Reports on the Human Rights Situation in Ukraine," (Geneva/ Kyiv: April 2014, June 2014, February 2015, August 2015, June 2017).

Pearlman, Wendy and Cunningham, Kathleen Gallagher, "Nonstate Actors, Fragmentation, and Conflict Processes," *Journal of Conflict Resolution*, 56, no. 1 (2012): 3–15

Perez-Diaz, Victor M., *The Return of Civil Society: The Emergence of Democratic Spain* (Cambridge, M.A.: Harvard University Press, 1993).

Petersen, Roger D., *Understanding Ethnic Violence: Fear, Hatred, and Resentment in Twentieth-Century in Eastern Europe* (Cambridge: Cambridge University Press, 2002).

Petro, Nicolai N., *Russia's Orthodox Soft Power* (Washington, DC: Carnegie Center, March 2015).

Petro, Nikolai N., "Understanding the Other Ukraine: Identity and Allegiance in Russophone Ukraine," in *Ukraine and Russia: People, Politics, Propaganda and Perspectives*, eds. A. Pikulicka-Wilczewska and R. Sakwa (Bristol: E-International Relations Publishing, 2015).

Pirani, Simon and Yafimava, Katja, "Russian Gas Transit Across Ukraine Post-2019: pipeline scenarios, gas flow consequences, and regulatory constraints," *The Oxford Institute for Energy Studies*, OIES paper: NG 105 (2016).

Pirie, Paul S., "National Identity and Politics in Southern and Eastern Ukraine," *Europe-Asia Studies* 48, no. 7 (1996): 1079–1104.

Pomerantsev, Peter, *Nothing Is True And Everything Is Possible: The Surreal Heart of the New Russia* (New York: Public Affairs, 2014).

Pomeranz, William E., "Ground Zero: How a Trade Dispute Sparked the Russia–Ukraine Crisis," in Elizabeth A. Wood, William E. Pomeranz, E. Wayne Merry, and Maxim Trudolyubov, Roots of Russia's War in Ukraine (Washington DC: Woodrow Wilson Center Press, 2016).

Popescu, Nicu "Eurasian Union: the real, the imaginary and the likely," *Chaillot Paper* 132 (Paris: EUISS, 2014).

Pribytkova I., "Миграционная Ситуация в Украине," in *Migration Situation in the CIS Countries,* ed. Janna Zayonchkovskaya (Moscow: Komplex–Progress, 1999).

Prizel, Ilya, "The Influence of Ethnicity on Foreign Policy: the Case of Ukraine," in *National Identity and Ethnicity in Russia and the New States of Eurasia,* ed. Roman Szporluk (New York and London: M. E. Sharpe, 1994).

Prizel, Ilya, *National Identity and Foreign Policy: Nationalism and Leadership in Poland, Russia and Ukraine* (Cambridge: Cambridge University Press, 1998).

Protsyk, Oleh, "Majority-Minority Relations in the Ukraine," *JEMIE* 7 (Flensburg: European Centre for Minority Issues, 2008).

Puri, Samir, "Human Security and Dialogue Challenges in Ukraine's Donetsk Region," Report (London: Peaceful Change Initiative, 2016).

Regan, Patrick M., *Civil Wars and Foreign Powers: Interventions and Intrastate Conflict* (Ann Arbor, MI: University of Michigan Press, 2000).

Regan, Patrick M., "Third Party Interventions and the Duration of Intrastate Conflicts," *Journal of Conflict Resolution* 46, no. 1 (2002), 55–73.

Reicher, Stephen, "The Context of Social Identity: Domination, Resistance, and Change," *Political Psychology* 25 (2004): 921–945.

Reid, Anna, *Borderland: A Journey Through the History of Ukraine* (London: Weidenfeld & Nicolson, 2015).

Rękawek, Kacper "Neither "NATO's Foreign Legion" Nor the "Donbass International Brigades:" (Where Are All the) Foreign Fighters in Ukraine?" *PISM Policy Paper* 108: 6 (Warsaw: the Polish Institute of International Affairs, 2015).

Rid Thomas and Hecker, Marc, *War 2.0 Irregular Warfare in the Information Age* (Westpoint: Praeger Security International, 2009).

Rumer, Eugene, "Sending Weapons to Ukraine Won't Help," *Defense One,* 2 June 2014.

Sakwa, Richard, "Russian Nationalism and Democratic Development," in *Russia After the Cold War* eds. Michael Bowker and Cameron Ross (Harlow, Addison Wesley Longman, 1999): 199–220.

Sakwa, Richard, ed. *Chechnya: From Past to Future* (London: Anthem Press, 2005).

Sakwa, Richard, *Russian Politics and Society*, 4th edition (Abingdon: Routledge, 2008).

Sakwa, Richard,*Frontline Ukraine: Crisis in the Borderlands* (London: I.B. Tauris, 2015).

Sakwa, Richard, "The death of Europe? Continental Fates after Ukraine," *International Affairs* 91, no. 3 (2015).

Sambanis, Nicholas, "Do Ethnic and non ethnic civil wars have the same causes?," *Journal of Conflict Resolution* 45, no. 3 (2001), 259–282.

Sasse, Gwendolyn, *The Crimea question: Identity, Transition, and Conflict* (Cambridge, Massachusetts: Harvard Ukrainian Research Institute, 2007).

Sasse, Gwendolyn, "New Hope in Ukraine Conflict?," *ZOIS Spotlight,* 7 June 2017.

Scheipers, Sibylle, *Unlawful combatants: A genealogy of the Irregular Fighter* (Oxford: Oxford University Press, 2015).

Scobell, Andrew and Hammitt, Brad, "Goons, gunmen, and gendarmerie: Toward a reconceptualization of paramilitary formations," *Journal of Political and Military Sociology* 26 (1998), 213–227.

Shevchenko, Taras "Kateryna," translated by Mary Skrypnyk (Toronto: 1960), http://sites.utoronto.ca/elul/English/248/Shevchenko-Kateryna-Skrypnyk-trans.pdf

Shulman, Stephen "Cultures in Competition: Ukrainian Foreign Policy and the 'Cultural Threat' from Abroad," *Europe-Asia Studies*, 50: 2 (1998): 287–303.

Silvius, Ray "The Russian State, Eurasianism, and Civilisations in the Contemporary Global Political Economy," *Journal of Global Faultlines*, 2: 1 (2014): 44–69.

Sinisa, Malesevic, *Identity as Ideology: Understanding Ethnicity and Ideology* (Basingstoke: Palgrave Macmillan 2006).

Slobodchikoff, Michael O., "Challenging US Hegemony: The Ukrainian Crisis and Russian Regional Order," *The Soviet and Post-Soviet Review* 44 (2017): 76–95.

Smith, Anthony D., *National Identity* (London: Penguin, 1991).

Smith, Anthony D., *Ethno-symbolism and Nationalism: A Cultural Approach* (London: Taylor & Francis, 2009).

Smith, Graham and Wilson, Andrew, "Rethinking Russia's Post-Soviet Diaspora: The Potential for Political Mobilisation in Eastern Ukraine and North-East Estonia," *Europe-Asia Studies* 49, no. 5 (1997): 845–886.

Solchanyk, Roman "The Politics of State Building: Centre-Periphery Relations in Post-Soviet Ukraine," *Europe-Asia Studies*, 46: 1 (1994): 47–68.

Speedie, David C., "Soft Power": The Values that Shape Russian Foreign Policy," *U.S. Global Engagement*, July 30, 2015.

Stepanova, Ekaterina, chapter "Russia," in *The Oxford Handbook of the Responsibility to Protect*, eds. Alex Bellamy, Tim Dunne (Oxford: Oxford University Press, 2016).

Stephenson, Svetlana, *Gangs of Russia: from Streets to Corridors of Power* (Ithaca: Cornell University Press, 2015).

Sutyagin, Igor, "Russian Forces in Ukraine," Research Report (London: RUSI, 2015).

Swain, Adam, and Mykhnenko, Vlad, "The Ukrainian Donbas 'in transition'," in *Re-Constructing the Post-Soviet Industrial Region: The Donbas in Transition*, ed. Swain Adam (London: Routledge, 2007).

Tajfel, Henri, *Human Groups and Social Categories: Studies in Social Psychology* (Cambridge: Cambridge University Press, 1981).

Tambiah, *Stanley, Leveling Crowds: Ethnonationalist Conflicts and Collective Violence in South Asia* (Berkeley: University of California Press, 1996).

Tereshchenko, Antonina, "Regional Diversity and Education for 'National' Citizenship in Ukraine: the Construction of Citizenship Identities for Borderland Youth," in *Naturalization Policies, Education and Citizenship: Multicultural and Multi-Nation Societies in International Perspective*, ed. Dina Kiwan (Basingstoke: Springer, Palgrave, 2013).

Toal, Gerard, *Near Abroad: Putin, the West and the Contest over Ukraine and the Caucasus* (Oxford: Oxford University Press, 2017).

Trenin, Dmitrii, *The Ukraine Crisis and the Resumption of Great-Power Rivalry* (Moscow: Carnegie Moscow Center, 2014).

Tsyganok, Anatolii, *Donbass: Unfinished War. Civil War in Ukraine (2014–2016)* (Moscow: Association of Researchers of Russian Society (AIRO–XXI), 2017).

Turkina, Ekaterina, "Russia-Ukraine Crisis: Value-Based and Generational Perspective," *Studies in Ethnicity and Nationalism* 15, no. 1 (2015).

Ugarriza, Juan E. and Craig, Matthew J. "The Relevance of Ideology to Contemporary Armed Conflicts: A Quantitative Analysis of Former Combatants in Colombia," *Journal of Conflict Resolution* 57, no. 3 (2012): 445–477.

"Ukraine–The Human Face of the Eastern Conflict," conference report, by ACF, DDG, DRC, PiN and NRC (Brussels: 23 January 2017).

Vlasov, Sergei and Popovkin, Valerii, "Проблема Регионализма в Структуре Государственной Власти и Политике Украины," in *Ethnic and Regional Conflicts in Eurasia*, Book 2: Russia, Ukraine, Belarus, eds. Zverev Alexei, Coppiters, Bruno and Trenin, Dmitrii (Moscow: Ves' Mir, 1997).

von Hagen, Mark, "Does Ukraine Have a History?" *Slavic Review* 54, no. 3 (1995): 658–673.

Walzer, Michael, "On the role of symbolism in political thought," *Political Science Quarterly* 82, no. 2 (1967), 191–204.

Way, Lucan, "Between National Division and Rapacious Individualism Ukraine before and after the Orange Revolution," *The Brown Journal of World Affairs*, 14, no. 2 (2008).

Whiteside, Craig, "Lighting the Path: the Evolution of the Islamic State Media Enterprise (2003–2016)," (The Hague: ICCT Research Paper, 2016).

"Who feels Scottish?' National identities and ethnicity in Scotland" (Manchester: University of Manchester, ESRC Centre on Dynamics of Ethnicity (CoDE), 2014).

Williams, Brian Glyn, *The Crimean Tatars: From Soviet Genocide to Putin's Conquest* (Oxford: Oxford University Press, 2015).

Wilson, Andrew, "The Growing Challenge to Kiev from the Donbas," RFE/RL Research Report 2, no. 33 (August 20, 1993).

Wilson, Andrew, "The Donbas between Ukraine and Russia: The use of history in political disputes," *Journal of Contemporary History*, 30, no. 2 (1995).

Wilson, Andrew, *Ukraine crisis: What it means for the West* (New Haven, CT: Yale University Press, 2014).

Wilson, Andrew, "The Donbas in 2014: Explaining Civil Conflict Perhaps, but not Civil War," *Europe-Asia Studies*, 68, no. 4 (2016): 631–652.

Winter, Charlie "Media Jihad: The Islamic State's Doctrine for Information Warfare," The International Centre for the Study of Radicalisation and Political Violence (London: Centre for Strategic Dialogue, 2017)

Winter, Charlie, *Documenting the Virtual Caliphate* (London: Quilliam, 2015).

Wood, Elizabeth Jean, "The emotional benefits of insurgency in El Salvador," 267–280, in *Passionate Politics: Emotions and social movements*, eds. Jeff Goodwin, James M Jasper and Francesca Polletta (Chicago: University of Chicago Press, 2001).

Yekelchyk, Serhy, *The Conflict in Ukraine: What Everyone needs to know*, (Oxford: Oxford University Press, 2015).

Yudina, Natalia, Al'perovich, Vera, "Затишье перед бурей? Ксенофобия и радикальный национализм и противодействие им в 2014 году в России," (Moscow: Sova Centre, 2015).

Zartmann, William, "Mutually hurting stalemate and beyond", in *International Conflict Resolution after the Cold War*, eds. Paul C. Stern and Daniel Druckman, Committee on International Conflict Resolution (Washington, DC: The National Academies Press, 2000), 225–250.

Zevelev, Igor, "The Russian World Boundaries: Russia's National Identity Transformation and New Foreign Policy Doctrine," *Russia in Global Affairs*, June 7, 2014.

Zevelev, Igor, "The Russian World in Moscow's Strategy," CSIS, August 22, 2016.

Zhukov, Yuri M., "Trading Hard Hats for Combat Helmets: The Economics of Rebellion in Eastern Ukraine," *Journal of Comparative Economics* 44 (2016).

Zhukov, Yuri M. and Baum, Matthew A., "Reporting Bias and Information Warfare," International Studies Association Annual Convention conference paper, Atlanta, GA, 16–19 March 2016.

Index

Abkhazia, 56, 197, 205, 208, 280, 287, 297;
  Abkhaz, 98, 197, 205, 287, 297
Accession Treaty with Russia, 64
Adalet Party, 52
Adleiba, Irakli, 197
Afghanistan, 10, 99, 103, 122, 196, 225, 226
agency, human, 9, 13, 16, 246
Akhmetov, Rinat, 71–73, 84, 85, 87, 188n6, 242, 251, 252
Aksyonov, Sergei, 59, 62, 63, 277
Alchevsk, 135, 152, 162
Aleprete, Michael, 271
Almaz-Antey, 157–58
Amnesty International, 124, 208
Anti-Terrorist Operation (ATO), 108, 121, 122, 127, 129, 145, 147–55, 159–62, 164, 170–72, 174, 199, 202, 209, 231, 243, 253, 255, 257
Antiufeev, Vladimir, 132–33, 162, 169
Arab Spring, 3, 94
armed groups, 12, 104, 164
Armstrong, Patrick, 292n75
asymmetric warfare, 14, 146
Autonomous Republic of Crimea (ARC), 47, 50, 51, 53, 54, 56, 59;
  Supreme Council, 56, 60, 63
Avakov, Arsen, 83, 123, 125, 241

Avdiivka, 150, 174, 186
Avidzba, Akhra, 187, 197, 222
Azov Sea, 69, 73, 165

Babitsky, Andrei, 208, 213n50
Bakhmut, 69, 174, 244
Bandera, Stepan, 27, 32, 200
Barabanov, Ilya, 173, 181
Baratelia, Stavros, 197
Barkashov, Alexander, 224
Basaev, Shamil, 208
Basurin, Eduard, 185
battalions:
  Aidar, 85, 123, 124, 151–52, 208, 245, 277;
  Azov, 126, 155, 174;
  Batman, 135, 196;
  Dnipro-1, 126;
  Donbas, 124;
  Kalmius, 134;
  Krivbas, 160;
  Kyiv-1, 124;
  Leshii (Troll), 135;
  Mirotvorets (Peacekeeper), 160;
  Oplot, 103, 134, 149, 160, 176, 204;
  Prizrak, 135, 136, 151, 152, 157, 162, 178, 197, 227, 231;
  Pyatnashka battalion, 187, 197;
  Russian Orthodox Army, 99;

Russian Orthodox Sunrise, 202;
Somali, 133–34, 160, 171, 193, 197;
Sparta squadron, 134, 161, 171, 197;
Svityaz', 160;
Viking, 99;
Vostok, 103, 134, 149, 150, 154,
    160, 171;
Zakarpattia, 160, 161;
Zarya (Dawn), 135
Bednov, Alexander, 135, 177, 196
Belarus, 34
Belgium, 6, 157, 233
Belousov, Oleg, 179
Benjamin, Walter, xvii
Beric, Dejan, 226
Berkut, 36, 38, 45n87, 59, 60, 83, 102
Berlin, Isaiah, 220
Beryoza, 100, 132, 133
Bezler, Igor, 116, 125, 128, 130–31,
    134, 149–51, 157, 206, 217
Bolotov, Valerii, 103–4, 116, 117n21,
    136
Bondarenko, Elena, 254
"Born by Revolution" Union, 80
Borodai, Alexander, 62, 64, 69, 83,
    94–96, 100, 105, 115–16, 126,
    128, 130, 132–34, 138–40, 150,
    161, 163, 184, 203, 204, 207, 216,
    218, 223, 227, 233, 234n17, 240,
    241, 252, 276, 293
Brezhnev, Leonid, 86
Buk missile system, 158
Busina, Oles', 255

CAF World Giving Index, 285
casualties:
    battlefield, 226;
    civilian, 226
Catherine the Great, 47, 79, 187, 199
ceasefire, 145, 147, 160, 169–75, 187,
    209, 216, 240–42, 247, 259, 261,
    263, 282
Chalenko, Alexander, 31, 33, 79, 109,
    114, 135, 188n5, 203, 282
Chalyi, Alexei, 60

Charity Aid Foundation (CAF), 285
Chechnya, 52, 106, 121, 126, 146, 148,
    208, 225, 228, 257, 259, 279, 294,
    296
Chervony Partyzan, 154
Chile, 200, 227
Chubarov, Refat, 59, 61, 62
Church:
    Christian Orthodox, 31;
    Kyiv Patriarchate of Ukrainian
        Orthodox, 31;
    Moscow Patriarchate of Ukrainian
        Orthodox, 31;
    Russian Orthodox, 194, 274;
    Ukrainian Autocephalous Orthodox,
        43n46;
    Ukrainian Orthodox, 31, 255
civil society, 33–34, 44n62, 78–79, 254,
    262, 273
civil war, 1, 2, 5, 11, 12, 26, 34, 70,
    86, 102, 103, 111, 114, 125,
    131, 167n34, 180, 229, 253, 298,
    309n1;
    participation in, 4
collective, 6, 8, 15, 38, 40, 48, 71, 73,
    77, 94;
    action, 2, 3, 7, 12, 15, 77;
    emotions, 10, 12, 13, 70, 179
    rituals, 14;
Colonel Cassad blog, Live Journal, 205,
    209–10;
    Rozhin, Boris, 60, 199, 209, 210
Committee on Public Support to the
    Residents of the Southeastern
    Ukraine at the Federation
    Council, 280
communication:
    campaigns, 205;
    channel, 247;
    line, 106, 154, 160, 161, 171;
    mass, xv, 33, 205;
    social, 211;
    strategy, 242
community, xii, 4, 7, 13, 33, 40, 48, 51,
    52, 55–60, 80, 95, 99, 113, 115,

140, 201, 210, 223, 224, 226, 308;
   discursive, 194;
   imagined, 12, 15, 70, 73, 75, 76, 194;
   international, 47, 52, 55, 77, 78, 112, 247, 250, 261, 277, 280, 286;
   security, 26;
   transnational, 40, 229;
   virtual, 40
The confederation of Mountain Peoples of the Caucasus, 52
conflict:
   conflict capital, formation of, 93;
   conflict divide, 225;
   conflict dynamics, 83, 262;
   conflict gestation, 80–85;
   conflict participants, 11, 193, 195, 200, 307;
   frozen conflict, 297;
   internal conflict, 175, 262, 296;
   mobilisation for conflict, 151, 278;
   post-Soviet conflicts, 93, 205, 286–87;
   resolution, 297
Coordination Council of South-East, 82
Cossacks, 52, 59, 61, 70, 73–74, 97, 108, 136–38, 140, 151, 171, 175–77, 195, 202–4, 206;
   Don Cossack Army, 136;
   Don Host, 73, 74;
   legacy in Donbas, 73–74;
   Luhansk Cossacks, 74;
   "Moscow Cossacks," 97;
   Neo-Cossacks, 180;
   State Policy Concept on, 74;
   Ukrainian (Zaporijie) Cossacks, 69;
   Union of Cossack Forces of Russia and Abroad, 97;
   Zaporizhian Host, 73
crime, 124, 133, 139–40, 176, 228, 249, 281, 296
Crimea, 30, 38, 84, 87, 93, 101, 102, 106, 107, 131, 150, 198, 199, 222, 273, 275–77, 287, 293;

Crimean Tatars, 48, 51, 51–54, 57, 61, 64;
Crimea Policy Dialogue (CPD), 58, 60, 65;
   faultlines in, 47–50;
   history, 64–66;
   Russian Bloc, 57, 60;
   Russian Community of Crimea, 57, 59;
   Russians in Crimea, 52;
   Ukrainians in Crimea, 48, 52
crowdsourcing, 207, 210
culture:
   cultural boundaries, 8, 47;
   cultural closeness, 31;
   cultural rivalry, 30–34;
   ethnocultural, 7, 25, 48, 56, 223;
   political, 3, 40;
   subculture, xvi, 15, 194, 210–11;
   and war, 33

Debaltseve, 99, 134, 137, 154, 160, 170–74, 217, 247, 278
Deep and Comprehensive Free Trade Agreement (DCFTA), 35
dialogue, 55, 58–60, 65–66, 135, 241, 260, 262
diaspora:
   Russian diaspora, 26, 224
discourse, 23, 26, 32–33, 37, 40, 50, 57–58, 60, 72, 87, 194, 199–200, 208, 221, 254, 271, 273–74, 286
Dnepr (Dnipro), 24, 86, 87, 79, 84, 113, 160, 179, 275
Donetsk, 24, 25, 28–30, 79, 83, 86, 102, 104, 107, 109, 111, 126, 130, 132–34, 139, 143n43, 150, 154, 155, 158, 159, 161, 164, 184, 202, 247, 248, 249, 251, 295;
"Donetskaya Respublica" organization, 80, 203
Donetsko—Krivorojskaya Respublika, 79–80
Donetsk People's Republic (DNR), 102, 110, 112, 132, 133, 134, 136, 154, 163, 164, 169, 171–73, 176,

179–82, 184, 185, 196, 203, 207,
    228, 244, 248, 250, 251, 259, 260,
    280, 282, 295
Dremov, Pavel, Commander, 135–38,
    140, 151, 177, 178
Drygaia Rossia (Different Russia),
    229
Dugin, Alexander, 217
Dutch Safety Board, 157
Dzerzhynsk. *See* Toretsk
Dziuba, Ivan, 26

economy:
    of Donbas, 240, 257, 287
elections:
    in Crimea, 57;
    in Donbas, 72, 75, 283;
    presidential, in Ukraine, 24, 25
elites, 2–3, 10, 25, 33, 37, 58, 67n25,
    70–72, 76, 81, 82, 84–86, 93, 97,
    100–102, 115, 138, 139, 181–84,
    188, 207, 215, 222, 232, 233, 240,
    241, 242, 250, 252, 256, 261, 271,
    272, 275, 276, 279, 280, 284, 286,
    294, 296;
    bargain, 17n22;
    business, 71–72;
    competition, 86;
    exodus, 88;
    intellectual, 58;
    political, 78, 275;
    regional, 78
emotions:
    collective emotions, 10, 12, 13, 15,
    70, 179, 233;
    emotional resonance, 7, 210, 215,
    220, 232;
    emotional shocks, 13
Eurasian Economic Union (EEU), 34
Euroatlanticism, 230
European Union, 34–36, 39, 88, 91n67,
    129, 226, 228, 230, 239, 243, 246,
    255, 275–77, 281, 284, 286;
    Association Agreement (EUAA),
    34, 35

Farage, Nigel, 223
fascism:
    anti-fascism, 200, 224, 229–32;
    Slav Antifascist Front, 59;
    symbols, 200
federalization, 78, 111, 239, 262, 276,
    295
field commanders, 16, 82, 98, 110, 133,
    146, 162, 175, 180, 188, 206, 210,
    216–17, 219, 226, 296
Filaret, 31
Finland, 227, 231, 233
Firtash, Dmytro, 54, 72, 242
foreign fighters, 11–12, 95, 215, 225–
    33;
    foreign fighters in Donbas, 229–33;
    Kyiv's foreign fighters, 227–28
fragmentation, 5
France, 36, 226, 231, 241, 252, 283
Free Aceh Movement, 5
frontline existence, reality of, 226–27
Frontline Ukraine, 86

Gazprom, 280, 284
geopolitics, 56
Georgia, 35, 103, 297
Germany, 27, 36, 207, 226, 233, 241,
    252, 283
Givi (Tolstykh, Mikhail), 134, 160–61,
    171, 178, 196, 207
Glaziev, Sergei, 275, 280
Gogol, Nikolai, 31, 43n44
Gorlovka, 130, 156
gosudarstvenniki, 223–24
group behavior:
    in-conflict, 8
Gubarev, Pavel, 82, 84, 114, 115, 138,
    143n43, 182, 203, 204, 221;
    Gubareva, Ekaterina, 82, 203
guerilla:
    guerrilla warfare, 11, 140, 218

history:
    historical memories, 14;
    history of Ukraine, 24–30

Horlivka, 126, 130–31, 139, 149, 157, 160, 161, 174, 247. *See also* Gorlovka
humanitarian, 97, 171, 232, 233, 249, 258, 280, 285
   humanitarian assistance/aid 96, 175, 207, 217, 243, 296
   humanitarian organisations/ community, 250, 252, 307
human rights:
   Human Rights Watch, 147, 156

ideas, xvi, 2, 11–14, 79, 95, 97, 105, 115, 194, 229, 273, 280;
   idealism, 5, 15, 128, 175, 226;
   power of, 13, 219–24
identity/ies:
   civilizational, 9;
   collective identity, 5, 12;
   construction of, 8;
   differences, 6, 25–26, 40, 254;
   faultlines, 34;
   fomenting, for conflict, 34–37;
   identity-based mobilisation, 11;
   individual, 195;
   layers of, 219;
   political, 6, 7, 14, 75, 184, 223;
   politicization of, 8, 9, 23–27;
   post-independence development of, 50–51;
   preservation of, 48;
   religious, 6;
   self-identification, 195;
   social, 6, 7;
   Soviet, 75;
   supra-national, 9;
   transnational, 12;
   and war, 5–9
ideology, 12, 27, 32, 86, 115, 139, 187, 221, 225, 230, 232, 255, 272, 274
Ilovaisk, 150, 160–62, 164, 165, 278
indigenous, 3, 37, 48, 51, 78, 83, 93, 99, 114, 115, 132, 179, 183, 194, 225, 229, 286, 298
industry, 250, 251;

Industrial Union of the Donbas, 71
information, 194;
   resistance, 209;
   resources, 308
insurgency:
   counterinsurgency, 4, 5, 15;
   insurgents, 15;
   transnational, 11
intelligentsia, 5, 30–34, 58, 61, 64, 78, 253, 255, 285
Interdvijenie (International Movement of Donbas), 79
internally displaced person (IDPs), 68n48, 77, 156, 242, 243, 245, 248
irredentism:
   grassroots, 79
Ishenko, Commander, 135
Izvestiya, 79

Joint Centre for Control and Coordination, 259
Joint Investigation Team (JIT), 157
Juchkovsky, Alexander, 79, 83, 101–2, 111, 127, 143n35, 145, 183, 187, 210, 223, 224, 247, 253
justice:
   idea of, 12;
   injustice, 64, 145, 305;
   social justice, 115–16

Karlivka, 150, 161, 174
Karlovka. *See* Karlivka
Kernes, Hennadyi, 87
Kerry, State Secretary, 289n23
Kharkiv, 79, 84, 103, 106, 107, 187, 228, 243, 251, 253, 275, 276, 107
Kherson, 84, 160
Khodakovsky, Alexander, 103, 134, 149, 162, 179, 180, 182, 247
Khrushchev, Nikita, 47, 48
Kiev/Kyiv, 30, 34, 35, 36, 38, 39, 43n45, 49–50, 53, 54, 56, 58, 59, 61, 65, 72, 77, 78, 80–81, 84, 85, 87, 93, 100, 102, 104, 105, 108,

109, 111, 113, 116, 122, 123, 131,
135, 137–39, 146, 147, 152, 158,
161, 163, 169, 171, 181, 186, 194,
199, 200, 216, 221, 225, 241, 244,
249, 251, 252, 258–63, 272, 275,
276, 277, 278, 280–84, 287, 288,
294–95, 297–98;
  foreign fighters of, 227–32;
  Patriarchate, 32
Kirill, Patriarch, 255
Klintsevych, Frantz, 63
Klitschko, Vitaly, 123
Kolisnichenko, Nikolai, 60
Kolomoyskyi, Ihor, 87, 116, 123
Kolstoe, Paul, 31
Kopat'ko, Yevgen, 248, 265n51
Kornilov, Vladimir, 33, 80, 202
Kosovo, 230
Kostyantynivka, 128
Kozak, Dmitry, 280
Kozitsyn, Nikolai, 136, 137, 175
Kramatorsk, 104, 109, 122, 128, 129,
148, 153, 160, 186, 244, 254
Krasnodon, 110, 154, 176
Kravchuk, Leonid, 24, 75
Kremlin, 1, 10, 33, 49, 61, 65, 88, 97,
106–7, 113, 157, 178, 215, 216,
275–77, 281, 282, 285
Krivoi Rog. *See* Kryvyi Rih
Kryvyi Rih, 252
Kuchma, Leonid, 24, 32, 50, 60, 71, 72,
131, 240, 241, 294
Kurchenko, Sergei, 84
Kushnarev, Yevgen, 78
Kuzio, Taras, 23, 33, 41n19, 52
Kyivan Rus, 201

label, 198
language:
  and fear of assimilation, 27–30;
  linguistic innovation, 198;
  linguistic sphere, 24;
  Russian, 27–30, 38, 40, 48, 53, 84,
    101, 272;
  Ukrainian, 28, 33, 49, 50, 53
Lavrov, Sergei, 282

Law:
  on Languages (2012), 53, 54;
  on Lustration (2014), 240;
  on Special Status, 261, 283
leadership:
  charismatic, 16, 128, 135, 181, 184;
  leaderless, 3, 88, 93, 180, 297;
  leaderlessness, 3
legitimacy:
  claim to, 186;
  illegitimate, 4, 11, 54, 135, 181,
    205, 283
Lenin, 74, 220, 253;
  statues of, 61, 249, 253, 254
Lenta, Victor Alfonso, 226
Levchenko, Nikolai, 84
Levochkin, Sergei, 71
Liberal-Democratic Party of Russia
  (LDPR), 135
liberalism:
  illiberalism, 232
Liberation Tigers of Tamil Elam, 5
Libya, 10, 208, 230
Logvinovo. *See* Lohvynove
Lohvynove, 173
Luganskaya. *See* Luhanska
Luhansk, 94, 104, 109, 116, 140, 147,
177, 184
Luhanska, 28, 30, 71, 72, 81, 97, 98,
103–5, 109, 112, 127, 135, 149,
151–53, 195, 199, 225–27, 242,
245, 247, 249, 251, 278, 279
Luhansk People's Republic (LNR), 98,
104, 112, 134, 136, 152, 154, 162,
164, 169, 172, 173, 175–85, 203,
206, 207, 227, 228, 231, 233, 248,
249, 251, 259, 260, 280, 282
Lukyanchenko, Alexander, 85, 139
Lyashko, Oleh, 254
Lynch, Dov, 289n17
Lysychansk, 151–53, 186

Maidan:
  anti-Maidan, 38–49, 60, 64, 78,
    80–81, 83–84, 101–103, 135, 200,
    209;

Euromaidan, 2–3, 9, 24, 34–37, 39,
    59, 75, 83, 87, 198–201, 205, 231,
    243, 253, 273–76, 306;
  first Maidan, 24, 32, 37, 78, 81, 273
Makiivka, 30, 126, 131, 134, 150, 161,
    202, 251
Malaysian Airlines Boeing/airliner, 38,
    241;
  Investigation, 157
Malet, David, 11–12, 95, 229
Malofeev, Konstantin, 62, 96, 217, 277
MANPAD:
  Igla complex, 157;
  Strela complex, 157
Mariupol, 79, 85, 112, 116, 125, 126,
    128, 138, 153, 163, 165, 170, 174,
    186, 251, 252
Marynivka, 150, 154, 155
Matveeva, Anna, 18n26, 267n94
Mearsheimer, John, 271
media resources, 208;
  Anna News, 208;
  new media, 15, 206, 207;
  rebel media websites, 226;
  Russian TV channels, 205, 210;
  RussVesna, 208;
  social media, 99, 124, 135, 197–200,
    203, 211, 224, 244–45, 250, 308;
  Sputnik i Pogrom (*S&P*), 86, 210;
  Television National Council of
    Ukraine, 205
Médicine Sans Frontiers (MSF), 247, 250
Medvedchuk, Viktor, 37, 240, 241, 259
Medvedev, Dmitrii, the then Russia's
    President, 74, 286
Merkel, Angela, 241
Mikhailo, 98, 134, 135, 148
Milli Mejlis, 51, 52, 55, 59, 61
Minsk Agreement, 176, 206, 227, 231,
    250, 251, 255, 257, 259–63, 282,
    268n102;
  Minsk-2 agreement (2015), 173,
    174, 282;
  Protocol, Minsk-1, 169, 171, 277,
    278, 297
mobilization:

  grassroots, 5, 9;
  identity-based, 11
Moldova, 35, 49, 84, 286
monism, 25
moral:
  beliefs, 10;
  duty, 219;
  outrage, 13
Mospino. *See* Mospyne
Mospyne, 150, 164
Motorola, 106, 122, 133, 161, 171, 178,
    220
Mozgovoi, Alexei, Commander, 115,
    128, 135–36, 151, 152, 157, 170,
    173, 177–78, 180
myth, 7, 11, 12, 37, 80, 193, 195, 203,
    253
  myth-making, 14, 13, 14, 197, 220

Nagorno Karabakh, 103
narrative, xv–xvi, 2, 13–16, 27, 32–33,
    87, 100, 194–95, 206–7, 285–86,
    296, 305–7;
  "clash of civilisations" narrative, 230;
  Cold War of, 1;
  historical narratives, 50;
  rebel narrative, 115, 186, 201, 220
national-democratic, 27, 31, 32, 37, 77
nationalism:
  ethno- or ethnic, 65, 223, 297;
  Russian, 223;
  Russian National Unity (RNU), 224;
  "state-ism", 223;
  Ukrainian, 25, 27, 57, 75, 78, 86–87
NATO, 275, 276
Nayyem, Mustafa, 36, 268n112
Non-Government Controlled Areas (of
    Donbas) (NGCA), 169, 178, 182,
    183, 186, 185, 188, 228, 242,
    244–46, 247–60, 262, 278, 280,
    281, 283, 294, 296–98
non-state actors, 4, 11, 15
Norin, Yevgenii, 101, 155, 185, 196,
    221
Novaya Gazeta, 63, 173, 177, 179, 228,
    278

Novoazovsk, 163, 165
Novorossiya:
　flag of, 202, 203;
　historical roots of, 79;
　idea of, 79, 82–83, 113, 179, 183;
　Novorossiya Movement, 14, 47,
　　79–80, 100, 113, 115, 153–54,
　　169, 172, 179, 180, 187, 195, 201,
　　202, 216, 218, 219, 221, 224, 225
Novorossiya News—Strelkov's *Briefs*,
　208

Odesa (Odessa), 79, 84, 100, 106, 146,
　251, 275;
　and "2 May Group", 38, 45n90;
　and Kulikovo Pole square, 38;
　and massacre 38, 39
Oleinik, Maria, 250
oligarchs:
　anti-oligarchic, 115
Onuphrii, Mitropolite, 31, 255
opportunity spaces, 14
Orange Revolution (2004), 32, 78;
　"Orange Coalition", 43n48
Organization for Security and
　Cooperation in Europe (OSCE),
　24, 247, 261, 282, 283;
　High Commissioner on National
　　Minorities , 41n1;
　Special Monitoring Mission
　　(SMM), 166n7, 174–75, 209,
　　213n52, 259, 284;
　Trilateral Contact Group, 240,
　　241
Organization of Ukrainian Nationalists
　(OUN), 27
"other":
　"othering", 75–77, 198
Ottomans, 69
Otunbayeva, Roza, 286

Palitsa, Igor, 45n90
paramilitaries, 10, 52
Party of Regions (PoR), 54, 55, 72, 78,
　81, 84, 93, 102, 245, 276, 288

patriotism, 97, 105, 210, 244, 250, 254,
　295
Pavliv, Mikhail, 203
Pavlov, Alexei, 135
Pavlov, Arsenii. *See* Motorola
peace:
　campaign, 285;
　peacebuilding, 58, 254, 262;
　process, 259–62, 272, 296;
　prospects for, 240, 253, 277
Peace Action, Training and Research
　　Institute of Romania (PATRIR),
　58
"People's Defence of Donbas" group,
　82
Pervomaisk, 137, 247
Pervomais'ke, 161
Peski. *See* Piski
Petlyura, Simeon, 43n53
Petrovsky, Sergei, 186
Pilavov, Manolis, 138
Pinchuk, Andrei, 100, 132, 133
Pinchuk, Sergei, 273
Piski, 150, 174, 186
Platov, Matvei, 137
Plotnitsky, Igor, 135, 137, 173, 177,
　181, 183
Pogrebinskii, Mikhail, 254
Poland, 36, 226, 227, 232
politics:
　absolute, 8;
　political and civic activism, 77–80;
　political economy perspective, 86;
　political order, 97, 100, 115, 128,
　　183, 188, 219, 232, 296
politization, of society, 243
Ponomarev, Vitalii, 110
Poroshenko, Petro, 100, 104, 113, 117,
　　129, 147, 148, 151, 169, 239, 240,
　　242, 273, 277, 284, 289n23, 294,
　　297;
　Bloc of Petro Poroshenko (BPP),
　　242
Potemkin, Count, 79
power-sharing, 62, 81, 260, 275

Prapor, Commander, 155
Prince, Commander, 82, 97–100, 109–11, 116, 122–24, 127–28, 130, 135, 136–37, 140–41, 147, 148, 162, 163, 176, 177, 207, 216, 220, 226, 276
prisoners:
    exchange, 258;
    war prisoners, 157, 208, 227, 258
Prosvirnin, Yegor, 86, 218
proto-statehood, 182–83
Prytula, Volodymir, 65
Purgin, Andrei, 80, 181, 182
Pushilin, Denis, 82, 182
Pushkin, Alexander, 26
Putin, Vladimir, 34–36, 63, 65, 68n42, 79, 87, 88, 107, 112, 163, 199, 215, 220, 222, 234n1, 240, 271, 277, 284–86, 297
Putzel, James, 18n22
Pyatt, Geoffrey, 274

Rada, Supreme or Verkhovna, 38, 56, 72
Radio Free Europe, 174
Rahr, Alexander, 158
rebellion:
    Kyiv's response and, 239–43;
    local momentum of, 102–6;
    motivations for, 99–102;
    NGCAs and, 247–59;
    peace and, 259–63;
    reason for joining, 9–13;
    social effects and, 243–46;
    in Ukrainian context, 239–63
referendum, 49, 75, 105, 111–17, 153, 186, 277
Rękawek, 236n57
religion, xvi, 6, 7, 9, 11–12, 31, 101, 201, 203, 210, 223–24, 255
resistance, 4, 10;
    symbols of, 14
"Responsible Citizens", 249–50
responsibility to protect, 12, 99–102, 230, 232

revolution, 3, 14, 32, 60, 74, 80, 82, 86, 114, 115, 181, 183, 194, 230, 232, 249, 252, 274, 277
revolutionary warfare, 11
Right Sector, 36, 38, 45n79, 62, 81, 200, 244, 255
Rogozin, Dmitrii, 57–58, 280
romanticism, 136, 229
Romashka, 108
Rostov, 107, 150, 157, 280–81
Rubezhnoe. *See* Rubizhne
Rubizhne, 151
Russian:
    Black Sea Fleet, 62;
    Civil Emergencies Ministry, 155;
    civilization, 40, 201, 273;
    Emercom, 280;
    Federal Migration Service, 248;
    Federal Security Service (FSB), 82, 95, 101, 129, 280, 281;
    government/ Moscow, x, 1, 14, 87–88, 233, 255, 271, 282, 293;
    Military Intelligence Directorate (GRU), 88, 129, 131;
    policy, 1, 208, 271, 286;
    Union of Russian Officers, 96
Russianness, 31, 94, 223, 254
Russians, in Ukraine, 26:
    Russian-speakers, 53;
    Russophones, 40, 77, 225;
    and schools, 28, 38
Russian Spring, 93–99, 133, 178, 202, 204, 215, 219, 221, 276, 278, 285, 298;
    autumn after, 216–19;
    significance of, 219–24
Russian Union of Afghanistan Veterans, 63, 96
Russian Union of Donbas Volunteers, 98, 218, 233, 234n7
Russian Unity, 57, 59, 62
Russian World, 40, 57, 94, 98, 99, 101, 111, 115, 132, 149, 196, 205, 208, 210, 215, 218, 220, 225, 260, 272–74, 286, 294, 273, 274

Russia. *See individual entries*
Russkaya Vesna. *See* Russian Spring
Russkyi Mir:
    Russonia, 40.
    See also Russian World

Sakwa, Richard, 1, 25, 35, 37, 40, 86, 260
Sanjarovka, 172
Savchenko, Nadia, 152, 258, 295
Savur Mohyla, 155, 159–60, 164
Schastia, 151–52, 160, 170, 174, 227, 277
security:
    guarantees, 275, 281, 288;
    insecurity, 62, 63, 112, 244–45, 263, 296, 308;
    sector, 73, 83, 133, 243;
    services, 16, 82, 103, 108;
    threat, 52
Security Service of Ukraine (SBU), 58, 65, 84, 103–4, 125, 138, 178, 240, 243, 245, 258
segmentation, 5
self, 8, 14, 15, 70, 193, 195, 202, 285, 298;
    concept of, 6;
    self-definition, 14, 70;
    self-rule, 112
Semyonovka, 110, 122, 147
Semyvolos, Ihor, 41n19, 254, 262
Serbia, 232
Sevastopol, 49, 56, 57, 59, 60, 62, 67n19, 147, 209;
    city council, 63
Severodonetsk. *See* Sievierodonetsk
Seversky. *See* Siverskyi
Shakhtarsk, 107, 134, 150, 160, 162
Shakhtyorsk. *See* Shakhtarsk
Sheremet, Pavel, 255
Shevardnadze, Eduard, 225
Shevchenko, Taras, 26, 198
Shtepa, Nelly, 138
Shufrych, Nestor, 240, 241
Shyrokyne, 174
Sievierodonetsk, 78, 82, 137, 140, 151–53, 186, 244, 254

Simferopol, 50, 55, 56, 59, 61, 62
Siversk, 136, 149
Siverskyi, 170
Skorkin, Konstantin, 85–86
Slavs, 55, 61;
    Slavonic Shield, 151;
    Slavophilism, 210, 224
Slavyanoserbsk, 195, 247
Slavyanskii Korpus (*Slavonic Corps Limited*), 279
Slobodchikoff, Michael, 271
Sloviansk, 98, 104, 106–11, 114, 122, 125, 127, 128, 134, 145, 147–49, 152–54, 157, 160, 166n2, 186, 202, 204, 206, 219
Smith, Graham, 41n8
Sneider, Noah, 114
Snejnoye, 110
Snezhnoye. *See* Snizhne
Snizhne, 110, 134, 140, 150, 156, 159, 160, 162
social movements, 12, 115, 193, 195, 222
sociopolitical norms, 13
solidarity:
    global solidarity movement, 225–28;
    international solidarity, 233
    solidarity fighters, 12;
Solovei, Valerii, 65
South Ossetia, 56, 96, 97, 280, 282
Sovietism, 115
Soviet Union, or USSR, ix–x, 23, 25–27, 40, 47–49, 74–75, 86, 93, 100, 104, 145, 187, 196, 204, 220–21, 223, 225–26, 229, 298
Spain, 226, 231–33;
    Spanish Civil War, 12, 102, 229, 298
spoiler, 217, 261
Stakhanov, 135, 137
Stanitsa Luhanska, 156, 162, 174
Starobesheve, 112, 164
Steinmeier, Frank-Walter, 283
Stepanivka, 155
St. George ribbon, 149, 199
Strannik (Pilgrim), 94, 95, 97, 100–101, 129, 176, 177, 179, 218

Strelkov, Igor, 62–64, 82, 95, 96, 100, 103, 106–11, 116, 121, 126, 128–30, 132–34, 136, 139, 147–51, 154–55, 157, 162, 163, 171, 179, 180, 196, 203, 204, 206, 208, 210, 215, 217–20, 223, 234nn. 1, 13, 278, 286, 290n30, 293
Sukhobok, Sergei, 255
Surkov, Vladislav, 277, 280, 286
surveys:
    Echo Moskvy, 234;
    IFAK Institut, 246;
    IFES, 35, 91n67;
    Kyiv International Sociological Institute, 41n11, 292n75;
    Osobyi Status (Special Status) center, 251;
    Razumkov Centre, 41n14, 66n3;
    Research and Branding Group, 80;
    ZOiS, 246, 251
Sverdlovsk, 154
Svoboda (Freedom) party, 38
symbolism:
    approach, 7;
    collective symbols, 204;
    communications and, 204–11;
    in digital era, 193–204;
    symbols, 13–14
Syria, 10, 208, 220, 226, 230
System Capital Management, 71

Taganrog, 107
Tagliavini, Heidi, 240, 241
Taruta, Sergei, 71, 85, 139, 251
technology, 195;
    peer-to-peer technologies, 15
Telegraph, 200
Terekhov, Vladimir, 57
Tereshchenko, Antonina, 90n28
Thought Factory Donbas, 264n24
threat:
    perception of, 53–54
Timoshenko, Yulia, 87
Tolstoy, Leo, 293
Torch of Novorossiya (Gubarev), 82

Toretsk, 174
Torez, 139, 159, 160, 162
Transdniestria, 49, 84, 94–96, 133, 136, 207, 219, 280, 286
Tsaryov, Oleg, 32, 102, 104, 112, 113, 138, 179
Tsekov, Sergei, 56, 60, 63
Tsyganok, Anatolii, 168n40, 221
Turchinov, Oliksandr, 85, 108, 123, 202, 293

Uglegorsk. *See* Vuhlehirsk
Ukraine. *See individual entries*
Ukraine's Choice, 37
Ukrainian Insurgent Army (UPA), 27
Ukrainian National Guards, 123, 125
Ukrainization, 28, 31, 32, 63, 252;
    of names, 53;
    policy of, 77;
    Ukrainophone, 40, 77
UN High Commissioner for Refugees (UNHCR), 156
UN Human Rights Monitoring Mission (HRMM), 156
Union of Serbian Veterans and Volunteers, 233
United Kingdom, 6, 207, 226
United States, 226, 231, 239, 284
UN Office for the Coordination of Humanitarian Affairs (UN OCHA), 248
UN Office of High Commissioner for Human Rights' (UN OHCHR), 38, 142n12, 182, 186, 258
UNSO (Ukrainian People's Self-Defense), 62
UN Working Group on Mercenaries, 228
Uppsala Conflict Data Program, 2
urbanization, 70, 248

Vakarchuk, Ivan, 28
Varyag club, 96
Vasquez, Sergio Becerra, 232–33
Vassiliyev, Alexander, 203
vatniks, 198

VCIOM (Russian Public Opinion
  Research Center), 64
Vejlivye liudi (polite people), 199
Veselova, Nataliya, 268n112
VGTRK TV channel, 152
violence, 38–41;
  trajectories of, 4–5.
  See also individual entries
V Kontakte social network site, 82, 205–6
Volnovakha, 165, 170
volunteers:
  Chechen, 98;
  combatant, xv, 11, 94, 97–99, 101,
    109, 111–12, 115, 126, 137, 149,
    170, 196, 205, 207, 216–18, 224–
    25, 286, 298, 306;
  Help Army movement, 244, 298;
  irregular fighters, 10–11;
  irregular war, 5
Voznik, Roman, 176
Vuhlehirsk, 172, 247

Walker, Shaun, 131, 236n58
Walter, Sergei, 266n79
warrior:
  elite, 181
Way, Lucan, 45n81
Web 2.0, 15
weapons:
  acquisition of, 126–28;
  lethal, 186
Williams, Brian Glyn, 66n4
Wilson, Andrew, 3, 40, 41n8, 69, 75,
    87, 115, 148
Winter, Charlie, 213n51
Wood, Elizabeth, 207, 213n51, 271

Yalta, 62, 63

Yampol, 148
Yanukovych, Viktor, ix, 24, 30, 32,
    34–38, 55, 56, 59–62, 65, 71, 72,
    78, 80, 83, 84, 87, 88, 100, 126,
    198, 200, 209, 261, 272–75, 277,
    278, 294
Yarosh, Dmytro, 87, 91n61
Yasinovataya. *See* Yasynuvata
Yasynuvata, 174
Yatseniuk, Arsen, 241, 268n103,
    168n50
Yatsuba, Volodymyr, 60
Yefremov, Alexander, 72, 84, 183
Yeltsin, Boris, 49, 121, 156, 286, 297
Yenakijeve, 131
Yermolayev, Andrei, 260
Yermolenko, Andrei, 201
Yevremov, Alexander, 103
Yugoslavia, 298
Yushchenko, Victor, 24, 25, 27, 28, 32,
    43n53, 50, 53, 55, 57, 78, 278

Zakharchenko, Alexander, 103, 134,
    149, 162, 170, 172–74, 176,
    180–84, 188n5, 202, 204, 216,
    240, 295
Zamilov, Timur, 204
Zaporizhe, 84
Zaroshenske, 158
Zelenopillya, 153
Zelenopolie. *See* Zelenopillya
Zharikhin, Vladimir, 273
Zhevlakov, Sergei, 137
Zhilin, Yevgenyi, 103
Zhirinovsky, Vladimir, 135
Zivkovic, Bratislav, 226
Zugres, 160
Zurabov, Mikhail, 240

About the Author

Anna Matveeva is a visiting senior research fellow at the Department of War Studies, King's College London. She works as an academic and a practitioner, specializing in conflict studies, and used to work for the United Nations Development Programme (UNDP). She acts as a consultant to international organizations, such as the UN, the EU and OSCE, international NGOs, and major donors. In 2010 Matveeva worked as a Head of Research Secretariat of the International Kyrgyzstan Inquiry Commission. Previously she was a research fellow at Chatham House, worked at the London School of Economics, and headed programs at International Alert and Saferworld. She was born in Moscow, and lived and worked in London since 1991. Matveeva is an author of numerous publications on post-Soviet politics and security including "No Moscow stooges: identity polarization and guerrilla movements in Donbass," *Journal of Black Sea and South European Studies*, "Russia's Changing Security Role in Central Asia," *European Security*, "North-Eastern Caucasus: Drifting Away From Russia," in Robert Bruce Ware (ed.) *Fire from Below: How the Caucasus Shaped Russian Politics since 1980s*, "Challenges of Minority Governance," in Oleh Protsyk, Benedikt Harzl (eds.) *Managing Ethnic Diversity in Russia*, "Shanghai Cooperation Organisation: A Regional Organisation in the Making," London School of Economics, "Exporting Civil Society: The Post-Communist Experience" and "Chechnya: Dynamics of War and Peace," *Problems of Post-Communism*, "Return to Heartland: Russia's Policy in Central Asia," *The International Spectator*, "Russia and USA increase their influence in Georgia," *Jane's Intelligence Review*, and "The North Caucasus: Russia's Fragile Borderland," *Chatham House Paper*. She contributed to *the Guardian's* Comment Is Free website and occasionally writes as a journalist.

Made in the USA
Middletown, DE
29 April 2022

65009169R00213